ART IN NATURE

ART IN NATURE

CLASSIC BOTANICAL PRINTS FROM THE EIGHTEENTH TO THE TWENTIETH CENTURY

Wm Edwards Del.   Pub by S. Curtis Walworth Feb 1 1812.   F Sansom Sc.

INTRODUCTION BY MARTYN RIX

RIZZOLI
NEW YORK

ACKNOWLEDGEMENTS

The Publishers would like to thank the following for their
help in the compilation of this book: Martyn Rix for his
introduction and editorial assistance, and Howard Swann
of Wheldon & Wesley Ltd.

The illustrations by Lilian Snelling on pages 40, 83, 84, 91,
123, 203, 204, 219, 225, 227, 228, 236 and 241 have been
reproduced by the kind permission of The Bentham-Moxon
Trust, The Royal Botanic Gardens, Kew; the illustrations
on pages 12, 22, 96, and 103 have been reproduced by the
kind permission of Stella Ross-Craig.

Text and illustrations originally
published from 1787 onwards
in the *Botanical Magazine*

This edition first published in the
United States of America in 1991 by
Rizzoli International Publications, Inc.
300 Park Avenue South, New York, NY 10010

ISBN 0-8478-1401-7
LC 91-82766

Printed and bound in Hong Kong

CONTENTS

PUBLISHER'S NOTE

The text and illustrations in *Art in Nature* have been selected from *The Botanical Magazine*, which was first published in 1787, later renamed *Curtis's Botanical Magazine*, and is today published as *The Kew Magazine*. William Curtis set up the magazine in response to 'the repeated solicitations of several ladies and gentlemen . . .' for 'a work in which Botany and Gardening, or the labours of Linnaeus and Miller, might happily be combined'.

Curtis's Botanical Magazine sought to popularise and encourage the cultivation of new and wild species which were being discovered on botanical explorations around the world. Many of these plants are now commonly seen in the gardens of the British Isles. During the two hundred years of its publication, *Curtis's Botanical Magazine* has contained over ten thousand splendid colour illustrations. A large number of the plants entered in the magazine had never been described, illustrated or indeed named, in any publication before. *The Botanical Magazine* is unique among journals for the influence it has had on gardening and the collection of plants shown in its many issues mirrors the developments of botanical exploration around the world and changing fashions of which plants have been in favour at a particular period.

Art in Nature brings together a selection of more than five hundred and fifty of the most beautiful of these plates, the majority of which appeared in the magazine's early years, between 1787 and 1820. The finest botanical illustrators were employed to faithfully portray the new species and the standard of scientific accuracy, maintained throughout the many years of its publication, has been outstanding. Sydenham Edwards and Walter Fitch, the two artists responsible for many of the entries in this edition, are particularly renowned for their botanical illustrations. The work of other contributors is also represented. Each plate is accompanied by an edited and abridged version of the original text.

For ease of reference the plants illustrated in *Art in Nature* have been alphabetically ordered according to genus. Each species carries both its latin and common name as it appeared in *Curtis's Botanical Magazine*. However, in view of subsequent botanical research many of these names have now altered, so a modern latin nomenclature has been added.

Example:

ACANTHACEÆ – genus
JUSTICIA ECBOLIUM – *Botanical Magazine* species nomenclature
LONG-SPIKED JUSTICIA – common name
Ecbolium linneanum – modern species nomenclature

In *Curtis's Botanical Magazine* the plates are numbered in order of publication. However, in *Art in Nature*, this has necessarily changed to accommodate the alphabetical ordering according to genus. The simple identification of each illustration is followed by the original plate number and the year of its publication; the initials of the artists are given, if their name appeared on the plate, and these can be cross-referenced with the appendix at the end of the book.

INTRODUCTION

The Botanical Magazine, later called *Curtis's Botanical Magazine*, or familiarly known as *The Bot. Mag.*, is unique among journals in the influence it has had on gardening. From its beginning in 1787, it sought to popularise and encourage the cultivation of new or rare wild plants in English gardens. It continued in regular publication until 1984, when it was renamed *The Kew Magazine*, and as such, is still published quarterly. During this period of 203 years, over ten thousand garden plants have been illustrated and described.

The period from the early-nineteenth century until the mid-twentieth was the great era of the expansion by the botanical colonial empires. This was accompanied by the botanical exploration of the tropics, the southern hemisphere, and the more inaccessible areas of North America and Asia. The Royal Botanic Gardens, Kew, at which *The Botanical Magazine* has been edited and written since 1841, had an important role in encouraging botanical exploration and the development of new crops in the colonies. Faster ships meant that living plants could be brought back, in addition to the seeds which had until then been the main means of the introduction of new species. Once the plants arrived in Europe, those which needed protection could be kept in glasshouses, heated by limitless supplies of cheap coal produced for the expanding industries based on iron and steel. Many of the great private gardens of the nineteenth century were supported by fortunes made by industrialists, and the prosperity resulting from the Industrial Revolution and the British Empire enabled gardening and an interest in rare plants, to become a national obsession which survives even today.

HISTORY OF THE BOTANICAL MAGAZINE

In the original preface to the first part of his *Botanical Magazine*, published on February 1st 1787, William Curtis said that it was produced in response to 'the repeated solicitations of several ladies and gentlemen, subscribers to the Author's Botanic Garden...' for 'a work in which Botany and Gardening, or the labours of Linnaeus and Miller, might happily be combined'. Curtis's garden was sited on Lambeth marsh, somewhere between present day Westminster Bridge and Waterloo railway station, and it contained displays of medicinal, culinary and crop plants, English wild flowers, and hardy ornamental trees and shrubs. Subscribers paid one guinea, and, in return, received plants and seeds in addition to free attendance at Curtis's lectures on botany.

Curtis was then aged forty-one, and although he had already published several small books, his major venture, the folio size *Flora Londinensis; or plates and descriptions of such plants as grow in the Environs of London*, had been a financial failure. It had been supported, in part, by Lord Bute, a wealthy patron of botany, called 'the Maecenas of the present age' because of his finance of this and other expensive botanical publications, but after 432 beautiful folio plates had been published, the *Flora* ceased for lack of support. By producing *The Botanical Magazine*, Curtis sought to remedy this loss, hoping that although there was insufficient interest in wild flowers, illustrations of the new garden flowers which he and his friends were growing, would prove more popular amongst the rich and fashionable members of London society.

Curtis was born in Alton, Hampshire, the son of a tanner, who was a member of the Society of Friends. When he was fourteen he was apprentice to his grandfather, an apothecary in Alton, and following this, he went to work for an apothecary in Gracechurch Street in the City of London. Although he succeeded in the business, his real love was Natural History, his interest having been aroused, as a boy, by James Lagg, an ostler at the Crown Inn in Alton. Lagg is said to have shown the young Curtis the flowers growing wild in that part of Hampshire, and to have been familiar with the works of Parkinson and Gerard; a knowledge of herbal plants was at that time an important part of the training of an apothecary. To give himself more time for the study of Natural History, Curtis soon took a partner in his London business, and shortly afterwards sold out to him completely, which enabled him to buy a plot of land in Bermondsey for a botanic garden.

Within a few years, in 1773, Curtis, presumably running short of money, was appointed *Praefectus Horti* and Demonstrator at the Apothecaries' Garden in Chelsea, now the Chelsea Physic Garden. This garden had been one of the most important in the country while under the influence of Phillip Miller. With his great curiosity and love of plants, Miller had corresponded with botanists and gardeners from all over the world, and his skill as a gardener had made Chelsea 'excell all gardens for excellence and variety'. Miller had died in 1771, but his *Gardener's and Florist's Dictionary*, first published in 1724, was still the major source of information on garden plants, and indeed a new, enlarged edition was published in 1803–1807, revised and updated by Thomas Martyn, Professor of Botany at Cambridge, and founder of the University Botanic Garden. Curtis held the post of *Praefectus Horti* for five years, long enough for him to publish a *Catalogue of Plants growing Wild in the Environs of London*, and begin his *Flora Londinensis*, and it was while at Chelsea that he conceived the idea of opening his own botanic garden to the public. He also put foreward to the apothecaries, a plan for a course of lectures on botany for medical students, and although this was approved, no lectures were ever given. Curtis later gave successful courses of lectures from his botanic garden at Lambeth, and it is from Lambeth that the early parts of *The Botanical Magazine* were published.

The first part of the magazine cost one shilling and contained three plates, of *Iris persica* from Turkey, *Echinacea purpurea* from North America and the European *Eranthis hiemalis*, (then much rarer than it is now). It was subtitled 'The Flower-Garden Displayed in which the most Ornamental Foreign

Plants, cultivated in the Open Ground, the Green-house and Stove are accurately represented in their Natural Colours'. There were soon over three thousand subscribers to the first part, exceeding the author's 'warmest expectations'. At first the artists were William Kilburn and James Sowerby, both of whom had already worked for Curtis on the *Flora Londinensis*, but in the same year a friend of Curtis's showed him some copies of plates from *Flora Londinensis*, done by young Sydenham Edwards, son of a schoolmaster from Abergavenny. Curtis recognised the boy's talent, brought him to London, and trained him in botanical illustration and in botany; Edwards's first illustration appeared in the magazine in the second volume in 1788, and he was almost the sole artist until 1815.

William Curtis died in 1799, and is buried in St Mary's churchyard, Battersea. The copyright of his magazine passed to his daughter, married to her father's first cousin, Samuel Curtis, who soon afterwards appointed Dr John Sims, one of William Curtis's executors as editor, a post he filled until 1827. Sims was a native of Canterbury, Kent and had studied both in Leiden, then one of the best universities in Europe, and in Edinburgh. He was a doctor of medicine and later a licentiate of the college of Physicians. Sydenham Edwards continued as the sole artist until 1815, when a disagreement with Dr Sims caused him to leave the magazine and with James Ridgeway, set up *The Botanical Register*, in competition. This was a very similar magazine, and lasted until 1847.

Under Dr Sims's guidance *The Botanical Magazine* became a journal of scientific as well as horticultural importance, and it was at the beginning of Sims's period as editor that the title of the magazine became 'Curtis's Botanical Magazine'. In an early preface, shortly after becoming editor, Sims stated that he wished 'to indulge our botanical readers with a representation and description of some of the novel and curious plants which are annually introduced, particularly from the Cape of Good Hope.' For the descriptions of many of these plants he relied on experts in their particular genera, so many plants, especially from the Cape, were first described in the magazine. John Bellenden Ker, who later changed his name to Gawler, (and so is generally known as Ker-Gawler), was an expert on the Iris family, and The Hon. and very Revd. William Herbert, Dean of Manchester, wrote the text for many of the Amaryllis family. R.A. Salisbury, a brilliant though somewhat maverick botanist, specialised in the Lily family, and it is owing to the influence of these three, who were keen gardeners as well as botanists, that the early parts of the magazine contain so many representatives of these families of bulbs. After the departure of Sydenham Edwards, Herbert himself provided many of the plates, as did a certain Samuel Curtis, apparently no relation of the founder.

During the latter part of Sims's period as editor, subscriptions to the magazine declined to fewer than a thousand, partly perhaps because of a lowering of the artistic standard of the magazine after Sydenham Edwards's departure, and partly because of the number of similar magazines which had arisen following the success of Curtis's original. Apart from *The Botanical Register*, already mentioned, which was supported by John Lindley and the Horticultural Society, there was Henry C. Andrew's *Botanists Repository*, which was published between 1797 and 1812.

In 1827 William Jackson Hooker took over as editor of *Curtis's Botanical Magazine*, beginning a family connection which lasted until 1906. Hooker was an outstanding botanist, and already Professor of Botany at Glasgow. He was also an accomplished botanical illustrator, and had started and published his own journal, *The Exotic Flora*, devoted to the study of tropical plants, which had been going for four years. Hooker introduced some minor changes to Curtis's magazine, including the tradition of dedicating each volume to an important horticultural person, and putting dissections of important details of the plant onto the plate. He discontinued his *The Exotic Flora*, and energetically tackled the problems of the magazine. His move to Kew as director in 1841 gave him even more access to suitable plants to illustrate, but less time to do the work himself. Much as Curtis had found and trained the young Sydenham Edwards, Hooker trained W.H. Fitch, an apprentice to a Glasgow calico designer. At first the young Fitch helped Hooker in the herbarium after work, but once Hooker realised the boy's talent for drawing, he paid off his master, and himself trained him as a botanical illustrator. From 1834 until 1877, Fitch drew and lithographed nearly all the plates in the magazine, and, in addition, produced the plates for most of the botanical monographs and travel books produced by Sir William Hooker and his son, Sir Joseph.

The joint production of the magazine between the Hookers and Fitch ended in 1878, when Fitch resigned because of his increasing disenchantment with Sir Joseph, the inadequate payment he received for his work (he was never paid a salary though he had worked at Kew for over forty years), and his failing eyesight. Although Hooker had earlier been unsympathetic to Fitch's complaints, he did approach Disraeli, and managed to get a government pension for Fitch from 1880 until his death in 1892.

Fitch's position on the magazine was taken over by his nephew, John Nugent Fitch, who became the lithographer for most of the plates originally drawn by other artists such as Sir Joseph's daughter, Lady Thistleton-Dyer, and, later, Miss Matilda Smith. Compared with the great stability of the nineteenth, the twentieth century produced many changes in both the editors, artists and the fortunes of the magazine. Sir Joseph was succeeded as editor, as he was in the directorship of Kew, by his son-in-law, Sir William Thistleton-Dyer, and the two positions were again combined under Sir David Prain, who was editor from 1907-1920. The text was written by members of the Kew staff, each according to his speciality, an arrangement which still continues.

The First World War nearly brought about the demise of the magazine, as the publishers decided, by 1920, that they could no longer afford the losses it was making. It was only rescued through the energetic intervention of Henry John Elwes of Colesborne, a keen naturalist, traveller, shot, and later plant collector and gardener, many of whose own new plants had already been figured in the magazine. Spurred on, perhaps, by rumours that the Smithsonian Institution in Washington, DC was interested in taking over the magazine, at a dinner on the evening of the Chelsea Flower Show in May 1921, Elwes persuaded his friends Lionel Nathan de Rothschild and William Cory to join him in purchasing the copyright from the publishers, for £250. After failing to get it taken over as an official Kew publication, it was presented to the Royal Horticultural Society. Production, however, continued to be associated with Kew, as the editorship was taken on by Otto Stapf, an excellent botanist who had recently retired as keeper of the herbarium. Lilian Snelling, who had already drawn many plants for Elwes, became the main artist, a post she filled until 1952.

Further strain was placed on the magazine by the Second World War. From its beginning until 1843, the plates were engraved in copper, often by an engraver, and hand coloured by a team of colourists, following the example of an original by the artist concerned. From 1845, Fitch not only painted, but lithographed the plates himself, lithography having taken over from engraving as the common method of reproduction. At the beginning, limestone was used as the base, but this was superseded in the twentieth century, by the use of zinc plates. Apart from one exceptional volume, all the plates up to 1948 had been hand coloured, but after the war, colourists were almost impossible to find, and impossibly expensive, so from 1949 colour printing was used. Nine thousand, six hundred and eighty-eight plates had been published using the old methods, and with the change to colour printing, a new series of numbers was begun.

After the retirement of Lilian Snelling, the plates for reproduction in the magazine were painted by Stella Ross-Craig, whose husband, Robert Sealy was on the staff of Kew and acted as editor; W.B.Turrill, Sir George Taylor and David Hunt also acted as editors during these last years. Many paintings were produced also by Ann C. Webster, and by Margaret Stones, who did the majority of the plates until 1984. Several, mostly younger artists, often trained at Kew, produced paintings for the last numbers of the old magazine. Christabel King, Pandora Sellars, Joanna Langhorne, Mary Grierson, and Ann Farrer, are, with Margaret Stones, some of the best botanical illustrators working in England and America today.

The end of the magazine in its original format and title, came in April 1984, when it was renamed *The Kew Magazine*, and each part included, as well as six plates as used in old magazines, articles on plant collecting, rare or threatened species and book reviews. W.T. Stearn has pointed out, in *The Flower Artists of Kew*, that there is a precedent for this; between 1845 and 1848, William Hooker published *A Companion to the Botanical Magazine*, which contained articles of botanical interest which did not fit the magazine's strict format, but were designed to be bound in with the magazine itself. Hooker did not, however, feel the necessity to change the title or begin a new numbering system, as was done in 1984. The association of the magazine with Kew had been almost unbroken since 1841, and the pointless change of title of the longest-running botanical magazine in the world is to be deplored.

PLANTS ILLUSTRATED IN CURTIS'S BOTANICAL MAGAZINE

During the two hundred years or so during which it was published, *Curtis's Botanical Magazine* contained over ten thousand illustrations of plants, mostly wild species, grown in gardens in the British Isles. The plants shown mirror the fashions in horticulture during this period, and demonstrate from which parts of the world new plants were being introduced, and which types of plant were in favour at a particular period.

Most of the plates reproduced here are from the early years of the magazine, between 1787 and 1820. Many of the plates in the first few volumes illustrated European or North American plants. Some of them had been grown in gardens for many years, and were introduced to the Chelsea Physic Garden, by Philip Miller who was chief gardener there from 1722 until 1770, for most of that time surpassing in experience and fame, the curator, *Praefectus Horti*, (a post later held by Curtis) who was nominally his superior.

In spite of the magazine's title, a few of the plants shown are natives of the British Isles. Plate 98 of this book, published in 1798, shows the Alpine Catchfly, *Lychnis alpina*, and says that it may be expected to be found in the mountainous parts of this island. It had, in fact, already been found above Glen Clova in Angus, by George Don in 1795, and it was also discovered on a mountain top in the Lake District in 1850. *Gentiana verna*, the Spring Gentian, (plate 187) was first grown in England from seed from the Alps, though it was, even in Curtis's time, known to grow wild in Teesdale in Co. Durham, and in western Ireland in Co. Clare and Galway.

Other plants are shown as garden rarities, which have now become commoner as wild plants. The Wild Lupin from Alaska and British Columbia, *Lupinus nootkatensis*, was illustrated in 1810, soon after its introduction by Archibald Menzies in 1794. Now it is seldom if ever seen as a garden plant, but can be found wild in considerable numbers, growing on shingle banks of the Dee and other salmon rivers in eastern Scotland.

The Himalayan Balsam, *Impatiens glandulifera*, was illustrated in 1881, as a garden plant; it is now naturalised by rivers and in damp woods throughout Europe, and is only found in the wildest of gardens.

Throughout its life *The Botanical Magazine* has concentrated on wild species and ignored garden hybrids or forms, however numerous or important they might be. It is interesting, however to see some of the species from which familiar garden flowers were later raised. Early single dahlias from Mexico, sweet peas from Sicily, a single pink camellia from Japan and Oriental poppies from Turkey, are among those illustrated in early volumes.

Plants from America had been popular throughout the seventeenth century, and particularly since the visits to Virginia of John Tradescant the younger in 1637. New plants continued to come in from America throughout the eighteenth century, and were raised and distributed not only by botanic gardens, but by specialist nurserymen, who became very prosperous and were happy to receive the publicity for their new plants which was provided by an illustration in *Curtis's Botanical Magazine*.

James Lee was one of the earliest of these great nurserymen, a partner with Lewis Kennedy in the Royal Vineyard Nursery in Hammersmith, founded around 1745 on the site of a former vineyard, now covered by the exhibition centre at Olympia, London. Lee supported collectors, both in America and the Cape, corresponded with botanists all over the world, and introduced the ideas of Linnaeus to England, by his translation in 1760, of Linnaeus's *Philosophia Botanica*. Redouté stayed at the Vineyard Nursery during his visit to England, and Lee was a prolific supplier of plants to the Empress Joséphine at Malmaison.

A story about the introduction of the first *Fuchsia*, illustrates Lee's enthusiasm for a new plant. He heard, from a customer, of a new and beautiful plant, seen that morning in Wapping, England. Hurrying there immediately, and he found that the plant belonged to a sailor's wife, whose husband had brought it back from South America, and gone to sea again, telling her strictly, to keep it safe for him until he should return. At first, afraid of what her husband would say, she refused to part with it, until Lee offered her all the money he had on him, eight gold sovereigns, and some small change, a considerable sum in 1788. Finally she gave him the plant, and he promised to give her back a plant from it the following year. As soon as he arrived back at the Vineyard, he stripped the plant of flowers and buds, and pushed into a hot bed as many cuttings as he could make, and by the following spring, had three hundred flowering plants for sale. These he released to the public a few at a time, charging a guinea a piece, and had soon sold the lot, not forgetting to take one back to the sailor's wife in Wapping. The same *Fuchsia* was introduced to Kew in 1788, and illustrated from there in the magazine in the following year. Lee and Kennedy also made a speciality of Australian plants, and received regular consignments of seed from Botany Bay, sent by Colonel Peterson who was in charge of the convicts who had been transported there. Conrad Loddiges, who founded a nursery in Mare St., Hackney in 1771, soon had almost as good a collection of plants for sale. He bought plants from Michaux and from John Bartram, collected in America, and his son, George, later published his own journal, with illustrations he drew himself, *Loddiges' Botanical Cabinet*, which ran from 1817–1834.

Both nurseries sold many plants from the Cape region of South Africa, and a number of them are shown in the early volumes of *Curtis's Botanical Magazine*. A trickle of Cape plants had arrived in Europe via the Dutch East India Company, and other ships which had called at the Cape, but the first systematic collections were made by Carl Thunberg, who sent plants and seeds back to Leiden and Amsterdam botanic gardens, and to Francis Masson, who was sent out by Sir Joseph Banks to collect bulbs and seeds for the Botanic Garden at Kew. Their first journeys were made between 1772 and 1774, and while Thunberg continued to Japan, Masson returned to England. He must have realised the unequalled richness of the Cape flora, for he went out there again in 1786, and set up a garden at the foot of Table Mountain, sending back plants to England by passing ships, until he finally returned to England himself in 1795. Masson died in 1805, while plant collecting in Canada for Kew. James Lee's son, also James, and now in charge of the Vineyard Nursery was a close friend and much saddened by his death, sent to the cold of Canada, 'in the decline of life after 25 years service in a hot climate, and all for a pittance.' Masson's collections, when grown in England, directly led to the vogue for Cape heathers, pelargoniums, and Cape bulbs which persisted into the nineteenth century. Succulents, which are most diverse in the drier parts of South Africa, and particularly in the Karoo, were a speciality of Masson's, and he published his own monograph of the Stapeliads.

Henry C. Andrews, whose *Botanist's Repository* sought to take advantage of the success of *Curtis's Botanical Magazine*, published 'The Heathery...' in 1804–1806, and '*Geraniums*' in 1805, in response to the great popularity of these two genera. The interest in the Cape geraniums persisted for at least two decades, as is shown by Robert Sweet's monograph, *Geraniaceae*, published in London in five volumes between 1820 and 1830. Pelargoniums, as most of the Cape species are now called, are enjoying increased popularity at present, both the large-flowered and colourful hybrids, and the species with more modest flowers but scented leaves.

When William Hooker became editor in 1827, the emphasis of the plants illustrated changed. Hooker was particularly interested in the flora of the tropics, and of America, and he had contacts in many parts of South America. There was a general increase of skill in growing plants in hothouses, or stoves as they were called, and epiphytic orchids, which until about 1800 had been short-lived in cultivation, became very popular among the rich. Many of the industrialists from Liverpool had business interests in Central and South America, and arranged for orchids to be collected and brought back alive, and the Horticultural Society of London, soon to become the Royal Horticultural Society, also sent out collectors. One of these was John Forbes, who joined a naval survey expedition to southern Africa. They landed first in Rio de Janiero, (apparently a regular stopping point en route to the Cape!), where Forbes collected several orchids which were sent home, including, *Cattleya forbesii* (t. 406 *Bot. Mag.*). They called at the Cape, then sailed to Madagascar, but after surviving an attack by tribesmen on the Lower Zambesi, Forbes died of fever at Senna in Mozambique, aged only twenty-three.

One of the most successful growers of the time was James Bateman of Biddulph Grange, Congleton. He employed T. Colley to collect orchids in British Guiana, and George Ure Skinner in Guatemala. Numerous plates in *Curtis's Botanical Magazine* were grown from his plants, and he published the largest ever botanical book, the elephant folio *Orchidaceae of Mexico and Guatemala*, with superb plates by Mrs Withers, who illustrated our *Cattleya pumila* (t.408 *Bot. Mag.*).

Nurserymen are frequently mentioned as the source of plants illustrated in the magazine. Both Lee and Kennedy and Loddiges of Hackney grew numerous orchids, but none acheived the pre-eminence of the Exotic Nursery in the Kings Road, Chelsea, founded by Joseph Knight, and bought by James Veitch in 1853. First under James Veitch, and then under his son, Sir Harry, the nursery sent out collectors all over the world to seek out new garden plants. Orchids were one of the firms specialities, and they were the first to produce orchid hybrids.

Veitch's were also particularly concerned with conifers, many of which were introduced by their collector William Lobb, and by David Douglas from the west coast of North America. Douglas was employed as a young man at Glasgow Botanic Garden under William Hooker, and on his recommendation was chosen by the Horticultural Society to collect seeds of conifers in British Columbia. He left England in 1823, and was extremely successful, sending back not only pounds of seed of important forest species, but several new ornamental shrubs and garden flowers, such as *Godetia purpurea* (t. 352 *Bot. Mag.*), one of the ancestors of the Garden Godetia.

The riches of the flora of the Himalayas were not realised until William Hooker's son, Joseph, visited Sikkim in 1848. Following his explorations there he brought back over thirty species of *Rhododendron*, which, together with other hardy shrubs, were to transform British gardening in the late-nineteenth and twentieth centuries, and become the mainstay of such great gardens as Exbury, Bodnant and Wakehurst Place, and of Botanic Gardens such as Edinburgh and the Arnold Arboretum.

One of the most prolific and influential of all horticultural collectors, E.H. Wilson, was first sent to China by Messrs. Veitch in 1899. Earlier horticultural collectors in China had not penetrated much beyond the Ichang gorges in the centre of the country, and it was the French missionary, botanist and zoologist, Pere Armand David, who visited the mountains on the border between what was then Tibet and Sichuan in 1865. Here he found ancient forests filled with completely new and beautiful plants, including the tree *Davidia involucrata*, and it was the seed of this tree, above all, that Wilson was instructed by Sir Harry Veitch to collect. David was also responsible for introducing, to France, another beautiful shrub from eastern China, *Xanthoceros sorbifolia*, shown on plate 522.

After the demise of Veitch's nursery in 1914, Wilson was sent to China again by Arnold Arboretum, and it was on one of these expeditions that he discovered *Lilium regale*. After his retirement from active collecting in 1919, he became assistant director and later keeper of the Arnold Arboretum, a post he held until his death in a car crash in 1930.

The Himalaya remained the centre of interest for collectors from Wilson's time until the communist takeover of China and Tibet made travelling there impossible. Rhododendrons and primulas were among the genera most sought after by men, George Forrest in Yunnan, Frank Kingdon-Ward in Tibet and Burma, and Ludlow and Sherrif in Bhutan, all of whom specialised in the particularly inaccessible, but botanically rich mountains and ravines of the eastern Himalaya.

Since the 1950's there has been no particular emphasis on any one part of the world for plant collecting, though new species suitably worthy to adorn European and American gardens have come from Turkey, Iran and Afghanistan, New Guinea and South America, and the choice of species illustrated in the last numbers of *Curtis's Botanical Magazine* has reflected this diversity. As fewer new areas of the world remain to be explored, the emphasis will moved towards finding better forms of already-known plants, and saving from extinction those species that are endangered because of the destruction of their native habitat.

ACANTHACEÆ

JUSTICIA ECBOLIUM.
LONG-SPIKED JUSTICIA.
Ecbolium linneanum.

PLATE 1

Linnæus, who has described only twenty species of Justicia in his *Species Plantarum*, divided these into two genera, naming one *Dianthera* from the circumstance of each filament bearing two anthers, one above the other; Jacquin and Vahl have united them into one genus; which however is so numerous as to require subdivision; the latter author having enumerated no less than one hundred and forty-seven species, though he separated the stemless species under the name of *Elytraria*. The first edition of Aiton's *Hortus Kewensis* contains only nine species, and the last but twenty-eight.

Justicia ecbolium is a native of the East Indies. Requires to be kept in the stove. Cultivated by Philip Miller in 1759. Propagated by cuttings. Flowers most part of the summer.

JUSTICIA NERVOSA.
BLUE-FLOWERED JUSTICIA.
Pseuderanthemum pulchellum.

PLATE 2

The late Professor Vahl, in his *Enumeratio Plantarum*, in which he has recorded no fewer than one hundred and sixty-seven species of Justicia, has arranged this under his 5th section, containing those that have a single calyx, and a nearly equal corolla. It seems however more properly to belong to his first section, those with a double calyx and parallel anthers. We have uniformly found, within the large bract, a glume-like two-valved outer calyx, closely embracing the tube of the inner or true calyx, as mentioned by Mr. Ker. In other respects, Vahl's description agrees with our own observations.

Perhaps the outer calyx in this and in every other *Justicia*, where it occurs, may be more properly considered as two smaller bracts. The structure is exactly the same in *Crossandra undulæfolia* of Salisbury, except that in the latter the two inferior bracts are

1 *Justicia ecbolium* (t. 1847 1816)

equal in length to the exterior. Indeed these two plants appear to us to have so near an affinity, as to throw great difficulty in the way of establishing *Crossandra* as a distinct genus; for the mere circumstance of two or four anthers does not seem sufficient to form a generic distinction, and on this account *Ruellia* is not easily separable from *Justicia*.

2 *Justicia nervosa* (t. 1358 1811)

As the specific name of *pulchella* was applied not only by the author of the *Botanist's Repository*, but by his reviewer, who reduced it to the genus *Justicia*, prior to Vahl's publication, and had been since adopted by Dr. Roxburgh, we think it should have been retained by the author of the *Hortus Kewensis*. But as the latter work will probably be considered as the standard for names of plants cultivated in this country, we give up our own opinion, rather than run the risk of adding to the confusion of the nomenclature.

Native of marshy places on the coast of Coromandel. Requires a bark stove, where it flowers very nearly the whole of the year. Introduced into Kew Gardens in the year 1796. Propagated by cuttings.

3 *Thunbergia fragrans* (t. 1811 1817)

THUNBERGIA FRAGRANS.
TWINING THUNBERGIA.
Thunbergia fragrans.

PLATE 3

Thunbergia fragrans has a climbing shrubby stem, which in the East Indies reaches the length of from four to six yards, but we have never seen it exceed that of a few feet in our hothouses, where, however, it well deserves a place, being almost constantly in blossom.

The flowers are quite scentless, nor have we observed any fragrance in any part of the plant; but Dr. Roxburgh in his *Plants of the Coast of Coromandel*, states positively, that "the *plant* possesses a peculiar and agreeable fragrance, and the beauty of its *flowers*, although not fragrant, entitle it to a place in the flower-garden;" so that the absurd notion, prevailing among the Nurserymen, which originated perhaps in the *Botanist's Repository*, that Dr. Roxburgh gave it the name of *fragrans*, because the place where it grew was sweet scented, though the plant was not so, seems to be entirely void of foundation. Perhaps the heat of a tropical sun is necessary to bring forth its odour.

Native of the East Indies; growing plentifully in the hedges and bushes on the banks of the water courses near Samulcotah, on the Coromandel coast. With us it is an inhabitant of the bark stove. Is propagated by cuttings or by seeds, which sometimes come to maturity in this country. Introduced into the Kew Garden by Mr. Peter Good, in the year 1796.

AIZOACEÆ

MESEMBRYANTHEMUM DENSUM.
GREAT BEARDED-LEAVED
FIG-MARIGOLD.
Trichodiadema densum.

PLATE 4

Mr. Haworth, the author of a monograph upon this genus, has, in our opinion, very properly separated the three varieties of M. *barbatum* in the *Species Plantarum*, into as many distinct species.

This plant, though not of difficult cultivation, is extremely shy of flowering; so much so, that Mr. Haworth, to whom we are indebted for the living specimen here figured, informs us that it is one and twenty years since he has seen it in blossom.

Native of the Cape of Good Hope. Requires the same treatment as other succulent plants from that country; which consists chiefly in taking care that they are not injured by damp in the winter, and in protecting them from frost.

4   *Mesembryanthemum densum* (t. 1220 1809)

MESEMBRYANTHEMUM DEPRESSUM.
DEPRESSED TONGUE FIG-MARIGOLD.
Glottiphyllum linguiforme.

PLATE 5

Mr. Haworth has for many years paid great attention to this extensive genus, and his names and characters have been almost entirely adopted in the new editions of the

5   *Mesembryanthemum depressum* (t. 1866 1816)

N. 1866.

Hortus Kewensis. We cannot but suspect, however, that this gentleman has made species of what, in many cases, had been better considered as varieties only. But as cultivators can alone determine, by careful observation, what are permanently distinct species, and as Mr. Haworth has himself been a considerable cultivator of these plants, we cannot do better, perhaps, at present, than to adhere to his names. We find, however, a great difficulty, in the present instance, in determining to which our present plant belongs.

We are informed by Mr. George Graves, that it is not very shy of flowering in the summer time, and that the blossoms expand in the forenoon, if the sun shine; but in cloudy weather, not at all. The leaves are remarkably brittle, and, when viewed through a lens, are observed to be covered with minute pellucid dots. Flowers in July and August.

ALSTRŒMERIACEÆ

ALSTRŒMERIA PELEGRINA.
SPOTTED-FLOWER'D ALSTRŒMERIA.
Alstroemeria pelegrina.

PLATE 6

Father Feuillée figures and describes three species of *Alstrœmeria*, viz. *pelegrina*, *ligtu*, and *salsilla*, common names by which they are severally distinguished in Peru: the present species, which is much valued by the natives on account of its beauty, he informs us is found wild on a mountain to the north of, and a mile distant from Lima.

From Peru, as might be expected, the present plant found its way into Spain, from whence by the means of his beloved friend Alstrœmer, Linnæus first received seeds of it; the value he set on the acquisition is evident from the great care he took of the seedling plants, preserving them through the winter in his bed-chamber.

Being a mountainous plant, it is found to be much more hardy than the *ligtu*, and is generally treated as a greenhouse plant; it is found, however, to flower and ripen its seeds better under the glass of a hot-bed frame, where air is freely admitted.

It flowers from June to October, and, though a perennial, is generally raised from seeds, yet may sometimes be increased by parting its roots, which somewhat resemble those of the asparagus: the seeds should be sown in the spring, in a pot of light earth, on a gentle hot-bed, either of dung or tan.

7   *Oplotheca floridana* (t. 2603 1825 JC)

8   *Amaryllis advena* (t. 1125 1808)

6   *Alstroemeria pelegrina* (t. 139 1790 SE)

AMARANTHACEÆ

OPLOTHECA FLORIDANA.
FLORIDA OPLOTHECA.
Froelichia floridana.
PLATE 7

Oplotheca belongs to the natural order of *Amaranthaceæ*, and has been established as a genus by Professor Nuttall, who unites with it, as a second species, the *Gomphrena interrupta; Gomphrena humboldtiana* of Roemer and Schultes, the *lanata* of Kunth, if it should not turn out to be the same, will certainly make a third. It is distinguished from *Gomphrena* chiefly by the form of the stigma.

Native of North America. Found on the banks of the Altamaho, by Dr. Baldwin; on the sandy beach of the Arkansa, by Professor Nuttall.

Communicated by Robert Barclay, Esq. of Bury Hill, In September, 1824. It was raised from seeds given to Mr. Barclay, by Mr. Nuttall.

AMARYLLIDACEÆ

AMARYLLIS ADVENA.
STREAKED-FLOWERED AMARYLLIS.
Hippeastrum advenum.
PLATE 8

A native of Chili; and till now, we believe, an entire stranger to our European gardens. Although described and figured in Feuillée's *Journal*, it has not been arranged in any of the systematic records of vegetation; nor had it before received a specific name.

Our drawing was made from a specimen, the produce of bulbs, brought by Mr. Brandt from South America. The whole plant is void of scent. Requires to be kept in the stove.

AMARYLLIS BELLADONNA (α).
BELLADONNA LILY.
Amaryllis belladonna.
PLATE 9

Amaryllis belladona (α) was introduced into this country from Portugal in 1712, but where native is yet doubtful; the channel through which the plant has been received makes it more than probable that it is a Brazil vegetable. The older Botanists call its country India, which with them may mean the East Indies, South America, or even some parts of Africa: β, which Miller tells us only differs in having paler flowers and blooming in the spring instead of the autumn, comes from the Cape of Good Hope where it was found by Sir Joseph Banks. This was also sent by Van Royen from Holland to Miller in 1754, and flowered at Chelsea Garden. (α) is very common in the gardens near Lisbon and Florence, at the last of which places it is sold in the markets under the name of the *Belladonna narcissus.*

Our seedsmen received the bulbs yearly in abundance from Portugal, and these when planted close to the foot of a southern wall will blow annually, after they are once settled, which they are not in less than two or three years; they then produce offsets in plenty: their time of expansion is October. This species is by no means so commonly cultivated as we should have imagined, from its beauty, fragrance, and easy culture, it would have been before this time.

N.º733

Syd Edwards del. Pub. by T. Curtis, S.t Geo. Crescent Apr. 1 1804. F. Sansom sculp.

9 *Amaryllis belladonna* α (t. 733 1804)

AMARYLLIS CURVIFOLIA.
GLAUCOUS-LEAVED AMARYLLIS.

Nerine curvifolia

PLATE 10

Blooms at various seasons; is generally treated as a stove plant; though we should think it would do better at the foot of a southern wall with *belladonna*, but not planted too shallow.

According to the Banksian Herbarium, our plant was brought into the Kew Gardens about 1788, from the Cape; Jacquin received it from the same place.

There is a gardening tradition that it was likewise received from Japan by the late Dr. Fothergill; if so, this, with *belladonna* and *sarniensis*, would make the third species of the genus that is common to the Cape as well as to countries immensely distant from it; but we confess that we place no reliance whatever on the story beyond its bare possibility.

AMARYLLIS HUMILIS.
DIVARICATE-PETALED AMARYLLIS.

Nerine humilis.

PLATE 11

This differs from A. *undulata* in having its leaves more bluntly pointed, the corolla more irregular, outer segments without the corniform mucro that exists in the other, the two lower of these divaricating edgeways, and further in having three very distinct filiform patent stigmas. Jacquin has figured two varieties, the smaller one of which approaches nearer to *undulata* in size

4

Syd:Edwards del   Pub. by T. Curtis, St Geo: Crefcent Mar. 1 1804.   F. Sanfom sculp.

10 Amaryllis curvifolia (t. 725 1804 SE)

than the other does; but is as distinct from it in every other part as this is.

It flowers freely every year towards the latter-end of the summer, it is often taken for *undulata*, and in some gardens is called

11 Amaryllis humilis (t. 726 1804 SE)

Syd:Edwards del   Pub. by T. Curtis, St Geo: Crefcent Mar. 1 2004.   F. Sanfom sculp.

crispa, the name of a very distinct species. We know nothing of the time when nor by whom it was imported. Jacquin received his bulbs from the Cape.

AMARYLLIS ORNATA (α).
CAPE COAST LILY.

Crinum zeylanicum.

PLATE 12

We lay before our readers the Sierra Leone variety of this species. The Sierra Leone plant has sometimes several flowers, with leaves several times broader than in the present specimen, and not acutely carinate; the edges are sometimes rough or obsoletely denticulate, but not always, nor all so on the same plant. Ehret supposes his specimen to have been imported from the Cape of Good Hope; but we are persuaded that it is the East Indian plant; at all events no spontaneous production of the Cape. Both *ornata* α and β require to be kept in the hothouse, and are very ornamental (see below).

NB   The reproduction of this illustration is greatly enlarged for the original is 198mm × 120mm.

AMARYLLIS ORNATA. (β.)
WHITE CAPE COAST LILY.

Crinum giganteum.

PLATE 13

After a diligent research (fully impressed with a contrary suspicion arising from their far distant, yet in fact not unanalagous, abodes) we are now satisfied of the specific identity of the Indian *zeylanica* of Linnæus and the African *ornata* of the *Hortus Kewensis* of which the present plant is an obvious variety. Linnæus most probably took up, as well as named, his species from the plates and descriptions of Commelin and Rudbeck. *Ornata* (α) is said to have been introduced in 1740 by Lord Petre, from whose plant Ehret designed his plate; but we more than suspect the exactness of his information, when he states it to be a native of the Cape of Good Hope. Among

the Gardeners it is known by the appellation of "the Cape-Coast Lily," and was certainly sent to us some years back from Sierra Leone. Dr. Roxburgh found spontaneous specimens on the Coromandel coast; Rumph mentions it as being an inhabitant of the gardens of Amboyna, where it had been received from Batavia, and there known by the name of the Java-Tulip.

Loureiro met with two varieties in China and Cochin-China: from Commelin we learn, that in Holland it was supposed to be a native of Ceylon: (β) was received by us also, from the colony of Sierra Leone; where it is said to grow in the water (most probably in spots that are only periodically inundated) and to be with great difficulty obtained, owing to the jealousy of the natives, by whom it is held in superstitious veneration, being used as an amulet or charm to preserve them in war, as well as almost every other species of danger. Both varieties agree in a decided predilection for low sandy situations, as well as of water, and we accordingly perceive in our stoves, that the size and number of flowers depend much upon the greater or less proportion of the latter element that has been supplied during the time of their vegetation.

In the adoption of the specific title of *ornata* in preference to the older one of *zeylanica*, we were influenced first by its being now as universally established as the other, and then by its being less liable to mislead.

AMARYLLIS REVOLUTA.
CHANGEABLE-FLOWERED AMARYLLIS.

Crinum giganteum.

PLATE 16

This very rare species has already made its appearance in the present work; but the specimen, from which the drawing was taken, had no leaves, and was altogether far less perfect than that which has been now figured by our draughtsman.

A. *revoluta* is very closely allied to A. *longifolia* (661); but has a corollat with the tube shorter, and not longer than the limb, as in that; also a proportionably smaller germen, which is oval, more even, furrowless, and polished.

Syd. Edwards Del. F. Sansom Jun. Sculp.   Pub. by T. Curtis St. Geo. Crescent Jun. 1. 1810.

N.º 923 ✻

Pub by T. Curtis, May. 1. 1806.

13 Amaryllis ornata β (t. 923 1806)

Amaryllis Tubispatha.
Mr. Griffin's Amaryllis.

Zephyranthes tubispatha.

PLATE 14

The species appears to have been first taken up by L'Heritier, from a specimen without leaves in Commerson's Herbarium, brought from Buenos Ayres. The present plant (probably the first living one that has been ever seen in Europe) was received by Mr. Griffin from a friend in Jamaica, who was informed that it had

Opposite:
12   Amaryllis ornata α (t. 1253 1810 SE)

been procured by a person residing "on one of the back settlements in the blue mountains of that Island."

The specimen, from which our drawing has been made, flowered last July for the first time; the corolla had a pinkish hue when it first showed itself in bud, but soon lost all vestige of that colour.— We have never met with the species in any Herbarium we have had access to. From the length of the peduncle, in relation to the scape, the spathe appears as if in the middle of the latter.

Brunsvigia Falcata.
Sweet-scented Brunswick-lily.

Cybistetes longifolia.

PLATE 20

Bulb round-ovate, integuments numerous membranous; outer *leaves* sometimes nearly two feet long, from half to an inch broad, quite flat, surrounded by a short white cartilaginous fringe; *scape* three to four inches high, in old many-flowered specimens very broad in proportion to its height; *corolla* about two inches and a half long, changing from greenish white to deep rose-colour; tube half an inch long; *capsule*

14   *Amaryllis tubispatha* (t. 1586 1813)

15   *Conanthera bifolia* (t. 2496 1824 JC)

with its continuous pedicel from six to seven inches long, brown, narrow-turbinate and shortly contracted at the top; *cells* about three inches long, with from one to three *seeds* of various sizes, which are fleshy but not outwardly herbaceous and irregularly rounded compressed. Native of the Cape of Good Hope. Blooms about August, diffusing a fragrance, which appeared to us to resemble that of the "Lily of the Valley."

CONANTHERA BIFOLIA.
VIOLET-FLOWERED CONANTHERA.

Conanthera simsii

PLATE 15

Conanthera bifolia is a native of the mountains of Chili, and our plant was raised from seeds, which came from that country, by the late John Walker Esq. of Southgate, where it flowered in June last year, 1823.

The figures in the *Flora Peruviana*, and in Feuillée, represent the petals narrower and more reflexed than they were in our plant; but the descriptions agree so well with it that we cannot consider them as distinct species. The leaves on the flowering plant decay before the blossoms ex-

pand; those represented in the figure, belonged to a bulb that did not flower, which is probably the reason of a third leaf being produced.

The bulbs are eaten by the natives both boiled and raw; and Feuillée found them very good in soup.

CRINUM ERUBESCENS.
BLUSH-COLOURED CRINUM.

Crinum erubescens.

PLATE 24

By Linnæus, if he really meant the same plant, this was thought to be a variety of *Crinum americanum*; by his son it has been separated into a distinct species, and so continued from his manuscript in the *Hortus Kewensis*. But we doubt if Linnæus had this plant in view.

A native of Spanish America. Requires to be kept in the hothouse. Differs chiefly from *americanum* in the colour of the bloom and the cartilaginous toothed edging of the leaves. Blooms at various seasons.

CRINUM MOLUCCANUM.
MOLUCCA CRINUM.

Crinum latifolium var moluccanum.

PLATE 25

Descr. "*Bulb* nearly sphærical, the size of a goose's egg, when stripped of its dead integuments of a pale purple colour, very different from the deep crimson of *Crinum zeylanicum.*" Leaves pale green, striate lanceolate, tapering to a point, undulated towards the base, nearly two feet long, and an inch and a half wide at the base, margin a little rough. *Scape* eight inches high, flat on one side and convex on the other, reddish purple. *Spathe* membranaceous, two-leaved, erect, obtuse, striate, flesh-coloured. *Flower* in our specimen four, sometimes six, large, showy. *Germen* sessile, green, unequally three-cornered: *tube* striate, flesh-coloured, equal in length to the *limb*, which is funnel-shaped, the laciniæ striate, flesh-coloured in the middle, with white margins, somewhat recurved at the point. *Stamens* and *style* declined, equal, shorter than the laciniæ.

The plant from which our drawing was taken flowered early in September at the Earl of Carnarvon's, and as we were informed by Mr. Gouen, his Lordship's Secretary, the bulb was received from Dr. Carey, of Serampore.

CRINUM SUBMERSUM.
LAKE CRINUM.

Crinum submersum.

PLATE 31

This is a most interesting plant, whether it be an intermediate link connecting two species, which are widely separated from each other in the two sections of its genus, so closely that it is difficult to say unto which it has most affinity, or a hybrid generated between them in the swamps of America. The bulb was discovered by George Hopkins, in the vicinity of Rio Janeiro, growing in water in a spot, which, after an unusual course of dry weather, was still inundated, in company with several plants of a smaller white *Crinum*, which appears likely to prove a variety approaching to the Corantyne variety, of

C. *erubescens*. The bulb was received at Spofforth, in August, having three dead scapes adhering to it, and it flowered about six weeks after, having been planted in drift sand and well watered; being in every point of bulb, leaf, and inflorescence, intermediate between C. *scabrum* and *erubescens*. The flowers of *submersum* have the fine nocturnal fragrance of *erubescens*, but less powerfully. The filaments are knobbed, and the connecting membrane visible between them as in *erubescens*, but less conspicuously. The upper filament detaches itself as in that species, but with less regularity, sometimes taking one of the laterals with it. The anthers before their inversion are of a paler ash colour than those of *erubescens*, mottled with the straw colour of *scabrum*. The petals have the channelled base and sharp-pointed long-oval form which belongs to the *Crina* of the first section, with the lesser expansion and the colouring which belongs to the second. The number of ovules is also intermediate between *scabrum* and *erubescens*. The ovules and pollen appeared perfect. Have we in this instance discovered a native mule in the wilderness? Have we lit upon the first origin of a new species? or, have we in this bulb an original link in the creation between two plants which have been placed by some writers in different genera? Whichever be the case, no unprejudiced botanist can now compare the three plants and not consider them of one genus. C. *scabrum* is known to grow on the woody hills near Rio, and its pollen may have been brought down to the lake on the plumage of a humming bird, and produced accidentally the same result in the wilds of Brazil, which art has effected in our stoves.

16   *Amaryllis revoluta* (t. 1178 1809)

Syd. Edwards Del.   Pub. by T. Curtis St Geo: Crescent Mar. 1 1809   F. Sansom Sculp.

CYRTANTHUS STRIATUS.
STRIATED CYRTANTHUS.
Cyrtanthus angustifolius.

PLATE 18

Our figure represents the inflorescence at two periods; the first flower never nodded, the others nodded before their expansion; and theirs is probably the true posture of the flower. It flowered in July, in the greenhouse, at Spofforth.

C. striatus was imported from the Cape, by the late Mr. Lee, and sold by him to many persons, labelled *Amaryllis falcata*, by the error of the collector. It was supposed at first to be a species of *Vallota*. *Vallota purpurea* has the capsule oval like *Cyrtanthus*.

17 *Cyrtanthus pallidus* (t. 2471 1824 JC)

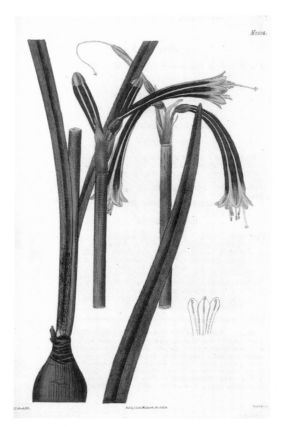

18 *Cyrtanthus striatus* (t. 2534 1824 WJH)

19 *Eucrosia bicolor* (t. 2490 1824 WJH)

CYRTANTHUS PALLIDUS.
PALE FLOWERED CYRTANTHUS.
Cyrtanthus pallidus.

PLATE 17

This appears to us to be an undescribed species of *Cyrtanthus*. It comes nearest to *C. ventricosus* (*angustifolius* of Jacquin) from which it differs in the paler colour of its flowers, in the regular diminution of size of the corolla from the limb to the base, without any sensible inflation of the middle of the tube, and especially in the nearly equal proportion of the limb to the tube including the faux, which latter character, as well as the absence of glaucescence in the leaves and scape, distinguishes it from *collinus*. From *Cyrtanthus spiralis* it differs totally in the form and colour of the leaves.

Native of the Cape of Good Hope, from whence it was sent in 1822, by Mr Villet, a gentleman in correspondence with the Horticultural Society. It flowered at their magnificent establishment in January 1823, but the leaves did not appear till sometime after the flower was quite decayed. Requires the protection of the greenhouse.

EUCROSIA BICOLOR.
PARTICOLORED EUCROSIA.
Eucrosia bicolor.

PLATE 19

We have paid the most minute attention to the drawing and description of this curious plant, because the only figure and account of it published are very inaccurate, the flowers being represented with a funnel-shaped limb and otherwise distorted (prob-

ably in consequence of having been forced out of their natural posture and form by the fingers of the curious) and the generic character being, in several respects, incorrect and imperfect. Bulbs of this species were imported from South America into the Hammersmith nursery, where one of them flowered in 1817. They were soon after lost by exposure in a cold frame, and we believe our specimen from the Spofforth collection is the only one that has been since produced in Europe. The flower has a singular resemblance to a winged insect, taking the germen for its head. The four flowers are placed back to back, nearly at right angles. The petals are bent upwards and pressed together sideways, and, if pulled apart, close again immediately.

The leaf of the full-grown bulb, which follows the flower, is near a foot long, and too large for the plate. The bulbs thrive in the stove in light loam, requiring moisture and shade while growing, drought and complete rest in autumn and winter. The plant flowered at Spofforth in April. We are, as yet, unacquainted with the seeds. The leaves are frequently solitary; probably, their number rarely exceeds three. This species should have been rather called *tricolor* than *bicolor*.

20 *Brunsvigia falcata* (t. 1443 1808 SE)

GALANTHUS LATIFOLIUS.
BROAD-LEAVED SNOWDROP.

Galanthus ikariae.

PLATE 21

Owing to the evacuation of books and specimens, and to other wartime difficulties, it has unfortunately not been possible to work out thoroughly the interrelations and distribution of the group of snowdrops with broad, lorate dark green leaves, recurved at the ends, grouped round *Galanthus latifolius* Ruprecht. The present article, therefore, must be regarded only as a tentative account pending further research.

The different species of snowdrops can be distinguished by several characters, namely the shape of the leaves, the shape of the outer perianth-segments, the marking of the inner perianth-segments, and the lengths of the pedicel and spathe. In *G. latifolius* the leaves are usually deep green, lorate, and recurved at the ends, the outer segments are oblong-oval acute at the apex and unguiculate at the base, the inner segments have a deep green marking round the sinus and usually extending halfway down the length of the segment, and the pedicel is shorter than the spathe. The green marking on the inner segment apparently varies to some extent, for in the specimen figured from the Rock Garden at Kew, it is much narrower and approximates to the narrow, horseshoe marking typical of *G. nivalis*. In the accompanying text-figure three types of marking are shown; type c is apparently rare.

G. latifolius was originally described from Transcaucasia and its distribution is given in the *Flora U.R.S.S. IV. 477* (1935) as endemic to the alpine and subalpine zones of eastern and western Transcaucasia. There are, however, two snowdrops from

21 *Galanthus latifolius* (t. 9669 1946 SR-C & LS)

other areas which appear to be best regarded as forms of *G. latifolius*, but which
require further study. The first was collected by E. K. Balls in 1933 near
Hamesekeui, south west of Trebizond, and
has been considered to be a variety of *G.
latifolius*. It is a smaller growing plant than
the Caucasian *G. latifolius*, but the flowers
are of the same size. The second was
described by J. G. Baker (*Gard. Chron. Ser.
3, XIII. 506*: 1893) as *G. ikariae* from the
island of Nikaria (classical Icaria), south
west of Samos. From Baker's description it
would appear to be very near *G. latifolius*
though the outer perianth-segments are
larger and the anthers more abruptly mucronate. Baker says that *G. ikariae* has the
apical green blotch on the inner segments
like *G. nivalis*, but in his description the
blotch is said to occupy half the outer-side
of the segment, and this character is also
shown in specimens from Mr. Bowles' garden which were figured in the *Botanical
Magazine*, t. 9474, and which are now
preserved in the Kew Herbarium. This is
one of the characters where it differs from
G. nivalis, in which species the apical
blotch is merely a green horseshoe marking
round the sinus.

There is another snowdrop, *Galanthus
fosteri*, also described by J. G. Baker (*Gard.
Chron. Ser. 3, V. 458*: 1889), which is
thought by some to be a form of *G.
latifolius*. Its likeness, however, ends at the
broad green leaves; the markings on the

inner segment are like those of *G. elwesii*
(*Bot. Mag.* t. 6166), that is, green markings round the sinus with a deep green
blotch at the base. This snowdrop came to
Professor M. Foster from Amasia in north-
central Asia Minor. It might be a natural
or garden hybrid between *G. latifolius* and
G. elwesii, or perhaps a large growing form
of *G. elwesii* with green instead of glaucous
leaves. *G. elwesii* is a somewhat variable
species.

Another snowdrop introduced by E. K.
Balls found at Soguk Su near Trebizond in
1934 (and also by Arthur Baker, near
Rizeh, fifty miles east of Trebizond along
the Black Sea) and known in gardens
under the name of *Galanthus latifolius* var.
rizehensis (or *rizensis*) is considered by some
to be a small form of *G. latifolius*. It would
appear rather to be a form or hybrid of *G.
nivalis*, having narrow linear leaves simply
channelled down the face, inner segments
marked with green only round the sinus,
and the pedicels longer than the spathes –
all characters of the *nivalis* group – but the
leaves are deep green and eventually recurved.

Galanthus latifolius, which was introduced into this country over seventy years
ago, flowers in English gardens in February
and the beginning of March and seeds
freely. Distribution. – Eastern and western
Transcaucasia.

22 *Haemanthus albiflos* (t. 1239 1809)

HÆMANTHUS ALBIFLOS.
WHITE-FLOWERED HÆMANTHUS.
Haemanthus albiflos.

PLATE 22

Leaves about four, one to two inches broad,
four to six long, somewhat shorter than
scape, of a deep green colour; *flowers* white
with very short *pedicels*; *anthers* deep tawny
yellow, incumbent; *style* rather thicker and
higher than *stamens*, upright; *berry* about
the size of a pea, roundish, trilocular, of a
bright shining red-lead colour; *loculaments*
one-seeded.

Introduced into this country from the
Cape of Good Hope. We did not perceive
that it had any scent.

23 *Haemanthus multiflorus* (t. 961 1806 SE)

HÆMANTHUS MULTIFLORUS.
MANY-FLOWERED BLOOD-FLOWER.
Scadoxus multiflorus

PLATE 23

From the first establishment of a colony at
Sierra Leone, the bulbs of this beautiful
flower have frequently been imported from
thence, and is rather common in our
stoves.

Being a native of so warm a climate as the Coast of Guinea, the bark stove is necessary to its preservation; and even there few have been so successful as to flower the same plant repeatedly; though imported bulbs will blow without the aid of artificial heat. Introduced into the Paris garden more than two hundred years ago by Mons. Robin, Jun.

LEUCOJUM AUTUMNALE.
AUTUMNAL SNOW-FLAKE.

Leucojum autumnale.

PLATE 26

This modest little plant is a native of Spain, Portugal, and the neighbourhood of Algiers, growing on the dry sandy hills; we have received specimens also from the rock of Gibraltar.

Brotero has another species or rather variety very similar to *Leucojum autumnale*, which he calls *trichophyllum*, in this the petals are acute, not tridentate.

Every author who has described this plant agrees that it has usually two, some-times one, but very rarely three flowers from the same spathe, yet all continue to say spatha *multiflora*; it appears to be much more constant to the character of two-flowered than *L. vernum* does to that of one-flowered.

It flowers, as the name denotes, in the autumn, coming up without leaves, which with us seldom appear till the flowering is entirely over, sometimes not till the spring; but in most of the specimens we received from Gibraltar the leaves appear with the flower, though much shorter than they afterwards grow; much the same as in Clusius's figure, from which all the other figures of the older authors were copied except our Parkinson, who however coarse, is usually original.

24   *Crinum erubescens* (t. 1232 1809 SE)

Nº 1232.

Syd. Edwards Del. F Sanfom Jun Sculp.

Pub. by T. Curtis St Geo: Crescent Oct.1.1809.

J. Sowerby. Del.

Pub. by S. Curtis. Walworth. Jan. 1. 1822.

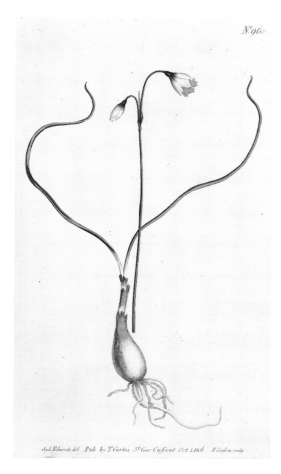

26 *Leucojum autumnale* (t. 960 1806 SE)

NARCISSUS BIFRONS.
JONQUIL-SCENTED NARCISSUS.
Narcissus intermedius var. *bifrons*.

PLATE 27

We have observed that the original *odorus* of Linnæus had been negligently converted by himself, in a subsequent work, into a species not really distinct from the *calathinus* of the same. The first was originally taken up in the *Amœnitates Academicæ*, but changed in the *Species Plantarum*, where the former synonymy is dropped, and a figure of the present plant alone quoted. This induced us to add it to that species as the variety γ. Now the plant itself is before us, its being a variety of that is out of the question: we have called it *bifrons*, from an almost equally proportioned resemblance to both *Joaquilla* and *calathinus*. Is it a mule production between these two species?

These bulbs were imported about two years ago from Holland, by a seedsman under the name which we have adopted above for our English one. Blooms in March and April. Has generally only two leaves, which are nearly two feet long, but sometimes shorter and equal to the scape.

OPPOSITE:
25 *Crinum moluccanum* (t. 2292 1822 JS)

It has from four to five flowers, larger than those of the Jonquil, but less than those of *calathinus*. Extremely fragrant. Seems to be as hardy as the others of the genus. If it has not been produced in the way we have guessed, then the native country is unknown to us.

NARCISSUS ORIENTALIS (α).
PALE-CUPPED WHITE GARDEN NARCISSUS.
Narcissus tazetta.

PLATE 28

This is the real *orientalis* of the *Hortus Kewensis*. Probably native of the Levant and Italy.

NARCISSUS MAJOR. β. γ.
LARGE YELLOW SPANISH NARCISSUS.
Narcissus hispanicus.

PLATE 29

NARCISSUS MOSCHATUS (δ).
SMALLER WHITE SPANISH DAFFODIL.
Narcissus moschatus.

PLATE 30

A very rare plant. We suspect that *major*, and *bicolor* are mere varieties of each other. *Pseudo-narcissus* and *minor* are evidently distinct from them all, but very probably varieties of each other. The three former are most probably native of Spain and other southern parts of the Continent, the latter of Great Britain and the more northern parts of Europe.

PANCRATIUM AMBOINENSE.
AMBOYNA PANCRATIUM.
Eurycles amboinensis.

PLATE 36

Requires to be kept in the stove, where it blooms about July. Mr. Brown, in his very

valuable *Prodromus of the Flora of New Holland*, observes that this species differs from its congeners in having a germen with dispermous cells, as well as by a crown that is six-parted to the base. In our plant this last character was not present, the dilated bases of the filaments cohering for nearly half the length of the crown they formed; such seems also to have been the case in the specimen delineated, accompanied with a dissection of the corolla, by Mr. Bauer, in the first volume of his *Sketches* in the Banksian Collection. We entirely agree with the author of the *Paradisus Londinensis*, in the opinion, that this is the species described and figured by Rumphius, although there is no appearance of the small staminilegous crown in his engraving. Mons. L'Heritier expressly notices the dilated bases of the filaments in his description of *Crinum nervosum*, citing Rumphius's figure for a synonym; and we suspect that he was induced to separate his plant from the *amboinense* of Linnæus, merely on account of that author's having added Trew's figure, as his variety β.; a figure which undoubtedly belongs to a very distinct species from his variety α.; which is our present plant.

L'Heritier gives the Philippine Islands as the native place of his plant.

PANCRATIUM CALATHINUM.
WHITE BRASIL PANCRATIUM.
Hymenocallis narcissiflora.

PLATE 32

We are informed that bulbs of this plant were received, together with many others, from the Brasils, by Lady Amelia Hume, in the year 1796. We are obliged to Sir Abraham Hume for the present specimen. In that gentleman's hothouse, the plant blooms every year, in March and April. Mons. Redouté, who had figured and described the species, tells us, that it is cultivated in the celebrated collection of Mons. Cels, at Paris; and that the place of its spontaneous abode is unknown. His specimen, judging from the figure, was stronger and more perfect than the one we received.

N. 2463

31 *Crinum submersum* (t. 2463 1824)

PANCRATIUM ROTATUM (α)
AMERICAN PANCRATIUM.

Hymenocallis rotata.

PLATE 33

Had we seen the present variety at the time we gave a name to the species, we should not have applied that of *rotatum*, which certainly does not characterize it in this state. The former specimen was raised by

Mr. Loddiges from American seed; the present is the produce of a bulb received by him from the same quarter. Both are exceeding fragrant, more peculiarly so in the night-time. Leaves about eight. Style green for a considerable way, as is the stigma.

PANCRATIUM SPECIOSUM.
BALSAM-SCENTED SEA-DAFFODIL.

Hymenocallis speciosa.

PLATE 41

Descr. *Bulb* depressed-sphærical, about the size of a turkey's egg, integuments numerous, membranous, brownish; *leaves* of a very dark green colour, from a foot and a half to two feet long, from three to four inches across the broadest part, in number uncertain, several fresh ones being produced each time the plant blooms, while the old ones do not decay in proportion, at least in our stoves; *scape* rather shorter than the foliage, compressed, ancipital, streakletted; *spathe* two inches or more in length, white-green; *umbel* seven to fifteen-flowered intermixed with *bracts* as long as the spathe but narrower; *flowers* pure white, nearly nine inches long, very ornamental, extremely fragrant, especially in the evening, retaining their scent for many months when dried; the *cells* of the

32 *Pancratium calathinum* (t. 1561 1813 SE)

germen in all the specimens we examined were dispermous, as in *Pancratium amboinense*. We do not know a more desirable stove plant than this. Has been confounded in the late edition of the *Hortus Kewensis* with the *caribæum* of t. 826 of the *Botanical Magazine* which had been mis-

33 *Pancratium rotatum* α (t. 1082 1808 SE)

taken by Redouté in his *Liliacèes* for the present species, and published by him under the appellation of *speciosum*.

34 *Strumaria crispa* (t. 1363 1811 SE)

STRUMARIA CRISPA.
GLITTERING-FLOWERED STRUMARIA.

Hessea cinnamomea.

PLATE 34

Bulb about the size of a walnut, outward membrane brown; *leaves* attaining at least six inches in length, one sometimes preceding the other and appearing nearly at the same time with the *scape*, which is about four inches high; *pedicels* dark green, rounded triquetral, about an inch and half long; *corolla* about nine lines in diameter, white suffused with rose-colour, transparent when viewed against the light; is a very beautiful object through a magnifying glass; *germen* shining, brownish; *anthers* brown, *pollen* yellow. Native of the Cape of Good Hope, from whence it was imported by Mr. Masson, in 1790. Requires to be kept in a greenhouse; blooms in November; has no scent that we could perceive.

ZEPHYRANTHES VERECUNDA.
MODEST ZEPHYRANTHES.

Zephyranthes verecunda.

PLATE 35

The bulb, from which our figure was made, formed part of a collection, consisting of seeds and a few bulbs, brought by Mr. Bullock from Mexico. It was accompanied by another species, apparently a *Zephyranthes*, with broader leaves, which we take to be *Amaryllis nervosa* of Humboldt; and a species with smaller striped flowers, which is perhaps his *Amaryllis minuta*: but it is impossible to decide with certainty, the specific characters of *A. nervosa* and *minuta*, being given briefly in Kunth, in precisely the same words; excepting that the corolla of the former is called white, and that of the latter approaching to rose-colour.

Zephyranthes verecunda, though of much smaller stature, comes very near indeed to *Zephyranthes atamasco*; the tube distinguishes it at once from *tubispatha*. Its foliage is narrower and thicker than that of *atamasco*, and sometimes spirally twisted. The flower, which was white at first, had begun to fade before it reached our draughtsman, and, consequently, had assumed a more erect posture than belongs to the genus,

35 *Zephyranthes verecunda* (t. 2583 1825 JC)

when the corolla is in its first perfection. The three filaments belonging to the outer petals are shortest, and their anthers attached nearer the middle than the other anthers.

Zephyranthes may be looked upon as the Crocus of hot countries. We learn from Dr. Carey, that *Z. tubispatha* and the hybrid *Hippeastrum splendens*, sent to him by us a few years ago, have multiplied so prodigiously, that they now form the ornament of most gardens near Calcutta.

36 *Pancratium amboinense* (t. 1419 1811 SE)

APOCYNACEÆ

ALLAMANDA CATHARTICA.

WILLOW-LEAV'D ALLAMANDA.

Allamanda cathartica.

PLATE 37

This beautiful stove plant (a native of Cayenne and Guiana, where it is said to grow by the sides of rivers) was introduced to this country in 1785, by Baron Hake; it has since flowered in many of our collections, usually in June and July.

Of this genus, which has a considerable affinity with that of *Vinca* and *Plumeria*, only one species is described in Linnæus's works, and this is usually increased by cuttings.

ECHITES NUTANS.

NODDING SAVANNAH-FLOWER.

Prestonia venosa.

PLATE 38

This plant was sent from the Botanic Garden at St. Vincents to that of the Horticultral Society at Chiswick, by Mr. George Caley, late superintendant of the former establishment. The red colour of the veins disppears in the older leaves, which then become more clothed with a very soft pubescence. There is a species of *Echites* described and figured in Tusac's *Flore des Antilles*, by the name of *sanguinolenta* (Bloody Savanna-flower of the inhabitants of Jamaica), which has similar red veins, but the shape of the corolla is totally

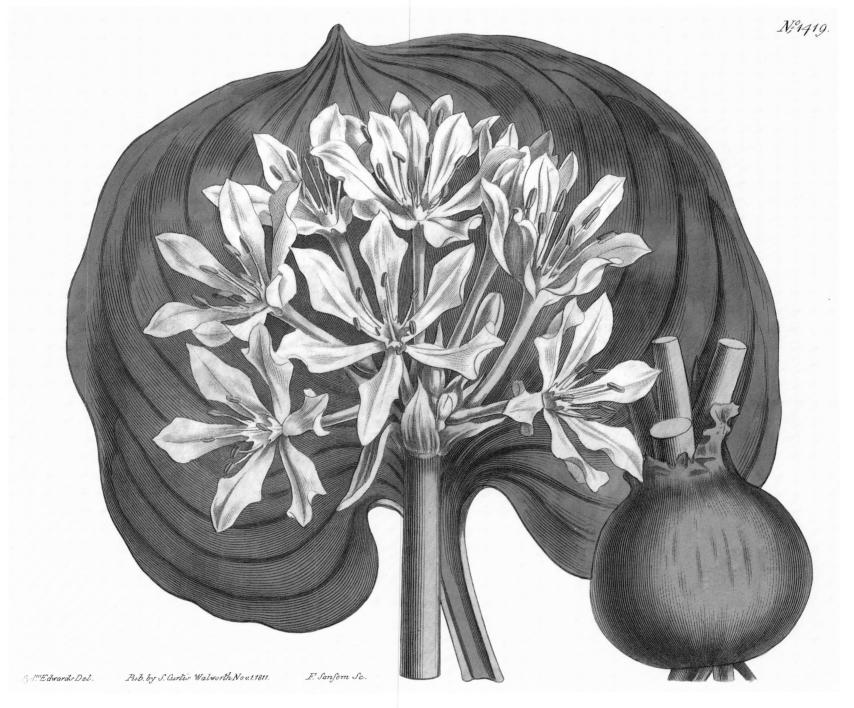

Gr.Mᵉˢ Edwards Del.   *Pub. by S. Curtis Walworth Novᵗ.1.1811.*   *F. Sansom Sc.*

Nº 1419.

19

37 *Allamanda cathartica* (t. 338 1796)

39 *Echites suberecta* β (t. 1064 1807 SE)

38 *Echites nutans* (t. 2473 1824 JC)

character is by no means constant.

Native of the West Indies. Requires to be kept in the stove. Our drawing was taken at the Horticultural Society's garden, in September 1823.

different, the laciniæ being terminated with a filiform point.

Mr. Caley informs us, that the garden at St. Vincents was in some places overrun with this plant, but that it flowered in one spot only; he observes, also, that there was a variety of it in the garden with white or silvery veins instead of red, so that this

ECHITES SUBERECTA (β).
LARGER SAVANNA-FLOWER.
Neriandra suberecta.

PLATE 39

This plant has been described by Jacquin, and more fully by Swartz in his *Observationes*; but neither of these authors have remarked the singular manner in which the footstalk of the leaf is inserted into the branch, through the medium of a kind of glandular stipule.

The stem is too weak to support itself. The flowers are large and showy; and in this variety not villous on the outside. The whole plant abounds with a milky juice, which is said to be very posionous to horses and cattle. Native of the savannas in Jamaica and St. Domingo, and also of dry heaths exposed to the sea-winds. Requires the heat of the bark stove. Flowers with us in July and August. Cultivated by Miller in 1759.

APONOGETONACEÆ
APONOGETON ANGUSTIFOLIUM.
NARROW-LEAVED APONOGETON.
Aponogeton angustifolius

PLATE 40

This had been confounded by Linnæus with *distachyon*, that having been made by him to vary with from six to twelve stamens. The *leaves* are here narrower than in *distachyon*, and tapered at each end. *Raches* pale-red. *Flowers* few. *Bracts* white, red at

40 *Aponogeton angustifolium* (t. 1268 1810 SE)

their base, two-parted almost to the bottom (or two, if you will), segments linear-oblong. *Stamens* six, three to four times shorter than bracts. *Styles* three. We did not see the plant in bloom, but have translated the description from *Hortus Kewensis*.

Introduced into this country in 1788, by Mr. F. Masson. Native of the Cape of Good Hope. A water-plant. The bulbs of *distachyon* are said to be eaten when roasted; so most probably are those of this closely allied species. Blooms most part of the year.

No. 1453.

<small>J⁵ᵗ Edwards Del.</small>   Pub. by S. Curtis Walworth Apr. 1. 1812.   F. Sansom Sc.

41   *Pancratium speciosum* (t. 1453 1812 SE)

Aponogeton distachyon.
Water Hawthorn.
Aponogeton distachyos.

PLATE 44

Root tuberous (G.), eatable when roasted; *leaves* radical, with long *petioles, blade* lanceolate-ovate, quite entire, smooth, floating, like that of *Potamogeton natans; spike* bipartite, imbricate inwards; *flowers* exceedingly fragrant, white, alternate, upright, placed within an ovate· *bract; stamens* six to twelve; *pistils* two to five. A water-plant. Native of the Cape of Good Hope. Introduced into Kew Gardens, by Mr. Masson, in 1788. Blooms most part of the year when placed in the greenhouse. Having had no opportunity of examining the living plant, we have trusted to the drawing and the *Hortus Kewensis* for what we have said.

Aquifoliaceæ

Ilex fargesii.
Père Farges' Holly.
Ilex fargesii.

PLATE 42

In its long and very narrow oblanceolate or oblong-oblanceolate leaves which are sparsely toothed only in the apical third or quarter, the typical form of this species is unique in the genus. In floral and fruit characters it is similar to our native holly, *I. aquifolium* L., and like it belongs to

21

Series *aquifolium* Maxim., though to a different section. Closely allied to the *I. fargesii*, *I. franchetiana* Loes. comes from the same geographical areas as *I. fargesii*, and differs only by its leaves being slightly shorter and relatively much broader (three to four times as long as broad against mostly five to seven times as long as broad), and usually toothed beyond the middle. The two species appear to be identical in floral and fruit characters, and the differences between them seem scarcely sufficient to warrant the retention of *I. franchetiana* as a distinct species.

I. fargesii was described from material collected between 1892 and 1896 by the French missionary Paul Farges in the "district de Tchen kéou tin", that is, in the neighbourhood of Chengkow ting, a city in the most easterly part of Szechwan. The species had previously (1888) been collected in that province (to the north of Wu shan, some eighty-five miles south-east of Chengkow) and in the adjacent part of Hupeh (near Hsingshan hsien, and Fang hsien) by A. Henry, whose material, though noted as a new species, remained undescribed. E. H. Wilson also collected the species at Hsingshan during his first journey for Messrs. Veitch (no. 1827) and either on that expedition or his next sent home seeds by which the species was introduced into cultivation (Wilson Veitch seed no. 946). The typical form has also been collected much farther west in Szechwan,

42   Ilex fargesii (t. 9670 1946 LS & SR–C)

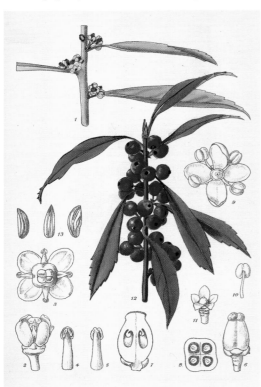

in the Mupin area, by Wilson (Veitch Exp. 3318a, Arn. Arb. Exped. 3098) and by Chu (no. 3259). Other material collected by Wilson in western Szechwan, west of Wên-chuan hsien (Arn. Arb. Exped. 1034), has broader leaves than typical *I. fargesii*, and was described as a variety, var. *megalophylla* Loes. To this variety Loesener also referred Wilson's 4094 collected in part near Kuan hsien, in part near Tachienlu, and in part west of Wên-chuan hsien.

In China *I. fargesii* is found in thickets and woodlands at altitudes of 1500–3000 metres. In cultivation it has proved hardy, and in October, 1926, it received the Award of Merit of the Royal Horticultural Society when shown by Mr. Armytage Moore, to whom we are indebted for the material here depicted.

Distribution. – China, provinces of Szechwan and Hupeh.

ARACEÆ

ARUM BICOLOR.
TWO-COLOURED ARUM.
Caladium bicolor.
PLATE 45

This plant, which has been frequently mistaken for the *Arum pictum* of Linnæus, was brought from Madeira, where it is cultivated in the gardens for the sake of the beauty of its leaves, which grow sometimes to a much greater size than the one represented in this figure. Said in the *Hortus Kewensis* to be introduced by Messrs. Lee and Kennedy, Nurserymen, at Hammersmith, in the year 1773, and flowered in the garden of Mr. Fonnereau, at East Sheen, in 1778. Thrives best when placed near the window in the most airy part of the stove.

Our drawing was made at Mr. Woodford's, Vauxhall, in whose store it flowered last.

43   Arum trilobatum (t. 339 1796)

ARUM TRILOBATUM.
THREE-LOBED ARUM.
Typhonium divaricatum.
PLATE 43

We learn from Mr. Miller, that roots of this arum were brought from Ceylon in the year 1752. It flowers in May and June, and is regarded both by Mr. Miller and Mr. Aiton as a stove plant; we have seen it succeed very well with the treatment of a tender greenhouse plant.

It is one of the least of the tribe; its root is like that of the common Arum, and extremely acrid: but the plant is more particularly distinguished by the rich, brown, velvety appearance of its flowers; the length of its tapering spadix, which on its lower part is full of little cavities, and resembles a piece of metal corroded by long exposure; and by the intolerable stench which the whole of the flower, but more especially the spadix, sends forth.

It is a native of Amboyna, as well as of Ceylon. Rumphius informs us that the roots, sometimes eaten raw by mistake, cause violent inflammations of the mouth and throat, and that they do not lose their acrimony even when boiled.

The plant increases freely by offsets from its roots.

Sydm Edwards Del. F.Sansom Junt Sc.   *Pubby T. Curtis St Geo: Crescent June 1.1810.*

44   *Aponogeton distachyon* (t. 1293 1810 SE)

CALADIUM SEGUINUM, β. MACULATUM.

POISONOUS CALADIUM
OR DUMB CANE.

Dieffenbachia seguina.

PLATE 48

Many of the plants of the family of *Aröidœ* are very acrid; but this perhaps exceeds them all in this quality. Sir Hans Sloane, in his *History of Jamaica*, gives the following account of the reason of the name by which it is known in the West Indies.

"If one cut this Cane with a knife and put the tip of the tongue to it, it makes a very painful sensation, and occasions such a very great irritation on the salivary ducts, that they presently swell, so that the person cannot speak, and do nothing for some time but void spittle to a great degree, or salivate, which in some time goes off; in this, doing, in a greater degree, what European Arum does in a lesser; and from this its quality, and being jointed, this Arum is called Dumb Cane."

It is said, that the masters sometimes inflict a severe punishment upon their slaves, by rubbing their mouths with this plant. It is, also, an ingredient in the highly acrimonious liquid used in the preparation of sugar.

Native of the West Indies, and the tropical part of the continent of America, growing in marshy places, where it attains the height of five or six feet. Cultivated in the stove. Flowers at different seasons.

Mr. Anderson, the curator of the Apothecaries' Garden at Chelsea, has three different varieties, or perhaps species under the name of Dumb Cane. The one here figured does not appear to be specifically different from that figured by Philip Miller, but to have just the same relation to it, as the Spotted Arum has to the plain variety. But a third kind in the same collection may perhaps be considered to be a distinct species, having broad-oval leaves, and stronger parallel ribs on the under side, running obliquely from the mid-rib to the margins.

Syd. Edwards del.   Pub. by T. Curtis, St Geo. Crescent Mar. 1 1805   F. Sansom sculp.

46 *Pothos foetida* (t. 836 1805 SE)

POTHOS FŒTIDA.

SKUNK-CABBAGE.

Symplocarpus foetidus.

PLATE 46

This singular plant, our figure of which, we suspect, may pass at first sight for a drawing of shells, is a native of North America, from Canada to Virginia.

We learn from Michaux, that in America it grows in the water, it has therefore been probably badly treated hitherto in our gardens.

In the first volume of the *American Memoirs*, the roots of this plant are recommended by Dr. Cutler as a useful remedy in asthma, with a very necessary caution to simplers, that they do not gather for it the roots of White Hellebore, as this likewise goes by the name of Scunkweed.

It flowered in Mr. Collinson's garden at Peckham, in the spring of the year 1736, from which plant Catesby's figure above quoted was taken. The leaves come up after the flowering is over.

OPPOSITE:
45 *Arum bicolor* (t. 820 1805 SE)

ARISTOLOCHIACEÆ

ARISTOLOCHIA LABIOSA.

MARCGRAVE'S BIRTHWORT.

Aristolochia cymbifera.

PLATE 56

Considering how easily errors may arise in drawing plants from imperfect dried specimens, we do not wonder that Professor Link conceived Vahl's *Aristolochia ringens* to be meant to represent this species; but the examination of Van Rohr's own specimen, preserved in Mr. Brown's Banksian Herbarium, and from which Vahl's figure was evidently taken, proves the two species to be distinct.

Aristolochia labiosa is a handsome climber, the leaves being of a delicate lively green and the flowers very large, beautifully variegated, and of a grotesque form; but its scent is very offensive, resembling that of some of the stapelias, and not very unlike the smell of decayed fish.

For an opportunity of offering to our readers a drawing of this very rare plant, we are indebted to the Count de Vandes, in whose splendid collection at Bayswater, this plant flowered in the hothouse, in September 1824. It is a native of Brazil, from whence it was introduced into the Kew Gardens, by Messrs. Cunningham and Bowie, the king's collectors.

ARISTOLOCHIA SEMPERVIRENS.

EVERGREEN BIRTHWORT.

Aristolochia sempervirens.

PLATE 47

In this species the flowers are solitary; the stems climbing and angular; but the flowers of *sempervirens* are smaller, of a pale yellow colour with deep red stripes, sometimes varying to dark purple on the outside; the peduncles twisted and hanging down, as if not able to support the weight of the flowers; the leaves are more acuminate and much waved, as well as of a thicker texture. Native of the Isle of Candia.

Both these plants stood out of doors, in a sheltered situation, through the winter; but

47 *Aristolochia sempervirens* (t. 1116 1808 SE)

coming from a southern clime, may be more safely considered as greenhouse plants. Cultivated in the Chelsea Garden, by Philip Miller, in 1739.

ASCLEPIADACEÆ

ASCLEPIAS NIVEA.

ALMOND-LEAVED MILKWEED.

Asclepias exaltata.

PLATE 49

The synonym of Dillenius, *Apocynum*, we consider as altogether doubtful, from the length of the peduncles, the too compact appearance of the umbel, the shortness of the corolla, the patent not reflex laciniæ, and the entire not five-toothed margin of the nectary.

The most remarkable feature of *Asclepias nivea*, is the very lax umbel, the flowers of which droop from the want of strength in the pedicels.

Native of Virginia and the Carolinas; is considered as a hardy herbaceous perennial, but is liable to be destroyed in severe winters, unless protected from the frost. Propagated by parting its roots. Flowers in July and August.

N.2606.

Pub.by S.Curtis Walworth, Oct.1825.

50 *Asclepias variegata* (t. 1182 1809 SE)

OPPOSITE:
48 *Caladium seguinum* β *maculatum* (t. 2606 1825 JC)

ASCLEPIAS VARIEGATA.
VARIEGATED MILKWEED.
Asclepias variegata.
PLATE 50

Michaux considering the *Asclepias variegata* of Walter as different from the plant so called by Linnæus, gave it the name of *hybrida*; but we can see no reason to believe that the A. *variegata* of the *Flora Caroliniensis* is different from the plant figured by Plukenet and quoted by Linnæus; nor do we see any thing contradictory in the specific character of the latter author, the very minute pubescence probably disappearing altogether in the dried specimen, to which alone Linnæus had access.

It is one of the most desirable species of the genus, and is esteemed to be hardy, but being a native of the southern states of North America, is liable to be destroyed in severe winters; and probably for this reason is still very rare, though cultivated by Philip Miller many years ago.

Our plant was brought from Carolina, by Mr. Fraser, Nurseryman, of Sloane Square. Flowers in July. Propagated by parting its roots.

CYNANCHUM DISCOLOR.
VIRGINIAN CYNANCHUM
OR ANGLE-POD.
Gorolobus obliquus.
PLATE 51

The *Cynanchum discolor* is very nearly related both to *carolinense* and *suberosum*, especially to the latter, from which it is principally distinguished by the common peduncle being longer than the petiole, and hairy, which in *suberosum* is shorter and villous. From *carolinense* it differs, in having longer, narrower, and less obtuse petals, and in its leaves being larger, broader, more hairy, and of a darker green colour.

Native of Virginia and Carolina in North America. We have no where seen this rare plant but in the very extensive collection of Messrs. Lee and Kennedy, at Hammersmith, where our drawing was made in August. It is probably a sufficiently hardy perennial to bear the cold of our ordinary winters.

51 *Cynanchum discolor* (t. 1273 1810 SE)

PERIPLOCA GRÆCA.
COMMON PERIPLOCA.
Periploca graeca.
PLATE 52

Periploca græca is a handsome climber, which under favourable circumstances will extend its branches from thirty to forty feet; and was once in great request for covering trellis work, arbours, &c. but is now more generally planted against a pole or the trunk of a tree; in the former case when it has overtopped its support and formed a spreading head with the branches entwined together, it makes a very handsome appearance, especially when in blossom, for the flowers, though chiefly of a sordid purple colour, yet being margined with green, are by no means void of beauty, and are interesting to the botanist from their very curious structure. It seldom bears seed in this country, but when it does the seed-pods are long, somewhat curved, and generally united at their points.

Native of Syria and the Grecian islands; is quite hardy; will grow in any soil; and is easily propagated by layers; flowers in July and August.

52   *Periploca graeca* (t. 2289 1812)

STAPELIA GEMINATA.
TWIN-FLOWERED STAPELIA.

Piaranthus geminatus.

PLATE 53

We received both this species and *punctata* from the Rev. Sackville Bale, at Withyam; near Tunbridge Wells, in September 1802. They had both flowered in very great

53   *Stapelia geminata* (t. 1326 1810 SE)

perfection, but owing to an accidental delay in the delivery of his letter, they did not arrive in a state fit for drawing. The figure here given was drawn from the collection of the late Jos. Walker, Esq. at Stockwell.

Although these plants for the most part grow in the hot sandy soil of the south of Africa, yet they will often flower better when supplied largely with water, provided the heat of the stove be sufficient. Mr. Bale had kept the pans of both the above-mentioned species constantly supplied with water and the stove very hot, to which he attributed their flowering better than they had ever done with him before. *Stapelia geminata* had grown so luxuriantly, that the branches hung over the edge of the pot and threw out roots into the water in the pan.

54   *Stapelia pedunculata* (t. 793 1804 SE)

STAPELIA PEDUNCULATA.
LONG-STALKED STAPELIA.

Tridentia pedunculata.

PLATE 54

This very distinct species of *Stapelia* may be at once known from all its congeners by the extraordinary length of the peduncles; and even when out of flower the appearance of

the branches is different from every other: the angles in these are so obscure as to render them almost cylindrical, and the teeth resemble warty excrescences, being nearly, and in many places entirely, obliterated. Found by the assiduous collector Masson in the dry country at the Cape, about Camies Berg, and introduced by him to the Kew Garden, about the year 1784.

Our drawing was taken at Mr. Woodford's Vauxhall, the latter-end of last June. Requires the same treatment as the rest of the genus, and is by no means so shy of flowering as some of the species.

55   *Stapelia picta* (t. 1169 1809 SE)

STAPELIA PICTA.
PAINTED STAPELIA.

Orbea variegata.

PLATE 55

We long ago remarked, that we could not agree with Jacquin and others, in considering these plants as properly belonging to the class Decandria; nor can we assent to the propriety of removing them to the class Gynandria. A perpendicular section of the flower of any of the *Stapelias*, through the centre of the germens, will show that the

OPPOSITE:
56   *Aristolochia labiosa* (t. 2545 1825 JC)

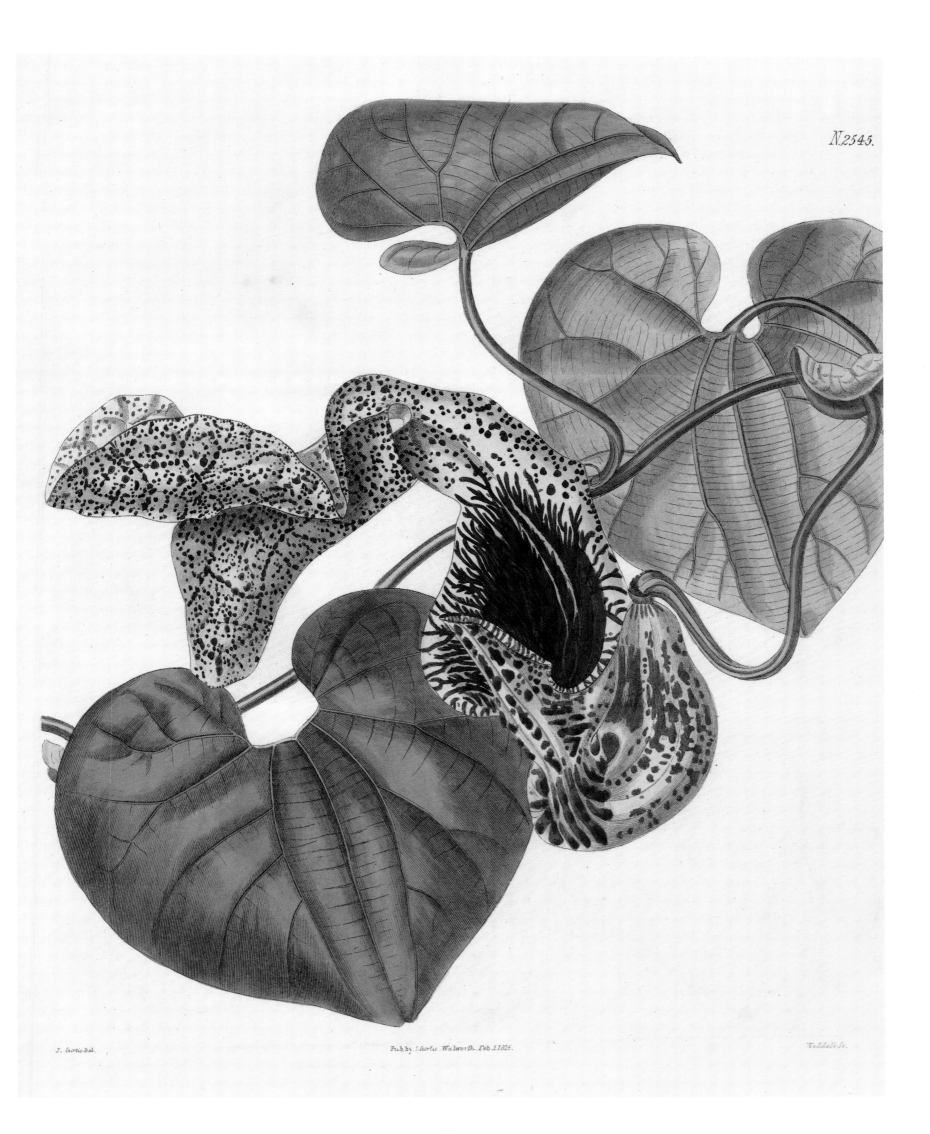

J. Curtis Del.   Pub. by S. Curtis Walworth. Feb. 1. 1825.   Weddell Sc.

stamens are supported entirely upon organs which take their rise from the corolla; and even in these cases where they appear to be most immediately incumbent upon the stigma, a thin membrane, which has its insertion in the corolla, is interposed between them and it. Indeed the stigma itself, which in the natural order of *Apocineæ* is so differently constructed from what is usual in this organ, appears to be rather an appendage of the corolla than of the germens. But as it seems destined to absorb the fertilizing fluid and convey it to the ovaries, it thus performs the office of the stigma, and we see no reason to call it by another name, as Haller has done.

All the species of this genus are natives of the Cape of Good Hope. Communicated by Mr. Loddiges, in September 1801.

STAPELIA RECLINATA.
RECLINING STAPELIA.
Duvalia reclinata.

PLATE 57

Stapelia reclinata, elegans, cæspitosa, and *radiata* of the *Botanical Magazine* very much resemble each other both in the herb and the flower. The last is most obviously distinguished from the others by the laci-

57　*Stapelia reclinata* (t. 1397 1811 SE)

niæ of the corolla being altogether without pubescence; *elegans* by the inside of the laciniæ being covered with hairs as well as the margin ciliated; *reclinata* and *cæspitosa* have the margin only ciliated, in the former the peduncle is longer than the flower, and the exterior stellula of the nectary (which in all four species is orbicular and quite entire) is of the same dark red as the laciniæ, but in the latter this part is green, and the peduncle only equal to the flower in length.

Native of the Cape of Good Hope. Discovered by Mr. Francis Masson. Introduced in 1795. Flowers through most part of the summer.

58　*Stapelia stricta* (t. 2037 1819)

STAPELIA STRICTA.
UPRIGHT STAPELIA
Stapelia stricta.

PLATE 58

There is a good deal of affinity between this species and *divaricata*. The shape and denticulation of the stems, as well as the colour of the corolla, are exactly similar, but in other respects there is great difference; the laciniæ of the corolla are not ciliated in *stricta*, nor rolled back at the margins, nor so sharp pointed as in *divarica-*

ta; the peduncles are shorter than the flower, and grow from near the base, and the branches are simple and quite erect, in both which characters it differs widely from *divaricata*.

It has been sometimes called in our collections *Stapelia rufa*; but has no similarity to the *rufa* of Masson; nor do we find that this species has been recorded by any author.

Native of the Cape of Good Hope. Requires a good greenhouse or dry stove. Flowers in October.

BALSAMINACEÆ
IMPATIENS COCCINEA.
GLANDULAR-LEAVED BALSAM.
Impatiens balsamina.

PLATE 59

Desc. *Stems* erect, somewhat branched: *branches* alternate. *Leaves* alternate, oblong-oval, smooth, pale underneath, sawed: teeth acuminate, rigid: *footstalks* nearly the length of the lamina, beset with a row of reddish glands on each side. *Peduncles* axillary, one-flowered, aggregate, after efflorescence lengthened, horizontal.

59　*Impatiens coccinea* (t. 1256 1810 SE)

Calyx two-leaved, falling, scarcely coloured. *Corolla* large, showy, crimson, variegated with white and dark stripes; *upper petal* roundish, concave, terminated with a greenish mucro; *lower pair* two-lobed, large, striped with white along the middle; *intermediate ones* small, nearly equal to the upper petal, and, like that, variegated with several dark red streaks, connate at the base with the lower petals. *Nectary* cowl-shaped, with a recurved spur, nearly as long as the flower.

Native of the East Indies, whence the seeds were brought by Dr. Roxburgh. Is a tender annual, requiring the same treatment as the common garden Balsam.

BEGONIACEÆ

BEGONIA FUCHSIOIDES.

FUCHSIA-LIKE BEGONIA OR

ELEPHANT'S EAR.

Begonia fuchsioides.

PLATE 60

A most lovely new *Begonia*, detected by Mr. Purdie on the Ocaña mountains of New Grenada, during his mission for the Royal Gardens of Kew. It is easily propagated by cuttings, grows rapidly, bears small but copious foliage, and is a plant to which he particularly requested our attention, on account of the copious, elegant, drooping, red flowers, at first sight resembling those of a *Fuchsia*; and because it is much eaten to allay thirst by the Arrieros (mule-drivers) of the country. He also observes that the globular buds (meaning, probably, the buds of the fertile blossoms, which are globular) contain a fluid, which, together with the acid of the flowers, proves highly grateful in the dry season and where there are no rivers. It has bloomed during the autumn months with Mr. Veitch of Exeter, and he has at this time (December 18th) one plant three feet high loaded with the richly-coloured flowers. It has been three months in bloom, and has abundance of buds yet to expand. Our plants are now, at mid-winter, beginning to flower. It is singular that, as far as they have yet blossomed, the plants have proved only male-flowered, except the tall one of Mr. Veitch, which has one cluster of female flowers at the top.

60   *Begonia fuchsioides* (t. 4281 1847 WF)

BIGNONIACEÆ

BIGNONIA GRANDIFLORA.

CHINESE TRUMPET-FLOWER.

Campis grandiflora.

PLATE 62

The *Bignonia grandiflora* is an extremely ornamental shrub, is easily propagated by cuttings, and blossoms more readily than *radicans*. It is considered as a greenhouse plant, and is observed to flower most freely, when forced by artificial heat. It is not improbable however that it may be found to be sufficiently hardy to bear our winters without shelter, being a native of Japan and China.

Our drawing was made from a specimen from the Royal Gardens at Kew.

BIGNONIA PANDORÆ.

NORFOLK-ISLAND TRUMPET-FLOWER.

Pandorea pandorana.

PLATE 61

Although naturally climbing, by the twisting of its stalks round whatever support comes in its way, is capable like the Hon-

eysuckle of forming a bushy shrub that can support itself. Blossoms freely and its foliage is lively and agreeable, but the flowers are apt soon to drop off, and with us it never produces fruit. It may however be easily propagated by cuttings.

B. pandorae is a native of Norfolk Island, in the South Seas, whence the seeds were brought to this country by Governor Patterson, from whose information it appears that a very destructive blight generally makes its first appearance upon the young shoots of this shrub, and spreads from thence over the whole vegetation of the island; from this relation the name we have adopted derives its origin. Requires the protection of a greenhouse.

61   *Bignonia pandorae* (t. 865 1805 SE)

BOMBACACEÆ

ADANSONIA DIGITATA.

ETHIOPIAN SOUR-GOURD

OR MONKEY BREAD.

Andansonia digitata.

PLATE 63

The *Adansonia digitata*, Ethiopian Sour Gourd, Monkey Bread, or Baobab, is a native of Senegal. It is said likewise to be

Pub. by S. Curtis Walworth Aug 1.1811.

N.º 1398.

Syd.ᵐ Edwards Del. F. Sansom Soulp.

62 *Bignonia grandiflora* (t. 1398 1811 SE)

found in Egypt and Abyssinia, and is besides cultivated in many of the warmer parts of the world. There seems to be no question that it is the largest known tree; the diameter of the trunk, Adanson says, being sometimes no less than thirty feet. Although it has been introduced into Britain, according to the *Hortus Kewensis*, so long ago as the year 1724, as may be supposed, so vast a tree is not likely, in our stoves, to arrive at that size, when its flowers and fruit may be expected.

Adanson, during his visit to Senegal, has given a full and interesting account of this tree, and, certainly, not the least striking circumstances respecting it are, its enormous size, and its great age, whence it

has been called "*Arbre de mille Ans*," and whence too, Humboldt has been led to speak of it as "*the oldest organic monument of our planet.*" Its trunk, indeed, great as is its diameter, has a height by no means proportionable to its breadth. The roots, again, are of a most extraordinary length, having numerous ramifications. In a tree, whose trunk was only ten or twelve feet high, with a trunk seventy-seven feet in circumference, Adanson has determined the main branch, or tap-root, to be one hundred and ten feet long.

The wood is pale coloured, light, and soft, so that, in Abyssinia, the wild bees perforate it, for the purpose of lodging their honey in the holes, which honey is reck-

oned the best in the country. I know not that the wood itself is applied to any particular purpose, but the Negroes on the eastern coast of Africa employ the trunks in a certain state to a very extraordinary purpose. The tree is subject to a particular disease, owing to the attack of a species of Fungus, which vegetates in the woody part, and which, without changing its colour or appearance, destroys life, and renders the part so attacked, as soft as the pith of trees in general. Such trunks are then hollowed into chambers, and within them are suspended the dead bodies of those who are

OPPOSITE:

63 *Adansonia digitata* (t. 2791 1828 WJH)

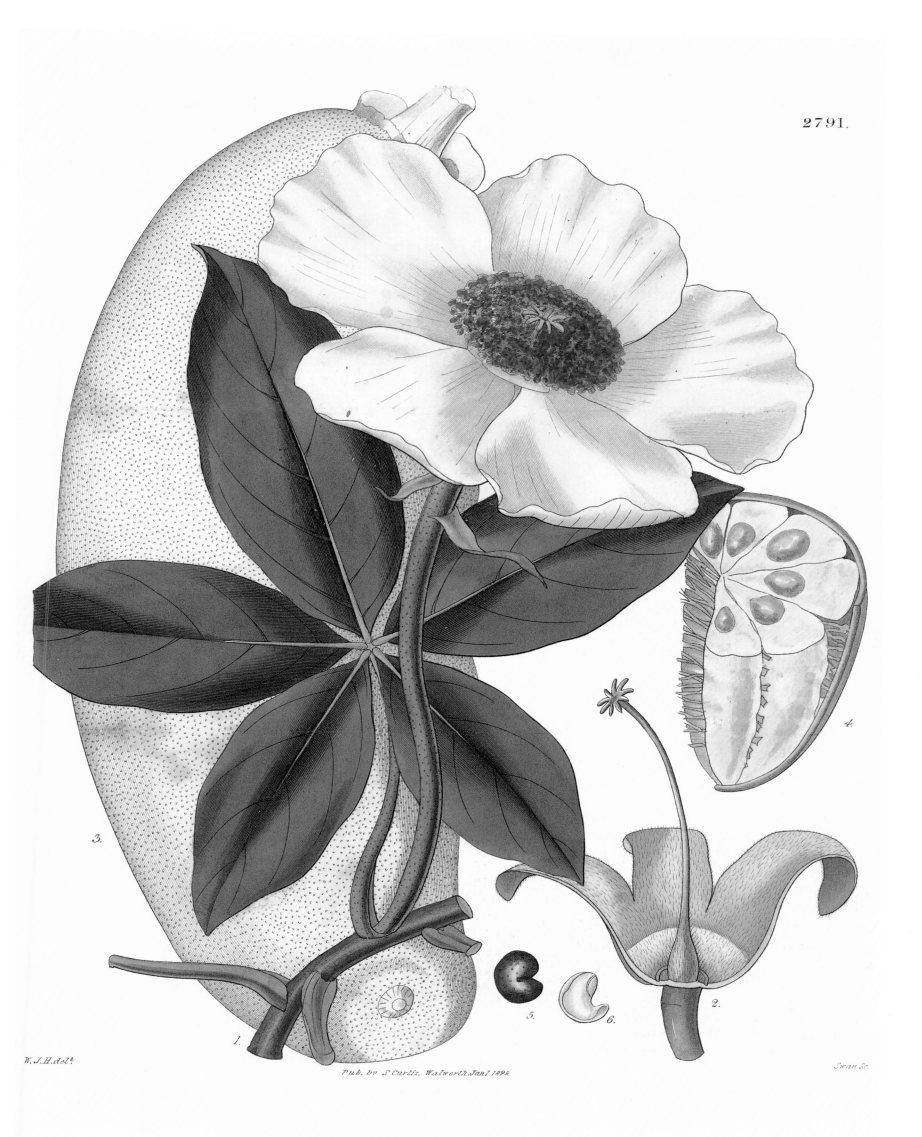

2791.

W.J.H. delt.

Pub. by S Curtis. Walworth Jan.1 1828.

Swan Sc.

refused the honor of burial. There they become mummies, perfectly dry and well preserved, without any further preparation or embalmment, and are known by the name of *guiriots*.

This plant, like all of the neighbouring order of *Malvaceæ*, is emollient and mucilaginous in all its parts. The leaves dried and reduced to powder constitute *lalo*, a favourite article with the natives, and which they mix daily with their food, for the purpose of diminishing the excessive perspiration to which they are subject in those climates, and even the Europeans find it serviceable in cases of diarrhœa, fevers, and other maladies.

The fruit is, perhaps, the most useful part of the tree. Its pulp is slightly acid and agreeable, and frequently eaten; while the juice is expressed from it, mixed with sugar, and constitutes a drink which is valued as a specific in putrid and pestilential fevers. Owing to these circumstances, the fruit forms an article of commerce. The Mandingos convey it to the eastern and more southern districts of Africa, and through the medium of the Arabs, it reaches Morocco and even Egypt. If the fruit be decayed or injured, it is burned: the leys are boiled with rancid oil of palm, and the negroes use it instead of soap.

CAROLINEA MINOR.
LESSER CAROLINEA.
Carolinea minor
PLATE 64

We received this elegant shrub from Messrs. Loddiges and Sons, under the names of *Bombax carolinoides*, an appellation given it by Dr. Anderson of the Botanic Garden at St. Vincent's, who was induced to refer it to that genus because its seeds are enveloped in a fine brown cottony substance. But it is so exact a representation in miniature of *Carolinea infignis*, that we cannot consent to separate it from the genus.

64   *Carolinea minor* (t. 1412 1811 SE)

Syd.ⁿᵉ Edwards Del.   *Pub. by S. Curtis, Walworth October. 1. 1811.*   *F. Sanfom Sculp.*

Carolinea minor, according to Dr. Anderson, is a native of Guiana, growing on the borders of rivers, and forming a very elegant tree; but is not common even there. The fruit, he says, is about the size of that of *Bombax ceiba*, is a woody capsule, one-celled, with five valves, and numerous kidney-shaped seeds disposed in five rows, and enveloped in fine brown cotton. Mr. Loddiges received the seed of this tree several years ago from Dr. Anderson, and has now several fine healthy looking plants.

BORAGINACEÆ

MYOSOTIDIUM NOBILE.

CHATHAM ISLAND FORGET-ME-NOT.

Myosotidium hortensia.

PLATE 65

This very lovely *Boragineous* plant, which cannot fail to call to mind the favourite Forget-me-nots of Europe, is an inhabitant of Chatham Islands, off New Zealand, S. Lat. 44°, whence it was introduced to Europe through the medium of Mr. Watson, of St. Alban's, by whom a living flowering plant was exhibited at a meeting of the Horticultural Society of London, in

65   *Myosotidium nobile* (t. 5137 1859 WF)

March, 1858, and attracted much attention. With the inflorescence of a *Myosotis*, it has a fruit which, in the state of ovary, induced Dr. Hooker to refer the plant to *cynoglossum*: but the fruit is quite different from the characters of both, approaching *omphalodes* in the winged achenia or nuts, yet differing in the nature of that wing, not being in any way introflexed, nor are the nuts attached to the style, as in that genus. Its foliage is quite unlike any species of those genera, and we think it may justly be considered a new genus, ranking very near the Forget-me-nots. The whole stock of this choice plant is (we believe) in the possession of Mr. Standish, who sent the plant here figured to us in April, 1829.

ONOSMA TAURICA.

GOLDEN-FLOWERED ONOSMA.

Onosma tauricum.

PLATE 66

This plant is not entirely new in our gardens, where it has generally passed for *Onosma echioides* of Linnæus, a much larger plant, greatly branched, clothed with very long yellowish hairs, and having entirely the habit of *Echium vulgare*. But fortunately in our search we met with specimens exactly corresponding with our plant, in a collection sent from Caucasus by Count Muschin Puschkin, under the name which we have adopted; we are informed that it is frequent in the open hills of Tauria, about Karassubasac and Sympheropolis, and also in the mountains of the Caspian Caucasus, flowering in May and June. A careful examination of the dried specimens left us almost without doubt, yet the observation of this author, that the flowers are of a full yellow colour, affords an additional proof of the identity of the plants.

It is a hardy perennial, but requires the same care as most other alpine plants, which are often preserved with more difficulty through our moist winters and variable springs, than the natives of warmer climes.

66   *Onosma taurica* (t. 889 1805 SE)

PULMONARIA MOLLIS.

SOFT LUNG-WORT.

Pulmonaria mollis.

PLATE 67

Pulmonaria mollis is very nearly allied to *angustifolia*, the chief differences observed by authors being the proportionately great-

67   *Pulmonaria mollis* (t. 2422 1823 JC)

er length of the calyx, broader sinuses of the laciniæ of the corolla, and the softer more silky pubescence of the leaves; but Mr. John Denson, the very intelligent curator of the Botanic Garden at Bury St. Edmunds, informs us, that these two plants are remarkably different in their mode of growth; *angustifolia* sending out its flowering stems horizontally, close to the ground, and even when the flowers open being only moderately assurgent, whereas the stems of *mollis* are in all their stages quite erect.

A hardy perennial. Native of the Pyrenees, particularly on Mount Llaurenti, in shady places. Communicated by N. S. Hodson, Esq. to whose exertions the Bury garden owes its existence and progressive advancement.

SYMPHYTUM ASPERRIMUM.
PRICKLY COMFREY.
Symphytum asperum.

PLATE 68

This species of *Symphytum*, a native of Caucasus, is by far the largest of the genus, growing to the height of five feet, and is really an ornamental, hardy perennial,

68   *Symphytum asperrimum* (t. 929 1806 SE)

which will thrive in any soil or situation. It differs from *Symphytum orientale* not only in stature and in the greater roughness of the leaves, but in the stems being not merely hispid, but covered with small curved prickles; the floral leaves are constantly opposite, which is seldom the case in *orientale*. The nectaries in both are flat, not filtulous.

According to Mr. Donn, it was introduced in 1801. Our drawing was taken at the Botanic Garden at Brompton, where we have observed it some years in the greatest vigour. Propagated by parting its roots or by seeds.

BROMELIACEÆ

BROMELIA ZEBRINA.
WHITE-BARRED BROMELIA.
Billbergia zebrina.

PLATE 69

This beautiful parasite was cut with a portion of the wood from the stem of a great tree in the neighbourhood of Rio Janeiro. Its hard and knotty stumps adhere inseparably to the trunk, at least they are not easily parted by a hammer and chisel. By the posture of the leaves when imported, the plant seems to have grown upon the side of a nearly upright trunk. Our plant flowered in the stove at Spofforth, in June, being planted in a small pot of peat on a warm flue. The growth of the inflorescence is singularly rapid. Twenty-four hours after its point had emerged from the leaves, it was in the state represented in our sketch. The leaves of this species are most singularly barred at uncertain intervals with white.

TILLANDSIA STRICTA.
FROSTED STIFF-LEAVED TILLANDSIA.
Tillandsia stricta.

PLATE 70

A parasitic plant; found by the late Dr. Solander in the Brazils, growing on trees near Rio Janeiro. There is nothing in the very little which Linnæus has left us concerning his *monostachya*, that does not tally with this species, except the synonymy.

Requires to be kept in the stove; but, we have been told, will live and blossom when suspended by a thread in a warm room. Our drawing was made from a plant that flowered at Messrs. Whitley and Brame's Nursery, in the King's Road, Fulham, in November last. Not recorded in any work known to us. First introduced into the European gardens by Lady Neale, in whose collection at Walhampton it has been cultivated for some years.

NB   The reproduction of this illustration is greatly enlarged for the original is 198mm × 120mm.

CACTACEÆ

OPUNTIA BRASILIENSIS.
BRAZILIAN PRICKLY PEAR.
Opuntia brasiliensis.

PLATE 71

The accompanying beautiful and very accurate delineation is the joint production of two ladies, whose talent in executing is only equalled by their zeal and readiness in undertaking whatever may be useful in the cause of Botanical science; the Hon. Miss Norton and Miss Young.

Though of comparatively recent introduction to Madeira, *O. brasiliensis* now occurs in several gardens at Funchal, flourishing without the slightest care or attention. Its principal flowering season is May or June; but blossoms are often produced more or less throughout the year. The fruit figured was ripe in May, simultaneously with the inflorescence; but August or September is its more abundant season.

The peculiar habit and mode of growth at once distinguish this species. It rises with a perfectly straight, erect, slender, but firm and stiff, round stem, to a height of from ten to twenty, or even thirty feet, very gradually tapering to a point from a diameter of two to six inches at the base, and furnished all the way up with short, mostly horizontal or declining branches, spreading round on all sides not more than a yard in any part from the main stem, and gradually becoming shorter upwards; often ceasing a little below the summit.

OPPOSITE:
69   *Bromelia zebrina* (t. 2686 1826 WJH)

W. Herbert. Del.   Pub. by J. Curtis. Walworth. Oct. 1826.   Weddell Sc.

b   a

Pub. by S. Curtis Walworth Feb.1.1813.

F. Sansom Sc.

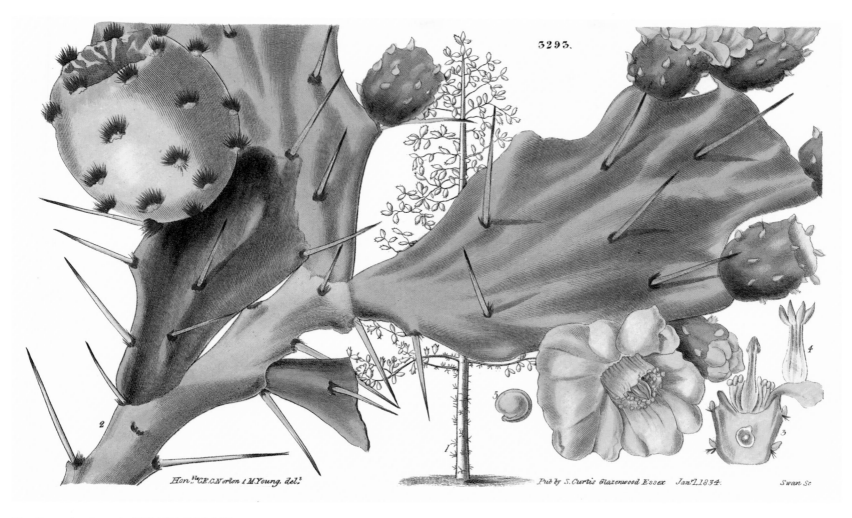

71 *Optunia brasiliensis* (t. 3293 1834 CN & MY)

OPUNTIA CYLINDRICA.
ROUND-STEMMED PRICKLY PEAR.

Optunia cylindrica

PLATE 72

I am indebted to the Hon. Miss Norton for a most admirable and truly artist-like drawing of this species of Prickly Pear, which was originally introduced into England in 1799, but has never flowered in Britain, the inflorescence being unknown to every author who has described the species. Thence it was sent to Madeira. It is truly intermediate between *Cereus* and *Opuntia*; having the filiform style and habit of the former, with the tubeless flowers of the latter. The bony, compact, central mass of seeds, (not diffused through the flesh, but distinct and separate,) is different from any thing I have observed in either of these genera: but the number of species which have fallen under my observation, is far too limited to justify more than a suggestion

OPPOSITE:
70 *Tillandsia stricta* (t. 1529 1813 SE)

whether this character may prove corroborative of Professor De Candolle's idea that the present plant with its allies may hereafter form a distinct genus.

72 *Optunia cylindrica* (t. 3301 1834 CN)

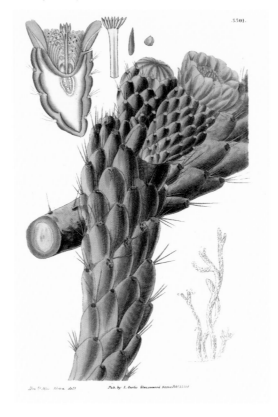

CAMPANULACEÆ

CAMPANULA AFFINIS

Campanula affinis.

PLATE 73

It is strange that there is no record of this species having been cultivated in Britain before 1934. In that year specimens and photographs were sent to Kew by Mr. T. Ashton Lofthouse of Middlesbrough, who was growing it in his garden, under the name of *C. bolosii*, from seed he had collected on Monserrat, above the Monastery. The same year he presented seed to Kew, where the plant has been in cultivation ever since. Our figure was prepared in 1937, when a fine group of plants, varying considerably in colour of the corollas, was on show in the Conservatory. At Kew, *C. affinis* is treated as a cool greenhouse plant. The seeds, which are sown in the late summer, produce rosettes of leaves which live through that and the following winter in cold frames. They are potted on into seven inch pots in the second spring and come into flower about the end of June, taking exactly two years to complete the

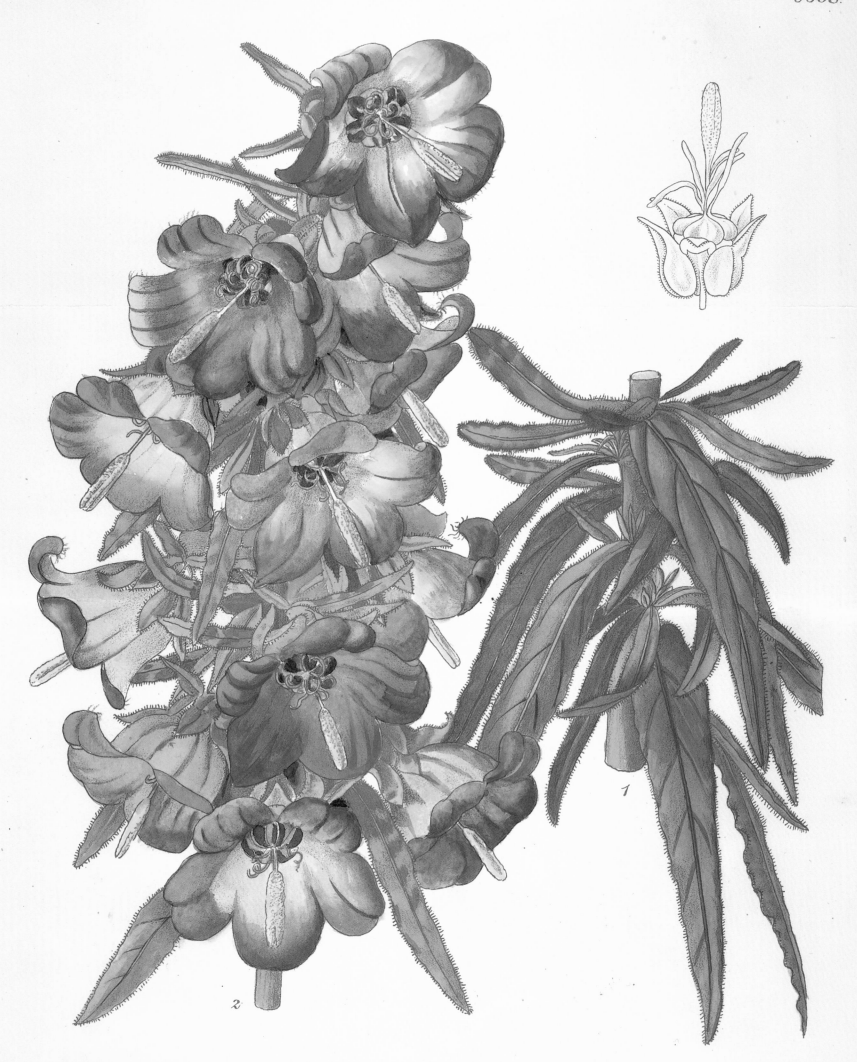

L. Snelling del. et lith.

cycle of growth. Cultivation outside has not been very successful at Kew, but in the warmer parts of the country C. *affinis* should prove a very valuable crevice plant for the limestone rock-garden.

Distribution. – Spain: mountains of Catalonia, Aragon and Valencia.

CAMPANULA CAPITATA.
CLUSTERED BELL-FLOWER.
Campanula lingulata.
PLATE 77

Having never seen a perfect capsule, we are not certain that it is five-celled, though from its five-cornered shape we have little doubt that this is the case. The calyx is divided into ten segments, five of which are erect, the other five broader, reflected. The whole plant is hispid. Root biennial.

This beautiful *Campanula* has not to our knowledge been hitherto noticed, but some account of it will probably appear when we are gratified with the *Flora Græca*.

Our drawing was taken at the Botanical Garden, Brompton, from a plant out of the very extensive collection of J. Swainson, Esq. at Twickenham, who informs us that he received the seeds of it from the Rev. Mr. Martin, of East Malling in Kent, to whom it was given by the late Professor Sibthorpe, soon after his return from his travels in Greece. Flowers in July, is a hardy biennial: loves a dry soil.

CAMPANULA GRANDIFLORA.
GREAT-FLOWERED BELL-FLOWER.
Platycodon grandiflora.
PLATE 78

Professor Jacquin is, we believe, the first author who has figured this species of *Campanula*, which he has done in his *Hortus Vindebonensis*; Linnæus the Son afterwards inserted it in his *Suppl. Pl.* assigning it the characters specified above in the synonyms, and expressing his doubts

whether it was not a variety of the *Campanula carpatica*. Professor Jacquin clearly demonstrates that it cannot be so, as it differs most essentially from that plant in a variety of particulars, *vid. Linn. Syst. Vegetab. ed. 14 Murr.* his specific description there given, agrees much better with the plants we have seen flower here, than that of Linnæus does, there being generally more than one flower on a stalk, and the leaves rarely growing three together.

The blossoms of this plant when it grows in perfection, are very large, nearly twice the size of those of the *Campanula carpatica*, whence its name of *grandiflora*; previous to their opening fully, they somewhat resemble an air balloon, from which circumstance it has been called by some the Balloon plant.

It is a hardy perennial, a native of Siberia and Tartary, and was introduced to this country by Mr. John Bell in the year 1782.

It flowers in July, is as yet a rare plant in this country, and likely to continue so, as it is not easily increased, multiplying but little by its roots, scarcely to be struck from cuttings, and rarely producing perfect seeds.

CAMPANULA MACROPHYLLA.
LARGE-LEAVED BELL-FLOWER.
Campanula allarifolia.
PLATE 79

For this new species of *Campanula* we are indebted to Mr. Loddiges, the product of seeds sent him from Mount Caucasus. Specimens of the same plant are in the collection transmitted from that country to Sir Joseph Banks, by Count Moushin Poushkin; but the ticket containing the name given by Dr. Adams having been lost, we are not certain that we apply from his list the one intended, and the leaves not appearing to us to bear a good resemblance to those in Aliaria, we have preferred that by which we saw the same plant designated in Mr. Vere's fine collection at Kensington Gore.

C. macrophylla is perfectly hardy. Flowers in July and August. Propagated by seeds. Being of large growth it requires room, and is, on that account, more adapted to ornament extensive plantations, than the confined parterre.

74 *Campanula peregrina* (t. 1257 1810 SE)

CAMPANULA PEREGRINA.
ROUGH-LEAVED BELL-FLOWER.
Campanula peregrina.
PLATE 74

The first account that we have of this species of *Campanula*, which appears to be a very distinct one, is, that it came up in the Botanic Garden at Upfal, amongst a number of young plants, produced from Cape seeds; whence it was supposed that it might be a native of Southern Africa. It is however so very unlike, in habit, to the vegetable productions of that country, that most probably it has a very different origin.*

The flowers are not unlike those of *Campanula pyramidalis*, but it differs materially in having usually only one simple stem, and in being altogether hairy.

It is a hardy biennial. Our drawing was taken at Messrs. Loddiges, who received the plant from Thomas Furley Forster, Esq.

*It is, indeed, a native of Turkey and the eastern Mediterranean.

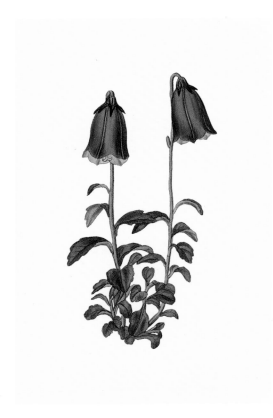

75 *Campanula pulla* (t. 2492 1824)

Campanula pulla.

Austrian Bell-flower.

Campanula pulla.

PLATE 75

Campanula pulla is a rare alpine plant, of very considerable beauty, and likely to be especially prized by the admirers of the diminutive productions of the vegetable kingdom, such as our predecessor and dear friend, the late Mr. William Curtis, used to compare to Cabinet Pictures.

We have designedly omitted the synonym from Caspar Bauhin's *Prodromus*, p. 35, generally referred to as variety β of this species, being convinced in our own mind that it must be totally distinct, not only from its bearing so many flowers upon the same stem, but more especially from the style being exserted so far beyond the corolla. The last circumstance will probably exclude also Lamarck's variety, γ.

A hardy perennial, native of the Austrian Alps. Flowers in July and August. Communicated by Messrs. Loddiges and Sons. Cultivated according to Mr. Aiton, in 1779, by John Blackburne, Esq.

Campanula thyrsoidea.

Long-spiked Bell-flower.

Campanula thyrsoides.

PLATE 80

This native of alpine stony pastures was first discovered by Clusius, and is described but not figured in his account of plants observed in Hungary, Austria, and Stiria.

The original representations of this plant by the older Botanists, are those of Dalechamp, John Bauhin, and Richier du Belleval. The last author, though now little known, was Professor of Botany at Montpelier, in the time of Henry IV. of France, and under the royal patronage established the first botanical garden there. He was very industrious in searching after new plants, and had described and engraved on copper several hundred species, but dying before he could give them to the world, they were long neglected, and have only within these few years been published by Gilibert, in his *Demonstrations Botaniques*.

Jacquin observes, that when plants of the first year were removed into the garden and planted in a shady damp border, they grew two feet high the next summer, and made a much more elegant appearance then in their native place. Introduced in the year 1785, by Dr. William Pitcairn. It is a hardy biennial, propagated by seeds.

76 *Canarina campanula* (t. 444 1799 SE)

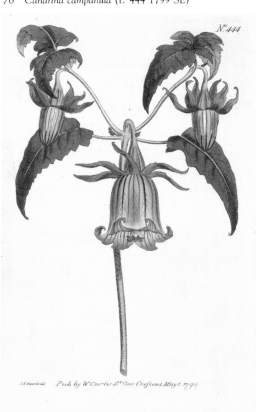

Canarina campanula.

Canary Bell-flower.

Canarina canariensis.

PLATE 76

The flowers of this plant so strongly resemble those of the *Campanula*, that it is no wonder the older Botanists regarded it as such, Linnæus himself did so at first, and Miller also; and even now it may perhaps be doubted whether it ought to be made a distinct genus of, since it is found to differ principally in the number of its parts of fructification.

It is a native of the Canary Islands, whence its name, was cultivated in the royal garden, Hampton Court, as long since as the year 1696, and is a tender herbaceous plant, to be found in most of our greenhouses; its stem rises to the height of six or more feet, its flowers produced singly from the fork of the stalk, are large and showy, they begin to open at the commencement of winter, and continue to blow till March.

"Is propagated by parting of its roots, which must be done with caution; for, as the root is fleshy, if they are broken or wounded, the milky juice will flow out plentifully; so that if these are planted before the wounds are skinned over, it occasions their rotting: the best time for transplanting and parting of their roots is in July, soon after the stalks are decayed; the soil should be a light sandy loam, mixed with a fourth part of screened lime rubbish." Miller.

Lobelia bicolor.

Spotted Lobelia.

Lobelia bicolor.

PLATE 81

In so extensive a genus as the *Lobelia*, so few of which have been accurately figured, or even fully described, it is not to be wondered at if some confusion should prevail. This is especially the case among the smaller species.

Opposite:

77 Top left: *Campanula capitata* (t. 811 1805 SE)

78 Top right: *Campanula grandiflora* (t. 252 1794)

79 Bottom left: *Campanula macrophylla* (t. 912 1806 SE)

80 Bottom right: *Campanula thyrsoidea* (t. 1290 1810 SE)

81 *Lobelia bicolor* (t. 514 1801 SE)

The pretty lively little plant which is here figured, flowered last summer in the Botanic Garden at Brompton, and in some other collections about town; the bright blue corolla distinguishes it at first sight from the *pubescens*, which has white flowers; we were, however, inclined to consider it only as a variety, but from a consideration of the description and figure, by Mr. Salisbury, in his *Icones plantarum rariorum*, it seems to differ in many material points, and possibly it may be the very plant that he has distinguished from his *alyssifolia*, the *pubescens* of the *Kew Catalogue*, under the name of *Lobelia erinoides*; but certainly is not the *erinoides* of Linnæus, a smaller, more delicate, trailing plant with flower-stalks shorter than the leaves. It agrees so well with the specific character of *Lobelia erinus*, as given in the *Mantissa Plantarum*, that we were once inclined so to determine it; but upon a careful examination of the specimens in Sir Joseph Banks's Herbarium, it appears to be certainly different from the one which is there marked, as having been compared with the Linnean Herbarium; nor does it appear perfectly to correspond with any specimen in Sir Joseph's extensive collection: we hope therefore to stand excused for having applied a new name and specific character. This we do always unwillingly, and never, when we can be tolerably satisfied that our

plant is the same that has been previously described.

It is an annual which readily perfects its seeds if brought forward by being sown in a hot-bed in the spring, and treated the same as other tender annuals.

LOBELIA MINUTA.
SMALL LOBELIA.
Laurentia minuta.
PLATE 82

We have before given a figure of a plant nearly related to this, under the name of *Lobelia minima* (*Bot. Mag.* t. 2077); from which this differs in being stemless, the leaves all radical, and the scapes naked, or without bracts; in all which characters, it agrees with Linnæus's description of *Lobelia minuta*, in his *Mantissa altera*.

The plant from which our drawing was made, was transmitted to us by our friend N. S. Hodson, Esq. from the Botanic Garden at Bury St. Edmunds. Native of the Cape of Good Hope. Flowers from June to September. Requires to be protected from frost, to be planted in a humid soil, and not too much exposed to the sun.

82 *Lobelia minuta* (t. 2590 1825 JC)

83 *Lobelia surinamensis* (t. 225 1793)

LOBELIA SURINAMENSIS.
SHRUBBY LOBELIA.
Centropogon surinamensis.
PLATE 83

The *Lobelia surinamensis*, a plant newly introduced here, is minutely described in the *Suppl. Pl.* of the younger Linnæus, under the name of *lavigata*, apparently from the smoothness of its flowers: in the year 1786, Mr. Alexander Anderson sent this plant to the Royal Garden at Kew, from the West Indies, where it grows spontaneously, as well as at Surinam; and Mr. Aiton has inserted it at the end of the *Hortus Kewensis* assigning to it a new specific description, and a new trivial name: our drawing was made from a plant which flowered in the stove of Messrs. Grimwood and Co. Kensington, to whom it was imparted by Richard Molesworth, Esq. of Peckham, a gentleman liberal in his communications, and anxious to promote the cause of Botany.

This species of *Lobelia* is a stove plant, having a somewhat shrubby stalk, growing to the height of several feet; its blossoms are very large, of a pale red colour, and its Antheræ, which might be mistaken for the stigma, usually hairy. It begins to flower in January and February, and continues to blossom during most of the summer. Is increased by cuttings.

LOBELIA TUPA.
MULLEIN-LEAVED LOBELIA.
Lobelia tupa.
PLATE 87

From a careful comparison of Father Feuillée's figure and description, we see very little reason to doubt but our plant is the same species as his, and consequently the *Lobelia tupa* of Linnæus, who probably took it up from that figure only. Although this represents the leaves as being quite entire, yet in the description, Feuillée observes, that the margins are serrate, with very small inconspicuous teeth, as is the case in our plant, though our draughtsman by a contrary fault has made the serratures much more evident than in fact they were.

This plant differs altogether from our *Lobelia gigantea* the *tupa* of the *Hortus Kewensis*. The inflorescence especially of that plant is totally different, the flowers growing in the axils of leaves twice the length of the peduncles and whole flowers together.

Lobelia tupa is a very handsome species, but if as poisonous as represented by Feuillée, would be dangerous to cultivate; the holy father, however, appears upon several occasions to have been too credulous of the exaggerated tales of the natives.

Our drawing was made at Mr. Brooke's nursery, at Ball's Pond, in October last, where it was raised from seeds received from Chili, and grew in the open ground, and continued a long time in flower.

PHYTEUMA BETONICIFOLIUM.
BETONY-LEAVED RAMPION.
Phyteuma betonicifolium.
PLATE 84

We were favoured with this plant by Mr. Jenkins, of the Botanical Nursery, Gloucester Place, New Road, in July last, under the name of *P. scorzonerifolium*, but we cannot find any distinguishing characters between this and the *betonicifolium* of Villars, which latter name we prefer, as having been adopted by Willdenow in his *Species Plantarum*. For although this author has afterwards taken up *scorzonerifolium* also in his *Enumeratio*, with his characters of which our plant corresponds, except that the radical leaves are more or less

84　*Phyteuma betonicifolium* (t. 2066 1819)

cordate, while those on the lower part of the stem are lanceolate, and supported on very long footstalks. Villars describes *betonicifolium* as having its radical leaves cordate, and *scorzonerifolium* as having all the leaves lanceolate; we consider both as mere accidental varieties. To the latter Villars applies as a synonym the *Phyteuma scheuchzeri* of Allioni, a very distinct species.

A hardy perennial. Native of the mountains of Dauphiny. Flowers in July.

CANNACEÆ

CANNA EDULIS.
TUBEROUS-ROOTED INDIAN REED.
Canna edulis.
PLATE 85

This very fine species of *Canna*, was raised by Mr. Lambert, at Boyton, from seeds gathered in Peru, near thirty years before they were sown. Pavon's own specimen of *Canna indica*, now in the Lambertian Herbarium, proves it to be this species, and not the *indica* of Linnæus, from which, indeed,

its tuberous esculent roots are alone sufficient to distinguish it.

The variable size and position of the inner laciniæ of the corolla, together with the petal-like filament and labellum, often so confuse the different parts of the flower in many of the species, that hardly any figure shows the whole distinctly; on this account we have given a rough sketch of one of the flowers of this species in which all the parts are brought into view.

CANNA INDICA.
COMMON INDIAN REED OR SHOT.
Canna indica
PLATE 86

The *Canna indica*, a native of both the Indies, is a plant greatly admired for the beauty of its foliage and flowers, and on that account generally cultivated; it has been called by some Indian Shot, from the roundness and hardness of its seeds.

We find it to have existed in our gardens in the time of Gerard, 1596. Parkinson was acquainted with that variety of it which has yellow spotted flowers: Professor Martyn, in his edition of *Miller's Dictionary* has quoted the chief of what these authors say of it, which as a matter of curiosity we shall here transcribe: "Gerard informs us, that in his time it was in the garden at Padua, that he had planted it in his garden divers times, but it never came to flowering; and that it must be set or sown in a pot, with fine earth, or in a bed made of horse-dung, in such manner as Cucumbers and Musk-Melons are: Parkinson says, in some kindly years this beautiful plant has borne its brave flowers, but never any ripe seed, and that it will not abide the extremities of our winters, unless it meet with a stove, or hot-house, such as are used in Germany; for neither house nor cellar will preserve it: Clusius saw it flowering by house-sides in Spain and Portugal, and says, that the inhabitants there use the seeds for making their rosaries."

"Being a native of the warmest part of America, it requires to be placed in a moderate stove in winter, where they always flower in that season, at which time they make a fine appearance, and in the summer place them abroad in a sheltered

85 *Canna edulis* (t. 2498 1824 JC)

86 *Canna indica* (t. 454 1799 SE)

situation with other tender exotic plants, where they generally flower again, and produce ripe seeds annually."

"These plants will continue many years with proper management, but as young plants always flower better than the old root, so it is scarce worth while to continue them after they have borne good seeds, which should be sown on a hot-bed in the spring." *Millers Dictionary*

CAPPARIDACEÆ

CLEOME DENDROIDES.

TREE-LIKE CLEOME.

Cleome dendroides.

PLATE 88

Though the colour of the flowers is rather singular than brilliant, this is a very striking plant, with its curious candelabrum-like flower-spike, and handsome foliage. It was raised from seeds imported in 1828 from the Brazils, by Mrs. Penfold of the Achada, to whose liberality I am indebted for its having been several years an inmate of my own garden. Miss Young has, in the narrow space of an octavo plate, admirably expressed all the leading characteristics of a plant, which would require a folio, to display it to advantage.

For the first two years, this *Cleome* has quite the appearance of an annual or biennial, herbaceous plant; rising with a single, erect stem to the height of from one to two or three feet, and producing, in the summer of the second year, a single, terminal spike of flowers. But after this, it puts forth one or two branches below the first spike; and the stem becomes more woody, brown, and decidedly shrubby: yet, even in this state, the plant attains no greater height than four or five feet, has seldom above two or three straggling branches at a time, (the rest dying away) and rather bears the aspect of an herbaceous plant, become by accident perennial, than of a really shrubby one: and, in fact, it rarely lasts altogether more than four or five years.

OPPOSITE:

87 *Lobelia tupa* (t. 2550 1825 JC)

J. Curtis del.   Pub. by J. Curtis, Walworth, Feb. 1.1825.   Weddell sc.

47

Miss Young del.   Pub by S Curtis Glazenwood Essex Jan.1.1834.   Swan Sc

88   Cleome dendroides (t. 3296 1834 MY)

89   Cleome pentaphylia (t. 1681 1814 SE)

CLEOME PENTAPHYLIA.
FIVE-LEAVED CLEOME.
Gynandropsis pentaphylla.

PLATE 89

The number of leaflets is so apt to vary in this genus, that it affords but a very bad specific character. Our plant being particularly strong, produced seven leaflets on each of the lower leaves; but retained its character of three in the floral leaves.

The genus is not less variable in the number and situation of the stamens in the different species, affording an instance of peculiar difficulty in arranging it satisfactorily in the Linnean system. Though inserted by Linnæus in his class Tetradynamia, Cleome has little affinity with the genera naturally belonging to that family. Jussieu inserts it in the natural order of *Capparides*, with which it associates well.

Native of both East and West Indies. A tender annual, requiring to be raised in a hot-bed, and kept in the stove or under a glass frame. Flowers in June, July, and August. Our countryman Parkinson had it in his garden so long ago as the year 1640. Drawn at the Right Hon. Charles Long's Brompton Hill, in Kent.

CRATÆVA FRAGRANS.
SWEET-SCENTED CRATÆVA.
Crataeva capparoides.

PLATE 90

First discovered in Africa, by our particular friend, Dr. Adam Afzelius, Botanical Demonstrator to the University of Upsal, who never met with it but twice, once in the Island of Bananas, in April, when it was in full flower, and afterwards at Sierra Leone, near Free Town, towards the mountains, in January, when the seeds were ripe. In both places it grew near water on rising and rocky ground, covering the rocks for a considerable extent with its widely-spreading stems and twining branches. He gave the seeds to T. Evans, Esq. Stepney, to whose liberality every possessor of this valuable acquisition to the stove is indebted. Is propagated easily by cuttings, but to thrive well requires more room for its roots than a pot.

It is at the desire of Dr. Afzelius that we have given it the specific name of *fragrans*, that of *capparoides*, equally applicable to other species of *Cratæva*, though hastily given by him to Mr. Evans, as something to remember it by, being never intended

90 *Crataeva fragrans* (t. 596 1802 SE)

for publication.

Our drawing was taken at the garden of Edward Woodford, Esq. at mid-summer 1801.

CAPRIFOLIACEÆ

LONICERA PUNICEA.

CRIMSON-FLOWERED HONEYSUCKLE.

Lonicera x brownii

PLATE 91

Descr. A low *shrub*, with scattered *branches* covered with a reddish-brown smooth bark. The *leaves* ovate and cordate-ovate, bright green on both sides, opposite on the flowering branches, but on the young vigorous shoots in our plant, ternate, a circumstance so singular in this genus, that we can hardly help considering it as a monstrosity. *Peduncles* two-flowered, solitary, growing from the axils of the upper leaves, than which they are shorter. *Germens* distinct, inferior, with two obtuse *bracts* at the base of each: *Calyx* minute, five-toothed, persistent, and increasing after the flower falls. *Tube* of *corolla* a little gibbous at the base, *limb* five-cleft: *laciniœ*

nearly equal, irregularly arranged, three looking one way, two another. Ripe *berries* not seen. It belongs to Jussieu's genus *Xylosteum*, and to his natural order of *Caprifolia*.

This pretty little shrub was communicated by Mr. Brookes, of Ball's Pond, Islington, in flower, in the month of April, 1882. Mr. Brookes received it from Mons. Parmentier of Brussels, under the name of *Lonicera canadensis*. But the plant recorded by that name, by Schultes in the new *Systema Vegetabilium*, from the late Professor Willdenow's manuscripts, appears to be different, and is probably the *Xylosteum ciliatum* of Pursh.

The detached sprig in our figure represents the end of a young shoot with ternate leaves.

91 *Lonicera punicea* (t. 2469 1824 JC)

LONICERA SEMPERVIRENS.

GREAT TRUMPET HONEYSUCKLE.

Lonicera semperivens.

PLATE 92

Miller enumerates two varieties; the present plant, which he says is a native of Virginia, and a smaller and much tenderer sort, native of Carolina. The latter rarely if ever occurs in our gardens at the present

92 *Lonicera sempervirens* (t. 781 1804 SE)

time; but the former is not uncommon, and if planted in a warm sheltered situation, and trained up a wall, paling, or lattice, is a very desirable plant both for its foliage and flowers, which latter are produced in June and continue in succession till the autumn.

It has not however the pleasing scent of the other honeysuckles, from which it differs in having nearly a regular corolla, except that one of the segments is a little separated from the rest by being more bent back.

Propagated by laying down the young branches, which readily take root. Cultivated by Mr. John Tradescant, Jun. in 1656.

VIBURNUM TINUS.

COMMON LAURUSTINUS.

Viburnum tinus.

PLATE 93

We scarcely recollect a plant whose blossoms are so hardy as those of the Laurustinus, they brave the inclemency of our winters, and are not destroyed but in very severe seasons.

93 *Viburnum tinus* (t. 38 1788 JS)

The beauties of this most charming shrub can be enjoyed by those only who cultivate it at some little distance from town, the smoke of London being highly detrimental to its growth.

Botanists enumerate many varieties of the Laurustinus, and so considerably do some of these differ, that Miller has been induced to make two species of them, which he distinguishes by the names of *Viburnum tinus* and *V. lucidum*; the last of these is the most ornamental, and at the same time the most tender; there are some other trifling varieties, besides those, with variegated leaves, or the gold and silver-striped.

It is only in very favourable situations that these shrubs ripen their seeds in England, hence they are most commonly propagated by layers, which readily strike root: Miller says, that the plants raised from seeds are hardier than those produced from layers.

It thrives best in sheltered situations and a dry soil. It is a native of Portugal, Spain, and Italy.

CARICACEÆ

CARICA CITRIFORMIS.
SMALL CITRON-FRUITED PAWPAW.

Carica citriformis.

PLATE 95

As far as can be judged from the brief character (and I know of no other) of *Carica citriformis*, given in Sprengel, the present plant may be safely referred to it: and it is a native of Guiana. A specimen, with the charming fruit here represented, was communicated from the stove of Charles Horsfall, Esq., Liverpool, in 1835. That gentleman procured it from the Curator of the Botanic Garden of Rotterdam, as the *C. monoica* of Desfontaines: but that species, as may be seen by the figure in the Ann. du Mus. d'Hist. Nat. v. 1. t. 18, is the same as the *C. microcarpa* of the *Hort. Schœnbr.*, and is easily distinguished by its small, deeply sulcated, and pointed fruit. Seeds from the fruit above-mentioned were raised in the Botanic Gardens of Glasgow and at Woburn, and so rapidly does the plant come to perfection, that it bore flower and fruit the first year.

Descr. *Stem* erect, three to five feet high, unbranched, woody below, herbaceous and succulent above, rounded. *Leaves* only from the upper part of the stem, on long rounded *petioles*, cordate, irregularly three- to five-lobed in a palmated manner, the lobes broadly oblong-acuminate, the middle lobe frequently trifid. On the nerves of the older leaves are scattered small, globose, white *glands*, sometimes in clusters. *Flowers* yellowish-white, in short *panicles* or *clusters*, from the axils of the leaves, much shorter than the leaf-stalks, monœcious? *Male flowers*, which alone have come under my observation, about an inch long. *Calyx* obsolete. *Corolla* with the *tube* long: the five oblong segments spreading. *Pistil* small, abortive. Stamens ten, in two rows, near the mouth of the tube. *Filaments* short, broader upwards; *anther-cells* applied to the inner face of the filament below the point. *Fruit* about the size of a hen's egg, and nearly of the same shape, but more inclining to oval, baccate, bright orange, containing several dark-brown *seeds*, muricated with large blunt spines. *Embryo* in a white waxy *albumen.*

CARYOPHYLLACEÆ

ARENARIA MONTANA.
MOUNTAIN SAND-WORT.

Arenaria montana.

PLATE 94

This plant is one of the largest of the genus, reaching sometimes, when supported by the bushes, amongst which it prefers growing, to the height of a foot and a half or two feet; its flowers are specious enough to attract attention, neither is it by any means uncommon in the mountainous districts in the south of France, particularly in the vallies of the department of the Hautes Pyrenées, in the mountains of Aragon, and in the northern parts of Portugal; all which circumstances considered, it seems surprising that the older Botanists should have left us no certain account of this plant. The first satisfactory account we find of the *Arenaria montana* is in Dr. Monnier's *Observations on the Natural History of the Southern Provinces of France*, published at the end of Mons. Cassini de Thury's Work on the Meridian of the

94 *Arenaria montana* (t. 1118 1808 SE)

OPPOSITE:
95 *Carica citriformis* (t. 3633 1838 WF)

3633.

W Fitch del.t

Pub. by S. Curtis. Glazenwood. Essex. Feb.y 1. 1838.

Swan Sc.

Observatory at Paris. He says that it occurs plentifully on the road from Orleans to Bourges, especially in the forest of Alloigni.

Brotero seems to hesitate whether he should consider the plant he has described under the name of *Arenaria montana* to be the same with that of Linnæus, but a comparison of his own with Monnier's descriptions, leaves no room to doubt of their identity. It is a perfectly hardy perennial, should be planted in bog-earth, in a shady and damp situation. Propagated by dividing its roots, or by seed. Flowers in April, May, and June.

DIANTHUS ARENARIUS.

SAND PINK.

Dianthus arenarius.

PLATE 96

Sir James E. Smith, in his remarks upon the genus *Dianthus* in the second volume of the *Transactions of the Linnean Society*, observes, that Linnæus was the only authority for this plant, and that the specimen in his herbarium is from Sweden. In

96 *Dianthus arenarius* (t. 2038 1819)

the herbarium of Sir Joseph Banks, the only specimen is from the collection of a Swedish botanist, which agrees very well with our plant, but is not very perfect. We have not ventured to add any of the synonyms usually affixed to this species, because none of them probably are correct, Linnæus, as we are informed by Smith, erased from his own copy of the species plantarum the synonyms of Bauhin and Clusius; that of Dodonæus he remarks ought also to be struck out, nor does he find any good reason to depend upon those of Le Monnier and Sauvages; and that of Scopoli, since added, must certainly share the fate of Clusius's.

Unwilling to run the risk of misleading with regard to a species so rare and so little understood by botanists in general, we have applied to our friend, the president of the Linnean Society, who is always ready to lend his assistance in establishing the Linnean species; and we have had the satisfaction of learning from him that our present subject is certainly the *Dianthus arenarius* of Linnæus.

The plant divides immediately from the root into a number of woody branches, terminated by fasciculated leaves, from the centre of which a single stem proceeds, bearing seldom more than two flowers, which are white: the petals are minutely cut to below the middle, and are marked with a faint greenish spot, covered with short dark purple hairs. A hardy perennial. Flowers in August.

DIANTHUS CARTHUSIANORUM, β.

CARTHUSIAN PINK.

Dianthus carthusianorum.

PLATE 97

Descr. *Stems* upright, a foot and a half high, simple, nearly smooth, though some roughness may be felt by the lips. *Leaves* linear-lanceolate, acute, without evident lateral nerves, but striated when dry, rough at the margins, pairs more distant at the upper part of the stem. *Flowers* collected into a close capitulum, eight or twelve together, but seldom more than one or two are expanded at the same time. *Involucrum* of several oblong oval leaflets, with a membranous margin, and an awn growing from a little below the point, somewhat shorter than the capitulum: *scales of the*

97 *Dianthus carthusianorum*, β (t. 2039 1819)

calyx ovate, awned, of a dark purplish rusty colour, shorter than the *tube*: *segments* erect, acute. *Claws* of the petals very long: *limb* wedge-shaped, serrated at the tip, of a rich purple colour, larger than those of the Sweet William.

A hardy perennial or rather biennial, propagated by slips or be seeds. Flowers in August and September. Communicated by Mr. Jenkins, from his Botanic Garden, Gloucester Place, New Road.

LYCHNIS ALPINA.

ALPINE LYCHNIS.

Lychnis alpina

PLATE 98

Of this genus there are many species cultivated for ornament; to the number of these we add the one here figured, a native of the mountainous countries of most parts of Europe, and which at a future period may possibly be found wild in some unexplored part of this kingdom. *

It is chiefly to the decoration of rockwork, that this diminutive species is applicable; for that purpose it has all the desirable requisites, being hardy, of ready growth, and forming a thick tuft of foliage, from which arise numerous flowering stems, four to six inches high, sustaining heads of flowers rather large in proportion to the plant, of a lively red colour, these appear in May, continue about three weeks, and are followed by seed-vessels with us, which contain abundance of ripe seeds; by these the plant may easily be propagated, it may also be increased by parting its roots, spring or autumn.

All plants kept in pots require to be regularly watered in dry weather; we have not found this Lychnis require an unusual quantity, though Miller was of that opinion.

*This plant was later discovered wild in Scotland and in the Lake District, England.

98   Lynchis alpina (t. 394 1798)

SILENE FIMBRIATA.
FRINGED-FLOWERED CAMPION.
Silene fimbriata.
PLATE 99

Silene fimbriata has altogether the habit of Cucubalus behen of Linnæus (Silene inflata

99   Silene fimbriata (t. 908 1806 SE)

of Smith) of which it is doubtless a congener. However averse from unnecessarily changing names, we entirely agree with our friend Dr. Smith in the propriety of separating these plants from Cucubalus bacciferus and uniting them with the genus Silene, of which the present species has altogether the character; nor is the behen perfectly free at all times from these processes, which forms what Linnæus calls the corona, as is observed by Dr. Smith, and before him by that accurate Botanist Pollich.

Native of Mount Caucasus; perfectly hardy; propagated by seeds, which it produces plentifully. Introduced by Mr. Loddiges, from whom we received it in flower in July last, under the name of Cucubalus fimbriatus.

SILENE VIRGINICA.
VIRGINIAN CATCHFLY OR FIRE PINK.
Silene virginica.
PLATE 100

In the Flora Bor. Americana, I expressed a doubt whether the S. virginica, of which I had then only very indifferent specimens at

my command, were really different from the S. pennsylvanica. But my valued friend, Dr. Short of Lexington, has cleared up all my difficulties on this point, and by a beautiful drawing of the former, (which though said in the Hortus Kewensis to be introduced to our collections by Mr. Loddiges in 1783, I have never seen in our gardens,) and by excellent specimens of both with remarks upon them, has enabled me to give the accompanying representation and description. "The S. pennsylvanica is always of humble growth, rarely rising more than six or eight inches from the ground, which it covers in dense patches of considerable size, and improves much under cultivation." The flowers too are of a rose colour. "The S. virginica is more solitary in its habit: there are fewer stems arising from one root, and they frequently exceed two feet in height." Mr. Elliott says, that this has sometimes entire petals; but Dr. Short has never seen the petals otherwise than bifid: a circumstance, together with the smaller size, narrower leaves, and smaller flowers, by which it may be known from S. regia (Sims, Bot. Mag. t. 1724.).

100   Silene virginica (t. 3342 1834 CWS)

101   *Euonymus latifolius* (t. 2384 1823 JC)

CELASTRACEÆ

EUONYMUS LATIFOLIUS.
BROAD-LEAVED SPINDLE-TREE.

Euonymus latifolius.

PLATE 101

Euonymus latifolius was considered by Linnæus as only a variety of *europæus;* from which, however, not only in the size and colour of the leaves, but in the greater comparative length of the peduncles, which are also more cernuous; in the flowers having, for the most part, five, more oval, petals, and five stamens; and in the angles of the capsule before bursting being more acute and wing-like. It grows to a considerably larger tree than the common sort; and the wood is applied to the same purposes, and especially adapted to turner's work.

A hardy shrub. Flowers in June and July. Native of the southern parts of Europe. First established as a distinct species by Scopoli, in his *Flora Carniolica,* confirmed by Dr. Solander in the *Hortus Kewensis,* and since generally adopted. Communicated, both in flower and fruit, by John Walker, Esq.

COMBRETACEÆ

COMBRETUM PURPUREUM.
MADAGASCAR COMBRETUM.

Combretum coccineum.

PLATE 103

This beautiful climbing shrub is a native of Madagascar, and was raised from seeds sent from the Mauritius to our friend Robert Barclay, Esq.; and flowered in his stove at Bury Hill in June last, among many other rare plants from that country.

This species is constantly decandrous, and has five petals and five wings to the seed-vessel; for it appears to us to be a five-winged capsule, containing a single seed about the size and shape of a barley-corn, rather than a naked seed with membranaceous angles.

Our drawing was taken by Mr. Duncombe, and kindly communicated by Mr. Barclay, together with a specimen of the foliage and a seed; but we had no opportunity of seeing the flowers.

This plant was first recorded as a *Combretum* by Lamarck, in the *Encyclopedie Botanique,* and a specimen of the plant was given by him to the late Professor Vahl, who changed the specific name to *purpureum:* but as there seems to be no good reason for this alteration, we should have certainly thought it right to restore the original appellation; only that of Vahl having been adopted in the popular systems of Willdenow and Persoon, the restoration might now tend to occasion confusion.

COMMELINACEÆ

TRADESCANTIA DISCOLOR.
PURPLE-LEAVED SPIDERWORT.

Rhoeo discolor.

PLATE 104

Descr. *Root* fibrous; *rootstock* lengthened upwards into a short *candex; leaves* from six inches to a foot long, green on the upper, crimson-coloured on the under surface, older ones more flatly expanded than the younger, upper forming a sterile coma. The *fruit* we did not obtain; but it has been minutely described by others. We did not

perceive any scent in any part of the plant.

Brought from the countries bordering the Gulf of Mexico to Jamaica; whence it has been imported into this country. Requires to be kept in the stove. Propagates abundantly both by offsets and seed. Of easy culture. Our drawing was made from a plant that bloomed last February in Mr. Vere's hothouse at Kensington-Gore.

NB   The reproduction of this illustration is greatly enlarged for the original is 198mm × 120mm.

COMPOSITÆ

ACHILLEA CLAVENÆ.
SILVERY-LEAVED MILFOIL.

Achillea clavennae.

PLATE 102

This plant varying with leaves more or less finely divided, and with the corymb of flowers more or less compact, Willdenow, in his monograph on the genus *Achillea,* distinguished them as two species; but, in the *Species Plantarum,* he again reduced them to varieties.

102   *Achillea clavenae* (t. 1287 1810 SE)

OPPOSITE:
103   *Combretum purpureum* (t. 2102 1819)

Pub. by S. Curtis, Walworth. Oct. 1. 1819.

Weddell. Sc.

Edwards Del. Sansom Sculp.
Pub. by T. Curtis, St. Geo. Crescent May 1. 1809.

It was first discovered on the summits of the lofty Alps of Austria and Stiria, growing in the crevices of the rocks and frightful precipices, by Clusius, who has given a description and good figure of it in his *Stirpes Pannoniæ*, drawn however, like ours, from a cultivated specimen, as he says he sent seeds and young plants to his friends in Holland, from which his figure was executed.

The *Achillea clavenæ* may be considered as a connecting link between this genus and *Artemisia*. According to Clusius it has not only the hoary appearance, but the bitter taste and scented seeds of the wormwood; Clavena however denies that this plant possesses either of these properties.

Cultivated by Mr. James Sutherland, in the Edinburgh Botanic Garden, in the year 1683. It is a rare plant, being, like most alpine plants, rather difficult to preserve. Planted on rockwork, or on a wall, in a shady situation, it would most likely endure longer than in a rich damp soil.

Flowers in June and July. Communicated by Mr. Salisbury, from his Botanic Garden in Sloane Street.

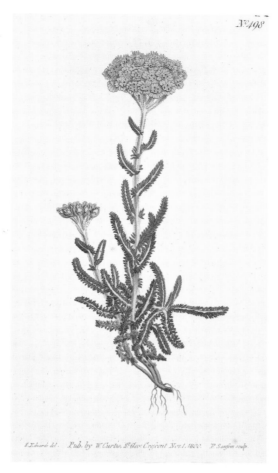

105   *Achillea tomentosa* (t. 498 1800 SE)

from the form of the pappus, which in the male plants somewhat resembles the antennæ of insects. To the above species *Antennaria contorta* has been since added in the *Botanical Register*. *Antennaria triplinervis* is a rather handsome herbaceous perennial, approaching *A. margaritacea*, and like it a good everlasting. Native of Nepal; and probably may be sufficiently hardy to bear our winters when not particularly severe, with little or no protection. Flowers in September and October. Communicated by Mr. Brookes from his nursery at Ball's Pond.

106   *Antennaria triplinervis* (t. 2468 1824 JC)

ACHILLEA TOMENTOSA.
WOOLLY MILFOIL.
Achillea tomentosa.
PLATE 105

This hardy perennial is a species of milfoil, a plant of very humble growth; its leaves, which are woolly, though probably much less so in gardens than in their wild state, spread on the ground and mat together; its stalks seldom rise above the height of nine inches, and produce on their summits umbels of flowers of a fine yellow colour, which continue during most of the summer.

Grows naturally in Spain, the south of France, the Valais, and Italy; was cultivated in the Oxford Garden in 1658.

It is well adapted to the borders of the small flower garden, or to place on rockwork; is a plant of very ready growth, and increased by parting its roots in the autumn or spring.

Opposite:
104   *Tradescantia discolor* (t. 1192 1809 SE)

ANTENNARIA TRIPLINERVIS.
NEPAL EVERLASTING.
Anaphalis triplinervis.
PLATE 106

Descr. *Stem* branched: *branches* rounded, woolly, white. *Leaves* alternate, half-stem-embracing, oblong, oval, quite entire, triply-nerved (or with three nerves uniting above the base), white-tomentose underneath, green but slightly woolly above. *Flowers* in a terminal compound lax corymb, with a small leaf-like bract at the base of each pedicel. *Involucrum* or *Calyx* imbricate: scales many, the interior ones elongated very narrow, acute, and forming a white ray. *Florets* yellow, minute, in our plant chiefly or altogether female. *Pappus* capillary. *Receptacle* naked, punctate.

The genus *Antennaria*, of which this is an unpublished species, was framed by Brown, from *Gnaphalium dioicumm alpinum, plantagineum,* and *margaritaceum* of Linnæus, and *carpaticum* of Wahlenberg, excluding G. *leontopodium* and *leontopdioides*, which Gærtner included in his genus *Antennaria*, a name given by him

ASTER ARGOPHYLLUS.
MUSK-SCENTED STARWORT.
Olearia argyrophylla.
PLATE 107

Fresh flowering specimens of this plant were kindly communicated to us, by Mr. Handscomb, of Newport-Pagnel, Buckinghamshire, on the 1st of May last, who informs us that they were taken from a fine shrub nine or ten feet in height, which had been at that time nearly a month in full flower.

Thriving plants of this *Aster* have for some years been to be seen in several collections about town; and are much admired for the delicate scent of musk, which the leaves retain for a long time after they are dried, as well as when recent.

We received a present of a very fine shrub of this kind from Mr. Knight, of the Exotic Nursery, King's Road, some time since, but it showed no signs of flowering, and with us soon lost its scent, probably from having the power which usually covers the upper surface of the leaves rubbed off; for to this substance the musky odour appears to be confined. We have not heard of this shrub having blossomed in this country before the present year. Mons. Labillardiere describes the flower as having three rays, in our cultivated specimens there were almost constantly five.

Native of Van Diemen's Island, where it grows to a small tree, the wood of which, as we are informed by Mr. Brown, is remarkably hard. Should be kept in the greenhouse. Propagated by cuttings. Introduced, according to Mr. Aiton, in 1804, by Messrs. Lee and Kennedy.

108 Aster salsuginosus (t. 2942 1829 WJH)

ASTER SALSUGINOSUS.
SALT-PLAIN MICHAELMAS DAISY OR FLEA BANE.
Erigeron salsuginosus.

PLATE 108

Descr. From a woody and fibrous perennial *root* spring one or more erect, simple, striated, pubescent, and purplish stems, about a foot high, leafy. *Leaves* mostly lanceolate, acute, those of the stem sessile, gradually smaller upwards, the lower ones often inclining to obovate, attenuated at the base into a long footstalk, entire, or more or less toothed, glabrous, especially on the upper surface, below often more or less hairy. *Flowers* solitary, or two or three at the extremity of the stem in luxuriant plants, large and showy. *Involucre* small in proportion to the size of the flower, purplish-green, its scales linear or inclining to subulate, pubescent, lax and squamose. *Florets* of the disk tubular, yellow, five-cleft. *Germen* slightly hairy, oblong, surmounted by the simple scabrous hairs of the *pappus*. *Florets* of the ray ligulate, three-toothed, purple. *Pistil* and *Pappus* as in the central florets.

This handsome species of *Aster* was first detected by Dr. Richardson on the Salt

Plains of the Athabasca, North America, and described in the Appendix to Franklin's first *Journal*. Mr. Drummond during the second journey found it among the Rocky Mountains, and from seeds brought home by him, our plants were raised which flowered in the Glasgow Botanic Garden, in May, 1829; and there cannot be a doubt but that so desirable a plant will soon become common in our collections. The early flowering and weak specimens produced but one flower on the stalk; but later in the season, in the month of June, from two to four blossoms were not unfrequent on the same stem. This might rather be called the Spring than the Michaelmas Daisy.

BERCKHEYA UNIFLORA.
ONE-FLOWERED BERCKHEYA.
Berkheya uniflora.

PLATE 109

The genus *Berckheya* was established by Fred. Ehrhart, in honour of J. F. Van Berkhey, author of a learned treatise on the structure of compound flowers, antecedently to the name of *Rohria* by

109 Berckheya uniflora (t. 2094 1819 JC) .

107 Aster argophyllus (t. 1563 1813 SE)

Thunberg, which it has accordingly superseded.

In one circumstance this plant does not altogether correspond with the above generic character; the leaflets of the calyx being divided quite to the base, but in other respects it agrees well. The seeds are sunk in the cells of the receptacle, are covered with long white hairs, and crowned with a pappus, consisting of a regular row of lanceolate paleæ, which are longer than the seed. The interior row of the leaflets of the calyx are narrow-lanceolate, quite entire, erect, and armed with an extremely sharp spine: the exterior ranks are wider, and armed, not at the point only, but at the margins, with spinous ciliæ.

The *Berckheya uniflora* is a herbaceous perennial. Flowers from August to October. Native of the Cape of Good Hope. Communicated by Mr. Jenkins, from his botanical garden in Gloucester Place, New Road.

CALLIOPSIS TINCTORIA:
VAR. ATROPURPUREA.
DYEING COREOPSIS;
DARK-FLOWERED VAR..
Coreopsis tinctoria.

PLATE 110

110   *Calliopsis tinctoria var. atropurpurea* (t. 3511 1836)

The ordinary state of this pretty plant is that the flower is a bright and full yellow colour, with a deep blackish-purple or blood-red eye. Cultivation shows that these colours are liable to vary, and has made us acquainted with a state of this plant of great beauty and richness as concerns the flower. In some specimens the whole of the ray is atro-sanguineous; in others there is a tawny narrow margin, forming, as it were, a kind of limb around it. Mixed with the common yellow sort in large patches, they add greatly to the charms of a flower-garden.

Our specimen here figured was from the garden of Mr. James Tait, Merry Flats, and was one of the twelve best species of hardy annuals which gained the prize at the September Meeting (1835) of the Glasgow Horticultural Society.

111   *Centaurea aurea* (t. 421 1798 SE)

CENTAUREA AUREA.
GOLDEN CENTAURY OR KNAPWEED.
Centaurea aurea.

PLATE 111

Though cultivated by Mr. Miller so long since as 1758, this species of centaury appears to have been but little known; it is

first described in the *Hortus Kewensis* of Mr. Aiton, without a reference to any author; it is there mentioned to be a native of the south of Europe.

It is a hardy herbaceous plant, growing to the height of about two feet, and producing on the summits of the stalks fine, bold, magnificent flowers, of a beautiful yellow or gold colour; these making their appearance in August and September, contribute not a little to enrich the borders of the flower-garden, at that time on the decline.

Grows readily in almost any soil or situation, and is easily increased by parting its roots.

CENTAUREA GLASTIFOLIA.
WOAD-LEAVED CENTAURY.
Chartolepsis glastifolia.

PLATE 112

Assumes the name of *glastifolia* from the similitude which the leaves bear to those of the *Isatis tinctoria*, or *Woad*, *Glastum* of the old Botanists.

In this plant we have an excellent example of the *Folium decurrens* and *Calyx secar-*

112   *Centaurea glastifolia* (t. 62 1788)

iosus of Linnæus, the leaves also exhibit a curious phenomenon, having veins prominent on both their sides; the scales of the calyx are moreover distinguished by a beautiful silvery appearance, which it is difficult to represent in colours.

It is a native of the East, as well as of Siberia; flowers with us in July, in the open border, and is readily propagated by parting its roots in autumn, which are of the creeping kind: requires no particular treatment.

Miller, in the last four to edition of his *Dictionary*, enumerates a *Centaurea glastifolia*; but his description in detail, by no means accords with the plant.

113 *Centaurea ochroleuca* (t. 1175 1809 SE)

CENTAUREA OCHROLEUCA.
CAUCASIAN CENTAURY.

Centaurea fischeri.

PLATE 113

This plant has affinity with *Centaurea montana* but is abundantly distinguished by the stem being much more winged by means of the undulated leaves, and by the long tawny ciliæ growing from the black margin of the scales of the calyx.

It is a hardy perennial, readily increased by seeds or parting its roots. Native of

Mount Caucasus, whence the seeds were received under the name of *Centaurea caucasica*, by Mr. Loddiges; who at the same time received seeds of another variety, or very nearly related species, by the name of *C. chlorantha*, which has pale purple or lilac coloured flowers, and leaves more woolly, softer, and not undulated. Flowers in May, June, and July.

CENTAUREA RAGUSINA.
CRETAN CENTAURY.

Centaurea ragusina.

PLATE 114

The *Centaurea ragusina*, a native of the isle of Candia, and of several places on the coasts of the Mediterranean, both in Europe and Africa, was cultivated here in 1714, by the Duchess of Beaufort, and is now a common greenhouse plant; it seldom exceeds the height of three feet; its stalks which are perennial, divide into many branches; the flowers are of a bright yellow colour, they appear in June and July, but the seeds seldom ripen in England: as this plant retains its leaves, which are extremely white all the year, it makes a pretty

114 *Centaurea ragusina* (t. 494 1800 SE)

variety among others. If planted in dry lime rubbish, Miller says, it will bear the cold of our ordinary winters, in the open air.

May be propagated by slips, or by planting the young branches, which do not shoot up to flower, in a shady border any time during the summer; in the autumn these may be removed into a warm border, or put into pots to be sheltered in winter.

CHRYSANTHEMUM INDICUM.
INDIAN CHRYSANTHEMUM.

Dendranthema indicum.

PLATE 118

We rejoice in the opportunity afforded us, of presenting our readers with the coloured engraving of a plant recently introduced to this country, which, as an ornamental one, promises to become an acquisition highly valuable.

This magnificent species of chrysanthemum, began to flower early in November last, 1795; and as there were many buds on the plant, at that time, yet unopened, it appeared as if it would continue to flower during the early part of the winter at least.

Rumphius, in his highly interesting work, the *Herbarium Amboinense* is minute in his information; he observes, that these plants were originally brought from China, where they flower in May and June; that there are two sorts principally cultivated in India, the white and yellow-flowered, and a third sort, differing only in the colour of its flowers, which are red (the variety, as we suppose, here figured) began to be known among them at Amboyna; the flowers there do not expand well, owing to their being produced at the rainy season, and they decay without producing any seed.

He tells us further, that it is cultivated chiefly for pleasure; that the natives and the Dutch plant it only in the borders of their gardens, in which it does not succeed so well as in pots; and that, if it remains more than two years in the same spot, it degenerates, becomes less woody, and often wholly perishes; that the Chinese, by whom it is held in high estimation, pay great attention to its culture; they set it in pots and jars, and place it before the windows of their apartments, and that it is not unusual for them when they invite their friends to an entertainment to decorate their tables with it; on those occasions, he that produces the largest flower, is considered as conferring the greatest honour on his guests; besides these three varieties already mentioned, they have a fourth, which is more rare, whose flowers are of a greenish ash colour (is not this the var. figured in the *Hort. Malab.?*) all these varieties growing in separate pots, they place in certain quarters which they particularly wish to decorate, and the effect they produce is highly pleasing: in the cultivation of this plant they spare no pains, the shorter it is and the larger its flowers, the more it is esteemed; to make it dwarfish, and at the same time productive of flowers, they check its growth; for, if suffered to grow rude, it assumes a wild nature, and produces little but leaves; when it is coming into flower, of the three blossoms which usually terminate each branch, they pluck off two, and thus the remaining flower grows larger; by this, and other management, they cause the flowers to grow to the breadth of one's hand: he enumerates still a fifth sort with white flowers, which is extremely rare, and smaller than the others, called *Tschuy say si*, that is the *drunken woman*; its flowers morning and evening flag, and hang down as if debilitated by intoxication, in the middle of the day they become erect, and follow the course of the sun; but this (most probably a distinct species) is not exported from China. Finally, he remarks, that the Chinese and Malays are so attached to these flowers, that they even decorate their hair with them.

Thunberg, in his *Flora Japonica*, enumerates it among the natives of that country, and describes it as growing spontaneously in Papenberg, near Nagasaki, and elsewhere, observing, that it is cultivated for the extreme beauty of its flowers in gardens and houses throughout the whole empire of Japan, and that the flowers vary infinitely in point of colour, size, and plenitude. Kæmpfer's account of it in his *Amaen. Exot.* is very similar.

This chrysanthemum appears to be a hardy greenhouse plant, and it is highly probable that, like the *Camellia* and *Aucuba*, it will bear the cold of our mild winters without injury.

As it flowers so late, there is but little prospect of its producing seeds with us, but it may be increased by cuttings, and parting of the roots.

115 *Chrysanthemum multicaule* (t. 6930 1887)

CHRYSANTHEMUM MULTICAULE.
MANY-STEMMED COLEOSTEPHUS.
Coleostephus multicaulis.

PLATE 115

The vast genus *Chrysanthemum*, including as it now does *Pyrethrum* and a host of monotypic or oligotypic genera, contains upwards of one hundred and twenty nominal species, of which Bentham considers that about eighty may be regarded as well established. The dividing these into sub-genera and sections is a great difficulty, founded as such divisions are chiefly on the varying form of the pappus. The subject of the present plate has been referred to *Coleostephus*, of which the type is C. *myconis*, L., and also to another genus *Glossopappus*, which hardly differs. C. *multicaule* is a native of various parts of Algeria; it was first found in the Oran province by Desfontaines, and has since been collected at Biskra and elsewhere growing in sandy fields, &c. Judging from a rather insufficient example, it extends to Morocco, whence a specimen collected at Tangier by Broussonet is in the Hookerian Herbarium at Kew.

I am indebted to Mr. Lynch, of the Cambridge Botanical Gardens, for the fine specimen figured here, which is much larger, more branched and succulent than are native ones in the Herbarium. It flowered in July and August.

CINERARIA PETASITIS.
BUTTER-BUR-LEAVED CINERARIA.
Senecio petasites.

PLATE 116

This gigantic *Cineraria* is a native of Mexico, and was raised from seeds sent from that country, at Boyton, the seat of Aylmer Bourke Lambert, Esq. where it flowered for the first time in this country last Christmas.

Our drawing was taken from a recent specimen communicated by the liberal possessor early in January. The same plant is in the collections of Mr. Vere, at Kensington-Gore, and of Mr. Evans, at Stepney; but in neither of them have the flowers yet come to perfection, owing probably to the difficulty of admitting a sufficiency of air at so cold a season of the year. The stems have the appearance at present of being perennial. The lower leaves grow upon long

116 *Cineraria petasitis* (t. 1536 1813 SE)

J. Curtis. Del.   Pub. by S. Curtis. Walworth. Jan. 1. 1822.   Weddell Sc.

Pub by W. Curtis St Geo: Crescent Feb. 1. 1796

Syd^m. Edwards Del.   Pub by S. Curtis Walworth Mar. 1 1813.   P. Sansom Sc.

118   *Chrysanthemum indicum* (t. 327 1796)

119   *Cosmea bipinnata* (t. 1535 1813 SE)

footstalks, and rival in size those of our butter-bur; some similarity to which suggested to Mr. Brown the name we have adopted; the edges are dotted with small cartilaginous excrescences, sometimes obsolete, which we rather call warts than glands, because they do not seem to be immediately connected with the veins. In the system this species may stand between *Cineraria tussilaginis* and *præcox*.

OPPOSITE:
117   *Cnicus afer* (t. 2287 1822 JC)

CNICUS AFER.

BARBAR CNICUS OR TWIN-THORNED THISTLE.

Cnicus diacantha.

PLATE 117

This is perhaps the handsomest species of all the thistle tribe, and is really worthy to be admitted into the flower-garden.

We see no reason to believe that the *Cardus diacantha* of Labillardiere and *afer* of Jacquin, are distinct species, or even worthy to be recorded as separate varieties; the first name has therefore the right of priority; but Jacquin's name of *afer* having been preferred by Wildenow and the authors of the *Hortus Kewensis* may now be considered as best established, on which account we have adopted it.

The large size and spreading of the persistent, coloured upper squamæ of the calyx may be considered as making a near approach to the genus Carlin. The receptacle is thickly covered with white soft hairs, amongst which the obovate seeds crowned with a feathery pappus are imbedded.

A hardy annual or biennial. Native of Barbary. Introduced by Mons. Thouin in 1800. Communicated by Mr. Joseph Knight of the Exotic Nursery, King's Road.

120 Cnicus spinosissimus (t. 1366 1811 SE)

CNICUS SPINOSISSIMUS.
FEATHERY-HEADED CNICUS.
Cirsium spinosissimum.

PLATE 120

Cultivation, as is usual in such cases, makes some change in the habit; instead of the flowers being crowded together at the extremity of a simple stem, they stand nearly single on short branches, but are each surrounded with beautiful feathery yellowish white bracts. Haller describes not only the florets but the anthers as yellow-white [*flosenti cum vagina ochroleuci*]; in our garden specimen the latter were blueish-purple, the former as described by Haller.

Though a native of the herbaceous regions of the Alps of southern Europe, the plant flourishes extremely in Kew Garden, from whence we were favoured, by Mr. Aiton, with the specimen from which our drawing was made, in July last. Dr. Smith gathered it on little Mount Cenis, in an expedition recorded in the third volume of his Tour of the Continent, on the 14th of August. "As I look on the specimen," (he says in his letter on the subject) "all the charming scene recurs to my memory." Everyone must have occasionally witnessed a similar feeling. The author has elegantly expatiated on the same idea in the second volume of his Tour, where he remarks that

"a plant gathered in a celebrated or delightful spot, is like the hair of a friend, more dear to memory than even a portrait; because it excites the imagination, without presuming to fill it."

COSMEA BIPINNATA.
FINE-LEAVED COSMEA.
Cosmos bipinnatus.

PLATE 119

This beautiful plant, native of Mexico, was raised from seeds, procured from that country, at Boyton, the seat of A. B. Lambert, Esq. by whom we were favoured with flowering specimens in the beginning of November last. The same species blossomed in the Royal Botanical Garden in Madrid, in October, November, and December, in the year 1789, and was described and figured by the late Rev. Ant. Jos. Cavanilles, in the year 1791, in the first volume of his *Icones*. This author gave it the name of Cosmos, from its ornamental appearance, since changed by Willdenow to *Cosmea*, such termination being more consonant with botanical usage.

Both external and internal calyx are described by Cavanilles as eight-cleft; but the number of segments of the former, in the specimens we have seen, have varied from six to seven.

The plant does not appear to be new in the country, as it is said by Donn to have been introduced in 1804. This author marks it as perennial; but, according to Cavanilles, it is annual. If brought sufficiently forward by artificial heat, it will certainly flower the first year, and then probably perish.

DAHLIA SUPERFLUA.
FERTILE-RAYED DAHLIA.
Dahlia rosea.

PLATES 121 AND 122

This species varies so much, not only in the colour of the flowers, but also in the form of the leaves and in general stature, that, at first sight, it might be supposed to be readily separated into several distinct ones. But attentive observation has shown that the seminal varieties are, like those of the China Aster, almost endless.

121 Dahlia superflua (t. 1885A 1817)

They have all large tuberous roots, not unlike those of *Helianthus tuberosus*, which should be taken up after the stem perishes, and preserved in sand or dry mould, protected from frost during the winter; and in the spring be planted out in the open border: or, in a warm situation and dry soil,

122 Dahlia superflua (t. 1885B 1817)

they may be left, without removal, only covering the border with dead leaves to defend them from severe frost. Plants raised from seeds in a hot-bed early in the spring, will sometimes flower the following autumn; when the flowers will begin to open early in September, and continue in succession till overtaken by frost.

Native of Mexico. Introduced in 1789, by the Marchioness of Bute. Both our drawings were made from specimens communicated by the Comte de Vandes, who imported these with several other varieties from France, where these plants have been cultivated for some years with great assiduity, particularly by Mons. Lelieur, at Sévre, near Paris.

ECHINOPS STRICTUS.
UPRIGHT GLOBE-THISTLE.
Echinops exaltatus.
PLATE 123

Descr. *Stem* erect, simple, three or four feet high, furrowed, somewhat woolly. *Leaves* alternate, half-stem embracing, unevenly pinnatifid, toothed; teeth terminated with

123 *Echinops strictus* (t. 2457 1824 JC)

a small spine. *Peduncle* terminal, elongated, rounded, bearing a large globular head of florets without any involucre. *Calyx* (proper) imbricate: *leaflets* lanceolate with a bristly point, the inner ones largest. *Florets* tubular: *tube* white: limb linear, revolute, bright blue. *Anthers* blue, soon turning brown: *stigma* deeper blue, bifid, revolute. *Germen* oblong, hairy, white. *Pappus* none. *Receptacle* bristly; but the bristles adhere to the bottom of the calyxes, and when these are pulled off the receptacle is left naked and honey-combed.

This appears to be an undescribed species. Native of Russia. Communicated by Aylmer Bourke Lambert, Esq. In September 1823, and was raised at Boyton, from seeds received from Dr. Fischer, late of Gorenki, but now Director of the Imperial Botanic Garden at St. Petersburgh.

GAILLARDIA ARISTATA.
WHOLE-COLOURED GAILLARDIA.
Gaillardia aristata.
PLATE 124

The principal difference between this and G. *bicolor* of our gardens, consists in the leaves being entire in the upper part of the stem, and in the ray of the flower being of one pale, uniform, yellow colour. Pursh described it from the Herbarium of Lewis, who found it in the Rocky Mountains, on dry hills. Mr. Douglas discovered it abundantly in dry soils, through a tract of country extending from the Rocky Mountains, to the Western ocean; everywhere retaining the characters above mentioned, which distinguish it from the G. *bicolor*. It varies in size: for intermixed with the common appearance of the plant, Mr. Douglas saw many which did not arrive to a height greater than ten or twelve inches, and having all the leaves entire. It flowers in July, and will soon become common: the seeds having been introduced by the Horticultural Society, and by them liberally dispersed among our gardens.

*Named in compliment to a French Botanic Amateur, Mons. Gaillard de Charentonneau. It is often incorrectly spelled Galardia.

HELIANTHUS SPECIOSUS.
SHOWY MEXICAN SUNFLOWER.
Tithonia rotundifolia.
PLATE 125

Along with the very beautiful drawing here figured, my obliging correspondent, Thomas Glover, Esq. of Manchester, sent me the following account of this charming *Helianthus*. "Mr. Edward Leeds of this place, who has lately commenced business as a Nurseryman and Florist, from among a packet of seeds from the Botanic Garden, Mexico, sent to him by W. Higson, Esq. of Manchester, has raised several plants that are not known in this neighbourhood. Only one, the subject of my present communication, has flowered, and an unfortunately early frost has cut it completely off. A single blossom which Mr. Leeds had given me to draw is all that is saved, and its beauty now is passed: I think, however, I have been successful in delineating its character and colour, and I send you the fragments for examination. Only one seed vegetated; and the title upon the paper was 'Composita speciosa:' – and it is said to have come from Jorullo. The plant came up to the height of about eighteen inches, very much like a common Sunflower, the outer and lower leaves being about the size of the one sent, and the inner ones smaller, and very close together at the top, as in the Sunflower, with all the leaves entire. It then threw out lobed leaves, and became a very different looking plant. It rose to the height of about five feet, beset with branches very thickly all the way from the bottom to the top, the lower ones projecting nearly horizontally from the plant, turning up at the ends, and about eighteen inches long, the rest gradually decreasing in length up to the top and forming a complete cone. The first flower which appeared was at the termination of the main branch, and quite erect, and afterwards each lateral one threw out a flower at its termination rather in a horizontal direction, the end of the flowering stalk inclining upwards. The stem is round, and covered with a fine silky substance, but the leaves are rather coarse, and very subject to be infested with *Aphis*."

124 *Gaillardia aristata* (t. 2940 1829 WJH)

125 *Helianthus speciosus* (t. 3295 1834 TG)

LIATRIS SPICATA.
BUTTON SNAKEROOT.

Liatris spicata.

PLATE 126

The *leaves* of this species vary much in length and breadth, and when cultivated are more or less ciliated at the base, or frequently naked: the broader ones have several longitudinal nerves, and when held to the light, are perceived, by the aid of a lens, to be full of transparent dots. The *spikes of flowers* vary much in length, and begin flowering at the top of the stalk; on which account, the appearance is much better when it first blossoms than afterwards, when the dead flowers at the sum-mit of the stem render the plant unsightly. The remarkable length of the *stigmas* is perhaps common to the genus, though this character would exclude some species that are at present arranged under it. Though not comparable with the fragrance of *Liatris odorata*, the leaves of this plant are by no means destitute of an agreeable smell when dried.

A hardy perennial. Flowers in August. Propagated by parting its roots or be seed.

OTHONNA AMPLEXICAULIS.
LEAF-CLASPED OTHONNA.

Othonna amplexifolia.

PLATE 127

The stems of this plant, though of a woody texture, are not properly strutescent, as they die down annually. It has much affinity with *Othonna bulbosa* or *pinnata*; so we are persuaded that the two last-named plants are the same.

The *Othonna amplexicaulis* is a very rare plant and we have never seen nor heard of its being in any collection in this country, but at Mr. Knight's Nursery in the King's Road, Chelsea, where our drawing was taken.

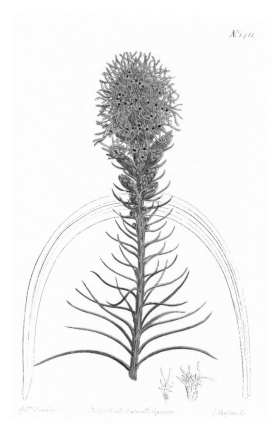

126 *Liatris spicata* (t. 1411 1808 SE)

RUDBECKIA COLUMNARIS.
HIGH-CROWNED RUDBECKIA.
Ratidbida columnaris.
PLATE 128

This new species of *Rudbeckia* was introduced, we believe, by Mr. Nuttall, from the country of the Missouri; our drawing was taken at the Nursery of Messrs. J. and J. T. Fraser, in Sloane Square. It is sweetscented, of low stature, and but little branched. Flowers in August and September. Root perennial and hardy, but it may be safest to preserve some under a frame during the winter.

128 *Rudbeckia columnaris* (t. 1601 1813 SE)

SERRATULA SIMPLEX.
ONE-FLOWERED SAWWORT.
Jurinea mollis.
PLATE 129

Serratula simplex and *cyanoides* appear to be so nearly related that some doubt may be raised whether they are not mere varieties of the same species. In our plant, the *stem* was upright, fluted, with a few side branches, bearing, like the main stem, a single

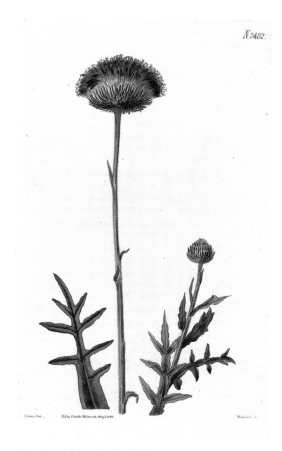

129 *Serratula simplex* (t. 2482 1824 JC)

flower at the termination of each. *Leaves* pinnatifid: lobes narrow with an undulated margin, much resembling those of the crisped variety of *Reseda lutea. Receptacle* bristly. *Seeds* inversely pyramidical, four-sided, tuberculated. *Pappus* bristly, rigid, unequal, scabrous.

Marschall van Bieberstein, describes *cyanoides* as having a strong, to him disagreeable, smell of musk, while *simplex* (his *blanda*) he says has very little scent; but, Jacquin observes, that his plant, which is referred by De Candolle to *simplex*, has a strong scent of musk, infecting the hands that touch it.

The chief distinguishing characters mentioned in the *Flora Taurico-Caucasica*, are, that in *cyanoides* the stem is divided towards the top into a sub-corymb, and the seeds are smooth.

A hardy perennial; native of Austria, Carniolia, and Caucasus. Communicated by Mr. William Anderson, from the Chelsea Garden, where it was introduced by Dr. Fischer, from Gorenki, in 1817.

127 *Othonna amplexicaulis* (t. 1312 1810 SE)

Native of the Cape of Good Hope. Propagated by seeds, and probably by cuttings of the root. Flowers in May and June.

M.S.del J.N.Fitch lith.

Vincent Brooks Day & Son Imp

SILPHIUM ALBIFLORUM.

WHITE-FLOWERED SILPHIUM
OR ROSINWEED.

Silphium albiflorum.

PLATE 130

This is one of two species of the North American genus *Silphium* which Gray includes under the "Compass Plants." *S. albiflorum* is not nearly so handsome a plant as *S. laciniatum*, being comparatively a dwarf, of robust rigid habit, with nearly white flowers. The cultivated specimens are much less scabrid, as might be expected, than the native, and have longer points to the involcral bracts, giving a squarrose look to the unopened heads. There is a further difference in the achenes; those of the native plant have the wings produced upwards into somewhat triangular teeth which are often adnate to a pair of subulate and more or less projecting rigid awns; in the garden plant the upward continuation of the wings are rounded at the tips, and there are no awns, in a young state at any rate.

I am indebted for living specimens of this very interesting plant to my old and valued correspondent, Mr. Thompson, of Ipswich, who has for so many years contributed objects of value and interest to this work; he sent it in September of last year, and informs me that his plants are seven or eight years old. Its native country is Reverhon in Texas.

SILPHIUM TRIFOLIATUM.

WHORL-LEAVED SILPHIUM
OR ROSINWEED.

Silphium trifoliatum.

PLATE 131

A native of Carolina, Virginia, and Georgia, and received at the Glasgow Botanic Garden (along with the preceding species *S. perfoliatum*) from Dr. Wray. It flowers at the same season, but is a less showy plant, having smaller and paler coloured flowers, and leaves more resembling those of several species of sunflower.

OPPOSITE:
130 Silphium albiflorum (t. 6918 1887 MS)

131 *Silphium trifoliatum* (t. 3355 1834 WJH)

Descr. *Stem* arising from a perennial *root*, erect, five to six feet high, purplish, smooth, angled, panicled above. *Leaves* mostly verticillate, spreading, three or four together, the lower ones often alternate, all of them scabrous, especially above, broadly lanceolate, toothed. *Panicle* branched in a di- or trichotomous manner, glabrous, with small leaves at the forkings. *Flowers* large, rather pale yellow. *Involucre* squarrose, the outer scales large, very leafy. *Corollas* of the ray about eighteen, bearing achenia, which are compressed, and distinctly bidentate.

TAGETES LUCIDA.

SWEET-SCENTED TAGETES
OR CHILI MARIGOLD.

Tagetes lucida.

PLATE 132

A native of Chili; of the greater value as, contrary to its more gaudy congeners, it has an agreeable smell. This plant has been accurately described by Cavanilles from the Madrid garden, whence it was introduced into this country. This author does not notice that the leaves are full of pellucid points, giving them an appearance as if

perforated when held up to the light; but this circumstance is common to some other species of tagetes. He describes the pappus as consisting of usually five unequal aristæ, but there are in fact but two, which are equal, somewhat divaricate upwards, about one-third the length of the seed, minutely jagged on the outside; except these, we could observe only the mere remains of the tube of the floret. The number of the aristæ must be therefore less limited in the generic character or this must be separated from the genus.

The root is perennial and may be increased by parting, or fresh plants may be raised from seeds, which it produces freely. Is sufficiently hardy to resist moderate frost, but if sheltered in the winter will be more secure, as well as keep longer in flower. Will live in any soil, but thrives best in a strong loam.

132 *Tagetes lucida* (t. 740 1804 SE)

VERNONIA FLEXUOSA.
ZIG-ZAG VERNONIA.

Vernonia flexuosa.

PLATE 133

Descr. *Radical leaves* on short, flat footstalks, ovate, quite entire, fleshy, rigid, covered above with closely adpressed hairs, and somewhat woolly underneath. *Cauline*

133 *Vernonia flexuosa* (t. 2477 1824 JC)

leaves lanceolate, margin quite entire and scabrous, narrowed towards the base, remote; upper ones smaller. *Stem* upright, straight, hairy, a foot and half high, dichotomously branched towards the top: branches spreading, zig-zag. *Flowers* in round heads, bright purple, sessile at the divisions and at the flexures of the branches, with a leaf-like bract at the base of each. *Calyx* ovate, imbricate, hairy: *leaflets* mucronate. *Receptacle* indented. *Limb of corolla* five-cleft: segments linear. *Anthers* purple: *pollen* white. *Style* exserted; *stigma* bifid. *Pappus* double, outer one shortest, rather bristly than chaffy. *Seed* angular, pubescent.

This handsome species of *Vernonia*, appears to us not to have been heretofore described; but has a near affinity with *sericea* and *remota*. It was raised from seed sent to us by Mr. Frederick Sello, from Brazil, in the garden of John Walker, Esq. of Arno's Grove, and flowered in September. Is probably annual or biennial. Requires to be raised in a stove or hot-bed.

XERANTHEMUM CANESCENS.
ELEGANT XERANTHEMUM.
Helipterum canescens.
PLATE 134

Our plant accords exactly with specimens of *Xeranthemum canescens* of Linnæus in the Herbarium of Sir Joseph Banks; though it does not agree so well in some respects with the Linnæan description as could be wished.

It is a weak, branched, and widely-spreading plant if left to itself, and does not appear to advantage in a collection, unless carefully tied up to a stick; nor is it a plant that succeeds well with every one: and his superior success appears to have arisen from his keeping it in a warmer situation than others, on a shelf in the front of his stove, for it requires more warmth than the greenhouse affords; thus situated, it begins flowering with him in the autumn, and continues in blossom all the winter and spring; when the flowers are out of bloom they droop, but will continue a long while in the plant in that state, and even continue to expand and look beautiful when the sun shines on them.

It is a native of the Cape, recently introduced, and is propagated by cuttings.

134 *Xeranthemum canescens* (t. 420 1798 SE)

CONVOLVULACEÆ

CONVOLVULUS CANARIENSIS.
CANARY BINDWEED.
Convolvulus canariensis
PLATE 138

This immense genus very much needs revising and requires dividing into several, which might be conveniently done, as proposed by Mr. Salisbury, from the various structure of the filaments, stigmas, and seed-vessel.

In our plant the *stigmas* are fully as long as the style, and entirely divaricate, filiform, and obtuse; ovary conical and covered with soft hairs; the *filaments* are best at the lower part with glandular hairs, and are united together at the base; the fasciæ of the *corolla* hairy. The *leaves* vary from ovate-cordate to oblong-cordate, and are sometimes acute, sometimes obtuse, and sometimes quite rounded at the point; all of them pubescent on both sides; soft, and, upon the upper surface especially, feel like a piece of fine cloth. The peduncles are from one to six-flowered.

Mr. Salisbury's *pannifolius* agrees in so many points with our plant, that we have been led to doubt whether it does not belong to the same species, though the flowers of that are larger than in *canariensis*; and Mr. Salisbury describes the stems as angular, which in our plant are perfectly rounded.

It is an evergreen with shrubby stems, and, if properly supported, will climb to a great height. Native of the Canary Islands. Requires the protection of a greenhouse. Propagated by cuttings or seeds; but Miller remarks, that those propagated in the former method, rarely bear seeds, whilst in the latter they seldom fail. Cultivated by the Duchess of Beaufort in 1690. Communicated by Messrs. Loddiges.

CONVOLVULUS CNEORUM.
SILVERY-LEAVED BINDWEED.
Convolvulus cneorum.
PLATE 135

The *Convolvulus cneorum* is a native of Spain and the Levant, was cultivated in the Botanic Garden at Chelsea in 1739,

135 *Convolvulus cneorum* (t. 459 1799 SE)

and flowers from May to September. *Ait. Kew.*

In size, habit, &c. this species has some affinity to the *Convolvulis linearis*, but differs from it, and other species usually cultivated with us, in the silky appearance of its foliage, which it is not in the artist's power to imitate, and for the beauty of which, more than that of its flowers, it is very generally kept in collections of greenhouse plants; its blossoms are nearly white and rarely or never productive of seeds in this country, hence it is increased by cuttings.

It is a hardy greenhouse plant, requiring a dry rather than a moist regimen.

CONVOLVULUS DAHURICUS.
DAURIAN BINDWEED.
Calystegia dahurica.
PLATE 136

Our specimen flowered in July, at Spofforth, where it was sent two or three years ago, by Mr. Cooper, botanic gardener to Lord Milton, who raised it from seed, received, we believe, from Dr. Fischer. *C. dahuricus* belongs to the same division of

the genus as *C. sepium*, having besides the five segments of the calyx, two broad calyx-like bracts, which cover the calyx. It differs from *C. sepium* in having the bracts proportionately broader and less acuminate, a smaller rose-coloured flower, downy stalks, petioles, and peduncles, the leaves downy on the margin and on the nerves underneath, more oblong, not so tapered at the point, nor so broad and auriculate at the shoulder.

It is a hardy perennial plant, flowering in July, with creeping fleshy roots. These troublesome species may be ornamentally cultivated in small plots insulated in the turf, under which their roots will not spread.

136 *Convolvulus dahuricus* (t. 2609 1826 WJH)

EXOGONIUM PURGA.
PURGA OR TRUE JALAP.
Ipomæa purga.
PLATE 137

Although Jalap has been used in European medicine for nearly two centuries and a half, it is only within a few years that its botanical source has been correctly ascertained. The plant long cultivated as yielding the true Jalap, in the stoves of Europe, and among the rest in the Botanic Gardens of Edinburgh, is the *Convolvulus jalapa* of

Linnæus and Willdenow, or *Ipomœa macrorhiza*, of Michaux, a native of Vera Cruz. But, between the years 1827 and 1830, it was proved by no fewer than three independent authorities, Mons. Ledanois, a French druggist, resident at Orizaba, in Mexico, Dr. Coxe, of Philadelphia, through information supplied by Mr. Fontanges, an American gentleman, who lived at Jalapa, and Schiede, the botanical traveller, from personal examination, that the drug of commerce is obtained, not from the hot plains around Vera Cruz, but from the cooler hill country near Jalapa, about 6000 feet above the level of the sea, where it is exposed to frost in winter-time; and that the plant which yields it is an entirely new species.

The plant belongs to the genus *Exogonium* of Choisy, as defined in De Candolle's *Prodromus*, although the author places it under the genus *Ipomœa*, from which it is at once distinguished by its exserted stamens. It grows on the Mountains of Mexico. Schiede found it at a great elevation, on the eastern slope of the Mexican Andes, near Chiconquinaco; and also on the eastern slope of Cofre de Perote. He gives an account of his discovery in the *Linnæa* for 1830. Hartweg gathered it in Mexico, and it has been described by Bentham, from his specimens.

137 *Exogonium purga* (t. 4280 1849 WF)

138　*Convolvulus canariensis* (t. 1228 1809 SE)

139　*Cornus florida* (t. 526 1801 SE)

CORNACEÆ

CORNUS FLORIDA.
GREAT-FLOWERED CORNEL
OR DOGWOOD.

Cornus florida.

PLATE 139

In the temperate regions of North America this tree is much spoken of for its beauty, rising from ten to twenty feet in height, agreeable in its foliage, and covered in the spring and early part of the summer with a profusion of white or sometimes rose-coloured flowers; nor does it want beauty even in the gloomy months of winter, from the quantity of red berries which it bears, and which at that season afford sustenance to the finest warbler of the woods of Amer-

ica, the celebrated mocking bird (*Turdus orpheus*) emphatically called in the Indian language, the Hundred-tongued Bird.

It is a tree of slow growth, and in Europe has, we believe rarely arrived to any very considerable size. That which afforded the subject of our present figure is, perhaps, almost the only one in this country that can be said nearly to rival those of its native soil. It grows in the Duke of Marlborough's garden at Syon Hill, is about sixteen feet high, and spreads at least eighteen, has a straight trunk about six feet in length before it branches, measuring two feet in circumference a yard from the ground; the bark much resembles an elm of the same size. This beautiful tree has flowered freely for many years past, but unfortunately produces no fruit. Its age is unknown, but as we have evidence of its

being cultivated at Chelsea by Miller, in 1739, it is probable that its origin may not be of much later date.

It is most certainly propagated by seeds sent from Virginia, which should be sown immediately after their arrival, in boxes or pans of sandy garden mould, and covered with wet moss, to prevent the earth from drying, and placed where they may be protected from frost. These precautions are the more necessary, as the seed will lie in the ground till the second or third year before they germinate; and as the young plants generally come up the latter-end of summer, they are then in too tender a state to resist the frost without some covering. A shady and sheltered situation promotes its growth and secures its preservation.

CRASSULACEÆ

BRYOPHYLLUM CALYCINUM.
PENDULOUS-FLOWERED BRYOPHYLLUM.

Bryophyllum pinnatum.

PLATE 140

The plant possesses the singular property of germinating from the dark spot observable at the base of every indentation in the margin of the leaf, not whilst growing, but as it decays. Thus, in attempting to dry a specimen, little germinating bulbs were produced in abundance, though there was no appearance of any before the plant was deposited between papers. We know of no other species which will come under this genus; the *Cotyledon pinnata* of Lamarck being probably the same; and his two varieties differing in nothing but that in the one the crenatures of the leaves had germinated and put forth radicles, while the other had not.

Native of the Moluccas, and brought into England from the Calcutta garden by Dr. Roxburgh. Requires a moderate stove. Flowers in May. Propagated by the crenatures of the leaves or by cuttings.

SEMPERVIVUM TORTUOSUM.
GOUTY HOUSELEEK.

Aichryson tortuosum.

PLATE 141

We know of no figure of this plant, the first and only account of which is to be found in the *Hortus Kewensis* of Mr. Aiton; there it is specifically described, and from thence we discover that it was introduced from the Canary Islands, where it is a native, by Mr. Masson, in 1779.

It is a shrubby plant of low growth, producing numerous fleshy leaves growing thickly together, which being evergreen, and making a pretty appearance the year

140   *Bryophyllum calycinum* (t. 1409 1811)

N.º 1409.

Pub. by S. Curtis Walworth Sep.ʳ 1. 1811.

F. Sansom Sculp.

141 *Sempervivum tortuosum* (t. 296 1795)

143 *Alyssum montanum* (t. 419 1798 SE)

142 *Sempervivum villosum* (t. 1809 1816)

Society, under the name of *stellatum*. Our plant was some years since very common in the Chelsea Garden, and in that of the late Dr. Pitcairn, at Islington; and, being an annual producing seeds readily, might be cultivated as hardy. Certainly the plant figured by Seguier as a native of Monte Baldo, appears to be very different, both from our plant and from Sir James Smith's description.

An annual plant. Native of the Island of Madeira. Flowers in the middle of summer, and ripens its seeds in August.

through, render the plant worthy a place in all general collections at least, of greenhouse plants; and though it cannot vie with many of the more showy high-priced novelties, it is an abiding plant, not subject to casualties, while many of those are here today and gone tomorrow.

It throws up its flowering stems, supporting numerous, starry, stonecrop-like flowers; in July and August, and is most readily propagated by cuttings.

which usually go off without producing any perfect seed, though in its wild state it is sufficiently fertile, as is evident from Professor Jacquin's figure.

Through want of seeds, it may be increased without difficulty from cuttings; requires the same treatment as other rare Alpine plants. Was cultivated by Mr. Miller in 1759. *Ait. Kew.*

SEMPERVIVUM VILLOSUM.
HAIRY HOUSELEEK.
Aichryson villosum.
PLATE 142

We have no doubt but that the plant here figured is the *Sempervivum villosum* of the first edition of Aiton's *Hortus Kewensis*; having compared it both with specimens from the Kew Garden and a native one from Madeira. At the same time we suspect that it is also the same plant which Sir James E. Smith described in the first volume of the *Transactions of the Linnean*

CRUCIFERÆ
ALYSSUM MONTANUM.
MOUNTAIN ALYSSUM OR MADWORT.
Alyssum montanum.
PLATE 143

The *Alyssum montanum* is a small procumbent plant, of the perennial kind, with hoary leaves curiously embossed with little prominent points, having the summits of its branches about the end of April covered with a profusion of bright yellow flowers,

BISCUTELLA HISPIDA.
HISPID BUCKLER MUSTARD.
Biscutella cichoriifolia.
PLATE 144

A hardy annual. Native of the south of France and the north of Italy. Communicated by N. S. Hodson, Esq. from the botanic garden at Bury St. Edmunds; where, we are informed by the intelligent curator, it was introduced by Mr. Fischer, of the Gottingen garden.

144 *Biscutella hispida* (t. 2444 1823 JC)

IBERIS SAXATILIS (β) CORIFOLIA.

SMOOTH-LEAVED ROCK CANDY-TUFT.

Iberis saxatilis var. *corifolia*.

PLATE 145

As this species has neither ciliated, pubescent, nor acute leaves, we were inclined to regard it as quite distinct from *saxatilis*, and supposed that it rather belonged to *Iberis garrexiana* of Allioni. But upon more mature consideration, we rather consider it to be a smooth variety of *Iberis saxatilis*. It seems pretty certainly to be the variety *coridis folio* of Villars, and we find an excellent representation of it, from a drawing sent by one Jacobi Plateau, in Clusius's History.

Native of the mountains of southern Europe, growing especially on limestone rocks. Flowers in the spring. Propagated by seeds.

CURCUBITACEÆ

FEUILLÆA PEDATA, FEM.

FEMALE PEDATE FEUILLÆA.

Telfairia pedata.

PLATE 147

The *Feuillæa pedata* is a native of some part of the east coast of Africa, where, we are

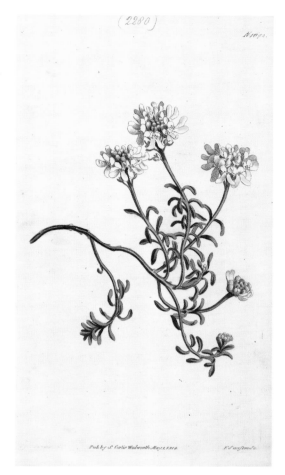

145 *Iberis saxatilis* β *corifolia* (t. 1642 1814 SE)

informed, it was discovered by M. Bojir, and has been successfully cultivated at the Mauritius. It is said to have spread over a large surface of ground there, producing much fine large fruit, containing each about a hundred seeds, the kernels of which are sweet and good to eat.

Charles Telfair, Esq. superintendent of the Royal Garden at the Mauritius, a most zealous collector of subjects of natural history, especially of seeds, bulbs, and plants from Madagascar and the east coast of Africa, to whom the splendid collection at Bury-Hill is indebted for so many of its rarities, sent seeds of this plant to Mr. Barclay, in June, 1825, from which our present subject was raised and planted out in the stove about the latter end of October, and has grown so vigorously, that the gardener informs us, one of its shoots is now fifty-six feet in length. In June last, one year after the seed was sown, it produced several blossoms; but for want of the male plant, the germens fell off soon after the decay of the flower.

DIPSACACEÆ

SCABIOSA ATROPURPUREA.

SWEET SCABIOUS.

Scabiosa atropurpurea.

PLATE 146

The Sweet Scabious has long and deservedly held a place as an ornamental plant in our gardens, the flowers are well adapted for nosegays, have a sweet musky smell, and are produced in great profusion from June to October.

It is a hardy biennial, requiring yearly to be raised from seeds, these should be sown about the latter end of May, or beginning of June, on a shady border of fresh earth, thinning the plants as they advance to the distance of three or four inches; in autumn they should be removed into the border, where they are intended to flower, thus treated they will become good strong plants against winter, flower early the ensuing summer, and produce abundance of perfect seeds.

The blossoms vary in colour, towards autumn the edge of the florets become paler.

146 *Scabiosa atropurpurea* (t. 247 1793 SE)

E.D.Del.   Pub. by S.Curtis, Walworth Sep. 1826.   Weddell Sc.

DROSERACEÆ

DIONÆA MUSCIPULA.

VENUS'S FLY-TRAP.

Dionæa muscipula.

PLATE 149

Great numbers of this very singular plant have been cultivated both this and the last year by Mr. Salisbury, at the Botanic Garden, Brompton, where our drawing was taken. Many of these have flowered and produced ripe seeds in an airy stove. They should be planted in bog-earth mixed with white sand, and the pot kept in a pan of water.

The plant may be kept very well in a window of a room that has a warm aspect if covered with a glass cylinder open at top, and has been known to flourish better with this treatment than when nursed in a stove. Introduced to the Kew Garden by Mr. William Young, in 1768.

150   *Andersonia sprengelioides* (t. 1645 1814 SE)

SCABIOSA CAUCASEA.

CAUCASEAN SCABIOUS.

Scabiosa caucasica.

PLATE 148

This species has very great affinity to *Scabiosa graminifolia*, but the stem is more erect, the flowers are much larger, the leaves broader and less silvery, with longer and more rigid hairs; but the most material difference appears to be in the length of the internal calyx, which in *graminifolia* is hardly longer than the external.

The flower exceeds in size that of any other known species of scabious, and continues long in beauty.

Raised by Mr. Loddiges from seeds received by him from Mount Caucasus. Is a hardy perennial. Flowers in July and August.

149   *Dionaea muscipula* (t. 785 1804 SE)

EPARIADACEÆ

ANDERSONIA SPRENGELIOIDES.

SPRENGELIA-LIKE ANDERSONIA.

Andersonia sprengelioides.

PLATE 150

The genus, of which our present plant is a species, was established by Mr. Brown in his *Prodromus Florae Novae Hollandiæ*. It differs from *Sprengelia* chiefly in the existence of scales at the base of the germen (nectaria of Linnæus); which are wanting in the latter genus, and in the greater length of the tube of the corolla, with laciniæ bearded at the base.

Mr. Brown gave it the name of *Andersonia*, in memory of Mr. William Anderson, Surgeon, who accompanied Captain Cook in two of his voyages, in the last of which he perished; and also to commemorate the merits of Dr. Alexander Anderson, Prefect of the Botanic Garden in the Island of St. Vincent, and of Mr. William Anderson, a most skilful gardener and assiduous cultivator of curious exotics, as also an acute observer of their peculiar habits, to whose abilities our pages bear frequent witness.

A hardy greenhouse shrub. Discovered on the southern coasts of New Holland, by Mr. Brown. Introduced in 1783, by Mr. Peter Good.

OPPOSITE:
147   *Feuillaea pedata*, Fem. (t. 2681 1826 ED)

151 *Andromeda axillaris* β (t. 2357 1822 JC)

ERICACEÆ

ANDROMEDA AXILLARIS, β.
FINE NOTCHED-LEAVED ANDROMEDA
OR FETTER-BUSH.
Leucothoe axillaris.
PLATE 151

Andromeda axillaris and *catesbœi* have been often considered as varieties of the same species, and, as both vary considerably in the form of the leaves, they may sometimes approach so near as to render it not easy to decide to which species some individuals belong, or at least not from the foliage alone; but we believe that our present plant in all its varieties may be generally distinguished by its shorter, more erect, and more clustered racemes. In *A. catesbæi* the racemes are longer, more or less cernuous, and are furnished with longer and more pointed bracts. We must not conceal however, that the accurate botanist Mr. Nuttall is decidedly of opinion that *A. axillaris* and *spinulosa* (our *catesbœi*) form but one species. To us however our present plant, which we take to be variety β of Pursh's *axillaris*, appears to be evidently distinct from the one we have given under the name of *A. catesbœi*.

Native of Carolina and Georgia, and though considered as hardy, is liable to be killed by our winters when severe. Flowers from May to August.

ANDROMEDA CALYCULATA, *VAR.*
VENTRICOSA.
GLOBE-FLOWERED CALYCLED
ANDROMEDA OR LEATHER LEAF.
Chamædaphne calyculata.
PLATE 152

By the two bracts at the base of the calyx, which have given occasion to its name, this species approaches to *Gaultheria*, but the fruit is that of an *Andromeda*.

There are several varieties of this shrub: in Mr. Loddiges's garden, besides the three mentioned in *Hortus Kewensis*, we have observed two others. The one (δ) is distinguished by its decumbent stem, rounder, somewhat more toothed leaves, and shorter racemes. The other (ε) by its smaller greenish flowers, with narrow pointed calycine leaflets, more erect branches, nearly linear dark-coloured leaves with undulate reflexed margins.

May be propagated by cuttings or seeds. Cultivated by the Duke of Argyll in 1748. Flowers in February and March. Communicated by Messrs. Loddiges and Sons.

152 *Andromeda calyculata var. ventricosa* (t. 1286 1810 SE)

153 *Erica andromedaeflora* (t. 1250 1809 SE)

ERICA ANDROMEDÆFLORA.
Erica holosericea.
PLATE 153

For this very rare heath, we are indebted to Mr. Knight, Nurseryman, in the King's Road. *Erica andromedæflora* grows with its branches erect, approaches in affinity to *glauca* and *elegans*, between which Mr. Dryander has placed it. Native of the Cape. Flowers in May.

ERICA ARISTATA.
BEARDED-LEAVED HEATH.
Erica aristata.
PLATE 154

This heath, which is one of the most beautiful, as well as singular in the whole genus, was communicated to us by Mr. Williams, Nurseryman, at Turnham-Green. In the new arrangement of the numerous species of this genus, framed by Mr. Dryander for the new edition of the *Hortus Kewensis*, it occurs under the division of *Coniflorœ grandes*, having the tube of the corolla dilated at the lower part and

154 *Erica aristata* (t. 1249 1809 SE)

155 *Erica grandiflora* (t. 189 1792)

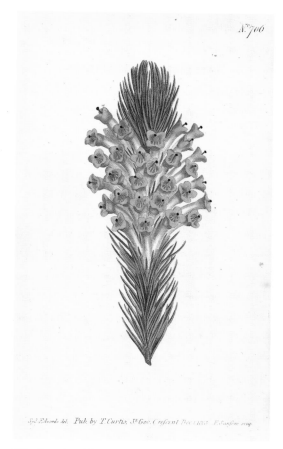

156 *Erica longifolia* vars. *carnea* (t. 706 1803 SE)

plant, that we should be led to consider it as another species, did not the respectable authority of the *Hortus Kewensis* silence all doubts on that head.

The blossoms of this species, whether we regard their magnitude, their colour, their smooth and glossy surface, or the regular position of the filaments, projecting beyond the corolla, and closing together by the antheræ, excite our notice, and claim our admiration.

Like every other heath, the hardy ones excepted, it is a greenhouse plant, and flowers from May to July.

Our drawing was made from a plant finely blown, in the choice collection of James Vere, Esq. Kensington-Gore.

slight footstalks, are scabrous at the margin and sharp pointed. Peduncles not half the length of calyx with three linear bracts close beneath and near the length of calyx. Calycine leaflets ovate far acuminate and very minutely serrated at the base. The germen turbinate, top very woolly. Corolla less curved than in the drawing, and when closely examined, especially when dried, is evidently ribbed. Blossoms in May. Raised from Cape seeds by Mr. Rollisson, Nurseryman, Upper Tooting.

Grows freely, flowering sometimes when only two years old. Requires the same treatment as the rest of the Cape species.

exceeding half an inch in length, and the second subdivision or such as have unarmed anthers. Each leaf is terminated with a recurved bristle which affords a remarkable character. The number of terminal flowers varies from two to four.

Native of the Cape of Good Hope. Requires the same treatment as the rest of the genus. Flowers in December.

Erica grandiflora.

Great-flowered Heath.

Erica grandiflora.

PLATE 155

The erica here figured, is one of the many new and beautiful species, which within these few years have been sent from the Cape by Mr. Masson, and which have contributed so greatly to enrich the Royal Garden at Kew.

The description given of the *grandiflora* in the *Suppl. Plant.* accords so ill with our

Erica longifolia, var^s. carnea.

Flesh-coloured Long-leaved Heath.

Erica longifolia.

PLATE 156

Although we are inclined with the accurate Mr. Salisbury to consider the *longifolia* and *vestita* as varieties of the same species, yet, as the former is the one originally given at the Royal Garden at Kew, and adopted by Mr. Salisbury, we rather give it under the present appellation. The leaves are very slender and tremulous from the

Erica resinosa.

Varnished or Lantern Heath.

Erica blenna.

PLATE 157

This heath having foliage of a full green and very thick set, and flowers of a shining colour (not to be well imitated by art) with deep green tips, makes a striking and beautiful appearance.

157   *Erica resinosa* (t. 1139 1808 SE)

We believe it to be an entirely new species, except the *Erica ardens* of Andrews be a variety of the same. It is one of the very extensive collection belonging to Messrs. Lee and Kennedy, at Hammersmith, where it is known by the appellation of *Erica vernix*. But as this word cannot be properly used as an adjective, and *vernicif-lua* has been already applied by Mr. Salisbury to another species, we have thought it necessary to give a different specific name. For although *Rhus vernix* is used by Linnæus, yet this is a mere translation of its vulgar name, the Varnish Tree; so *Rhus sumach*, because that species had been before called *sumach*; but it is in such cases only that the use of a substantive for a specific name is admissible.

Native of the Cape of Good Hope; flowers from May to August. Requires the same treatment as other Cape heaths.

ERICA VENTRICOSA.
PORCELAIN OR WAX HEATH.
Erica ventricosa.
PLATE 158

Of the many new heaths which have been introduced within these few years, none have excited greater admiration than the present one; its blossoms, though they cannot boast the grandeur or richness of colour so strikingly displayed in the *cerinthoides*, and some others, please more on a near inspection, they have indeed a delicacy and beauty which are indescribable; we have given to it the English name of Porcelain Heath, as the flowers have somewhat the appearance of porcelain, or enamel.

This species has been introduced from the Cape, since the publication of the *Hortus Kewensis*; we saw it in blossom many years since, in the Royal Garden at Kew; several varieties of it have been raised from Cape seeds by Mr. Loddiges, Nurseryman, at Hackney, differing in the hairiness of their leaves, size and colour of their blossoms; but the best variety we have seen is the one here represented.

It is with heaths, in some respects, as it is with fruit trees; one season they will produce blossoms most abundantly, they seem indeed to overblow themselves, the next few appear; in different years the blossoms of the same heath will vary also considerably in size. The *ventricosa* is a free blower, and will in general produce flowers in abundance, for two or three months, from June to September.

Those who possess the knack of striking heaths, raise it by cuttings without much difficulty.

KALMIA ANGUSTIFOLIA.
LAMBKILL OR SHEEP LAUREL.
Kalmia augustifolia.
PLATE 159

In this work we have already given three different species of *Kalmia*, two commonly, and one more rarely cultivated with us, we mean the *hirsuta*, and which indeed we are sorry to find it scarcely to be kept alive in this country by the most skilful management; to these we now add another species, a native also of North America, introduced by Peter Collinson, Esq. in 1736, two years after he had introduced the *latifolia*; Cates-

158   *Erica ventricosa* (t. 350 1796)

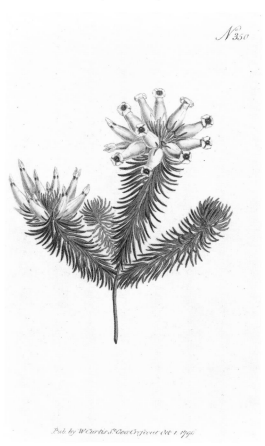

159   *Kalmia angustifolia* (t. 331 1796)

by mentions its having flowered at Peckham in 1743; it is a low shrub, rarely rising above the height of two feet, growing spontaneously in swampy ground, and flowering with us from May to July; there are two principal varieties of it, one with pale and another with deep red flowers; these two plants differ also in their habits, the red one, the most humble of the two, not only produces the most brilliant flowers, but those in greater abundance than the other; Mr. Whitley, who has these plants in great perfection, assures me that it usually blows in the autumn as well as summer.

This shrub is extremely hardy, thriving best in bog earth, and is propagated most commonly by layers. Like the *latifolia*, it is regarded in America as poisonous to sheep.

KALMIA HIRSUTA.
HAIRY KALMIA OR SANDHILL LAUREL.
Kalmia hirsuta.
PLATE 160

This new species of kalmia which we have called *hirsuta*, the stalk, leaves, and calyx, being covered with strong hairs, was im-

ported from Carolina in the spring of 1790, by Mr. Watson, Nurseryman at Islington, with whom several plants of it flowered this present autumn, about the middle of September, from one of which our drawing was made.

The plants were brought over with their roots enclosed in balls of the earth in which they naturally grew, which on being examined appeared of a blackish colour, and full of glittering particles of sand; similar indeed to the bog-earth which we find on our moors and heaths; there is therefore little doubt (for no account accompanied the plants) but this kalmia grows on moorish heaths, or in swamps.

It is propagated by layers, and requires the same treatment as the rest of the genus, that is, to be planted in bog-earth, on a north border: as this however is a new, and of course a dear plant, it will be most prudent till we know what degree of cold it will bear, to keep it in a pot of the same earth, plunged in the same situation, which may be removed in the winter to a greenhouse or hot-bed frame.

161   *Menziesia ferruginea* β (t. 1571 1813 SE)

MENZIESIA FERRUGINEA (β).
CAROLINA MENZIESIA OR MINNIE BUSH.
Menziesia pilosa.
PLATE 161

The plant we have figured was brought from Carolina, by Mr. Fraser, of Sloane Square, and, at first sight, seems to differ from the figure given by Dr. Smith, in having broader and blunter leaves, terminated with a large yellowish gland; but we have dried specimens taken from the same shrub, in which the leaves resemble those in Dr. Smith's figure, and the gland at the point is shrunk so much as not to be very observable. The same gland at the point of the leaf is visible in Mr. Menzies's own specimens, with a sight of which we have been obligingly favoured. In both, the leaves are hairy on the upper surface and naked underneath, except a few strong bristles along the midrib, which in the living plant grow from a gland similar to that at the point of the leaf, but much smaller. Of the form of the corolla nothing certain can be said until the flowers of both shall have been examined in a recent state.

Upon the whole, we scarcely think that there is any ground for considering these plants as entitled to be distinguished, even as varieties.

RHODODENDRON ARBOREUM,
VAR. ALBUM.
TREE RHODODENDRON; WHITE-
FLOWERED VAR.
Rhododendron arboreum
subsp. *cinnamomeum* var *roseum.*
PLATE 162

The drawing here figured of this beautiful Tree Rhododendron was communicated by Robert Baxter, Esq., Dee Hills, Chester, in whose conservatory it flowered in very great perfection in February, 1831. It was raised from seeds sent by Dr. Wallich to Mr. Shepherd of Liverpool, about twenty years ago.

In the *List of Plants* of the Hon. the East India Company's Museum, Dr. Wallich gives this as a native of the high mountains of Nepal, where he gathered it in 1821. I have followed the same author in consider-

W. J.H. del.ᵗ   Pub. by S. Curtis. Glazenwood Essex   Jan.ʸ 1.1834.   Swan Sc

ing it a variety of *R. arboreum*, not having had an opportunity of seeing the plant myself. But it is only fair to observe, that Mr. Don and Mr. Sweet, following Dr. Hamilton, have described it as a distinct species; observing that it derives its most essential specific character from the circumstance of every alternate filament of the stamen bearing an appendage a little above the base, sometimes one on each side.

Dr. Hamilton appears to have first discovered the plant on a mountain at Narainhatty. It flowered for the first time in Europe in Mr. Baxter's Collection.

RHODODENDRON DAURICUM.
DOTTED-LEAVED RHODODENDRON.
Rhododendron dauricum.

PLATE 163

This very beautiful shrub is, according to Pallas, peculiar to the subalpine tracts of eastern Asia, occurring chiefly in the northern parts of Siberia between the Jenisea and Lena rivers, where the northern sides of the mountains in the beginning of May are entirely empurpled by it. It must of course be considered as a very hardy plant, though like many other inhabitants of the coldest regions, when cultivated in this country, from the greater mildness of our winters it is apt to expand its flowers prematurely, which are usually destroyed by subsequent frosts and cold winds. On this account it is better, as soon as the blossoms begin to appear, to remove the plant under shelter, where it will prove exceedingly ornamental in the very depth of winter; but should the frost begin early and continue so long as to retard the opening of the blossoms till its natural season, it might be suffered to continue in the open border.

Our drawing was made at the garden of E.J.A. Woodford, Esq. of Vauxhall, from a very fine specimen, which began to expand its blossoms in the open air in the beginning of January, and was then removed under shelter.

OPPOSITE:

162 *Rhododendron arboreum var. album* (t. 3290 1834 WJH)

163 *Rhododendron dauricum* (t. 636 1803 SE)

RHODODENDRON FULVUM.
Rhododendron fulvum.

PLATE 164

Rhododendron fulvum is very closely allied to *R. fulvoides*, differing in its less elongated leaves and redder indumentum. These differences do not amount to much, however, judged from a large series of specimens collected by Rock, though there is in addition a difference in the number of ovary cells, usually eight in *R. fulvum*, and four to six, or occasionally seven, in *R. fulvoides*.

The series is found only in western Yunnan and the adjoining parts of south-eastern Tibet and Burma. It shows relationship with the *Arboreum* and *Lacteum* series, being distinguished by the glabrous or nearly glabrous ovary and sickle-shaped fruits. *R. fulvum* was first collected by Forrest in August 1912, on the western flank of the Shweli-Salween divide, lat. 25° 20′ N., at an altitude of 3000–3300 metres, where it grows to a tree twenty to twenty-five feet high. Plants are in cultivation raised from Forrest's seeds. The species is classed as being hardy anywhere in the British Isles.

The specimen figured here was grown by the Marquess of Headfort, Kells, Co. Meath, with whom it flowered early in March, 1938. Three colour-forms were received, one with white flowers with faint bands of pink, another with bright pink flowers with deeper bands (as shown in our plate), and a form intermediate between these two.

Distribution. – Western Yunnan, south-eastern Tibet, Upper Burma.

164 *Rhododendron fulvum* (t. 9587 1939 LS)

RHODODENDRON HIRSUTUM.
HAIRY RHODODENDRON
OR ALPEN ROSE.
Rhododendron hirsutum.

PLATE 165

Rhododendron hirsutum and *ferrugineum* are very much alike. By the older Botanists they seem to have been considered as varieties only, and are for the most part described together, as the smooth and hairy Mountain Rose. They are, however, permanently distinct species. The flowers of *hirsutum* are not so large, and rather less intense in colour than those of *ferrugineum*; nevertheless, a large shrub of the former, when covered with blossoms, is a highly ornamental object.

165   Rhododendron hirsutum (t. 1853 1816)

Native of the Alps of Switzerland, Dauphiné, Austria, and Stiria. Flowers in May and June. Should be planted in peat mould. Propagated by offsets, layers, or seeds, which, however, are but rarely perfected with us. As the natural situation of these plants is among the rocks on the summits of lofty mountains, where they insinuate their roots between the crevices of stone, we should recommend a trial of them on old walls, which, when such occur, might be beautifully decorated by planting them with well-chosen subjects.

RHODODENDRON MAXIMUM.
LAUREL-LEAVED RHODODENDRON OR ROSEBAT.
Rhododendron maximum.
PLATE 167

This elegant tree, according to Catesby, adorns the western and remote parts of Pennsylvania, always growing in the most

sterile soil, or on the rocky declivities of hills and river banks, in shady and moist places. Michaux says it is found from New England to North Carolina. In its native soil it attains the height of sixteen feet.

Requires a moist soil with an admixture of bog-earth and a shady situation. Bears forcing as well as the *ponticum*, but is not so well adapted to this purpose from the paleness of the flowers, which, in this state, become white, except the upper lacinia. Is rather more apt to be disfigured by the cold easterly winds occurring late in the season.

Our drawing was made in the spring of 1785, at Messrs. Whitley and Brame's, Old Brompton, when every shrub both of this and *ponticum* produced abundance of flowers in the greatest perfection. This year not a complete umbel was to be seen in the whole collection! Introduced in 1736, by Peter Collinson, Esq.

RHODODENDRON NUDIFLORUM; *VAR.* SCINTILLANS (HYBRIDUM).
GHENT AZALEA 'SCINTILLANS'.
Rhododendron x azalcoides scintillans.
PLATE 168

The hybrid varieties of the *Azalea* group of *Rhododendron* are almost endless, but few are more beautiful than the present, when growing vigorously, as was the case with the individual from which our figure was taken in the American border of the Glasgow Botanic Garden.

The origin of this variety, first reared by Mr. Gowen, the gardener at High Clere, is thus given in his own words, in the *Botanical Register*. "This *Azalea* was raised at High Clere in the same year with those already figured in previous parts of this work, and is a seedling from *Azalea coccinea, (nudiflora,* var. *coccinea,) major*, impregnated by the pollen of *Azalea Pontica.*"

No where perhaps are the varieties of *Azalea, Rhododendron*, and other choice American shrubs cultivated upon a larger scale, or more successfully, than in the Nursery of our friend Mr. Curtis at Glazenwood, where the present hybrid makes a very splendid appearance.

RHODODENDRON PUNCTATUM. (α.)
CAROLINA DOTTED-LEAVED RHODODENDRON.
Rhododendron minus.
PLATE 169

Rhododendrum punctatum was first described by Michaux under the name of *minus*; an appellation applicable enough if only compared with *maximum*, but not at all so in reference to the whole genus.

It seems to vary considerably in the form and colour of its flowers. Andrews's figure, in the *Botanist's Repository*, represents the flower as smaller and much deeper coloured; in the variety *Rhododendron punctatum* β. of the *Botanical Register* the flower is much larger, but is free from all spotting; in our plant the flower in size was intermediate between the two, and two or three of the laciniæ in each were spotted with yellow, not green, dots.

Native of Carolina and Georgia. Flowers in June and July. Introduced in 1786 by Mr. John Fraser. Is considered as a hardy shrub, but its blossoming cannot be secured without protection in the early part of the spring; our late frosts frequently destroying the buds before they open. Thrives best in sandy peat.

166   Rhododendron saluenense (t. 9095 1926 LS)

N.º951

Pub by T.Curtis Aug 1 1806   Edwards del. Sansom sculp

167   *Rhododendron maximum* (t. 951 1806 SE)

RHODODENDRON SALUENENSE.

SALUEAN RHODODENDRON.

Rhododendron saluenense.

PLATE 166

When writing in the *Botanical Magazine* of the *saluenense*-group I said that the affinities of this group "are so close as to be bewildering, and one wonders how the tangled skein of forms will be unravelled." The present plate and the accompanying text may be acceptable as a contribution towards the problem, because *R. saluenense* is the first member of the group to be known, and because it is now, owing to recent accretions of field-specimens, well

represented in the collections at Kew and Edinburgh. *R. saluenense* was discovered by the Abbé Soulié in 1894 at Dong in an eastern tributary valley of the Upper Mekong (24° 40′ N.) and on the Sie-la (Séla of Franchet), a pass in the Mekong-Salween divide about sixty km. farther south (28° 3′ N.).

The area of the *saluenense*-group is confined to the high mountains of western Yunnan (from 28° 40′ N.) and the adjoining ranges of Burma (here *R. charidotes* and *R. calostrotum*). *R. saluenense* itself inhabits stony, often moist, pastures and meadows or cliffs and boulders from 3600–4200 m. within an area roughly bounded by 28° 40′ N. and 27° N., and by 98° E. and 99° E.

Forrest describes it in his field-notes as a small shrub, twenty to sixty centimetres high, with purple flowers often verging to rose or crimson. We are indebted to the Marquis of Headfort for the material from which the plate was prepared. He grew it from seed, collected by Forrest, in the open in his garden at Headfort, Kells, Ireland, where it flowered for the first time towards the end of April 1924. It is, of course, perfectly hardy.

Distribution. – North-west Yunnan: Mountains of the Yangtse-Mekong-Salween divides between 3600–4200 m.

168   *Rhododendron nudiflorum var. scintillans (hybridum)* (t. 3667 1838)

169   *Rhododendron punctatum α* (t. 2285 1821 JC)

VACCINIUM CRASSIFOLIUM.
THICK-LEAVED WHORTLE-BERRY OR CREEPING BLUEBERRY.

Vaccinium crassifolium.

PLATE 170

Whether this little shrub be really a *vaccinium* or an *andromeda*, as the author of the *Recensio Plantarum* suspected, can only be positively determined from the fruit, which we have never seen; from the habit, however, we should suspect that it belongs to the former genus.

A native of South Carolina, whence it was introduced by Mr. Fraser, about the year 1794. It is sufficiently hardy to live in the open air during mild winters, but for safety should be protected from frost. Flowers in May and June. Communicated by Mr. Loddiges.

VACCINIUM MACROCARPON.
AMERICAN CRANBERRY.

Vaccinium macrocarpum.

PLATE 171

We do not enter into the consideration of the propriety or otherwise of separating *Oxycoccus* as a distinct genus from *Vaccinium*. Most of the American species of *Vaccinium* belong to the class Decandria, but of the English species some are decandrous and some octandrous; yet, other characters forbid their separation.

Several authors have considered *Vaccinium macrocarpon*, as a mere variety of *V. oxycoccus*; but they are undoubtedly distinct, and always may be readily distinguished by the peduncles of the latter being terminal; growing for the most part two together; sometimes only one, and now and then three or four; whereas, in *V. macrocarpon*, the peduncles are always lateral; growing alternately from the axils of smaller leaves, or bracts, below the extremity of the branch. There is likewise, besides the difference in the foliage, a considerable diversity in their habits, the stems of *V. oxycoccus* being entirely prostrate; whereas, in *V. macrocarpon*, the flowering branches are assurgent. Both species are cultivated with success in a soil, by no means damp, at the Fulham Nursery.

The American Cranberries are larger and fairer to the eye than the European, and by some they are preferred in tarts or preserves; but in our opinion the taste of the English Cranberry is pleasanter than that of the American.

Native of North America, from Canada to Virginia. Flowers with us in June and July.

170 *Vaccinium crassifolium* (t. 1152 1808 SE)

171 *Vaccinium macrocarpon* (t. 2586 1825 SE)

172 *Vaccinium reflexum* (t. 5781 1869 WF)

VACCINIUM REFLEXUM.
REFLEXED-LEAVED WHORTLE-BERRY.
Vaccinium crenatum.
PLATE 172

A beautiful little Andean rock-plant, conspicuous for its pendulous habit, the deep glossy green hue of the leaves, which are reflexed on the stem and branches, the bright pale red hue of the young foliage, and deep red flowers. It was introduced by Messrs. Veitch, through their late energetic collector, Mr. Pearce, from Bolivia, and flowered in their establishment in the King's Road, Chelsea, in January of the present year. I have examined Herbarium specimens, labelled from the hills between Cuenca and Loxa, collected by Professor Jameson, others from the sources of the Maranon by Warsewitz, and from Equador by Seemann. As a species it approaches *V. densiflorum*, Benth., which is described as having shortly-awned anthers, and is a very much larger and more robust plant, with slightly serrated leaves, which are not reticulated as are those of this species.

VACCINIUM RESINOSUM (β.)
RED-FLOWERED CLAMMY WHORTLE-BERRY OR BLACK HUCKLEBERRY.
Gaylussacia baccata.
PLATE 173

The *Vaccinium resinosum* is a native of Canada and Pennsylvania, and the mountains of Virginia and both the Carolinas.

It forms a pretty little shrub, is usually planted in pots and protected from frost during the winter; but is sufficiently hardy to bear our climate in the open air, at least in a sheltered situation.

Introduced into the Kew Garden in 1772. Communicated by Messrs. Loddiges and Sons, Hackney. Flowers in May and June. Thrives best in a mixture of bog-earth and loam.

173 *Vaccinium resinosum* β (t. 1288 1810 SE)

EUPHORBIACEÆ
EUPHORBIA MELLIFERA.
HONEY-BEARING EUPHORBIA.
Euphorbia mellifera.
PLATE 174

The *Euphorbia mellifera* is a native of Madeira, whence it was introduced to the Royal Garden at Kew in 1784 by Mr.

174 *Euphorbia mellifera* (t. 1305 1810)

175 *Euphorbia variegata* (t. 1747 1815 SE)

Masson. It forms a very handsome shrub, growing with a straight stem and branching at the top. The branches are well clothed with leaves, very much resembling those of the Oleander, and bear the flowers in panicles at their extremities. The name was given it from the extraordinary quantity of honey secreted by the petals, the odour of which spreads far around. Except the figure in the *Jardin de Malmaison*, published at Paris, under the auspices of the Empress Joséphine, we know of no representation of this plant. It requires to be carefully protected from frost.

It is propagated by cuttings. Flowers in April. Communicated to us by Mr. Barr, Nurseryman, a skilful and experienced horticulturist, to whose urbanity we are frequently indebted.

EUPHORBIA VARIEGATA.
PYE-BALLED SPURGE
OR SNOW-ON-THE-MOUNTAIN.

Euphorbia marginata.

PLATE 175

All the parts of this hitherto unnoticed plant are smooth, except the stem, which is hairy. A few of the lower leaves are plain, but as soon as the flowers begin, though they preserve the same form, take on an appearance of bracts, the margins being surrounded with a band, which, like the petals, is perfectly white, and becomes broader and broader towards the extremity of the branch, till the uppermost leaves are all white except a narrow line along the

midrib. The styles are united half-way up, then become bifid and revolute with obtuse stigmas. The filaments also are bifid.

This species approaches to *nudiflora*, but differs essentially in having solitary flowers; besides that, the petals and every part of the fructification are larger, while the plant itself is much smaller.

It is an annual; propagated by seeds only. Native of Upper Louisiana. Introduced by Mr. Nuttall.

FUMARIACEÆ

FUMARIA CAVA.
HOLLOW-ROOTED FUMITORY.
Corydalis cava.

PLATE 176

The Hollow-rooted Fumitory differs from the *solida*, in a variety of particulars; its root is always, as far as we have observed, hollow, appearing sometimes, as Parkinson informs us, "like a shell, every part of which when broken will grow;" frequently acquiring a very great size; the plant itself usually grows to twice the height of the *solida*, bearing foliage and flowers proportionably large; its bractæ or floral leaves, which in the *solida* assume a kind of finger'd appearance from the manner in which they are divided, in this are entire or but slightly indented; it flowers also about three weeks earlier.

Of the *Fumaria cava* there are three principal varieties in point of colour, viz. the white, the blush-coloured, and the purple, which, though plentiful in our gardens formerly, are now rarely met with; Mr. Chappelow informs me, that he found them all this spring, in an old plantation at Teddington, where they produced the most pleasing effect.

It begins to flower in March and continues in bloom three weeks or a month,

176   Fumaria cava (t. 232 1793)

rarely produces any seed, so that it is to be propagated only by dividing its roots; it is a hardy herbacous plant, a native of Germany, and will grow in almost any soil provided it be planted in a shady situation.

177   Fumaria cucullaria (t. 1127 1808 SE)

FUMARIA CUCULLARIA.
TWO-SPURRED FUMITORY
OR DUTCHMAN'S BREECHES.
Dicentra cucullaria.

PLATE 177

The remarkable structure of the flower in this species, may seem to justify those Botanists who have considered it as forming a genus distinct from *Fumaria*. The difference however is not so great as at first sight appears, for the curtailing one of the spurs and uniting the six filaments into two would leave very little difference; and it may be noted that there is something anomalous either in the flower or fruit of almost every species of *Fumaria*.

The change in the specific character was suggested to Mr. Dryander by a very nearly related species, found by Mr. Archibald Menzies, on the west coast of North America, and preserved in the Banksian Herbarium, under the name of *erubescens*, distinguished from *F. cucullaria*, "calcaribus incurvis."

Communicated by Mr. Loddiges. Flowers in May. Propagated by separating the bulbs. Loves a shady situation and light somewhat loamy soil. Native of Virginia and Canada. Cultivated by Philip Miller in 1759.

FUMARIA FORMOSA.
BLUSH FUMITORY.
Dicentra formosa.

PLATE 178

This species approaches very near to *Fumaria cucullaria*, and is the same that is there mentioned, as being preserved in the Banksian Herbarium, under the name of *erubescens*. It was discovered by Mr. Archibald Menzies at Nootka Sound, and introduced by him into the Royal Garden at Kew, from whence it has most probably extended to the nurseries about town. Has a creeping fleshy root, by which it increases rapidly.

We received very fine specimens from Mr. Knight in the King's Road, who has observed it to be an excellent detergent, the juice of it rubbed on the hands getting out any stains, much more expeditiously than soap; but in a single trial with the stain of the outer coat of walnuts, we did not find it succeed.

178   Fumaria formosa (t. 1335 1810 SE)

GENTIANACEÆ

CHIRONIA ANGUSTIFOLIA.
NARROW-LEAVED CHIRONIA.

Orphium frutescens var. *angustifolium.*

PLATE 183

The flower of this species very much resembles that of *Chironia decussata*, but the segments of the corolla are more wedge-shaped with a longer acumen; they are as in that covered with a clammy shining balsam; the tube is longer, extending considerably beyond the calyx, which is oval, not globose, with segments that connive at the points; the leaves are long and linear, of a dark green, without the least pubescence, as is every part of the plant. Raised from Cape seeds by Mr. Whitley at Old Brompton; is one of the most beautiful of the genus, flowers freely during the summer months; requires the same treatment as *Chironia fruticosa*, of which perhaps both this and *decussata* may be the offspring, changed by culture.

179 *Chironia decussata* (t. 707 1803 SE)

CHIRONIA DECUSSATA.
CROSS-LEAVED CHIRONIA.

Orphium frutescens.

PLATE 179

Mons. Ventenat, in his accurate work, distinguishes this chironia from the *frutescens*, by the stalk being more simple, the branches very short, the flowers larger, the calyx more globose and deeply divided into five segments, the leaves wider, more obtuse, growing in two ranks, and covered with a close short pubescence. There are however so many intermediate varieties as to leave room for doubt whether it be a genuine species or not.

It has been long known in our nurseries by the name of *latifolia*. Is a very ornamental greenhouse shrub, occupying but little space and continuing long in blossom.

GENTIANA CAUCASEA.
CAUCASIAN GENTIAN.

Gentianella caucasea.

PLATE 184

We received this species last year, under the name we have adopted, from Mr. Loddiges, who raised it from seeds he received from Mount Caucasus. Flowers in July. Propagated by seeds only. Hardy.

GENTIANA MACROPHYLLA.
LONG-LEAVED GENTIAN.

Gentiana macrophylla.

PLATE 180

Desc. *Stalk* assurgent, rounded, mostly naked in the middle part, but often having a pair of small imperfect leaves near the bottom, and another pair, somewhat larger, towards the upper part. *Radical leaves* lanceolate, five-nerved, pale underneath, quite entire, some of them equalling the stalk in length. *Flowers* verticillate, crowded together at the summit of the stalk, sessile. *Floral leaves* several, four long growing crosswise, others smaller intermingled with the flowers; one or two flowers sometimes grow in the axils of the upper pair of cauline leaves. *Calyx* truncate, split-

ting on one side. *Corolla* somewhat inflated upwards: *limb* divided into four or five segments, soon becoming erect and more acute. The corolla is blue at first, but changes green, and persists in this state till the seeds are ripe. *Stamens* four or five, shorter than *germen*, which is spindle-shaped. *Stigmas* flat, at first applied close together, afterwards revolute. The taste of this plant is slightly bitter, but dwells long on the tongue.

Native of Siberia, according to Pallas, where, especially in the eastern parts, it is very common, in the pastures, in woods, and in the mountains. In all this tract of country *Gentiana cruciata* does not occur.

Communicated by Messrs. Loddiges and Sons. Flowers in June. Is a perfectly hardy perennial. Propagated by seeds.

180 *Gentiana macrophylla* (t. 1414 1811 SE)

GENTIANA OCHROLEUCA.
PALE-WHITE GENTIAN.

Gentiana villosa.

PLATE 181

Gentiana ochroleuca has a near affinity with G. *saponaria*, from which however it differs not only in the colour of the corolla, which is white with green veins, but this part is also longer, sharper pointed, and has the alternate laciniæ shorter and quite entire, not fringed as in *saponaria*; the segments of the calyx are more spreading and acute; the anthers are distinct, not united at the apex; leaves narrower and less evidently three-nerved. The flowers, in all the specimens we have seen, are crowded together at the extremity of the stem, and have none growing from the axils of the leaves, as represented in Plukenet's figure. After all, these two plants approach too near to each other.

Introduced into the Kew Gardens, according to Mr. Aiton, in 1803. Native of North America: growing, according to Mr. Pursh, from Pennsylvania to Florida, but not so common as G. *saponaria*, on dry sandy fields and gravelly hills: Michaux gives woods as the native situation of his plant. Flowers in September.

GENTIANA SAPONARIA.
BARREL-FLOWERED GENTIAN OR SOAPWORT GENTIAN.

Gentiana saponaria.

PLATE 185

This very handsome species of gentian is a native of North America, where it is very common in grassy places in the woods. The *fimbriata* of Vahl is supposed not to differ from this species. In fact the folds on the inside of the corolla terminate in small teeth somewhat jagged, between the larger teeth, but owing to the involution of the margins of the larger laciniæ, these smaller teeth do not appear; for the flower never expands, but remains always closed at the point; which circumstance, added to the size and barrel-like form of the corolla, at once distinguishes it from every other known species. We suspect the *Gentiana ochroleuca* may be a mere variety of this plant, but this we have at present no means of ascertaining.

A hardy perennial, requires a shady situation and a mixture of bog-earth or rotten leaves with a loamy soil. Introduced to the Kew Garden in 1776, by Mr. William Young.

that out of many thousands, he could not meet with a single one: the usual number is five.

Our plant was communicated by Messrs. Loddiges, with whom no species of gentian thrives better or flowers more freely.

GENTIANA TRICHOTOMA.

Gentiana trichotoma.

PLATE 182

This beautiful species was first collected in the year 1890 by Pratt at Tatsienlu on the Tibetan border of Szechwan growing at an altitude of 3000 to 4300 metres. Since then other collectors have sent home material but it does not appear to have been in cultivation until it was raised from seed collected by Captain Kingdon Ward near Glacier Lake Camp, Szechwan, in July, 1921. Plants raised from this seed obtained an Award of Merit in May, 1923, when exhibited at the Royal Horticultural Society by Messrs. Bees, Chester, under the name of *Gentiana hopei* Hort.

Herbarium material shows a wide diversity of forms varying considerably in the

182   Gentiana trichotoma (t. 9638 1942 LS)

181   Gentiana ochroleuca (t. 1551 1813 SE)

GENTIANA SEPTEMFIDA, VAR. (β.)
SPOTTED-FLOWERED CRESTED GENTIAN.

Gentiana septemfida.

PLATE 186

The plant here figured has wide leaves; the gores of the corolla are more finely cut, and the limb is spotted with white: circumstances probably owing altogether to cultivation. We should not, therefore, have thought this variety of sufficient importance to have given a separate figure of it; but that, for want of more early attention, the whole impression was coloured under an idea of its being another species, which we have not yet been fortunate enough to meet with.

The name of *septemfida* is a very improper one; a corolla with seven laciniæ being a very rare occurrence; Bieberstein observes

91

length and colour of the corolla and in the height of the plant. The height varies from less than ten centimetres to over forty centimetres, the length of the corolla from 2.5 centimetres to about five centimetres and the colour from white or white and blue together through pale blue to deep blue. Undoubtedly, the finest form is that with steel-blue flowers which appears to remain constant, although a white form has appeared in cultivation with flowers of similar length. These variations were noted by Captain Kingdon Ward who writes in the *Gardeners' Chronicle*, Ser. 3, XCV. 263 (1934), of having found plants varying from pale sea-blue to deep prussian-blue, and in his book *A Plant Hunter in Tibet*, p. 198, of it ranging from pale blue or almost white to a deep sea-blue.

Gentiana trichotoma was placed by Kuznezow in his section *Frigida*. Later, Marquand (*Kew Bull.* 1937) when subdividing the section *Frigida* placed our plant in his series *Multiflorae*. In his key to the section *Frigida*, Kusnezow (*Acta Horti Petrop.* XV. 255) separated G. *trichotoma* from all the other species in the section by the character of the corolla in bud, as seen from inside, twisting to the right. Marquand, from his examination of the specimens in the Kew Herbarium states (*Kew Bull.* 1928, p. 59) that this character does not appear to be constant. Examination of the specimens at the Edinburgh Herbarium, and of cultivated material confirms Marquand's statement. Its closest ally is G. *przewalskii* Maxim., from which it differs in the more slender habit, in having the flowers borne (as a rule) in threes with the lowermost flowers on long peduncles, thus forming a lax raceme-like inflorescence, in the blue colouring of the corolla, and in the narrower calyx-lobes recurved at the tips. In G. *przewalskii* Maxim. the flowers are borne in a loose terminal head, the colour of the corolla is whitish and the calyx-lobes are broad and erect.

Regarding the behaviour of this attractive plant in cultivation, although it cannot be considered a plant for every garden, it can be grown successfully, if given certain conditions. It is definitely perennial and while not of long duration in the south

of England, it survives several years in Scotland. In his garden in Perthshire, Mr. A. Harley, who supplied the material from which the plate was prepared, states that he has had plants survive for over five years. From this it may be concluded that the conditions there are suitable. The plants are grown in full exposure to sun, in a water-retentive soil where also there is sufficient moisture below to keep the soil cool, and to which the roots can penetrate; even in the summer time, there is never any of the blistering heat that is experienced in the south of England. While accepting these conditions of free moisture, the plant does not require and will not tolerate the amount of moisture that other Chinese species, such as G. *sinoornata*, enjoy. The flowering period is during the latter part of June, and throughout July.

Distribution. – The western provinces of China and the adjoining parts of Tibet.

GENTIANA VERNA.

VERNAL GENTIAN.

Gentiana verna.

PLATE 187

187   *Gentiana verna* (t. 491 1800 SE)

S. Edwards del.   Pub. W. Curtis St George: Crescent Sep. 1.1800.   F. Sansom sculp.

This elegant hardy perennial, a native of the Alps of Switzerland, Austria, and the Pyrennees, hath, as we are informed by Dr. Smith, in his *Flora Britannica*, been discovered by Mr. Heaton, on the mountains between Gort and Galway, in Ireland; and in Teesdale-Forest, Durham, by the Rev. Mr. Harriman, and Mr. Oliver.

Its flowers have a very agreeable scent, and will decorate either the open border or rockwork; they appear in April or May, and may be brought forward at least six weeks earlier, by being placed in the greenhouse. It succeeds well in a mixture of peat-earth and loam.

188   *Erodium gussonii* (t. 2445 1823 JC)

GERANIACEÆ

ERODIUM GUSSONII.

GUSSONE'S HERON'S-BILL.

Erodium gussoniei.

PLATE 188

Descr. *Root* perennial. *Stem* herbaceous, decumbent, rounded, hairy: hairs pointing downwards. *Cauline leaves* opposite, unequal, one being generally larger than the other, petioled, cordate-ovate, obtuse, somewhat lobed, crenate, soft-villous on both sides. *Peduncles* axillary, alternate, three or four times longer than the hairy petiole. *Umbel* about ten-flowered. *Involucre* scariose, two-leaved kidney-shaped. *Pedicels* horizontal. *Calycine leaflets* unequal, streaked, each of them furnished with a short arista or mucro, inserted a little below the apex. *Petals* rounded, quite entire (Tenoré says emarginate), purple, veined, two of them stained with a deeper colour towards the base. *Filaments* five fertile, bearing dark purple two-celled anthers, opening internally, and five sterile, alternating with the fertile. *Stigma* five-rayed, persistent.

This species has considerable affinity with *Erodium malacoides*, of which very variable species it perhaps may be thought to be only a variety. It differs however in having larger flowers; much longer seed vessels; pedicels longer and more horizontal; leaves softer and more glaucous.

Communicated, in flower, in July last, by Philip Barker Webb, Esq. to whom we are entirely indebted for the above synonymy. This gentleman informs us, that the plant was sent to Professor Tenoré by his pupil, Don Giovanno Gussoné, from Avellino, in Sicily, where Mr. Webb gathered both specimens and seeds. Gussoné, a zealous, active, and accurate botanist, was at that time curator of the Duke of Calabria's garden at Palermo, and gave Mr. Webb reason to expect from him before long, a *Flora Sicula*, with descriptions of many new species.

MONSONIA LOBATA.
BROAD-LEAVED MONSONIA.
Monsonia lobata.
PLATE 189

In the third volume of this work we have given a figure and account of the *Monsonia speciosa*, to which the present species, in its general habit, bears a great similitude, differing principally in its foliage, which is undivided; the flowers are smaller than those of *speciosa*, and more handsome in bud than when open; they are more frequently produced, but require the influence of the sun to make them expand fully.

It is a native of the Cape, and was introduced by Mr. Masson in 1774. Flowers in April and May; requires the same treatment and is propagated in the same manner as the *speciosa*.

189 *Monsonia lobata* (t. 385 1797)

PELARGONIUM ACETOSUM.
SORREL CRANE'S-BILL.
Pelargonium acetosum.
PLATE 190

Mons. L'Heritier, the celebrated French Botanist, who, in the number, elegance, and accuracy of his engravings, appears ambitious of excelling all his contemporaries, in a work now executing on the family of *Geranium*, has thought it necessary to divide that numerous genus into three, viz. *Erodium*, *Pelargonium*, and *Geranium*.

The *Erodium* includes those which Linnæus (who noticing the great difference in their appearance, had made three divisions of them) describes with five fertile stamina, and calls *Myrrhina*; the *Pelargonium* those with seven fertile stamina, his *Africana*; the *Geranium* those with ten fertile stamina, his *Batrachia*.

They are continued under the class Monadelphia, in which they now form three different orders, according to the number of their stamina, viz. Pentandria, Heptandria, and Decandria. If the principles of the Linnean system had been strictly adhered to, they should perhaps have

been separated into different classes; for though the *Pelargonium* is Monadelphous, the *Geranium* is not so; in consequence of this alteration, the *Geranium peltatum*, and *radula*, must now be called *Pelargonium peltatum* and *radula*, and the *Geranium reichardi* be an *Erodium*.

The leaves of this plant have somewhat the taste of sorrel, whence its name; it flowers during most of the summer, and is readily propagated by cuttings. Miller mentions a variety of it with scarlet flowers.

It is a native of the Cape, and known to have been cultivated in Chelsea Garden, in the year 1724.

190 *Pelargonium acetosum* (t. 103 1789)

PELARGONIUM TRISTE (β)
FILIPENDULIFOLIUM.
DROP-WORT-LEAVED NIGHT-SMELLING PELARGONIUM.
Pelargonium triste
PLATE 191

The corolla of this variety of the Nightsmelling Pelargonium is irregular and the petals are long and lax, looking two upwards and three downwards. The leaves are far less hairy than in variety (α), indeed almost smooth, except along the footstalk

191 *Pelargonium triste β filipendulifolium* (t. 1641 1814 SE)

and main ribs, and are more like those of common drop-wort; on which account we have added the additional name of *filipendulifolium*. We have been induced to do this, more especially, as we are not sure that it may not turn out to be a distinct species. The synonyms we have assigned to this variety in particular come considerably nearer to it than the others, but none of them resemble it so exactly as to leave no doubt.

In the daytime the flowers of this plant are without smell; but after sunset and through the night emit a powerful scent, which conveys the idea of some delicious fruit.

Flowers most part of the summer. Propagated by seeds or by cuttings of the root. Communicated by Messrs. Whitley Brame, and Milne, of the Fulham Nursery.

GESNERIACEÆ

GESNERIA PURPUREA.

Gesneria maculata.

PLATE 192

During the present winter my attention has been directed to a state or variety of this plant, which has been the pride and ornament of our stoves during the winter months. Of it we received the tubers from Mr. Millosovich, of Rio Janeiro, last year; and I was not a little surprised to find it taken up as a new species, both by Dr. Lindley, in Paxton's *Flower Garden*, under the name of *G. purpurea*, and by Dr. Planchon, in the *Fore des Serres*, under that of *Dircœo-Gesneria purpurea*; the former, its introduction being unknown to him, suspects it to be a hybrid, "perhaps between *G. Douglasii* and *G. discolor*;" the latter traces its parentage, but unaccompanied by any proof, to *Gesneria Douglasii* and *G. (Diceœa) lobulata* (a rich scarlet-flowered species) of both of which excellent figures are given by the author in the same volume. To Dr. Lindley is due the merit of distinguishing the *G. purpurea* as a species; and since I am able to prove that this has been imported three different times and by as many different persons, direct from the

192 *Gesneria purpurea* (t. 5115 1859)

Brazils, I think a legitimate parentage will be henceforth conceded to it. I may add too that my herbarium possesses native specimens of both the species now under consideration, gathered by Gardner, in Brazil, and exhibiting all the characters, as figured and described by Lindley. The one is no. 251, of *Gardner's Herb. Bras.*, from the trunks of trees, on the Pedra Bonita Tejuca, 1836, and correctly named *Gesneria douglasii*, Lindl. The other is his n. 466, from the Organ Mountains, marked *Gesneriæ sp.* "At all events," Dr. Lindley concludes, "*G. purpurea* is one of the most striking of the whole race to which it belongs," and we heartily concur with him in that opinion.

193 *Sciadacalyx warszewiczii* (t. 4843 1855)

SCIADACALYX WARSZEWICZII.

WARSZEWICZ'S SCIADACALYX.

Isoloma warszewiczii.

PLATE 193

The genus *Sciadacalyx* Reg., deriving its name from the umbrella-like expansion of its calyx, is allied to *Hepiella*, Reg., and *Brachyloma* Stanst. We are only acquainted with one species of this fine genus, viz. *S. warszewiczii*, which the collector, whose name it bears, discovered in the mountains about Santa Marta, New Granada, and transmitted to the Botanic Garden at Zürich, where it was first brought to flower, and whence it was diffused over the different gardens of England and the Continent. Its chief merits as an ornamental stove plant consist in flowering from July until almost the end of the winter, and its gay-coloured blossoms.

Descr. A perennial herb, three to four feet high, with catkin-like *stolons*. *Stem, petioles, leaves,* and *calyx* villoso-hirsute. *Leaves* opposite, with long petioles, oval-shaped or cordate, generally with an irregularly-sided base, crenate at the margin, and accuminate at the apex. *Flowers* arranged in axillary umbels, three to six. *Calyx* attached to the ovary, five-lobed; lobes expanded almost horizontally, like an umbrella. *Corolla* nearly straight, almost oblique at the base, with a slightly inflected tube, and a five-lobed limb, hirsute, scarlet, with the exception of the base of the tube, which is yellow, and the lobes, which are either bright yellow or yellowish-green, dotted with red or brown. *Stamens* five, four of which are fertile, bearing bilocular *anthers* connate with each other. *Ovary* hirsute, surrounded by a glandular five-lobed ring. *Stigma* bilobed. *Capsule* unilocular, many-seeded, two-valved.

STREPTOCARPUS POLACKII.

POLACK'S STREPTOCARPUS.

Streptocarpus polackii.

PLATE 194

Streptocarpus polackii is another addition to the horticulturally pleasing but botanically puzzling group of species which centres, at any rate from the standpoint of botanical history, around *S. rexii* (Hook.) Lindl. In point of fact if we wish to get a true picture of this interesting species-group, we must abandon the idea that *S. rexii* is its central species, for, whilst the group as a whole is distributed along the mountain ranges of South-east Africa from Knysna in Cape Province to the Zoutpansberg in northern Transvaal, *S. rexii* itself comes from the extreme southern end of the range.

S. polackii is a plant of eastern Transvaal and has been collected at Tzaneen in Pietersburg District (*v.d. Merwe* 479) and at Graskop (*Reynolds* 2659) and Sabie

194 *Streptocarpus polackii* (t. 9668 1946 S.R-C & LS)

(*Koeleman s.n.*) both in the Lydenburg District. Mr. A.J.R. Polack of Pretoria, after whom the plant is named, found it further south, in and around Barberton, where he collected seeds. Plants were raised from these seeds by Mr. Lawrence, who kindly sent a specimen to Kew in April, 1940, and this served as the model for the present plate.

GOODENIACEÆ

GOODENIA GRANDIFLORA.

LARGE-FLOWERED GOODENIA.

Goodenia grandiflora

PLATE 195

As soon as the flower opens, the stamens are bent quite away from the stigma; but the anthers in this genus, as in most, if not all, the family of *Campanulaceæ*, shed their pollen before the corolla is expanded. If the flower-bud in this species be carefully opened a day or two before its proper season of expanding, a most curious spectacle offers itself, the stigma will be found erect, open, in the shape of a cup, and

sometimes completely filled with the pollen, shed from the anthers, which now connive over its mouth. Before the flower opens, the style is much lengthened, and the stigma closes, the filaments at the same time shrinking away.

The flowers have a sweet, but not very agreeable, smell, and the whole plant partakes of the same. If brought forward by sowing the seeds in a gentle hot-bed in the spring, and the young plants be afterwards set out in open ground, they will flower about the beginning of August, and continue to blossom till the frost sets in. The seeds will ripen in October. Requires a plentiful supply of water.

We received this plant from Mr. Whitley, of Old Brompton, who raised it from seeds from New South Wales.

195 *Goodenia grandiflora* (t. 890 1805 SE)

GRAMINÆ

COIX LACHRYMA.

JOB'S TEARS.

Coix lacryma-jobi.

PLATE 196

This very remarkable plant has been known in our gardens from the time of Gerard; but being a tender annual, rarely

197 *Coix lachryma* (t. 2479 1824 JC)

perfecting its seeds with us, is not very common. Its seeds, however, are often imported from the warmer parts of Europe, and from the East Indies. These are contained singly in a stony involucre or calyx, which incloses the female flower, and never opens till committed to the earth; the style, however, is exserted, and a pedicel supporting the spike of male flowers issues with it from the bottom of the involucre. This stony calyx, which, when ripe, is very like a drop of white porcelain, with a bluish tinge, is generally supposed to be the seed itself. Its shape, round at bottom and pointed at top like a drop of liquid, readily suggested a name for the plant.

It is said to be cultivated as an esculent, and that a coarse bread is made of the seed; but the principal use to which it is put is to make necklaces or rosaries, which gives occasion to old Parkinson to make a rude remark in his usual quaint language. It is said to grow spontaneously in Candia, Rhodes, and in Syria, as well as in the East Indies. With us it must be treated as a tender annual, and raised in the spring in a hot-bed, to afford any chance of its producing perfect seeds.

GUTTIFERÆ

HYPERICUM BALEARICUM.
WARTY ST. JOHN'S-WORT.

Hypericum balearicum.

PLATE 197

Is according to Linnæus a native of Majorca, Miller says that it grows naturally in the Island of Minorca, from whence the seeds were sent to England by Mr. Salvador, an Apothecary at Barcelona, in the year 1718.

The stalks of this species are usually of a bright red colour, and covered with little warts; the leaves are small with many depressions on their upper sides like scars; the flowers are not always solitary, but frequently form a kind of Corymbus.

It is a hardy greenhouse plant, and readily propagated by cuttings. It flowers during most of the summer.

Clusius informs us in his *Hist. pl. rar. p.* 68 that he received from Thomas Penny, a Physician of London, in the year 1580, a figure of this elegant plant, and who the next year showed a dried specimen of the same in London, which had been gathered in the Island of Majorca, and named by him μυρτο-κιζον, or Myrtle-cistus; it appears therefore that *Hypericum baleari-*

197 *Hypericum balearicum* (t. 137 1790 SE)

cum has long been known, if not cultivated in this country.

We may remark that Clusius's figure of this plant is not equally expressive with many of his others.

HYPERICUM MONOGYNUM.
CHINESE ST. JOHN'S-WORT.

Hypericum chinense.

PLATE 198

Of this genus twenty-eight species are enumerated in the *Hortus Kewensis* of Mr. Aiton, forty-two in Professor Murray's ed. of the *Systema Vegetab* and sixty-four in Professor Gmelin's fourteenth ed. of *Linn. Syst. Nat.* of the latter number fourteen are described with five styles, forty-six with three, two with two styles, and two with one; when the term *monogynum* was first applied to this species it was a proper one, there being then only one in that predicament, another having since been discovered it ceases to be so now; some have indeed doubted the propriety of using the word *monogynum* at all, alleging that in reality there are five styles, which man-

198 *Hypericum monogynum* (t. 334 1796)

ifestly show themselves above, though they coalesce below; such is the opinion of my friend, Dr. Gwyn; this is a point on which botanists will think differently.

This elegant native of China, now common in our greenhouses, appears from Mr. Miller to have been first introduced to this country in 1753, by Hugh, Duke of Northumberland; he tells us, that the plants were raised in his Grace's curious garden at Stanwick, from whence the Apothecaries garden at Chelsea was furnished with it.

Mr. Miller has given us a minute description of this plant, which he observes is the more valuable, as it continues in flower great part of the year; he observes further, that if planted in a very warm situation, it will live in the open air, but that those plants which stand abroad will not flower in winter, as those do which are removed into shelter in autumn. It may be propagated by slips from the root, or by layers.

HAEMADORACEÆ

ANIGOZANTHUS PULCHERRIMUS.
BEAUTIFUL YELLOW ANIGOZANTHUS.

Anigozanthus pulcherrimus.

PLATE 201

One of the most beautiful of this fine genus from its copious and richly coloured flowers and flowering branches; the former being bright yellow, the latter clothed with scarlet hairs, curiously branched on a yellow ground. It is a native of the Swan River settlement, where it was detected by our indefatigable friend Mr. James Drummond. From seeds sent by him it has been raised by Mr. Lowe, to whom the Royal Botanic Garden owes the possession of a fine plant. It has not yet, however, as far as I am aware, bloomed in this country, and our flowering specimen is taken from a dried native specimen sent by Mr. Drummond, in which, from the nature of the plant and pecularity of its vestiture, the form and colours are as well preserved as if seen in a living state. Perhaps in the general structure of the blossoms it comes nearest to A. *flavidus*; but the flowers are much shorter, and the panicle and leaves and clothing are all very different in the two species. It loves a light sandy soil and the protection of a good greenhouse, and will prove a highly ornamental plant to our gardens.

199 *Wachendorfia brevifolia* (t. 1166 1809 SE)

WACHENDORFIA BREVIFOLIA.
DINGY-FLOWERED WACHENDORFIA.

Wachendorfia paniculata.

PLATE 199

We believe this to be specifically distinct from that of the name of *hirsuta*; but as we missed the opportunity of examining the living plant, after Mr. Edwards had drawn it; we cannot, with precision, determine the differences. Breynius describes the stem of *brevifolia* as being a foot high, round, green, and hairy; the flowers as crimson intermixed with a tawny yellow colour, with some soft hairs on the outside; the leaves in his figure are distich, one placed above the other edgewise, about half a foot long, and diverging salcately.

In our drawing, besides the difference of colour, the stem appears thicker, rounder, and less flexuose; the branches far more numerous, and placed with much shorter intervals from each other.

Dr. Solander has left no further description but the specimen from which he took it is preserved in the Banksian Herbarium.

Our drawing was made some years ago at Mr. Woodford's garden at Vauxhall. Native of the Cape of Good Hope; a greenhouse plant.

WACHENDORFIA HIRSUTA.
HAIRY WACHENDORFIA.

Wachendorfia paniculata.

PLATE 200

Flowers, quite scentless, open in succession, close towards evening; expand in the month of July. We have never observed the six stamens mentioned by some authors and figured in one species by Breynius, nor the rudiments of any more than the usual three. The genus is remarkable in this natural order for its inferior corolla, and is perhaps one of its connecting links to the hexandrous liliaceous plants; in the habit of its leaves it approaches *Babiana*, in that of the flower and capsule it comes nearer to *Cyanella*. If Burman's figure is attentively examined, it will be found to come nearer to this than *paniculata*; the lower leaves not being seen nor described it is impossible to be so certain as we could desire; the plant was only known to Burman by a drawing taken at the Cape, from which his engraving was made. Introduced amongst us by Mr. Williams, Nurseryman at Turnham-Green, who received the bulbs three or four years back from the Cape. Requires the same treatment as *Ixia* and other Cape *Ensatæ*.

200 *Wachendorfia hirsuta* (t. 614 1803 SE)
OPPOSITE:
201 *Anigozanthus pulcherrimus* (t. 4180 1845 WF)

Tab. 4180.

Reeve, Bro. imp.

Fitch. del.

HYPOXIDACEÆ

HYPOXIS STELLATA (β).
WHITE-FLOWERED STAR HYPOXIS.

Hypoxis stellata.

PLATE 202

The present specimen of *Hypoxis stellata* (ß) was unknown to us; we have since learned that it comes from Sierra Leone; has been most probably introduced by Professor Afzelius.

202   *Hypoxis stellata* β (t. 1223 1809 SE)

ILLICIACEÆ

ILLICIUM FLORIDANUM.
RED-FLOWERED ILLICIUM
OR ANISEED-TREE.

Illicium floridanum.

PLATE 203

Of the genus *Illicium* there are at present only two known species, viz. the *Illicium anisatum* and *Illicium floridanum*, the former a native of China and Japan, the latter of Florida; both of them are cultivated in this country, but the latter more generally, on account of the superior beauty of its flowers, which are of a fine deep red colour, and have the appearance of being double.

According to Mr. Aiton, this species was introduced by John Ellis, Esq. in 1776; but Isaac Walker, Esq. of Southgate, was the first who possessed it in this country, he informs me by letter, that he received plants of its from Pensacola in 1771, by the hands of Mr. John Bradley, and that he communicated some of them to Dr. Fothergill, Dr. Pitcairn, and Mr. Ellis. It flowers from April to July.

Cultivators differ widely as to their treatment of this plant, some keeping it in the stove, others in the greenhouse, while some have ventured to plant it in the open ground in warm situations; it probably is more hardy than we imagine; all agree in propagating it by layers, or by seeds if they can be procured.

Linnæus, contrary to his usual practice, distinguishes the two species by their colour only, and Thunberg is disposed to regard them as mere varieties.

203   *Illicium floridanum* (t. 439 1799 SE)

204   *Antholyza merianella* (t. 441 1799 SE)

IRIDACEÆ

ANTHOLYZA MERIANELLA.
DWARF ANTHOLYZA.

Watsonia coccinea.

PLATE 204

This very rare species is perfectly distinct from the *meriana* of more humble growth, the flowering stem seldom rising to more than a foot in height, and producing from four to six flowers, which are proportionably longer, more closed, and of a deeper red colour than those of *meriana*.

Was introduced from the Cape by Captain Hutchinson, in 1754. *Ait. Kew.* Is readily increased by offsets, and requires the same treatment as the *anthol. Meriana* already figured. Flowers in May and June.

Our drawing was made from a plant which flowered with Mr. Fairbairn, at the Apothecaries Garden, Chelsea, 1798.

205 *Aristea cyanea* (t. 458 1799 SE)

ARISTEA CYANEA.
GRASS-LEAVED ARISTEA.
Aristea africana.
PLATE 205

It will be seen, on consulting the synonyms, that this native of the Cape, though introduced to the Kew Garden by Mr. Masson in 1774, was long before known to a considerable number of Botanists, and it is curious to see the different opinions which they entertained of it; we abide by that of Mr. Aiton, who has called it *Aristea*, from the bearded appearance, we apprehend, of the spathæ.

It is a small fibrous-rooted plant, rarely exceeding when in bloom the height of six or eight inches, and would be too insignificant for a greenhouse collection, were not its flowers of a very brilliant blue colour; indeed Miller, who appears evidently to have cultivated it, says, the flowers make little appearance, and so the plant is only kept for the sake of variety. *Dict.* 4to. ed. 6. *Ixia africana.* Mr. Aiton tells us, that it flowers from April to June, yet Mr. Andrews, intent on giving to Messrs. Lee

and Kennedy the credit of flowering it first, disregards this information and is pleased to conjecture that the plant never flowered at Kew, because Mr. Aiton, as he alleges, has not given to it any specific character; not aware that, as a new genus, its parts of fructification are described at the end of the *Hortus Kewensis* and that no specific character is ever given to a plant, where there is only one of a genus, and that for the most obvious reason.

The *Aristea* is a plant easily propagated by parting its roots, as well as by seeds, will succeed in a small pot, and though a greenhouse plant, will not be hurt by the moderate heat of the stove, but flower the better for it. The blossoms do not expand fully unless the sun shines hot on them.

206 *Aristea melaleuca* (t. 1277 1810 SE)

ARISTEA MELALEUCA.
MOURNING-FLOWERED ARISTEA.
Aristea lugens.
PLATE 206

Root fibrous, perennial; *root-sheaths* membranous sphacelate, short; *leaves* perennial, three to four inches high, two to three lines broad; *stem* annual, about a foot high, striate; *corolla* three inches or more in

diameter; *style* twice shorter than the larger segments; *anthers* about equal to filaments, upright, yellow. Native of the Cape of Good Hope, where it was found by Thunberg on and near the Paarleberg, growing among the bushes.

Introduced by Mr. Masson into Kew Gardens, where it flowered in 1788. A greenhouse plant of great beauty.

BABIANA SAMBUCINA.
ELDER-FLOWER-SCENTED BABIANA.
Babiana sambucina.
PLATE 207

This fine species was lately received by Mr. Hibbert, from the Cape of Good Hope. Our drawing was made when the bloom was rather too far advanced; and which, before we obtained the specimen for description, was entirely withered. Differs from *spathacea*, its closest relative, in having the tube scarcely longer than the spathe, which last is also pubescent. The flowers are exceeding fragrant.

207 *Babiana sambucina* (t. 1019 1807 SE)

BABIANA VILLOSA.
CRIMSON BABIANA.
Babiana villosa.
PLATE 208

Stem declined. *Flowers* scentless. Outer segments of the *corolla* are traversed by a hairy subcarinate line on the outside, and terminated by a small mucro. *Anthers* deep violet or black, at first surrounding the *stigmas*, but ultimately inclining to a parallel front, though not ascendent.

Differs from *Babiana* (*Ixia*) *rubro-cyanea*, chiefly in not having the stigmas so broad and rounded, nor so markedly curled and fringed. – Are they really distinct species?

Flowers in May. Introduced into Kew Garden by Dr. Patrick Russell, in 1778.

208 *Babiana villosa* (t. 583 1802 SE)

CROCUS BIFLORUS.
SCOTCH CROCUS.
Crocus biflorus subsp. biflorus.
PLATE 209

Why this is called the Scotch Crocus we are equally at a loss to account for, as for the adoption of the specific title. It is

209 *Crocus biflorus* (t. 845 1805 SE)

certainly no native of Scotland, but, as Mr. Salisbury informs us, most probably of Italian or Asiatic origin, but on what authority he believes so he does not tell us. This gentleman says he has a variety with quite white spathes, not tawny as in our plant, and with higher coloured flowers. Is one of the earliest blowers and perfectly hardy.

If our synonym from Parkinson be correct, it is a very old inhabitant of our gardens, and is certainly one of the most desirable of the genus.

˙Now known to occur in Italy from Verona southwards, in Sicily, North-west Turkey and on Rhodes, with related subspecies throughout Greece and Turkey.

CROCUS SEROTINUS.
MOUNTAIN CROCUS.
Crocus serotinus.
PLATE 210

Desc. *Bulb-tuber* larger and flatter in the cultivated than in the spontaneous plant, yet twice smaller than that of Saffron (*sativus*); *root-sheaths* somewhat tawny; *corolla* of a faint violet-purple; *stigmas* of a bright orange colour; blooms with us in

mild seasons from the end of October till December. Although known in our gardens for more than two centuries, is now but very rarely to be met with in them. Had been entirely overlooked by more modern Botanists, until lately described in the *Paradisus Londinensis*. Found by Clusius in Portugal, where it grows on rocks near the sea-coast; by Pallas and Georgi in the Crimea and more southern departments of the Russian empire, along with the "Cloth of Gold species" (*susianus*, No. 652), the "Scotch Crocus" (*biflorus*, No. 845) and *nudiflorus*. We have to thank Mr. Haworth for the specimen from which our drawing was taken; we saw others in the nursery of Messrs. Gibbs and Co. at Old Brompton.

210 *Crocus serotinus* (t. 1267 1810 SE)

CROCUS SIEHEANUS.
Crocus sieheanus.
PLATE 211

The known history of C. *sieheanus* is soon told. Corms were sent to Messrs. Barr and Sons by Siehe as "a species from the same locality as C. *tauri*," that is from the Taurus Mountains in south-eastern Asia Minor. That was in 1927, and in the spring of 1929 Mr. E. A. Bowles reported to Mr. Barr that the crocus did not belong to any

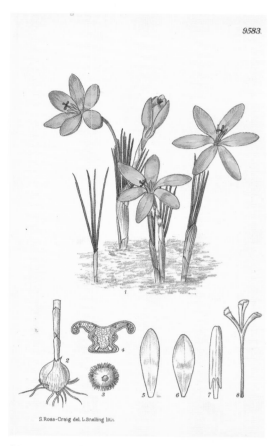

211 *Crocus sieheanus* (t. 9583 1939 S R-C & LS)

nurseries twenty-five had black barbs while twenty-eight were without them.

Whatever its true taxonomic status may prove to be, *C. sieheanus* is a most attractive garden plant. It comes into bloom in the cold house in late January and early February, and its clear orange-yellow flowers are delightfully fragrant. The plants from which our figure was taken flowered in the Alpine House at Kew in February, 1937.

Distribution. – Taurus Mountains, Asia Minor.

CROCUS VERSICOLOR.
PARTY-COLOURED CROCUS.
Crocus versicolor.
PLATE 212

Differs from *maesiacus* in having the filaments devoid of all pubescence, the anthers not so remarkably divaricate nor the filaments so closely pressed to each other, the stigmas longer, not flattened nor crested and fringed; from *vernus* again in having a bivalved spathe and the mouth of the tube of the corolla without any glandu-

212 *Crocus versicolor* (t. 1110 1808 SE)

lar pubescence; as well as in several other characteristics. It is the most fragrant species known to us, having a scent resembling that of the Violet. We suspect it to be a native of the south of France. The bulb-tuber is large and covered with dark brown scariose membranes streaked with close straight parallel nerves. In this genus two fertile bulbs are generally evolved from the summit of the mother-bulb; but these are sometimes grown into one; when the number of leaves and flower-stalks are doubled, although that of the root-sheaths remains the same.

GALAXIA GRAMINEA.
NARROW-LEAVED GALAXIA.
Galaxia fugacissima.
PLATE 213

For the drawing of the present plant, as well as of *Melanthium monopetalum* and *Aponogeton distachyon*, we are obliged to the kindness of Sir Joseph Banks, for whose library the original drawings were made. It is a native of the Cape of Good Hope. Has several times flowered at Messrs. Lee and Kennedy's, but as we never had an oppor-

213 *Galaxia graminea* (t. 1292 1810 SE)

species known to him, and on his advice they named it *C. sieheanus*. This name, however, has not hitherto been formally published.

Mr. Bowles has suggested to me that *C. sieheanus* may be a hybrid, the corm-tunics being such as might result from a cross between a "reticulate" and an "annulate" species. The most probable parent from the section with reticulate corms is undoubtedly *C. ancyrensis*, whose range extends as far east as Marash, though I have not actually seen any specimens from the Taurus mountains. Among the members of the section *Annulati*, *C. sieheanus* most closely resembles *C. chrysanthus* (Herb.) Herb. The form of this species found in the Taurus is usually referred to *C. danfordiae* Maw, which is distinguished by its small pale yellow flowers. There is a specimen in the Kew Herbarium, however, which has deep orange-yellow flowers, and the gap between *C. chrysanthus* and *C. danfordiae* is further bridged by colour forms collected round Ankara by Balls and others.

Some relationship between *C. sieheanus* and *C. chrysanthus* may be indicated by the occurrence in both species of black-barbed anthers. This is a well-known feature of *C. chrysanthus*, though by no means constant, and Mr. P. R. Barr tells us that in flowers of *C. sieheanus* examined at his firm's

tunity of seeing it while in bloom, we shall not attempt any further description than is given in the specific character. Is said to vary with a yellow tube and violet-coloured limb. Grows on hills between Cape Town and the Table Mountain.

214 *Galaxia ovata γ purpurea* (t. 1516 1812 SE)

GALAXIA OVATA (γ.) PURPUREA.
PURPLE-FLOWERED GALAXIA.

Galaxia ovata.

PLATE 214

The drawing of the present variety was made from a plant imported from the Cape of Good Hope, by Mr. Griffin, in whose conservatory at South Lambeth it flowered last summer.

GEISSORHIZA OBTUSATA.
YELLOW-FLOWERED GEISSORHIZA.

Geissorhiza imbricata.

PLATE 215

Our plant has a *prima facie* resemblance to *Sparaxis bulbifera, supra*; but if critically examined, will be found to differ in almost every particular.

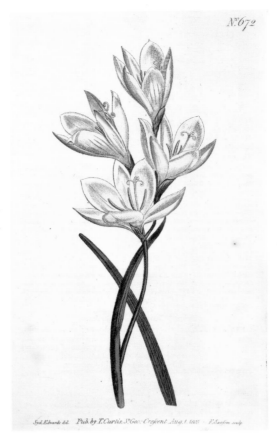

215 *Geissorhiza obtusata* (t. 672 1803 SE)

This very rare species was received from the Cape by Mr. Hibbert, in whose conservatory it flowered in May, most probably for the first time in Europe; indeed all the species of this genus are rare with us, *secunda, supra*, being the most common in our collections; they may all be easily known on their first arrival from the Cape, by the singularity of their bulbs, from amongst those of the rest of their order.

Our generic name is composed of γεισσειν, in *subgrandae modum conformare*, and ζιζα, *radix*; from the appearance of the bulb as above described. Requires the same treatment as *Ixia*.

GEISSORHIZA SETACEA.
NARROWEST-LEAVED TILE-ROOT.

Geissorhiza setacea.

PLATE 216

Upon comparing live specimens of *rochensis* and *obtusata* with the present plant and with each other, we can see no reason for retaining them as distinct species. But others may think differently; by them, the varieties here given, may be preserved as species, with the names by which we have

already distinguished them in the present work. *Leaves* from bristle-form threads to blades half an inch in breadth; *stem* from one to eight or ten inches high. In *secunda* the *rachis* is clothed with a short dense nap; here the whole stem is naked. Bloom scentless. Native of the Cape of Good Hope, from whence our present specimens were imported by Messrs. Lee and Kennedy of Hammersmith.

216 *Geissorhiza setacea* (t. 1255 1810 SE)

GLADIOLUS ANGUSTUS.
NARROW-LEAVED CORNFLAG.

Gladiolus angustus.

PLATE 217

Leaves narrow, upright, shorter than stem, with a single prominent midrib. *Stem* flexuose, reclined upwards from a foot to two feet high. *Flowers* three to five, about four inches long, straight, narrow, funnel-formed, one-ranked, scentless. Upper segments broader, middle one broadest, lower ones rather narrower; all flat and somewhat patent. Cultivated by Miller in 1757. A native of the Cape, and seems to have been one of the first denizens of Europe in this family. Has been confounded with the *Gladiolus augustus* of Thunberg. Is closely

217 Gladiolus angustus (t. 602 1802 SE)

allied to a species that we have never yet met with in any collection, though cultivated by Miller, viz. the *Gladiolus involutus* of De La Roche – probably no longer existing in this country.

The specimen from which our drawing was taken flowered in unusual perfection at Messrs. Grimwood and Wykes, Kensington, in the month of June. Propagates with the greatest facility both by seed and offsets, and is one of the commonest, though seldom seen to flower so perfectly as the present specimen, except from recently imported bulbs.

GLADIOLUS BYZANTINUS.

TURKISH CORNFLAG.

Gladiolus byzantinus.

PLATE 219

This and *Gladiolus segetum* have usually been accounted varieties of *Gladiolus communis* but, as appears to us, more from remissness in the observers, than from want of distinctive marks; this a comparison of their specific characters will show,

for which purpose we have subjoined a reformed one of *communis*.

The present species has by far the largest and most ornamental corollas of the three; is a somewhat earlier blower than *communis*, somewhat shorter, but more robust, and never seeds in our gardens, which both the others do freely. Blooms in June. By the above synonyms seems to have been imported from the neighbourhood of Constantinople. Is perfectly hardy and grows any where, except in the shade; but does not propagate so rapidly as the other two.

GLADIOLUS CARNEUS.

FLESH-COLOURED CORNFLAG.

Gladiolus carneus.

PLATE 218

Leaves ensiform, nerved, sheathing at the base, shorter than the stem, edged with a slender white filiform cartilage. *Stem* one to two feet high. *Flowers* three to five, narrow funnel-form below the segments. Upper segment broadest, lanceolate, concave, acuminate, convolute above, where it is also recurved and sometimes slightly undulate; the three lowest narrower, nearly linear, lowest straighter, narrowest. Differs from *Gladiolus cuspidatus* besides in colour and in being less waved, in having its spathes more inflated and not so convolute, spike more decidedly distich, flowers not so upright, tube shorter, more curved, less filiform; segments proportionally longer, being nearly the length of the tube, leaves more conspicuously margined.

Native of the Cape. Flowers in May and June, earlier than *Gladiolus cuspidatus*. Scentless; blows freely, and is easily propagated either by seed or offsets. The spikes being too large for our page, one rank of its flowers was necessarily omitted, leaving the spathes to show the distich character of the inflorescence.

GLADIOLUS COMMUNIS (β.) CARNEUS.

FLESH-COLOURED COMMON CORNFLAG.

Gladiolus communis.

PLATE 221

Stem from one to near three feet high; flowers six to twenty. Hardy and of easy

culture. *Communis* differs from *byzantinus*, in having the flowers so inclined as to form a single flexuose rank, the spathes bent forward beyond the rachis and mutually inclining towards each other; while in that the spike is arranged in two distant rows with diverging spathes that are parallel with the rachis; in *communis* the two lateral upper segments of the corolla are obtuse and mucronate, and the two lower lateral ones shorter and narrower than their middle one, which is not the case in *byzantinus*. *Segetum* differs from both, besides in the distinction of the seed, in having the upper side-segments of the corolla much shorter than any of the rest, the upper middle one wholly elevated over these and twice the broadest of any, and the three lower ones equal to each other in length and nearly so in breadth. Mr. Schulte has separated this plant from his *communis*, (the *segetum* of this work,) under the name of *neglectus*; he says, that both are found in the neighbourhood of Cracow, and that this flowers nearly a month later than the other. Our drawing was made at the Nursery of Messrs. Gibbs, Brompton.

GLADIOLUS CRUENTUS.

BLOOD-RED GLADIOLUS.

Gladiolus cruentus.

PLATE 220

This very beautiful plant, a native of the Colony of Natal, in South Africa, was flowered by Mr. Bull, at his nurseries in Chelsea, in September, 1868. It is specifically allied to G. *cardinalis*, which is indigenous in the same district of South Africa, but differs in the much larger flower, colour, and notched perianth segments. The original plants that have hitherto flowered are, we are given to understand, made over to be hybridized, so that in all probability the pure race will soon be lost to cultivators.

Considerably upwards of one hundred species of gladiolus have been cultivated in Europe; indeed upwards of one hundred and ten reputed species have been figured from living specimens: the greater proportion of these are no doubt lost to cultivation, and probably no horticultural establishment boasts more than a fraction of them: the genus belongs to that immense class of South African and other plants

218 *Gladiolus carnœus* (t. 591 1802 SE)

219 *Gladiolus byzantinus* (t. 874 1805 SE)

which were the favourites of our fore-fathers, were suited to the atmosphere of their plant-houses heated by currents of dry air, and the cultivation of which is not understood by the generality of gardeners of the present day. It is greatly to be desired now that such amateurs as are disposed to leave the beaten track of ordinary green-house and stove culture, should take up the culture of these and similar tribes, which would well repay all their care, and advance our knowledge of some of the most interesting and beautiful of our Colonial floras.

NB. The reproduction of this illustration has been enlarged for the original is 252mm by 158mm.

GLADIOLUS CUSPIDATUS.
TALL CORNFLAG.
Gladiolus undulatus.

PLATE 222

Leaves ensiform, generally shorter than the stem, and narrow in proportion to their height. *Stem* two to three feet high, erect, round. *Tube* filiform, straight, nearly twice the length of the spathe, above which it is gradually enlarged into a faux; segments lanceolate, far-attenuate, much shorter than tube, and generally waved, upper ones broadest, uppermost nearly straight, recurved at the end. *Flowers* vary much in colour and in the form of the mark on the lower segments, which is sometimes obsolete as well as the undulation.

Linnæus, in his *Mantissa*, fixes upon this species as the link that unites *Gladiolus* and *Ixia*, which he would hardly have done had he seen the numerous species that have

been since discovered, many of which seem to approach much nearer to *Ixia*. This magnificent species is a native of the Cape, flowers in May and June. Our drawing was taken from the collection of Messrs. Grimwood and Wykes, at Kensington. Its time of introduction uncertain; but since the publication of *Hortus Kewensis*.

GLADIOLUS HIRSUTUS (VAR. β.)
ROSE-COLOURED HAIRY CORNFLAG.
Gladiolus caryophyllaceus.

PLATE 223

We have seen many other intermediate varieties, but have, as usual, only enumer-

OPPOSITE:
220 *Gladiolus cruentus* (t. 5810 1869 WF)

5810.

W. Fitch, del. et lith.

Vincent Brooks, Day & Son, Imp.

221 *Gladiolus communis* β *carneus* (t. 1575 1813 SE)

222 *Gladiolus cuspidatus* (t. 582 1802 SE)

ated the most striking, and as such many will probably reckon distinct species. *Watsonia humilis*, a standing synonym to this, is a real Watsonia, and a very distinct plant with smooth leaves. The present variety flowers in May, and smells very like the flowers of Hawthorn or May. It scarcely ever blows two years together of the same size or colour, varying from a deep purplish rose colour to a pale pink nearly white. Much of its beauty depends upon skilful cultivation. Mr. Williams, Nurseryman, at Turnham-Green, has an exceeding large variety without the purple edge to the leaves. Is at all times very impatient of moisture. Was most probably introduced among our Nurserymen by the way of Holland; we have seen many specimens of it among the late Cape arrivals. Our figure was taken at Messrs. Grimwood and Wyke's, Kensington, where it flowered in great perfection.

IRIS CHINENSIS.

CHINESE IRIS.

Iris japonica.

PLATE 224

The public are indebted to Mr. Evans of the India House, for the introduction of this plant from China, where it is a native.

It flowered last year, at different periods, for the first time, in many collections near London; this irregularity of its blowing was occasioned, we presume by its being kept in different degrees of heat, in the stoves of some, and the greenhouses of others; there is no doubt but it will bear the cold of our ordinary winters, and thrive better in the open ground, in a moist situation, than in the stove, or greenhouse, in either of which, however, it will flower very well; and, where the plant is luxuriant, continue to do so for a considerable length of time,

the blossoms being numerous, and unfolding gradually: in a strong plant at Mr. Colvill's Nursery we counted seven blossoms expanded at one time on its different branches.

It differs from all other known iris's, in having a root perfectly of the creeping kind, sending out shoots to a considerable distance, by which it is rendered very easy of propagation; its flowers, in form and colour, come nearest to those of *Iris cristata*, and have a considerable degree of fragrance.

223 Gladiolus hirsutus var. β (t. 574 1802 SE)

224 Iris chinensis (t. 373 1797)

IRIS CRISTATA.
CRESTED IRIS.
Iris cristata.

PLATE 225

It appears from the *Hortus Kewensis* where this plant is first and minutely described, that it is a native of North America, and was introduced by Peter Collinson, Esq. in 1756.

Authors have described this plant as having a creeping root, but perhaps not with strict propriety; to us it appears to increase much in the same way as most others of the genus, with this difference, that when it grows luxuriantly it throws out longer shoots; as these are always above ground and throw out fibres from their under side, they are to be regarded as stalks rather than roots; in the *Iris chinensis* it is very different, there the root is truly creeping.

If the *Iris cristata* be planted in bog-earth, in a moist situation (for it will not succeed at all in a dry one) and has the shelter of a hand-glass in severe weather, it will grow readily in the open border. It blossoms about the middle of May.

The tube of the flower in this species is unusually long, tender, and brittle in the extreme; the flowers are delicate, with little or no scent. It is increased by dividing its roots.

225 Iris cristata (t. 412 1798)

IRIS FLORENTINA.
FLORENTINE FLAG.
Iris germanica 'Florentina'.

PLATE 226

A native of Italy and other parts of the south of Europe; grows plentifully on the walls of Florence; cultivated here by Gerard in 1596. Desfontaines found it in Algiers, where it is sown with *germanica* about graves; he doubts if they are specifically distinct.

The dried root of this plant was formerly used in medicine, but is now confined to some insignificant lozenges as an expectorant, and to the manufactory of the perfumer, to whom it is known by the name of Orris or Orrice-root, being used to give to certain articles, such as hair-powder, the scent of violets; that which is used for these purposes however is imported from Leghorn, as what is produced in our climate has neither the flavour nor other qualities of the Italian root. Ray says the pigment called *Verdelis* or *Iris-green* is made from the flowers of this species, while Haller and others say from those of *Iris germanica*.

It is perfectly hardy; is propagated by parting its roots in autumn; not quite so common in our gardens as *Iris germanica*, from which it differs in the colour of its flowers and leaves, in the scent of its dried root, in having its spathes more sphacelate or membranous, and the tube of its corolla not so much longer than its germ as in that. Skynner has derived Orrice from Iris.

IRIS GERMANICA.
GERMAN FLAG.
Iris germanica.

PLATE 227

Native of Germany, Switzerland, Dauphiny, and Italy, growing in uncultivated spots and on old walls; *Iris germanica* β. is found near Halle, the stem of this is scarcely the length of one's finger and about the length of the leaves, yet sufficiently distinct from *Iris pumila*. Desfontaines found the species in Algiers.

The commonest *Iris* in our gardens, where it flowers in May and June, is perfectly hardy, and to be propagated by dividing its roots in autumn; seldom seeds.

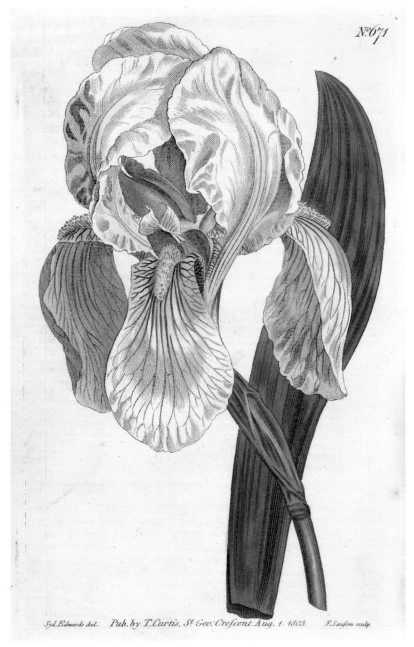

226 *Iris florentina* (t. 671 1803 SE)

227 *Iris germanica* (t. 670 1803 SE)

Cultivated here by Gerard in 1596. Clusius observes that in his time it was much less frequently met with in the gardens of Austria and Hungary than *Iris sambucina*, and that he procured a supply of seeds for them from the Low Countries.

A pigment, chiefly used by miniature painters, called *Verdelis, Vert d'iris* or *Iris-green*, is made from its flowers, which are macerated and left to putrify, when chalk or alum is added.

The root first tasted is slightly bitter, presently producing a most insufferable heat in the throat, as do the flowers in a lesser degree.

IRIS GRAMINEA.
GRASS-LEAVED FLAG.

Iris graminea.

PLATE 228

Herb very closely cespitose. *Leaves* ensiform-linear, narrow, grass-like, nerved-streaked, deep green. *Stem* shorter than these, from about nine inches to a foot high, ancipital, simple, with one flower-fascicle. Involucre herbaceous, valves acuminate, sometimes foliaceously elongated and equal to the leaves; a single membranous valve separates the flowers; *pedicels* longer than the germ, which is two to three times shorter than the flower, ventricosely oval and winged-hexagonal; *tube* very short, green, suburceolate; exterior ungues suborotately patent, oblong-oval, convolute-concave, broader than the

stigmas, three times longer and even somewhat broader than the laminæ, which are ovate and subconvolute; inner segments about equal to the stigmas, straight and somewhat upright, ungues linearly conduplicate, laminæ oblong, subconvolute, twice longer than these; stigmas arched-patent, oblong, narrow downwards, keeled, with their sides but slightly turned back, equal to the outer ungues, exterior lip bifid, segments mucronate, deflected; filaments brown, flat-subulate, nearly twice the length of the anthers. Style even shorter than tube.

The flowers expand in June and have a scent something like that of fresh plums. A native of Austria, perfectly hardy, and will grow in any situation.

Our drawing was taken at the Nursery of Messrs. Whitley and Co. Brompton, Cultivated here by Gerard, in 1597.

228 *Iris graminea* (t. 681 1803 SE)

229 *Iris halophila* (t. 875 1805 SE)

IRIS HALOPHILA.
LONG-LEAVED FLAG.

Iris spuria subsp. *halophila*.

PLATE 229

We confess that we are unable at present to detect any other distinctions between this and *Iris spuria* (see below) than that this is altogether a much larger plant and possesses considerably more rigidity both in the leaves and stem than that; to which may be added a far greater elongation of the outer valve of the spathe; yet there is a difference in their general appearance, though not easily expressed, that makes it difficult for us to consider them as mere varieties of each other; besides that their habitats are widely distant, this being a native of the salt marshy spots of Siberia, the other of the moist meadows in Germany.

Our species is among the tallest of the genus, the stem being three feet or more high and the leaves sometimes four; these yield the same offensive smell, when bruised, as those of *spuria*; they are very smooth, even, striated, and linear.

None of its characters have as yet varied by culture, though introduced into our gardens as far back as 1780, by Dr. Peter Pallas. Is not very common in our collections, though of as easy culture and as hardy as any of the genus. Approaches *ventricosa*, but that is shorter with a leafless stem and a more inflated spathe.

IRIS LURIDA.
DINGY FLAG.

Iris × *lurida*.

PLATE 230

Flowers early in May: its bloom is sweetish, and not entirely scentless, as described in *Hortus Kewensis* where it is suspected to be a variety of *Iris sambucina*; native of the southern part of Europe; cultivated by Miller in 1758.

Our specimen had rather a large flower, and its laminæ were rather more undulate than usual. The drawing was taken at the Nursery of Messrs. Grimwood and Wykes, Kensington.

230 *Iris lurida* (t. 669 1802 SE)

IRIS PRISMATICA.
NEW JERSEY IRIS.

Iris prismatica.

PLATE 231

Leaves, in the specimens we saw, from six to eight inches high, and little more than two lines in breadth; *scape* dotted over with purple. We are inclined to believe it to be a mere variety of *virginica*, a species which we sometimes find varying with peduncles to the full as long as in the present plant; and sometimes with a stem many times shorter than the leaves, and quite simple. We have however followed Mr. Pursch (by whom it was discovered and lately introduced) in considering it as specifically distinct. Found in North America, growing in deep swamps in New Jersey, near Egg-Harbour.

Our drawing was made from a specimen which bloomed in July last, at Messrs. Lee and Kennedy's, Hammersmith, at the same time with two varieties of *virginica*; which are also said to be natives of the boggy parts of North America.

231 Iris prismatica (t. 1504 1812 SE)

232 Iris pumila var. violacea (t. 1261 1810 SE)

233 Iris ruthenica β (t. 1393 1811 SE)

scription gives no clue beyond the above synonym. We should observe, that the length of the leaves and stem, in relation to each, is in this genus of no avail in specific distinction. The present is the handsomest of all the varieties of *pumila*, as well as one of the rarest. We have usually found it preserved in a frame; perhaps it is tenderer than the others.

IRIS PUMILA, *VAR.* VIOLACEA.
VIOLET-BLUE DWARF FLAG.
Iris pumila.

PLATE 232

Among the gardeners, the present plant has pretty generally passed for the Linnean *biflora*; and, if we are to take the species from the specimen deposited by Linnæus in Clifford's Herbarium, and made to refer to the species in his *Hortus Cliffortianus* corresponding with the *biflora* of his *Species Plantarum*, the gardeners may be right; for that is certainly *pumila*. But if we found the species on the plant cited by Linnæus from Besler's *Hortus Eystettensis* as a synonym, and assume that he has erroneously judged the above specimen to be the same with the plant represented in that work; then *biflora* certainly is a very distinct species from *pumila*, and most probably a dwarf specimen of the *subbiflora*. From a specimen out of the Kew Gardens preserved in the Banksian Herbarium, we have little doubt but that the *biflora* of *Hortus Kewensis* is likewise the same species with our *subbiflora*. We have never seen the specimen in Linnæus's Herbarium, and his de-

IRIS RUTHENICA. (β.)
PIGMY IRIS.
Iris ruthenica.

PLATE 233

The publication of the present plant, was unintentional. We had long wished to procure a drawing of *Iris verna* for the present work; when Mr. Whitley, of Brompton, kindly informed us that he had numerous specimens of it in bloom, which he said had been raised from American seed; and the present plate was ready for publication, before we had convinced ourselves that the plant represented could not be the one we were in search of, although generally but erroneously passing

for it. *Verna* was first instituted a species by Gronovius in his *Flora Virginica*.

Ruthenica thrives well in the open border, where it flowers in April and May; the corolla has the scent as well as colour of the violet.

IRIS SPURIA (ζ.) STENOGYNA.
CREAM-COLOURED BASTARD-IRIS.
Iris spuria subsp. *halophila.*

PLATE 234

In a preceding article we have reduced to one as many plants as have afforded to others five distinct species; leaving to each its former specific name, as a mark of its variety, along with the immediate synonymy; for the use of those who differ from us, and are competent to find specific distinctions for each. They are all met with in various parts of the continent, from Denmark to Siberia, from the South of France to Mount Caucasus; near which mountain both the blue and yellow ones were discovered by Mr. Marschal of Bieberstein, who says they differ from each other in nothing but colour. They are likewise natives of the

234 *Iris spuria ζ stenogyna* (t. 1515 1812 SE)

some minds not apt to be caught by gaudy attire, these sombre tints have their charms. In this respect it strongly contrasts with *Bot Mag* t. 532.

It is a native of the Levant, and with respect to the cold of our climate is perfectly hardy, flowers best, according to Miller, in an eastern aspect, and if the soil be light it will be proper to put some rubbish at the bottom to prevent the roots descending too deep, in which case they seldom produce flowers.

It blossoms in April or May, rarely produces seed with us, but is easily propagated by offsets from the roots, which may be taken up when the leaves decay, but should not be kept long out of the ground.

235 *Iris tuberosa* (t. 531 1801 SE)

find so commonly given to it by the elder Botanists and even by the modern Florists, was acquired from the plant's having been first introduced into the Low Countries from England, most probably without any notice of its true habitat, and hence presumed a native of our country by those that received them: Clusius says, that on his first arrival here in 1571, he sought for it wild, until he was informed by Lobel of its being only cultivated in certain gardens near Bristol, where it had been most probably imported by some vessel from Spain or Portugal. Gerard includes it among the British plants, in which he has been followed by Dr. Withering in his *Botanical Arrangements*; but Parkinson was aware of its real habitat.

Flowers in June. Hardy and of easy culture, seeding freely. The best bulbs are imported yearly by the seedmen from Holland, and should be put in the ground early in the autumn.

236 *Iris xiphioides* (t. 687 1803 SE)

coast of Barbary. All are said to affect either maritime situations, or such inland ones as are moist and have the soil impregnated with salt. Mr. Donn speaks of the present variety as a native of Germany; but we do not know on what authority. Mons. Redouté is incorrect in attributing to the corolla of this variety a tube any ways longer than in that of the others. By speaking of the *enlarged part* of this portion of the flower, we see that he has taken the neck of the germen for a part of the tube. Our drawing was made from a specimen sent us by Mr. Donn from Cambridge, where it blooms in the Botanic Garden about July. The flower is scentless.

IRIS TUBEROSA.

SNAKE'S-HEAD IRIS OR

VELVET FLOWER-DE-LUCE.

Hermodactylus tuberosus.

PLATE 235

This species of *Iris*, readily distinguished from every other by its quadrangular leaves, is more remarkable for the singularity than for the beauty of its flowers; yet, to

IRIS XIPHIOIDES.

PYRENEAN FLAG.

Iris latifolia.

PLATE 236

A native of the Pyrenees. We are uncertain if Desfontaines means precisely this species or *xiphium*, or some other that has been usually deemed a variety.

The name of "English Iris," which we

IXIA ARISTATA.
SALVER-FLOWERED IXIA.

Ixia longituba

PLATE 237

Nearly allied to *Ixia patens* and *flexuosa*, but a far more robust plant; segments quite flat, rotate, and blunter; spathe more dentate, less membranous, and the parts of fructification more erect and collected. Scentless. Flowers in May.

The specific name was undoubtedly suggested to Thunberg by the spathes, which however he describes as "*aristato-dentatae*;" and we guess that the inappropriate application of the word "*aristata*" was in some measure the cause of the mistake in *Hortus Kewensis* where *Sparaxis grandiflora* (*Ixia grandiflora*, Bot. Mag. t. 541, and *Ixia bulbifera, var. purpurea*, Thunb.) is taken for the present species. When a weakly plant, it bears a strong *prima facie* resemblance to *Ixia capillaris, var.* γ. but differs in the spathe and tube.

In the Banksian Herbarium we find a Cape specimen of this plant, marked *Ixia patens*, placed as a synonym by the side of the one from Kew Gardens, from which the description of that species was taken by Dr. Solander. In fact, the several in-

termediate varieties we have seen, lead us to suspect, that *Ixia patens, flexuosa,* and *aristata*, can scarcely be retained as distinct species.

Found by Thunberg, at the Cape, growing in moist sandy places. Is very impatient of drought, and should be set in a pan of water when near flowering. Varies with white, pale pink, and purple-rose-coloured flowers.

The *Ixia leucantha* of Jacquin is a variety of *Ixia patens*, agreeing with that in proportion of the limb to the tube, but approaching this in size and robustness of growth.

237 Ixia aristata (t. 589 1802 SE)

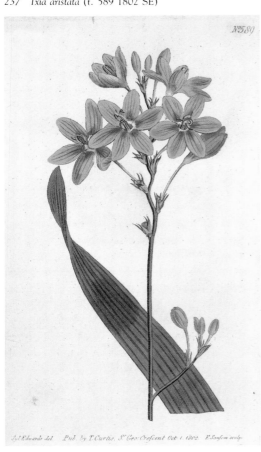

IXIA GRANDIFLORA.
VELVET-FLOWERED IXIA.

Sparaxis grandiflora.

PLATE 238

Descr. *Bulb* ovate, about the size of a hazel nut, covered with a white silky fibrous tunic, base umbilicated. *Leaves* from five to eight, ensiform, shorter than the scape, distich, outer ones gradually shorter. *Scape* from six inches to a foot long, thickish, stiff, and nearly of equal thickness. *Rachis* very flexuose. *Spathe* membranous, light

238 Ixia grandiflora (t. 541 1801 SE)

brown with dark edges, more or less torn into irregular awn-like jags, according to the time it has been in flower (for, if not at first, it is sure to be so sooner or later). *Flowers* from one to five, never more, large, showy. *Tube* short, nearly the length of the spathe. *Segments* several times longer than the tube, sometimes ending with a small point more or less obsolete. *Branches*, when any, one or two flowered. *Parts of Fructification* lateral (i.e. inclined to one side without being ascendent). *Stamens* diverging, whitish. *Stigmas* large, exceeding the anthers, recurved, complicate, ciliate. *Stem-Bulbs* one or two, slender, oblong, from the axils of the inner root-leaves.

It is propagated easily by seeds and bulbs. Flowers in May. Was introduced into the Kew Garden in 1758.

IXIA ROCHENSIS (α.)
PLAID IXIA.

Ixia paniculata var *rochensis.*

PLATE 239

Our drawing of this very rare and beautiful little plant was taken from a specimen kindly communicated by R. Salisbury, Esq.

239 Ixia rochensis α (t. 598 1802 SE)

by whom the bulbs were received from the Cape.

We have given a trivial name in remembrance of Dr. Daniel de la Roche, author of a small tract, entitled, "*Specimen inaugurale sistens descriptiones plantarum aliquot novarum, Lugd. Bat. 1766*," confined to this natural order, of which he has described many Cape species with great minuteness, chiefly from the Herbariums of the Dutch, and has added five good plates of such as he saw flower in the gardens of Holland.

Lapeyrousia fissifolia.
Leafy-spiked Lapeyrousia.
Lapeyrousia pyramidalis.
PLATE 240

Our figure does not show the outer campanulate shell of the Bulb-tuber; it had been taken off previous to planting. *Stem* four to six inches high; lower *leaves* one to three inches long, upper ones shorter, enveloping the spathes, splitting open and diverging from the inner to near the outer edge they lose their ensiform appearance; *spathe* very short, sphacelate, about the

length of the *germen*; *corolla* varying from pale purple to white, about an inch and half long, fragrant, brittle. Both varieties were introduced this year from the Cape of Good Hope, by Messrs. Lee and Kennedy of Hammersmith, in whose greenhouse they flowered in September.

241   *Moraea angusta* (t. 1276 1810)

Moræa angusta.
Rolled-leaved Moræa.
Moræa angusta.
PLATE 241

Nearly allied to *tripetala*, *Bulb-tuber* ovate; outer *integuments* reticulate, dark brown, fibres thick and woody; cauline *leaflet* spathaceous about an inch long, usually sterile; *spathe* about two inches long, outer valves sphacelate and reddish at their point; *corolla* near two inches long, yellow, purple veined on the outside. As we had no opportunity of inspecting the living plant, we are uncertain whether the stamens have united or separate filaments, or if the outer ungues have the small melliferous cavity at their base, so usual in this genus; Thunberg calls the flower *imberbis*, but he has more than once overlooked this character, which is far less conspicuous here than in *Iris*, and is sometimes not to be ascertained

without the aid of a glass. Native of the Cape of Good Hope, where it was found by Thunberg on hills below the Duyvelsberg and Lewekop. We have to thank Sir Joseph Banks for his very liberal permission to copy the original drawings of this plant, as well as of *Aristea melaleuca*, *Moræa spicata* and the curled-leaved variety of *crispa*, which two last will appear in the next fasciculus.

Moræa sisyrinchium.
European Moræa or Spanish Nut.
Gynandriris sisyrinchium.
PLATE 242

Descr. *Bulb tuber* about the size of a small chestnut, with coarse brown reticulated cartilagineo-fibrous integuments; *leaves* six to nine inches long, narrow; flowers about an inch and half long, three to five opening in succession; *seeds* numerous, small, of a reddish brown colour: varies with blue, purple, white, and with yellow corollas. In the later botanical works the corolla of this species is described, and even exhibited in dissections annexed to the figures of it, as

240   *Lapeyrousia fissifolia* (t. 1246 1809 SE)

242   *Morea sisyrinchium* (t. 1401 1811 SE)

furnished with a long tube; but a careful inspection shows, that what has been mistaken for the tube of the *corolla* is in reality the upper sterile part of the *germen*, in which the *septa* are perceptible although the *ovula* are obliterated or nearly so; and when the corolla decays, it is seen to part from the summit of its supposed tube, leaving the same cicatrix that is usually perceptible on the ends of the germens of this genus when the corolla has fallen from them. Notwithstanding the plant has been known from the days of Gerard (1597) in our gardens, we had never met with it until this summer at Mr. Vere's, where it had been received from Gibraltar.

The interior of the Bulb-tuber is said to be eaten by the children in Spain and Portugal, by way of nuts; whence the appellation given it by Parkinson and Gerard of "Spanish Nut." Native of Spain, Portugal, Sicily, the Grecian Islands, and the Coast of Barbary. Blooms in May. Should be sheltered in the greenhouse or garden-frame from severe frost.

243   *Morea spicata* (t. 1283 1810 SE)

MORÆA SPICATA.
FLEXUOSE MORÆA.
Homeria elegans.

244   *Patersonia sericea* (t. 1041 1807 SE)

PLATE 243

Differs from *collina* in having a several-jointed flexuose stem, with a one-valved?, one-flowered? spathe situated at each joint, forming a kind of remotely-flowered spike; in *collina* the inflorescence is disposed in a several-valved several-flowered terminal spathe, the valves being arranged one within the other on a short receptacle, in a convolutely equitant fascicle; in *spicata* the receptacle is drawn out into a several-jointed rachis with a single flowered? spathe at each joint; the upper spathe is besides lengthened into a point that reaches beyond the flower; which is not the case in *collina*. As we did not examine the living plant of *spicata*, we cannot say in what other respects they may differ. Nearly allied to *virgata* and *elegans*. Found at the Cape of Good Hope by Mr. Masson.

PATERSONIA SERICEA.
SILKY PATERSONIA.
Patersonia sericea.

PLATE 244

Our specimen was furnished us by Messrs. Lee and Kennedy, of Hammersmith, who received the seeds, from which they raised it, from Port Jackson; we believe it to be the first species of this order from that country that has bloomed in any European garden. Requires the shelter of a greenhouse, and appears to be of easy culture. Without scent.

This genus has the closest affinity with *Aristea, Witsenia, Tapeninia,* and *Diplarrena*, between the two first of which we should place it. Notwithstanding some apparently material discrepancies, upon the face of Labillardiere's description and figure, between *Patersonia* and *Genosiris* (which discrepancies, by the bye, we think are in some measure increased by the defectiveness of that description and figure) we have no doubt that the latter must one day merge in the one we are now treating of.

SISYRINCHIUM GRAMINEUM.
GRASS-LEAVED SISYRINCHIUM.
Sisyrinchium angustifolium.

PLATE 245

In a former Number of the *Botanical Magazine*, we gave a figure of the large variety of *Sisyrinchium bermudiana.* of *Linn.* regarding it as a distinct species, and naming it *iridioides*, conformably to Dillenius's specific description; we regret now that we did not continue to it the name of *bermudiana* (it being the true Bermudas plant) and which cannot with propriety be applied to the present species, a native of Virginia, far more diminutive, with flowers much smaller, of a paler blue colour, a much hardier plant also, and of more ready growth; it is indeed a truly hardy perennial, adapted to the open border, in which it will grow readily, and produces abundance of flowering stems in June and July; the flowers expand to the sun, and are followed by numerous seed-vessels which ripen their seeds, by which the plant may be increased, or by parting its rots in the autumn.

N.º464

S. Edwards del. *Pub. by W. Curtis St. Geo. Crescent, Dec. 1, 1799.* *F. Sansom sculp.*

245   *Sisyrinchium gramineum* (t. 464 1799 SE)

SISYRINCHIUM MACULATUM.
SPOTTED-FLOWERED SISYRINCHIUM.

Sisyrinchium graminifolium var. *maculatum*.

PLATE 246

Descr. *Stem*, in our plant, scarcely more than a foot high, remarkably compressed, green, bearing four to five linear-ensiform, acuminated, striated, equitant leaves, the lower ones the longest, and about a span in height, all of them full yellow-green, scarcely at all scabrous. From the upper and shorter leaf arises a panicle of several *flowers*, three or four of which proceed together from a common spathe, only one however, flowering at once. *Spathes* lanceolate, conduplicate, green, with a broad, white, membranaceous margin, within which are a few membranaceous bracts. *Pedicels* equal in length with the spatha, or scarcely exceeding it. *Perianth* of six obovate and somewhat cuneated, acute, spreading segments of a full deep yellow colour, pale at the claws, and with a deep blood-red spot just above the claw; the three alternate ones with a large horse-shoe-shaped spot or cloud of the same hue occupying the whole width. The back of the segments of the perianth is of a paler colour, and the spots and clouds less distinctly marked. *Stamens*

three, yellow. *Filaments* monadelphous. *Anthers* oblong, versatile. *Germen* inferior, broadly ovate, somewhat angled, glandular. *Style* shorter than the filaments of the stamens: *Stigmas* three, subulate, spreading.

A native of Chili, where, in the neighbourhood of Valparaiso, it was found by Alexander Cruickshanks, Esq. and by him introduced to the Glasgow Botanic Garden. It produced its bright and lively coloured flowers in May, 1832, being treated as other plants of the same genus, in the greenhouse. Its nearest affinity is with *S. graminifolium* (*Bot. Reg.* t. 1067); but it is, with us at least, a smaller and less vigorous plant, the leaves are scarcely at all scabrous, the flowers larger, of a deeper yellow, and marked with dark blood-coloured spots, the spathas smaller, sharper, and more membranaceous at the margins.

W. J. H. del. *Pub by E Curtis Glazenwood Essex Nov. 1 1832* *Swan Sc.*

246   *Sisyrinchium maculatum* (t. 3197 1832 WJH)

TRICHONEMA PUDICUM.
BLUSH TRICHONEMA.

Romulea pudica.

PLATE 247

Contrary to the more general habit of the genus, the entire stem in this species is protruded from the ground, while the plant

N.º1244.

Syd. Edwards Del. *Pub. by T. Curtis St. Geo. Crescent, Dec. 1, 1809.* *F. Sansom Jun. Sc.*

247   *Trichonema pudicum* (t. 1244 1809 SE)

is as yet only in a flowering state; in most others, the stem-like peduncles alone appear during that period; the real stem, as in *Crocus*, emerging gradually while the fruit ripens. *Leaves* three to four; *flowers* two to three, scentless; *stem* three to four inches high. Not recorded in any general system of vegetables; and most probably now first known in our European gardens. Brought from the Cape of Good Hope by Miss Symonds, sister to the late Lady Gwyllim, and given by her to Messrs. Whitley and Brame, in whose greenhouse at Brompton it flowered last August.

TRITONIA CAPENSIS (β.)
LESSER TRUMPET TRITONIA.

Tritonia flabellifolia.

PLATE 248

We met with this variety last summer (for the first time) in Mr. Griffin's conservatory at South Lambeth. That gentleman had received several of its bulbs in the spring from the Cape of Good Hope, some of which flowered with him in August and October. The *leaves* were from three to six inches high, outer ones gradually shorter;

248   *Tritonia capensis* β (t. 1531 1813 SE)

TRITONIA ROCHENSIS (α.)
BENDING-FLOWERED TRITONIA.

Ixia bellendenii.

PLATE 249

The nearly-allied species *longiflora, rochensis, capensis,* and *pallida,* are all natives of the Cape of Good Hope; have oblately rounded bulb-tubers, which sometimes produce others at the end of their roots; and all flower nearly at the same time. *Pallida* differs from *longiflora* and *rochensis,* in having a white corolla, a striate tube, an irregular limb, the upper middle segment being twice broader than the others, and anthers that are collaterally and not trifariously placed; from *capensis* in having the outer valve of the spathes equal to the inner, and blunt and tridentate, while in that this is much longer than the inner, and sharp-pointed and entire. The *Gladiolus longiflorus* of the *Supplementum* of the younger Linnæus seems rather to belong to *capensis* than either of the other three, the spathe being described as linear.

250   *Tritonia squalida* (t. 581 1802)

stem eight or nine inches long, bending (particularly before the bloom springs from the spathes), simple or one-branched; *flowers* rather more than two inches long, scentless. It is, we believe, sometimes one-flowered.

249   *Tritonia rochensis* α (t. 1503 1812 SE)

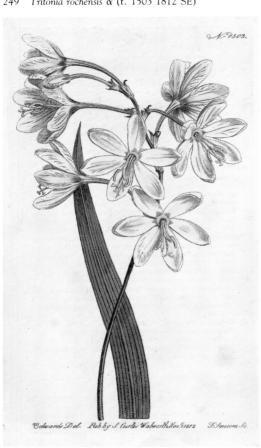

TRITONIA SQUALIDA.
SWEET-SCENTED TRITONIA.

Tritonia squalida.

PLATE 250

The present species, although too closely allied to *Tritonia* (*Ixia*) *crocata,* differs in having outer leaves rather more blunt and falcate, corolla smaller and less patent, veins more prominent, laminas narrower, more rounded, often retuse and incurved, claws less hyaline; besides in smelling very sweet, whereas *crocata* is perfectly scentless. In the *Hortus Kewensis* the *Tritonia* (*Gladiolus*) *lineata,* is made a variety of this; but upon what foundation we know not, as besides the numerous differences above ground the habits of the bulbs are very distinct. Name derived from *Triton,* in the signification of a vane or weathercock, in allusion to the variable direction in the stamens of the different species. We have not adopted Thunberg's trivial name of *lancea,* for although, taking circumstances together, we have little doubt but this is his plant, yet the description is too vague to apply with certainty to any species. Flowers

in May. Introduced by Mr. Masson, in 1774. Our figure was drawn at the nursery of Messrs. Grimwood and Wykes, Kensington.

WATSONIA ALETROIDES.
ALETRIS-LIKE WATSONIA.

Watsonia aletroides.

PLATE 251

The name of watsonia was first given by Miller, in honour of our friend, the late Sir William Watson, and was adopted by Jussieu in that invaluable work his *Genera plantarum,* and will be found to form a very natural genus, sufficiently distinct from *Antholyza.* This very elegant species, which does not appear to have been noticed by Willdenow, is readily distinguished from every other by the distinct form of the corolla, which strongly resembles some species of *Aletris, Lachenalia,* and *Aloe.* The alternate segments are interior; the bulb is compressed and tunicated. It is very subject to vary, having in one instance a single scape six or eight inches high, with three or four distant, sometimes one-ranked, flowers; in another, a three or four-branched stem two feet high, with a terminal spike of from twenty to thirty closely imbricated distich flowers, and adpressed spikelets in proportion. The same bulb will one year produce pale pink, the next deep crimson, and the following variegated or striped corollas, as in the figure, always scentless. One of these varieties has been figured in the *Botanical Magazine*, under the name of *Antholyza merianella*, but the real *Antholyza merianella* of Linnæus, or *Gladiolus merianellus* of Thunberg, is a different plant, having pubescent leaves, fewer in number, nearly sheathing the whole stem, flowers differently formed, with larger and rounder segments, stigmas entire and complicate; and is in fact a *Gladiolus* nearly allied to *Gladiolus hirsutus* by leaf, and to *Gladiolus watsonius* by the tubular throat.

251 *Watsonia aletroides* (t. 533 1801 SE)

Watsonia Marginata (β.) Minor.
Lesser Broad-Leaved Watsonia.
Watsonia marginata.
PLATE 252

The present variety was introduced last year from the Cape of Good Hope, by Mr. Griffin, in whose conservatory at South Lambeth we saw it in bloom in October last. Seems to come very near to *rubens*.

252 *Watsonia marginata* β *minor* (t. 1530 1813 SE)

Watsonia Roseo-Alba (β.)
Variegated Long-Tubed Watsonia.
Watsonia humilis.
PLATE 253

For the present variety we are indebted to Mr. Woodford, with whom it bloomed, some years since; as did variety *roseo-alba* (γ). Flowers six to fourteen; stem simple; no part of the plant has any scent. Native of the Cape of Good Hope.

Watsonia Strictiflora.
Straight-Flowered Watsonia.
Watsonia strictiflora.
PLATE 254

Descr. *Bulb-tuber* about the size of a large nutmeg, covered by thick brown membrano-fibrous *integuments*; *leaves* four to six inches long, about half an inch broad; *stem* rather higher than these in the present specimen, two-flowered; *flower* scentless, of a cherry-red colour, about three inches long, opening of the faux marked with a deep violet-purple coloured star of six short broadish-pointed rays (nec-

253 *Watsonia roseo-alba* β (t. 1193 1809 SE)

tarostigmata) one on the base of each segment; *anthers* dark purple with yellow pollen; *stigmas* deep rose-colour; when the flower begins to fade, the segments of the corolla, which are about the third of an

254 *Watsonia strictifolia* (t. 1406 1811 SE)

inch broad, converge subbilabiately. We have not found any traces of the species in any work known to us; it agrees with *marginata* in having trifarious upright divergent stamens, but disagrees with all the species yet known to us in the straightness and uprightness of the corolla, length of the tube, and proportionate shortness of the faux. Introduced into this country from the Cape of Good Hope, by the Hon. W. Herbert, in whose collection it flowered this summer; to that gentleman we are also obliged for the specimen from which the drawing was made, as well as for his observations on the species.

*This species is now reported to be very rare or even extinct in the wild, because of agriculture and building on its restricted natural habitats to the north-east of Cape Town.

LABIATÆ

MOLUCCELLA LÆVIS
SMOOTH MOLUCCA BALM
OR BELLS OF IRELAND.
Molucella laevis.

PLATE 255

Molucella lævis is an annual plant, and, unless in favourable seasons, does not perfect its seeds with us, which accounts for its being so rarely met with in our gardens. To insure the ripening of its seeds, Miller directs that it should be raised in the autumn, and the young plants preserved through the winter under a frame. In the spring, they may be planted in the open air, in a warm situation, sheltered from the high winds. These plants, which have been preserved through the winter, will flower towards the end of June, and may be expected to produce ripe seeds, should the weather be at all favourable.

The *calyx* in the whole genus is bell-shaped and much larger than the corolla, with teeth more or less mucronated: in this species they are described as being without mucro; but this is not the fact: the mucro is indeed small, and though not pungent when green, becomes so in drying. The whorls are generally five-flowered, and under each calyx is a bract of from three to five spines united at the base, which, though at first innocuous, become rigid and pungent; these together form an in-

255 *Moluccella laevis* (t. 1852 1816)

volucre surrounding the stem, beneath each whorl.

Authors differ in their opinion of its scent; Parkinson observes, that the smell thereof is nothing like balm, but rather fulsome: to us the scent is very agreeable; as it was to John Bauhin.

Native of Syria. Cultivated by Lobel in 1570. Flowers in July and August. Communicated by our kind friend, Alexander McLeay, Esq.

PLECTRANTHUS FORSKOHLÆI.
FORSKOHL'S PLECTRANTHUS.
Plectranthus forskohlei.

PLATE 256

Descr. Stem frutescent at the lower part: branches herbaceous, obtusely four-cornered, hairy: hairs pointing upwards. *Leaves* oval, crenate towards the apex, rugose, reticulately veined, seven-nerved, smooth on the upper surface, tomentose on the under; fleshy not flexile, continued down the *petiole*, which is ciliated. *Raceme* terminal, a foot long, verticillated, without

bracts or floral leaves. *Pedicels* hairy, longer than the calyx. *Calyx* bilabiate, gibbose at the base, hairy: *upper lip* trifid. Middle segment broad, round-oval acuminate, two lateral ones very narrow, acute, ciliated with glandular hairs: *under lip* bifid, segments narrow acute like the lateral segments of the upper lip, but a fourth part longer. *Corolla* ringent; *tube* refracted, gibbose above. *Upper lip* short, three lobed, rounded, bearded: *lower lip* canoe-shaped, acute, hairy along the keel, containing the *stamens* which are declined; *filaments* not toothed, united half-way, inserted at the entrance of the tube: *anthers* four-lobed, one-celled. *Pollen* globose. During æstivation, that is in the bud, in its unexpanded state, the upper lip is superincumbent on the lower. Obs. The leaves are extremely bitter to the taste, the calyxes aromatic and pungent.

Flowers in October and November. Propagated by cuttings. Native of Arabia-Felix and Abyssinia. Introduced in 1806 by Viscount Valentia, now Earl of Mountnorris, whose ardour in the pursuit of natural knowledge is well known. Communicated from the stove of James Vere, Esq. of Kensington Gore, by Mr. William Blake, his gardener.

PRUNELLA GRANDIFLORA.
GREAT-FLOWERED SELF-HEAL.
Prunella grandiflora.

PLATE 257

The plant here figured, which we have several years cultivated in our garden at Brompton, without discovering in it the least disposition to vary, is undoubtedly the same as is figured by Professor Jacquin, in his *Fl. Austr.* under the name of *grandiflora*; he regards it as a distinct species, and as such it is introduced in Professor Gmelin's ed. of the *Syst. Nat.* of Linnæus: Mr. Aiton, in his *Hortus Kewensis* following Linnæus, makes it a variety of the *vulgaris* a common English plant, which we have never seen to vary much in the size of its flowers.

Professor Jacquin informs us, that it grows wild, mixed with the *laciniata* (a

OPPOSITE:
256 *Plectranthus forskohlaei* (t. 2036 1819)

Pub. by S. Curtis. Walworth. Jan. 1. 1819.

Weddell. Sc.

257 *Prunella grandiflora* (t. 337 1796)

kindred species with yellowish flowers) on the Alps; it is found also in similar situations in various other parts of Europe.

In July and August, it puts forth its large showy blossoms, of a fine purple colour. Such as are partial to hardy herbaceous plants, of ready growth, which are ornamental, take up but little room, and are not apt to entrench on their neighbours, will be induced to add this to their collection. It is propagated by parting its roots in autumn.

SALVIA AMŒNA.

PURPLE-FLOWERED SAGE.

Salvia amœna.

PLATE 258

This species of sage approaches very near to Dr. Smith's *amethystina*, from which it differs in its leaves not being tomentose underneath, in the length of its footstalks, in the more shrubby and more branched stalks. Its foliage resembles very much the *tubiflora* of the same author, but the flowers are totally different.

Those *Salvias* which have the upper lip of the calyx undivided, including most, if not all, the South American and West Indian species, might, perhaps, be advantageously separated from the European ones, having a five-cleft calyx, and formed into a distinct genus. This separation would be a great relief, in a genus so extensive, that Professor Vahl has enumerated one hundred and thirty-seven species; and has not even divided them into sections. Donn, in his catalogue of the Cambridge garden, has the present species under the name of *violacea*, but the *violacea* of Vahl is an annual and quite distinct from this.

Native of the West Indies: has been cultivated in the stove by Mr. Loddiges these ten years or more, and is easily propagated by cuttings. Flowers in May and June.

258 *Salvia amoena* (t. 1294 1810 SE)

SALVIA AUREA.

GOLDEN SAGE.

Salvia africana-lutea.

PLATE 259

Such as are delighted with the singular rather than the beautiful appearances of plants, cannot fail of ranking the present

species of sage among their favourites.

It has been called *aurea*, from the colour of its flowers, *ferruginea* would perhaps have been more expressive of them; when they first open indeed they are of a yellow colour, but they quickly and constantly become of the colour of rusty iron.

The leaves are nearly round, and have a pleasing silvery hue; a few of them only, and those chiefly at the extremities of the young shoots, are of the form described by Linnæus in his specific character of the plant, and hence Commelin's description (*vid. Syn.*) is to be preferred, as leading us with more certainty to a knowledge of the plant; the colour of the leaves, the colour and unusual magnitude of the blossoms, are indisputably the most striking features of the species, and therefore to be resorted to: for my own part, as a friend to the advancement of the science, rather than as the follower of this or that great man, I see no good reason why colour should not in many instances, especially where expressive characters are wanting, form a part of the specific character in plants, as well as in animals: we are told indeed of its inconstancy. I would ask – who ever saw the colour of the leaves or blossoms of the present plant to vary? and, on the contrary, who ever saw its leaves constant in their form?

259 *Salvia aurea* (t. 182 1792 SE)

The *Salvia aurea* is a native of the Cape, and was cultivated by Mr. Miller in 1731, it is a hardy greenhouse plant, is readily propagated by cuttings, and flowers from May to November. If suffered to grow, it will become a shrub of the height of six or seven feet.

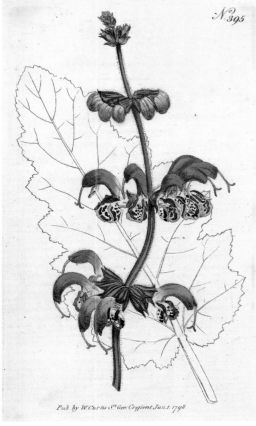

260   *Salvia indica* (t. 395 1798)

SALVIA INDICA.
INDIAN SAGE.
Salvia indica.
PLATE 260

Though a native of India, as its name implies, this magnificent species of sage is found to be a hardy herbaceous plant, requiring, indeed, a little extraordinary care to be taken of it in severe winters; we have had it flower in great perfection in a large garden pot, but it will succeed as well, or better, in the open border, where it will grow to the height of four or five feet, and produce during the months of June and July abundance of flowers, singularly and beautifully marked.

It may be increased by parting its roots in the autumn or spring, and also by seeds; the latter we have found to be but sparingly produced in our garden at Brompton,

though we consider it as peculiarly favourable to the seeding of plants.

The beauty of tall plants, like the present, depends greatly on the pains taken in sticking them; this business in general is not sufficiently attended to, being frequently deferred till it becomes a matter of necessity rather than of choice; we would therefore recommend it to our readers to set about it early, soon after the plant emerges from the ground, especially in respect to all those which are furnished with tendrils, or have twining stalks; the due execution of this work requires judgment, and will admit the display of some taste.

It appears that Mr. Miller cultivated this sage at Chelsea, in the year 1731, and yet even now it is a plant rarely seen in gardens.

SALVIA INVOLUCRATA.
LARGE-BRACTED SAGE.
Salvia involucrata.
PLATE 261

Communicated by the kindness of the Hon. and Rev. William Herbert, of Spofforth, from his splendid conservatory: where, planted in the border, it has

261   *Salvia involucrata* (t. 2872 1828 WJH)

attained a height of from twelve to fourteen feet, and makes a brilliant appearance, with its numerous heads of richly-coloured blossoms, scarcely less beautiful than those of the well-known *Salvia splendens*. Mr. Herbert received the plant from Mr. Tate of the Sloane Street Nursery, who imported the seeds from Mexico. The plant smells not unlike the Common Sage (*Salvia verbeneca*) of England.

There can be no question, I think, as to the propriety of considering the S. *lævigata* of Humboldt, synonymous with the S. *involucrata*. The plates and the descriptions agree in every essential particular.

262   *Salvia spathacea* (t. 9640 1942 LS)

SALVIA SPATHACEA.
HUMMINGBIRD SAGE
Salvia spathacea.
PLATE 262

This coarse, sticky, but decorative plant is locally common in the coastal counties of California, occurring southwards from a point in Solano County a short distance north-east of San Francisco but apparently disappearing before reaching San Diego County on the Mexican border. Here, in the Upper Sonoran Zone, it is found flowering in April and May at low altitudes in canyons and on the slopes of hills, either in the open or in the partial shade of oak woodland.

Our plate was drawn from a specimen received from the Cambridge Botanic Garden in 1938. The plants at Cambridge originated from cuttings obtained from Mr. Clarence Elliott, who had collected seed of the species in California in 1931 and cultivated it in a cool greenhouse at Stevenage. Mr. Elliott tells us that he tried it in the open but it did not prove hardy, and this was also Mr. Preston's experience at Cambridge, where the plants are grown in a cool greenhouse with a minimum temperature of 40° in winter. Pots of fairly large size are required as the species is a strong grower and produces many suckers. It is readily propagated from cuttings and by division.

Distribution. – Coastal counties of California.

263   Scutellaria altissima (t. 2548 1825 JC)

SCUTELLARIA ALTISSIMA.
TALL SKULL-CAP.

Scutellaria altissima.

PLATE 263

Obs. *Stem* erect, square, smooth, from two to four feet high. *Branches* slender. *Leaves* cordate-ovate; (lower ones cordate-oblong), with large serratures. *Flowers* in terminal spikes, secund, growing by pairs, sessile, or on very short pedicels. *Bracts* shorter than the calyx, lanceolate. *Calyx* increased after deflorescence. *Corolla* large, upright, purple, not blue; *tube* several times longer than calyx: *limb* two-lipped: *lips* unequal, entire.

From the very imperfect specimen of Tournefort's plant, in the Banksian Herbarium, we cannot decide respecting it; but our plant agrees with the garden specimen in the same herbarium, and, we have no doubt, is the species cultivated by Ph. Miller.

Scutellaria altissima differs from *peregrina* in having smaller bracts, and in the entire, not trifid, under-lip. In the length of its tube it exceeds most of the other species. We believe that no figure of this plant has been heretofore published.

Native of the Levant. Propagated by seeds, being rather a biennial than perennial, as we are informed by Mr. John Denson, the intelligent curator of the botanic garden, at Bury St. Edmunds, from whence we received specimens in September 1824, by favour of N. S. Hodson, Esq. to whose energy this thriving establishment owes its existence.

ZIZIPHORA SERPYLLACEA.
SWEET-SCENTED ZIZIPHORA.

Ziziphora serpyllacea.

PLATE 264

Seeds of this alpine plant were received from Mount Caucasus, by Mr. Loddiges, who kindly sent it us in flower in July last. It continues several weeks in blossom, and is at the same time agreeable to the eye and grateful to the smell.

Having compared our plant with the specimens sent from Caucasus by Mr. Adams to Sir Joseph Banks, under the name we have adopted, we are certain of the identity of their species. In these specimens as well as in ours the bracts are not exactly similar to the leaves, being smaller, rounder, and more acuminate, without notches, ciliated at the edge, and more strongly nerved. The filaments in this species are extremely short, the anthers being nearly sessile in the faux of the corolla. In the same collection is another plant very nearly resembling this, except that the calyx is thickly covered with stiff hairs; as far as we can judge in the dried state it appears to be a mere variety of this; Mr. Adams however considers it as a distinct species, and calls it *Ziziphora pouschkini*. We have preserved as a synonym the name by which Mr. Loddiges received it, as we have sometimes found that the plants of these very distant countries have been published under these names long before we have known of it.

Native of Mount Caucasus; perfectly hardy; propagated by seeds, which it produces plentifully. Introduced by Mr. Loddiges, from whom we received it in flower in July last, under the name of *Cucubalus simbriatus*.

264   Ziziphora serpyllacae (t. 906 1806 SE)

LEGUMINOSÆ

ACACIA NIGRICANS.

UNEQUAL-WINGED ACACIA.

Acacia nigricans.

PLATE 265

This is a very beautiful shrub, with delicate and singular foliage. Native of the south-west coast of New Holland. Different individuals vary considerably in the number of leaflets on each pinna. Does not bear fruit in our conservatories, but may be propagated by cuttings. Flowers from April to July. Introduced about 1803, by Mr. Peter Good. Communicated by the Comtesse de Vandes from her very fine collection at Bayswater.

265　*Acacia nigricans* (t. 2188 1820 JC)

BOSSIÆA SCOLOPENDRIA.

FLAT-STEMMED BOSSIÆA.

Bossiæa scolopendria.

PLATE 266

Bossiæa and *Platylobium* are, as we have before observed very nearly allied; and unfortunately Dr. Smith's principal generic character, derived from the Legumen, does not hold true; consisting, in this species at

266　*Bossiæa scolopendria* (t. 1285 1810 SE)

least, of one cell, perfectly free from every sort of division, and only differing from that of *Platylobium formosum*, in having both margins thickened and the want of any wings.

We are however inclined to believe that the genera are really distinct; for all the species of *Bossiæa* have alternate leaves with articulated petioles without very evident or permanent stipules: whilst the leaves of platylobium are opposite with stipules longer than the petiole.

Native of New Holland, and is a rather hardy greenhouse shrub. Is propagated by seeds, but not easily in any other way.

Our drawing was made from a very fine living specimen communicated by Mr. Loddiges, with whom this shrub sometimes produces perfect seeds.

CASSIA AUSTRALIS.

NEW-HOLLAND CASSIA.

Cassia australis.

PLATE 267

Descr. Stem fruticose, erect, simple or very little branched towards the top. *Stipules* two, at the base of the petioles, subulate,

incurved. *Leaves* abrupt pinnate: *rachis* channelled: *leaflets* ten or twelve pair, oblong-elliptical, obtuse at both ends, emarginate, with a minute mucro, smooth, about an inch long when full grown. *Glands* erect, subulate, black at the point, one between each pair of the leaflets. *Peduncles* axillary, naked, shorter than the leaf, sometimes growing two together, sometimes single, bearing generally four large golden-yellow flowers. *Pedicels* cernuous, with a small oval *bract* at the base of each. *Calycine leaflets* round-oval, concave, nearly equal, but two a little the largest. *Petals* obovate, with a short claw, nearly equal. *Stamens* ten: *filaments* very short and thick: *anthers* oblong, all connivent, brown; the lower-most one the longest. *Germen* stipitate, linear, and together with the style curved into a semicircle: *stigma* simple.

This handsome *Cassia* was raised at Bury-Hill, from seeds received from Mr. Telfair, early in 1824, with an observation, that he had just got them from New Holland. Mr. Barclay also raised the same species from a packet of New Holland seeds, given him by Mr. Stillwell of Dorking. It has been raised also from seeds received from New Zealand. Has been hitherto cultivated in the greenhouse, where it blossoms in May and June, but has not as yet produced seeds.

CASSIA CORYMBOSA.

CORYMBOUS CASSIA.

Cassia corymbosa.

PLATE 268

Lamarck has given an accurate description of this beautiful shrub from a plant that flowered in the Botanic Garden at Paris, adding that of the seed-vessel from an imported specimen. The leaves are without stipules, consist generally of three pair of leaflets, between the two lowermost of which is a small conical sharp-pointed gland: the bunches of flowers, about eight in each, stand upon peduncles the length of the leaves to which they are axillary. According to Lamarck is a native of Buenos Ayres, in South America.

Our drawing was taken at the garden of E. J. A. Woodford, Esq. at Vauxhall, in August, from a plant purchased of Mr.

C.M. Curtis Del.

Pub.by J.Curtis Walworth Aug.t 1826.

126

N.º 633

268 Cassia corymbosa (t. 633 1803 SE)

North, Nurseryman at Lambeth, who says he raised it from seeds received from the West Indies about seven years ago. We are informed by Mr. Watson, Gardener to Mr. Woodford, that whilst confined in a pot and kept in the stove it never flowered, removed into the greenhouse it suffered from the cold, but when planted in the border of the conservatory it throve exceedingly and flowered freely, making a very ornamental shrub about five or six feet high. May be increased by cuttings.

COLVILLEA RACEMOSA.
SPLENDID COLVILLEA.

Colvillea racemosa.

PLATES 269 and 270

This truly splendid plant, worthy of bearing the name of his late Excellency Sir Charles Colville, Governor of the Mauritius, to whom it was dedicated by its discoverer, is probably a native of the east coast of Africa: but was only seen by Professor Bojer in 1824, in the Bay of Bombatoe, on the western coast of Madagascar, where a single tree was cultivated by the inhabitants. That indefatigable

OPPOSITE:
267 Cassia australis (t. 2676 1826 CMC)

naturalist raised it from seeds which he took to the Mauritius, where it has perfectly succeeded: and we may soon expect to add this most ornamental plant to the stoves of our own country. Its flowering season in the Mauritius is April and May. I am indebted to Professor Bojer for the excellent drawing, of which a portion is here represented, as well as for the description and for speciments.

Descr. *Tree* fourty to fifty feet high, with the general aspect of *Poinciana regia*, (*Bot. Mag.* t. 2884,) but with a thicker trunk and more ample foliage: the *bark* is reddish-grey, smooth; the *wood* white, rather fragile. *Branches* very long and spreading, rounded, grey, the younger ones greenish, rough with elevated points. *Leaves* alternate, remote, very patent, the lower ones reflexed, bipinnate with twenty to thirty pairs, oblong-oval in their circumscription, three feet long: pinnæ opposite, four inches long, with twenty to twenty-eight pairs of horizontal, linear *leaflets*, half an inch long, shorter at the base and at the extremity of the pinnæ, rather unequal, on very short petiolules, slightly pubescent. The common *petiole* is swollen at the base, channelled above, green or purplish. *Stipules* minute, setaceous, deciduous. *Flowers* bright scarlet, racemose. *Racemes* from four to twelve, partly arising from the apex of

269 Colvillea racemosa (t. 3325 1834 WB)

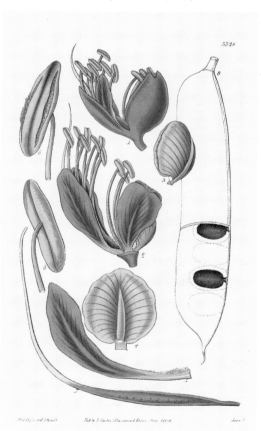

the branches and partly from the axils of the superior leaves, a foot and a half long, simple or branched. *Peduncles* crowded, jointed upon the stem, reddish: *bracts* coloured, very deciduous. The buds are obliquely globose, somewhat acute, beautifully velvety, red. *Calyx* greenish within, including the alæ and vexillum. The *vexillum* is singularly small, convolute, and almost wholly covered by the alæ: it has a broad nerve with a white downy tubercle at the base, and is of a yellowish colour, marked with veins. Of the ten free stamens, three are inserted beneath the vexillum, two under the alæ, one under the carina, and the rest beneath the ovary. *Ovary* glabrous green, ending in a very long style. (Bojer.)

CORONILLA VARIA.
PURPLE CORONILLA.

Coronilla varia.

PLATE 271

Clusius, in his work above referred to, informs us that he found this plant growing wild in various parts of Germany, in meadows, fields, and by road sides; that it flowered in June, sometimes the whole summer through, and ripened its seeds in July and August; the blossoms he found subject to much variations of colour, being either deep purple, whitish, or even wholly white: Casp. Bauhine notices another variety, in which the alæ are white and the rostrum purple; this variety, which we have had the honour to receive from the Earl of Egremont, is the most desirable one to cultivate in gardens, as it is more ornamental than the one wholly purple, most commonly met with in the nurseries, and corresponds also better with its name of *varia*; it is to be noticed however that this variety of colour exists only in the young blossoms.

The *Coronilla varia* is a hardy, perennial, herbaceous plant, climbing, if supported, to the height of four or five feet, otherwise spreading widely on the ground, and frequently injuring less robust plants growing near it; on this account, as well as from its having powerfully creeping roots whereby it greatly increases, though a pretty plant, and flowering during most of the summer, it is not to be introduced without caution, and is rather to be placed in the shrubbery,

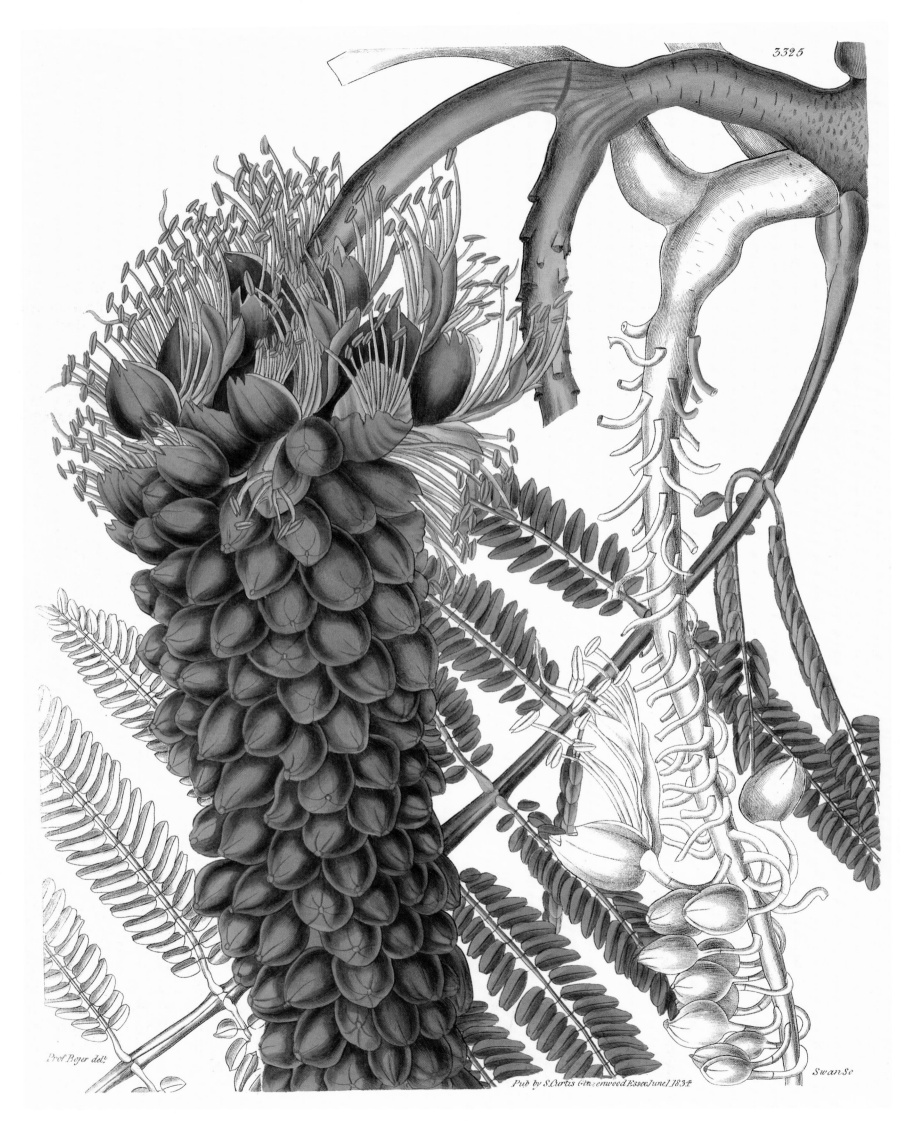

Prof Beyer delt.

Pub by S.Curtis Glazenwood Essex June 1 1834

Swan Sc

or outskirts of the garden, than in the flower border.

It will grow in any soil or situation, but blossoms and seeds most freely in a soil moderately dry.

Parkinson, in his *Theatre of Plants*, mentions its being cultivated as an ornamental plant. *Ait. Kew.* Its bitterness, will be an objection to its being cultivated for the use of cattle, for which purpose it has been recommended.

CROTALARIA JUNCEA.
CHANNEL'D-STALK'D CROTALARIA
OR SUNN HEMP.

Crotalaria juncea.

PLATE 272

This annual is a native of the East Indies; the seeds were brought to Mr. Miller, at Chelsea Garden, from the coast of Malabar before 1768, *Ait. Kew.* It rises with an angular, rushy, stiff stem, from three to

OPPOSITE:
270 *Colvillea racemosa* (t. 3326 1834 WB)

272 *Crotalaria juncea* (t. 490 1800 SE)

four feet in height, dividing into branches. The leaves are oblong-lanceolate, alternate, covered with soft silvery hairs, which are much diminished in number by culture, as we found on comparing a native specimen from the coast of Coromandel, in the possession of Sir Joseph Banks, Bart. The flowers are terminal and disposed in racemes, each flower being furnished with a short peduncle, they are large, of a deep yellow, and resemble those of the Spanish Broom.

These are succeeded by large turgid pods, containing reniform or kidney-shaped seeds. This plant requires the treatment of the tan-stove.

CYTISUS FOLIOLOSUS.
LEAFY CYTISUS.

Adenocarpus foliosus.

PLATE 273

The stalks in this species of cytisus are thickly covered with small leaves, which gives the whole plant an outré appearance, hence Mr. Aiton's name of *foliolosus*, so happily hit off; many other peculiarities attend this charming shrub, of which its

long deciduous bracts are not the least remarkable.

It is a native of the Canary Isles, where it was found by Mr. Masson, and introduced in 1779; if suffered to grow, it will acquire a great height, become indeed too large for a small greenhouse, and more fit for a conservatory, for which it would appear to be a most desirable plant; it produces flowers abundantly during May and June, which are not only ornamental but deliciously fragrant.

Strong established plants usually produce perfect seeds, by which this shrub is increased; cuttings rarely succeed.

273 *Cytisus foliolosus* (t. 426 1798 SE)

CYTISUS PURPUREUS.
PURPLE-FLOWERED CYTISUS

Cytisus purpureus.

PLATE 274

The Purple-flowered Cytisus is a humble shrub with weak stems, which in the month of May are covered with a profusion of flowers; these, in cultivation, we have observed generally to come in pairs, though described from native specimens as being solitary. The whole plant is smooth except the mouth of the calyx and the keel of the corolla, which are villous. The *calyx* is bilabiate: the *upper lip* emarginate, the *lower* appears to be entire, but when the villosity shrinks by drying is seen to be minutely three-toothed.

A native of Carniola, where it was first discovered by Wulfen, and a figure and description of it were published by Jacquin, in the *Appendix* to his *Flora Austriaca*. Is perfectly hardy. Introduced about the year 1790, we believe by Mr. Loddiges.

275 *Dalea mutabilis* (t. 2486 1824 JC)

274 *Cytisus purpureus* (t. 1176 1809 SE)

Dalea mutabilis.
Changeable Dalea.
Dalea mutabilis.
PLATE 275

Descr. A slender shrub; *branches* smooth. *Leaves* alternate, odd-pinnate: leaflets from seven to fifteen, obovate, with the point sometimes rounded, more frequently emarginate, dotted with transparent glands, which, when held to the light, give an appearance as if the leaf were perforated, as in the common St. John's Wort. *Stipules* small, subulate, inserted within the footstalk. *Peduncles* terminal, solitary, bearing the flowers in a close spike, lengthening as the flowers expand. *Bracts* ovate, concave, mucronate, persistent. *Calyx* of one leaf, five-toothed, hairy, membranaceous, with ten green streaks. Standard white, ovate-cordate, with a slender claw, longer than the limb; *wings* and *keel* shorter by half than the standard, white tipped with purple, colour encreasing with age. *Filaments* all connected downwards, free above: *Anthers* oval, dark purple: *pollen* orange-coloured. *Germen* oval, hairy: *Style* longer than the stamens: *Stigma* acute.

We have no doubt but that the *Dalea bicolor*, figured in Willdenow's *Hortus Berolinensis* is the same plant as the *Psoralea mutabilis* of Cavanilles; we have, therefore, retained the specific name of the latter author, this having the right of priority.

Native of Cuba and Mexico. Cultivated with us in the stove. Communicated by Mr. Anderson from the Chelsea Garden, in October, 1823, where it was introduced by Mr. Otto, in 1821.

Dillwynia obovata.
Cross-leaved Dillwynia.
Eutaxia myrtifolia.
PLATE 276

Whether our present plant properly belongs to the genus *Dillwynia*, or ought rather to be considered as a *Pultenæa* on account of its bracts, which, though minute and not so close to the calyx, are nevertheless very analogous to those of that genus, or whether it should be considered as distinct from both, we cannot determine. From the similarly formed calyx, the oblong hairy ovarium, the truncate stigma, which is neither acute nor pubescent, we should be inclined to think that it must belong to the same genus as *D. glaberrima*, notwithstanding the vexillum has not the long transverse diameter of the latter.

Our drawing was made from a plant communicated by Messrs. Loddiges and Sons. Flowers in May. Gathered at King George's Sound by Mr. A. Menzies, and in Van Dieman's Land by Labillardiere. Requires the shelter of a good greenhouse.

276 *Dillwynia obovata* (t. 1274 1810 SE)

277 *Dolichos lablab* (t. 896 1806 SE)

DOLICHOS LABLAB.
BLACK-SEEDED DOLICHOS.
OR HYACINTH BEAN
Dolichos lablab.

PLATE 277

Although always considered as a native of Egypt, Hasselquist assures us, that this plant is only cultivated there, and was most probably introduced from Europe, as it is called by the inhabitants the European Bean. Is cultivated for the table in several warm countries, in the same manner as the kidney-bean is with us; indeed Phaseolus and Dolichos are very nearly allied. Is usually considered as a stove plant, but is marked by Mr. Donn as a hardy annual.

Alpinus describes his lablab as a climbing evergreen tree, as large as a vine, enduring a hundred years or more, and in frequent use in the gardens of Egypt for making shady bowers. Surely this must render it very doubtful if his plant be the same as ours; more especially as he describes the pods as being long.

Flowers from July to September. Said in the *Hortus Kewensis* to have been cultivated by the Duchess of Beaufort, in 1714.

DOLICHOS LIGNOSUS.
PURPLE DOLICHOS.
Dipogon lignosus.

PLATE 278

The plant here represented has very generally been regarded as the *Dolichos lignosus* of Linnæus, and we are confirmed in the idea of its being so from his own figure in the *Hort. Cliff.* and that in the *Herbar. Amboin.* to which he refers, rather than from its according with his specific description, for with that the plant is evidently at variance, the seed-vessels being neither straight nor linear, but evidently curved, as represented on the plate: in their natural situation the concave part is turned upwards. Rumphius describes the germen under the term *corniculum fursum elevatum,* and the seed-vessels as *parum incurvæ*: Dr. Smith, on the contrary, taking no notice of the impropriety of Linnæus's description, says they are a little *recurved*; whether this term be strictly applicable to the seed-vessels in the *Linnæan* sense of the word, may perhaps admit of a doubt.

Rumphius informs us, that the seed-vessels of this plant are a common food throughout India, eaten as our French or kidney beans are, to which however he observes, that they are far inferior; of that

278 *Dolichos lignosus* (t. 380 1797)

Pub. by W.Curtis St.Geo: Crescent Aug. 1. 1797

extensive country it is considered as a native, there are good grounds for regarding it also as a native of Spain and Portugal: we were favoured with seeds of it by Mr. John White, of Fleet Street, which 'had been gathered at Gibraltar by his brother, Lieutenant White, of the 82d regiment.

This plant, so far from requiring a stove, is hardy enough to bear our ordinary winters, when placed against a wall in a sheltered part of the garden; but it is usually kept in the greenhouse as a climber, for which it is well adapted, as it continues if it has plenty of pot room, during most of the summer to throw out abundance of bright purple flowers, in succession; these soon fade, and are followed by seed-vessels, which have produced ripe seeds in my garden at Brompton, and by these the plant is readily increased.

*It is a native of the southern Cape region of South Africa.

279 *Erythrina herbacea* (t. 877 1805 SE)

ERYTHRINA HERBACEA.
HERBACEOUS CORAL-TREE.
Erythrina herbacea.

The branches though they appear shrubby are annual, dying in general down to the rootstock every winter; yet it sometimes happens that a branch does not perish in this manner, but continuing to vegetate becomes as it were an elongation of the root stock, and thus the plant puts on somewhat of the habit of *Erythrina Corallodendron*.

Being a native of South Carolina, is generally considered as a greenhouse plant; but Miller has observed that, unless nursed in the stove, it seldom flowers, yet in too much heat it is apt to fall a prey to insects and by the loss of its foliage to be deprived of much of its beauty.

Communicated by Mr. Loddiges of Hackney. Flowers from June to September.

GLYCINE APIOS.
TUBEROUS-ROOTED GLYCINE OR POTATO BEAN.
Apios americana.

PLATE 280

Glycine, as it now stands, certainly contains an assemblage of several distinct genera; but as a partial reform is apt to increase the confusion, we leave this as we found it, though a very doubtful species from the time of Linnæus himself.

G. *Apios* is considered as a hardy peren-

280 Glycine apios (t. 1198 1809 SE)

nial, but it should be remembered that, being a native of the southern states of North America, Carolina, and Virginia, it is liable to be destroyed by our winters, unless the roots are protected from the frost by a covering of tan or mulch, as recommended by Miller, who observes, that when planted against a southern wall, and properly supported, it will rise ten feet high, and flower abundantly in August and September. Is propagated by its tuberous roots, which are sweet and edible. Drawn at Mr. Salisbury's Botanic Garden, Brompton.

GOMPHOLOBIUM VERSICOLOR; *VAR.* CAULIBUS PURPUREIS.
CHANGEABLE GOMPHOLOBIUM; PURPLE-STEMMED VARIETY.
Gompholobium polymorphum.

PLATE 281

Gompholobium versicolor is a pretty greenhouse Swan River suffruticose plant, from the rich collection of Messrs. Lucombe, Pince, and Co., Exeter, who raised it from seeds sent home by Mr. James Drummond. It derives its specific name from the circumstance of the flowers becoming paler in age. But at all times the plant is extremely beautiful and most profuse in its blossoms, if it be kept well cut in, and not allowed to send out shoots that are too long and too luxuriant. Dr. Lindley has well distinguished the species from G. *etnue* and G. *sparsum*. It varies with purple stems, as represented in our plate, and flowered, in May 1845.

Descr. An upright, rather twiggy, small *shrub*; with subangular *stems* and *branches*, deep purple in our variety, glabrous, as is every part of the plant. *Leaves* alternate, nearly sessile, trifoliolate; *leaflets* linear, rather broadly so in the older parts of the plant, acute, almost apiculate at the extremity, the margins slightly recurved, costate, but with no evident nerves or veins, dark-green above, paler beneath. *Racemes* axillary (from the upper leaves), and terminal, few (two to three)-flowered; *pedicels* furnished with minute bractoles. *Flowers* large, handsome, peculiarly beautiful just before expansion, when the rich and deep scarlet of the *standard* alone is seen. *Calyx* of five deep, oblong-acute, or almost muc-

ronate segments. *Standard* long, somewhat reniform, deep red externally, pale within, yellow in the disk and with a deep red line bordering the yellow. *Wings* also deep red. *Keel* paler below, red towards the apex. *Stamens* ten, nearly as long as the pistil. *Filaments* ten, free. *Ovary* oblong, compressed, shortly stipitate. *Style* almost as long as the ovary, curved upwards. *Stigma* obtuse.

IBBETSONIA GENISTOIDES.
SPOTTED-FLOWERED IBBETSONIA.
Cyclopia genistoides (L.) Vent.

PLATE 282

Desc. *Stem* shrubby, with long, erect, furrowed branches. *Stipules* cartilaginous projections, from the hollow of which the leaves arise. *Leaves* ternate, sessile, crowded together: *leaflets* linear, smooth, longer than the flower. *Peduncles* about the length of the calyx, furnished at the base with three or four roundish convace bracts, resembling a second calyx, persistent. *Calyx* intruded at the base, five-toothed, lowermost tooth longer than the rest. *Corolla* papilionaceous: *vexillum* large, orbicular, emarginate, yellow with an irregular purplish brown spot at the base, from which slightly coloured veins extended near to the margin: *carina* incurved at the point and terminated with a beak (giving it somewhat the appearance of a bird's head) covered by the *alæ*, which are oblong, very obtuse; shorter than the vexillum. *Stamens* ten, distinct, inserted into a fleshy receptacle surrounding the base of the *germen*, which is oblong, attenuated at both ends: *style* long, ascending: *stigma* hairy. *Legumen*, in a native specimen, nearly two inches long, rather less than half an inch broad, flat, rugose, woody, black, terminated with the recurved persistent style, and marked by the impression of the kidney-shaped *seeds*, attached along the upper future. The outline added to our figure was taken from an imperfect pod, produced here, which contained no seeds. It was sufficient to show that the shrub was no *Gompholobium* as had been imagined.

Mr. Salisbury, in the ninth volume of the *Transactions of the Linnean Society*, has very judiciously remarked that the genus *Sophora*, as framed by Linnæus, contains

Tab. 4179.

N.º 1259.

Reeve, Bro. imp.

Fitch, del.

b. by T. Curtis S.t Geo. Crescent 1. Jan. 1 1810.

E. Sanfom Jun.r Sc.

281 *Gompholobium versicolor* var. *caulibus purpureis* (t. 4179 1845 WF)

282 *Ibbetsonia genistoides* (t. 1259 1810)

several very distinct genera, and that *Sophora genistoides*, to which, he says, may probably be added *ternata* and *triphylla* of Thunberg, will constitute one genus, of which, however, he has not favoured us either with the characters or a name. These deficiencies we have attempted to supply; wishing to dedicate this genus to Mrs. Agnes Ibbetson, the author of several very ingenious and instructive papers on vegetable physiology published in Nicholson's *Philosophical Journal*.

Besides Thunberg's species, we think two or three very distinct ones have hitherto been confounded under the name of *genistoides*.

Native of the Cape of Good Hope. Flowering with us at Midsummer, and requiring the protection of a greenhouse. Our drawing was taken at Mr. Whitley's, Old Brompton.

INDIGOFERA ANGUSTIFOLIA.

NARROW-LEAVED INDIGO.

Indigofera angustifolia.

PLATE 283

This small, delicate, and rather elegant species of indigo, is to be found in most collections of greenhouse plants near town, rises with an upright, shrubby stem, to the height of several feet; its leaves, of a lively green colour, are furnished with pinnæ, which are numerous and unusually narrow, whence its name; its flowers, produced on long racemi springing from the sides of the stem or branches, are of a singular dull red colour, and rarely followed by seeds with us.

It is a native of the Cape, from whence it was introduced by Mr. Masson, in 1774; flowers from June to October, and is usually increased by cuttings.

There is a description of this species in the *Mantiff. Pl. Linn.* but we know of no figure of it that has yet been published.

LATHYRUS ARTICULATUS.

JOINTED-PODDED LATHYRUS.

Lathyrus articulatus.

PLATE 284

The seed-vessels are of the first importance in ascertaining the several species of lathyrus, some being naked, others hairy, some long, others short, some having a smooth and perfectly even surface, others, as in the present instance, assuming an uneven or jointed appearance.

S.Edwards del.   Pub. by W.Curtis, S.t Geo. Crescent Dec.1.1799.   F.Sansom sculp.

283   Indigofera angustifolia (t. 465 1799 SE)

Pub. by W.Curtis, S.t Geo. Crescent Feb.1.1794.   V.Edwards del.Sansom sculp.

284   Lathyrus articulatus (t. 253 1794 SE)

Of this genus we have already figured three annual species, common in flower-gardens, viz. *odoratus*, *tingitanus*, and *sativus*; to these we now add the *articulatus*, not altogether so frequently met with, but

meriting a place on the flower-border, as the lively red and delicate white so conspicuous in its blossoms, causes it to be much admired.

It is a native of Italy, and was cultivated at the Chelsea Garden, in the time of Mr. Rand, 1739.

It is a hardy annual, requiring support, and rarely exceeding the height of two feet, flowering in July and August, and is readily raised from seeds, which should be sown in the open border at the beginning of April.

LATHYRUS TINGITANUS.

TANGIER PEA.

Lathyrus tingitanus.

PLATE 285

The Tangier Pea, a native of Morocco, cannot boast the agreeable scent, or variety of colours of the Sweet Pea; nor does it continue so long in flower; nevertheless there is a richness in the colour of its blossoms, which entitles it to a place in the gardens of the curious, in which it is usually sown in the spring, with other hardy annuals. It flowers in June and July.

The best mode of propagating it, is to sow the seeds on the borders in patches, where the plants are to remain; thinning them when they come up, so as to leave only two or three together.

285   Lathyrus tingitanus (t. 100 1789)

Pub.d as the Act directs, Nov.1.1789. by W.Curtis Botanic Garden, Lambeth Marsh.

Syd.Edwards del. Pub by J.Curtis, S.t Geo. Crescent. Oct.1.1806. F.Sansom sculp.

286   Loddigesia oxalidifolia (t. 965 1806 SE)

LODDIGESIA OXALIDIFOLIA.

OXALIS-LEAVED LODDIGESIA.

Loddigesia oxalidifolia.

PLATE 286

We believe that this delicate little shrub was first introduced into this country by George Hibbert, Esq. of Clapham Common, in whose conservatory our drawing was taken. We likewise received it from Mr. Loddiges, Nurseryman, at Hackney, who raised it some years ago from seeds he received from the Cape of Good Hope. This excellent cultivator, from his extensive correspondence with several far-distant countries, has been the means of introducing many rare exotics into our gardens, and to his experience and skill in horticulture, the preservation and propagation of more, that would have been otherwise lost, is to be entirely attributed. Of his liberality in communicating his possessions, for the promotion of science, the numbers of our magazine bear ample testimony, and in return, we consider it as a duty imposed upon us, thus to record his merits, by naming a genus after him. That the one we have chosen is very distinct, we apprehend the singular form of the corolla will sufficiently decide, although we have not yet been so fortunate as to meet with a seed-vessel.

It is a tolerably hardy greenhouse shrub, flowers freely, and is readily propagated by cuttings. Blossoms in May and June.

Linnæus sometimes amused himself with fancying a resemblance between the genus and the person to whose honour it is dedicated; and such conceits may at least serve to assist the memory. So in Loddigesia, the minute white standard may be considered as the emblem of the modest pretensions of this venerable cultivator; the broad keel, of his real usefulness to science; and the far-extended wings, as that of his two sons.

LOTUS HIRSUTUS.
HAIRY BIRD'S-FOOT-TREFOIL.
Dorycnium hirsutum.
PLATE 287

The *Lotus hirsutus*, according to Linnæus, is a native of the south of France, Italy, and the East.

287   Lotus hirsutus (t. 336 1796)

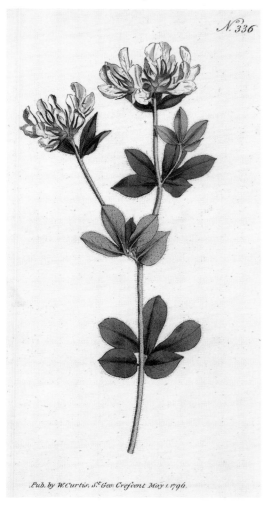

In mild winters it will bear the open border with us, but it is more generally kept in the greenhouse, of which indeed it has long had possession, being cultivated, according to Mr. Aiton, in 1683, by Mr. James Sutherland. It flowers from June to August.

Its blossoms are of a white colour, which being contrasted with the redness of the calyx, gives them a pleasing appearance; Caspar Bauhin informs us, that they are purple also.

This shrub will acquire the height of several feet; its flowers are usually succeeded by seed-vessels, which in favourable situations produce perfect seeds, by which the plant is easily propagated, as also by cuttings.

288   Lupinus arboreus (t. 682 1803 SE)

LUPINUS ARBOREUS.
TREE LUPINE.
Lupinus arboreus.
PLATE 288

Lamarck has enumerated in the *Encyclopœdia* several species with a shrubby stalk, all natives of South America; the one he calls *multiflorus* appears to resemble our plant in its foliage, but to be very different in its flowers: all the others are quite dissimilar.

Our drawing was made at Messrs. Grimwood and Wykes's, Kensington, in July 1801. It is usually treated as a greenhouse plant, but at the Botanic Garden, Oxford, we observed in the same year a large shrub growing in the open ground in a sheltered situation, in front of the greenhouse, where it produced abundance of ripe seeds. Its native country is unknown to us.

LUPINUS INCANUS.
HOARY LUPINE.
Lupinus incanus.
PLATE 289

The beautiful genus of lupine, of which the greater number of species, hitherto enumerated in our universal *Floras*, are natives either of the south of Europe or of the Andes of Peru, has been greatly increased by the discoveries of Mr. Douglas on the north-west coast of America, where that indefatigable Naturalist has detected no less than seventeen species in his first visit to the shores of the Columbia, and several have rewarded him on his second visit, as well as in California. Thus the genus may be considered to have its maximum on the western side of the Cordillera of North America. The present very handsome species is a native of South America, and "was raised by Mr. Nill, from seed sent by Mr. Tweedie of Buenos Ayres, and flowered freely in the greenhouse at Canonmills in June, 1833. It approaches very near to *Lupinus multiflorus* of *Encyclop. Méthodique*, vol. iii. p. 624, and had it not been for the very conspicuous pedicels in Mr. Neill's plant, I should scarcely have separated them."

Descr. "Whole *plant* silky, excepting only the corolla, stamens, and style. *Stem* suffruticose, erect, branched. *Leaves* (about six inches across) digitate, leaflets about nine, linear-lanceolate, silky on both sides, carinate below, entire, very acute. *Petiole* nearly twice the length of the leaflets, compressed vertically. *Stipules* (an inch and a quarter long,) adhering for about half their length, subulate. *Raceme* (a foot and a half long) terminal, elongated. *Pedicels* scattered equally over the rachis to within a little way of its base, which is naked, spreading when in flower, when in fruit erect, springing from the axil of a subulate,

3285

M. J. Macnab. del.

Pub. by S. Curtis, Glazenwood, Essex. Dec. 1. 1833.

Swan Sc.

caducous bracta. *Calyx* bilabiate, the upper lip two-, the lowest three-toothed, bibracteate towards the base, bracta small, subulate, adpressed, inconspicuous. *Corolla* pale lilac; *vexillum* reflected upwards and at the sides, subrotund, emarginate, cordate at the base, orange, and slightly spotted in the middle, keeled behind; *claw* short and rigid; *alæ* rather longer than the vexillum, straight in the upper edge, curved in the lower, and there cohering towards the apex, slightly turned up at the point, claws short; *keel* half the length of the alæ, more rigid and shining than the outer parts of the flower, and of deeper purple colour at its point, which is raised above the upper edge of the alæ, dipetalous, petals cohering only near their apices. *Stamens* monadelphous, included, the five with rounded anthers only a little longer than the others; *anthers* orange-coloured; *pollen-granules* very small and nearly spherical. *Pistil* longer than the stamens; *stigma* very small, capitate; *style* subulate, glabrous, shining; *germen* silky; *ovules* several. Unripe *Legumes* erect, silky-woolly, subcylindrical, tapering and connivent at their apices." *Graham.*

MEDICAGO CARSTIENSIS.
CREEPING-ROOTED MEDICK.

Medicago carstiensis.

PLATE 290

This species of medicago is undoubtedly distinct from all the supposed varieties of *Medicago polymorpha*, particularly in having a perennial creeping root and upright, square, almost shrubby stalks.

Found by Bursati in the Carstian mountains in Carniola, by whom seeds were sent to Professor Jacquin. Although seemingly considered by him as entirely new, it was known to some of the older Botanists; Ray gathered his plant in the mountains of Carinthia. Reichard, in his edition of the *Species Plantarum*, added the Synonyms of Ray and Morisson to the *ciliaris*, in which he was followed by Professor Martyn, in his edition of *Miller's Dictionary*; but Willdenow is certainly right in having applied them to this plant.

OPPOSITE:
289 Lupinus incanus (t. 3283 1833 JM)

290 *Medicago carstiensis* (t. 909 1806 SE)

Flowers in June and July; is a hardy perennial, but like other alpine plants, apt to perish in our humid winters.

Our drawing was taken from a plant sent us by Mr. Loddiges. We had also a specimen some years before from the Botanic Garden at Brompton. We learn from Mr. Donn, in his *Hortus Cantabrigiensis*, that it was introduced in 1790, probably by himself.

MIMOSA PUBESCENS.
HAIRY-STEMMED MIMOSA.

Acacia pubescens.

PLATE 291

Jussieu has remarked, that the numerous species of mimosa must hereafter be divided into distinct genera, according to the number of their stamens and the form of their seed-pod. Willdenow, by restoring Tournefort's Acacia and Plumier's Inga, has done this in part. But his division appearing to us insufficient, we prefer the continuing to give the species, as they may occur, under mimosa, until some Botanist

shall have made a scientific arrangement of the whole, as the only way to avoid the frequent changing of names.

When planted in the border of the conservatory, this makes a very elegant tree, with long pendent branches, thickly clothed with a beautiful foliage, and covered in the spring with a profusion of fragrant flowers. Altogether, it is one of the greatest ornaments of the greenhouse; but being difficultly propagated, except by seeds, which it will not produce in this country, it is not likely to become very common. Native of New South Wales. Our drawing was made at Messrs. Lee and Kennedy's nursery at Hammersmith.

291 *Mimosa pubescens* (t. 1263 1810 SE)

MIMOSA STRICTA.
TWIN-FLOWERED MIMOSA.

Acacia stricta.

PLATE 292

Willdenow has thought fit to restore the old name of Acacia, considering the sensitive plants as a distinct genus, for which he retains the name of mimosa; but as other divisions of this too extensive genus must be made, which cannot be properly executed without comparing the seed-pods, we think it safest at present to arrange all

292 *Mimosa stricta* (t. 1121 1808 SE)

these plants, as heretofore, under the name of mimosa; for as few of them ever produce ripe seed in Europe, no attempt to divide them can be successful, till some Botanist, who has an opportunity of examining their fruit, shall undertake it.

All the simple-leaved mimosas show pinnated leaves in the seedling plant; whence it may be doubted whether they are not in reality leafless, having only dilated leaf-stalks; but, as these are veined like leaves, there can be no doubt but that they perform the function of such; we have not hesitated to adopt the common language, without entering into the question whether they are properly leaves or not.

ONONIS NATRIX.
YELLOW-FLOWERED REST-HARROW.
Ononis natrix.

PLATE 293

The *Ononis natrix*, a plant usually to be met with in all general collections of greenhouse plants, is a native of Spain, and the South of France, where it is said to grow wild in the corn fields.

The general practice sanctioned by that of Mr. Aiton, is to consider this species as tender; Mr. Miller says it is very hardy, and recommends it to be planted in the open border, a treatment likely to suit it in mild winters; there is, however, one part of his account evidently erroneous, he describes the root as perennial, and the stem as herbaceous, this is not only contrary to Linnæus's specific description, but to fact, the stalk being undoubtedly shrubby.

As this plant in the course of a year or two is apt to grow out of form, it is advisable either to renew it frequently by seed, which it produces in abundance, or to keep it closely cut in.

It flowers from the middle of summer till towards the close, and is propagated readily either by seeds or cuttings.

It is no novelty in this country, having been cultivated by Mr. James Sutherland in 1683.

293 *Ononis natrix* (t. 329 1796)

ONONIS ROTUNDIFOLIA.
ROUND-LEAVED REST-HARROW.
Ononis rotundifolia.

PLATE 294

Professor Jacquin, and most modern writers on Botany, consider the *Ononis* here figured, as the *rotundifolia* of Linnæus; it accords certainly with the figure of Dodon. to which that author refers, but is irreconcileable with his description; the leaves for example are neither *parva, integerrima,* nor *glabra,* the words by which Linnæus describes them; they are indeed evidently serrated in the figure of Dodon. which he quotes: by the name of *rotundifolia,* however, this plant is now very generally known in our nurseries, to which its beauty has gained it admission. Lobel tells us in his *Adversaria,* printed in 1576, that the plant was then growing in the garden of a Mr. Morgan; as it is not enumerated in Mr. *Miller's Dictionary,* ed. 6, 4to. We suspect that it has been lost out of the country and re-introduced.

Baron Haller informs us, that it is found wild in abundance at the bottom of the Alps in Switzerland; it is found also in other parts of Europe.

It flowers in our open borders from May to July, in which it ripens its seeds, by which it is in general propagated, as also by slips; it grows to about the height of a foot and a half, is very hardy, and easy of culture.

*The flowers of his *rotundifolia* are yellow, and therefore cannot be our plant.

OROBUS VARIUS.
PARTICOLOURED BITTER-VETCH.
Lathyrus pannonicus subsp. *varius.*

PLATE 295

Orobus angustifolius, albus, and *varius,* have so near an affinity to each other, that some Botanists have considered them as mere varieties; they appear to us however to be sufficiently distinct species. Our plant is distinguished by the winged stalk, which is more spreading and branched, by the greater number of pairs of leaflets and of flowers on one peduncle, and by the colour of the latter, which does not seem disposed to vary.

294 *Ononis rotundifolia* (t. 335 1796)

295 *Orobus varius* (t. 675 1803 SE)

It appears to have been known to Miller before the year 1759, but was probably soon lost. In the new edition by Professor Martyn, we find no trace of it, though we have frequently observed it in different collections about London for these five years past. A native of Italy, and sufficiently hardy to bear the cold of our winters. Easily propagated by offsets from the roots, but rarely produces seed with us. Is worthy of culture, both to ornament the parterre and particularly for mixing with other flowers in the formation of bouquets.

Orobus versicolor of Gmelin is probably our plant, but as we have not had it in our power to examine the figure he refers to, and as neither Willdenow nor Martyn have adopted it, we have rather chose to retain the name by which it is well known in our gardens, than upon uncertain grounds to

follow an author whose innumerable blunders have rendered his work nearly obsolete.

OXYTROPIS PILOSA.

HAIRY OXYTROPIS.

Oxytropis pilosa.

PLATE 296

This herbaceous perennial is clothed in every part except the corolla with longish, patent, grey hairs. *Stem* upright, rounded, but little branched. *Stipules* lanceolate, somewhat oblique, inserted below the petioles. *Leaves* alternate, pinnate: *leaflets* about nine pair with an odd one, lanceolate, rounded at the base, reflexed.

Peduncles axillary, stout, cylindrical, longer than the leaves. *Flowers* sessile, in an oblong spike, yellowish green. *Bracts* subulate, the length of the five-toothed *Calyx: teeth* subulate, the two lateral ones the longest. *Vexillum* oval, with sides reflexed, emarginate, *alæ* shorter than the vexillum. *Carina* equal to the *alæ*, sharp-pointed, one-petaled. *Stamens* diadelphous $9/1$. *Germen* linear, silky: *Style* ascending, half the length of the germen.

Native of Austria, Caucasus, and Siberia. Flowers in June. Communicated by Mr. William Anderson from the Chelsea Garden, where it was introduced by Dr. Fischer, late of Gorenki, now of the Royal Botanic Garden, St. Petersburgh.

296 Oxytropis pilosa (t. 2483 1824 JC)

PLAYTLOBIUM TRIANGULARE.

TRIANGULAR-LEAVED FLAT-PEA.

Platylobium obtusangulum.

PLATE 297

297 Platylobium triangulare (t. 1508 1812 SE)

The separation of *Bossiæa* from *Platylobium* has limited very much the number of species of the latter. We know of only three that will now come under this genus, *P. formosum*, *P. parviflorum*, of which we intend soon to give a figure, and our present plant, which was not known to Dr. Smith when he published his account of the genus in the ninth volume of the *Transactions of the Linnean Society*.

The flowers of *Platylobium triangulare* are less brilliant than those of *formosum*; the back part of the vexillum being of a slate colour instead of fine dark red; on which account the buds are totally destitute of that richness of colouring so much admired by Mr. Curtis in his account of the latter.

Native of Van Diemen's Island, from whence it was introduced into the Kew Garden, by Mr. Brown, in the year 1805. Flowers in June and July. Propagated by seeds, which rarely come to maturity in this country; and not being easily increased in any other way, will probably never be very common. Out of Kew Garden we have not observed it in any collection, except that of Messrs. Loddiges and Sons in Hackney, by whom it was communicated to us.

PODALYRIA LUPINOIDES.

LUPINE-LEAVED PODALYRIA.

Thermopsis lupinoides.

PLATE 298

Podalyria lupinoides, though introduced to this country by the Duke of Northumberland as early as 1775, is still very rare. Mr. Loddiges, to whom we are indebted for the plant from which our drawing was taken, has been in possession of it several years, having raised it from seeds procured from Siberia, but was never so fortunate as to flower it till June 1810, and then but imperfectly; for, when in perfection, it has a long verticillate spike. Some of Pallas's specimens, however, in the possession of A. B. Lambert, Esq. have, like our drawing, a single whorl of flowers only.

The leaves and stipules are covered with a soft silky pubescence; the former, in our plant, were mostly imperfect, consisting of a single sessile leaflet, besides the leaf-like stipules: when perfect, the leaf is ternate, with a footstalk.

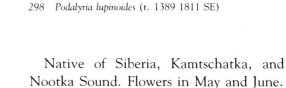

298 Podalyria lupinoides (t. 1389 1811 SE)

Native of Siberia, Kamtschatka, and Nootka Sound. Flowers in May and June. Hardy; but requires to be carefully protected from slugs.

299 Psoralea bracteata (t. 446 1799 SE)

PSORALEA BRACTEATA.

OVAL-SPIKED PSORALEA.

Psoralea bracteata.

PLATE 299

The old authors, and indeed Linnæus himself at first, regarded this plant as a *Trifolium*; afterwards the latter changed it to *Psoralea*, and minutely described it in his *Mantissa*.

As a greenhouse plant, this small and delicate species has long been cultivated, and still continues to hold a place in all collections of note.

Its inflorence to us has more the appearance of a *capitulum* than a *spike*, and which when the plant is in full bloom, is by no means ovate, but rather hemispherical; the purple colour of the vexillum, contracted with the white of the alæ, gives to the flowers a very pleasing particoloured appearance. In its leaves we have a good example of the *folium mucronatum*.

It is a native of the Cape, flowers in June and July, and is usually propagated by cuttings.

300   *Psoralea melilotoides* (t. 2063 1819)

PSORALEA MELILOTOIDES.

MELILOT-LIKE PSORALEA.

Psoralea melilotoides.

PLATE 300

Mr. Nuttall, chiefly on account of the absence of glands and the small size of the carina, refers this to Tournefort's genus *Melilotus*; but as it has as many of the characters of *Psoralea*, and may, as Mr. Nuttall allows, be considered as a connecting link between the two genera, we rather retain it in the latter genus, to which it has already been referred by Michaux, Persoon, and Ventenat.

It does not appear that this very rare plant has ever been known in our gardens till introduced by Mr. John Fraser, of Sloane Square, to whom we are indebted for an opportunity of giving a drawing of it, as it is not to be found in the catalogues of the Kew or Cambridge gardens, nor in Mr Sweet's excellent *Hortus Suburbanus*.

Native of North America, from Carolina to Florida, also of the open forests of Ohio, Kentucky, and Tennessee. Is not sufficiently hardy to bear our winters unprotected. Flowers in August, and continues long in blossom.

PULTENÆA BILOBA.

LOBED-LEAVED PULTENÆA.

Pultenæa scabra.

PLATE 301

Descr. *Stem* shrubby, branched; *branches* patent, clothed with white branched hairs: *branchlets* short, alternate, subequal, bearing from two to four flowers, in a terminal capitulum. *Leaves* wedge-shaped, ciliated, divided at the apex, into two lobes with a short recurved mucro between them, tubercular on the upper surface, and silky on the under, with recurved margins. *Stipules* deciduous, black, patent. *Calyx* campanulate, with a five toothed border; *teeth* acute, lengthened: *bracts* (appendixes of Smith) two, lanceolate, attached to the upper part of the tube of the calyx. *Corolla* papilionaceous: *vexillum* suborbiculate, emarginate, subconnivent, golden yellow. *Alæ* smaller, oblong, of the same colour. *Carina* two-petaled, dark purple. *Filaments* distinct. *Style* longer than these: *stigma* simple.

Pultenæa biloba is a very pretty lively little shrub, producing from April to July, abundance of golden yellow flowers with a dark purple keel. It is most nearly allied to

Pultenæa scabra of the *Hortus Kewensis*, from which however it is very distinct, the leaves of the latter being oblong-wedge-shaped, and truncated, not dilated into two lobes at the apex, as in our plant, in which also the stipules are not recurved, but patent, or sometimes upright.

We are indebted to our friend Mr. Robert Brown, for his assistance in determining this species, by whom it was first discovered in New South Wales. Raised from seeds by Messrs. Loddiges and Sons some years ago, by whom it was communicated to us.

301   *Pultenaea biloba* (t. 2091 1819 JC)

PULTENÆA STIPULARIS.

SCALY PULTENÆA.

Pultenæa stipularis.

PLATE 302

The name of *Pultenæa* has been given to this genus by Dr. E. Smith, in honour of Wm. Pulteney, M. D. of Blandford in Dorsetshire, whose various writings have so essentially contributed to the introduction and establishment of Linnean Botany in this country, and to the promotion of the useful arts connected with Botany, more especially Agriculture. It takes the name of *stipularis*, from its stalk being covered with scale-like stipulæ.

N.º 475

302   *Pultenaea stipularis* (t. 475 1800 SE)

Seeds of this species have been introduced to this country with some of the first productions of New Holland, the plant has flowered in several collections near town. It is but seldom, however, that this species can be brought to blossom, or even be kept alive here for any length of time, if treated in the way that greenhouse plants usually are; possibly it would succeed better with a warmer regimen. It flowers in April and May, and is to be raised only from imported seed.

ROBINIA HALODENDRON.

SALT-TREE ROBINIA.

Halimodendron halodendron.

PLATE 303

Lamarck has divided the genus *Robinia*, and arranges this species under his *Caragana*; but, whilst we confess that it ought to be separated from *Robinia pseudacaria, hispida*, &c. we think it will no more unite with *Caragana* than with them; nor do we know any other species of which it is properly a congener: we therefore follow the generality of Botanists, and refer it, for the present, to robinia.

This beautiful shrub thrives well with us in the open air, but is said to be in general very shy of flowering, which has been attributed to the want of salt in the soil, as its native place is in the dry barren salt fields on the borders of the River Irtis, in Siberia.

Introduced by the late Dr. William Pitcairn, in 1779. Our drawing was made at Messrs. Whitley and Brame's, Old Brompton. Flowers in June and July. Propagated by seeds, also by layers and grafting.

SCHOTIA TAMARINDIFOLIA.

BROAD-LEAVED SCHOTIA.

Schotia afra (L.) Thumb.

PLATE 304

Although the leaflets of this plant are considerably broader than in *Schotia speciosa*, more obtuse, even frequently emarginate, and rarely mucronate, and have the internal margin hollowed, so as to give them somewhat of a kidney shape, we should nevertheless have been inclined to consider them as mere varieties, had not our learned friend. Professor Afzelius, in a paper long since read before the Linnean Society but not yet published, made them distinct. The confidence we have in his accuracy will not permit us to doubt but that he had sufficient grounds for so doing, and perhaps the legumen may afford sufficient distinctive characters, but unfortunately we have not been able to see that of *S. speciosa*. In *tamarindifolia* the legumen is large, broad, extremely flattened, much arched, with a remarkable thick margin at both sutures, depicted with veins, which take their rise from both margins, and branching into a beautiful network, entirely cover the sides of the legumen. The germen is pedicellated, but the pedicel not increasing in length with the growth of the legumen, becomes in the latter nearly obsolete. In the Banksian Herbarium there is a third species with four pair of obcordate leaflets, and a legumen much less curved.

Our drawing was made at Mr. Woodford's, in whose collection at Springwell only, except at Kew, have we heard of this beautiful species being seen.

A native of the Cape of Good Hope, and requires the protection of a good greenhouse. Is propagated with difficulty by layers.

SPARTIUM JUNCEUM.

SPANISH BROOM.

Spartium junceum.

PLATE 305

Grows naturally in France, Spain, Italy, and Turkey; bears our climate extremely well; is a common shrub in our nurseries and plantations, which it much enlivens by its yellow blossoms: flowers from June to August, or longer in cool seasons. Is raised by seeds, which generally come up plentifully under the shrubs.

Miller mentions a variety of it, which, as inferior to the common sort, does not appear to be worth cultivating.

TEMPLETONIA GLAUCA.

GLAUCOUS-LEAVED TEMPLETONIA.

Templetonia retusa.

PLATE 307

The plant from which our drawing was taken was communicated by Mr. William Kent, from his curious collection of exotics at Clapton. It differs from *Templetonia retusa* chiefly in the glaucous colour of the *leaves*, which are obcordate-cuneate, slightly emarginate, with a small mucro: those on the young shoots are yellowish green and not at all glaucous. The *flowers* are large, of a deep scarlet colour, axillary, solitary, on short *peduncles*, which are furnished with two concave bracts close to the calyx, but not attached thereto. These bracts in *retusa* are described as being situated in the middle of the peduncle, and, if constant, this circumstance may afford a good distinguishing character. The *petals* are all nearly equal in length: *vexillum* oblong-ovate, emarginate, concave, in our plant not at all reflexed: *alæ* linear lanceolate: petals of the *carina* united at the tip. *Stamens*, which in *retusa* are described as monadelphous, were not altogether so; one of the filaments being shorter than the rest, and though slightly united, was easily separated to the base. *Germen* linear, pedi-

OPPOSITE:
303   TOP LEFT: *Robinia halodendron* (t. 1016 1807 SE)
304   TOP RIGHT: *Schotia tamarindifolia* (t. 1153 1808 SE)
305   BOTTOM LEFT: *Spartum junceum* (t. 85 1789)
306   BOTTOM RIGHT: *Virgilia capensis* (t. 1590 1813 SE)

Syd. Edwards Del.   Pub by T. Curtis St Geo Crescent Nov. 1 1808.   F. Sansom Sculp.

Pub. as the Act directs, June 1 1789, by W. Curtis, Botanic Garden, Lambeth Marsh.

Pub. by S. Curtis Walworth Oct 1 1813. Syd. Edwards Del. F. Sansom Sc.

cled: *ovula* several. *Style* nearly twice the length of the germen.

Native of the south-west coast of New Holland, where it was discovered by Robert Brown, Esq. who first established the genus *Templetonia*, Ventenat having referred it to *Rafnia*. Flowers in April and May.

307 *Templetonia glauca* (t. 2088 1819 JC)

Trifolium Lupinaster.
Lupine Trefoil.
Trifolium lupinaster.

PLATE 308

Our drawing, being taken from a specimen which grew in a pot, represents the plant of a much smaller size than usual; for when planted in the open ground it grows to the height of a foot and a half, and has larger leaves, is also branched and bears a number of heads of flowers on longer peduncles. The flowers growing from one side of the flattened end of the peduncle give the head a cristated appearance, forming what Linnæus calls *capitulum dimidiatum*; but in a more vigorous growth, the extremity of the peduncle turning further round, the head becomes globular, and the above appearance is confined to the more early state of the flowering. In habit this species

308 *Trifolium lupinaster* (t. 879 1805 SE)

approaches very near to the *Trifolium rubens*, the leaflets being very similar, except that they appear entirely sessile, from the membranous stipule running the whole length of the peduncle and closely embracing the stem. It is a singular deviation from the rest of the genus that it bears for the most part five, rarely six or seven leaflets upon one footstalk, nor can the two lower ones, as sometimes happens in Lotus, be well considered as enlarge stipules. The seed-pods are represented by *Buxbaum* as very long, but in our plant they are contained within the decayed remains of the flower, as described by Amman.

Raised from Siberian seeds by Mr. Loddiges of Hackney, but has several times been in our gardens before; is said in the *Hortus Kewensis* to have been first introduced by Mr. James Gordon in 1763, and we saw it in the late Dr. Pitcairn's collection in 1789. It has a susiform root and is but little disposed to produce offsets; hence if care is not taken to preserve the seed, of which very little will usually ripen with us, it must be liable to be soon lost. Is perfectly hardy.

Virgilia Capensis.
Vetch-leaved Virgilia.
Virgilia oroboides.

PLATE 306

Virgilia is distinguished from *Podalyria* by its compressed, not inflated, legume; by the vexillum not being reflexed at the sides; and widely by its habit.

This species varies much in the size of the leaflets; in some native specimens they are very narrow and small and seldom more than twelve-paired.

It is a very handsome greenhouse shrub, native of the Cape of Good Hope. Propagated by cuttings. Flowers in July and August. Introduced in 1767, by Thomas Cornwall, Esq.

Liliaceæ-Alliaceæ

Allium Flavum.
Yellow Garlic.
Allium flavum.

PLATE 309

Bulb with but a slight degree of the usual flavour of garlic; *integuments* thin, brow-

309 *Allium flavum* (t. 1330 1810 SE)

nish; *stem* one to two feet high; *valves* of the *spathe* three to nine inches long; the *bloom*, which has little or no scent while in the open air, is said, when placed in a room, to diffuse considerable fragrance. Differs from *paniculatum* and *pallens*, to both of which it is closely allied; from the first by its glaucous leaves and yellow umbel, as well as the roundness of the former, which are not strongly striate or ribbed on the back, as in *paniculatum*; from the second by the far greater proportionate length of both stamens and style. Native of Austria and the south of France. The specimen was communicated by Mr. Haworth.

310 *Allium obliquum* (t. 1408 1811)

ALLIUM OBLIQUUM.
TWISTED-LEAVED GARLIC.
Allium obliquum.
PLATE 310

Descr. *Bulb* scarcely of greater circumference than the stem with its sheathing leaves, of which it appears a mere continuation, integuments membranous brownish; *leaves* sheathing a stem one to three feet high for nearly half its length, six to eight, base of the blade in lower one nearly

an inch broad, in the upper ones gradually narrower; *flowers* of a greenish yellow colour, rather small; the whole plant, when bruised, emits a very rank smell of garlic. Native of Siberia. Blooms in May. Hardy. Cultivated by P. Miller in 1759. Our drawing was made from a plant in the collection of Mr. Haworth, the only one in which we have ever met it.

ALLIUM TARTARICUM.
TARTARIAN GARLIC.
Allium ramosum.
PLATE 311

There can be no doubt but that this is the *umbellatum* of Haller; scarcely any of its being the plant cited by Gmelin; and, as his figure corresponds well with the specimen of *ramosum* in Linnæus's Herbarium, this species of that author likewise. The specific name of *ramosum* seems to have had its rise from Gmelin's remark, that it has often, besides the fertile scape, a kind of false branch or sterile excrescence, which he calls "*crus solidum tenue;*" an excrescence which we have often seen

311   *Allium tartaricum* (t. 1142 1808 SE)

issue from the middle of the umbel of other species. Both authors describe the stamens of their plant as longer than the corolla, while the figure given by the one and cited by the other, shows the reverse to be the fact. A very common plant in most parts of Siberia. Introduced into Kew Gardens by Mr. Haneman in 1787. Blooms in May and June; the flowers are sweet-scented, but the plant, when bruised, emits a very rank smell of garlic. Varies greatly in the number and closeness of the radii of its umbel. One of the most ornamental of the genus.

312   *Allium victorialis* (t. 1222 1809 SE)

ALLIUM VICTORIALIS.
LONG-ROOTED GARLIC.
Allium victoriale.
PLATE 312

Descr. *Bulb* within the loose outer netted coverings of a deep purple colour, growing out into long thick fleshy sistular stem-sheathing *petioles*, which terminate in broad flattish elliptically-lanceolate green blades, from four to six inches long, from half an inch to near two in breadth; *corolla* of dirty subdiaphanous white colour, sometimes suffused with red; the whole plant, when bruised, has a very rank scent of garlic. Native of Spain, Italy, France,

Switzerland, and Germany. The root was considered by the Bohemian miners, when worn as an amulet, to be a safeguard against the attacks of certain impure spirits, to which they deemed themselves exposed; among them it was surnamed *siegwurz* (Root of Victory); hence *victorialis*. By the shepherds of other districts it has been used internally as a preservative against the effects of fogs and noxious exhalations; a purpose to which every species of garlic is more or less adapted.

Our drawing was taken at Mr. Salisbury's Botanic Garden.

lar; one on each alternate filament, and not, as described in the *Linnean Transactions*, two on each fertile filament. Our view of these parts has, besides the appearance we have mentioned, the sanction of analogy, as well as the opinion of a very accomplished Botanist, who has repeatedly examined them in specimens collected by himself in their native regions. Of easy culture, and blooms freely.

This undoubtedly is the *Aloë vera* of Miller, and the *perfoliata var. succotrina* of Mr. Aiton, that which produces the Succotrine Aloes of the shops, and is said to grow in the Island of Zocotra or Socotora, in the Straits of Babelmandel; it is therefore highly interesting as a medicinal plant, and very desirable as an ornamental one.

It is propagated by offsets, which it does not produce in any great plenty, and to have it in perfection, it must be treated as a dry stove plant.

LILIACEÆ-ALOEACEÆ

SOWERBÆA JUNCEA.
RUSH-LEAVED SOWERBÆA.

Sowerbæa juncea.

PLATE 313

Sowerbæa juncea is native of New Holland. Although now common in our greenhouses, it has so happened that we have missed every opportunity of examining the bloom. From a dissection of the stamens, given in the *Botanist's Repository*, the anthers appear to us to be three and bilocu-

ALOE LINGUA.
COMMON TONGUE-ALOE.

Gasteria maculata.

PLATE 315

Native of the Cape of Good Hope. One of the commonest ornaments of our greenhouses and parlour windows. Cultivated by Miller. Blooms most part of the summer. Propagated with the greatest facility by offsets. We are obliged to Mr. Haworth for the specimens of all the varieties here engraved.

ALOE RETUSA.
CUSHION ALOE.

Haworthia retusa.

PLATE 314

Though the flowers of this aloe have little to recommend them, there is much to admire in the form and structure of its leaves; and this pleasing circumstance attends it, it is perfectly distinct from all the other species: when first introduced, it was no doubt an object of great admiration; Fairchild, the celebrated Gardener of Hox-

313 Sowerbæa juncea (t. 1104 1808 SE)

314 Aloe retusa (t. 455 1799 SE)

ALOE PERFOLIATA, *VAR.* SUCCOTRINA.
SUCCOTRINE ALOE.

Aloe succotrina.

PLATE 316

The figure here given was drawn in January 1799, from a plant in full bloom in the dry stove of the Apothecaries Garden at Chelsea; Mr. Fairbairn informs me that it flowers regularly each year: the plant itself, supposed to be fifty years old, has a stem the thickness of one's arm, naked for the space of about four feet from the ground, then dividing into several large heads, formed of the leaves growing in clusters, from the centre of which arise the flowering-stems, two feet or more in length, producing spikes of flowers frequently much longer than those represented on the plate; these before they open are upright, when fully blown they hang down, and when out of bloom they turn upwards.

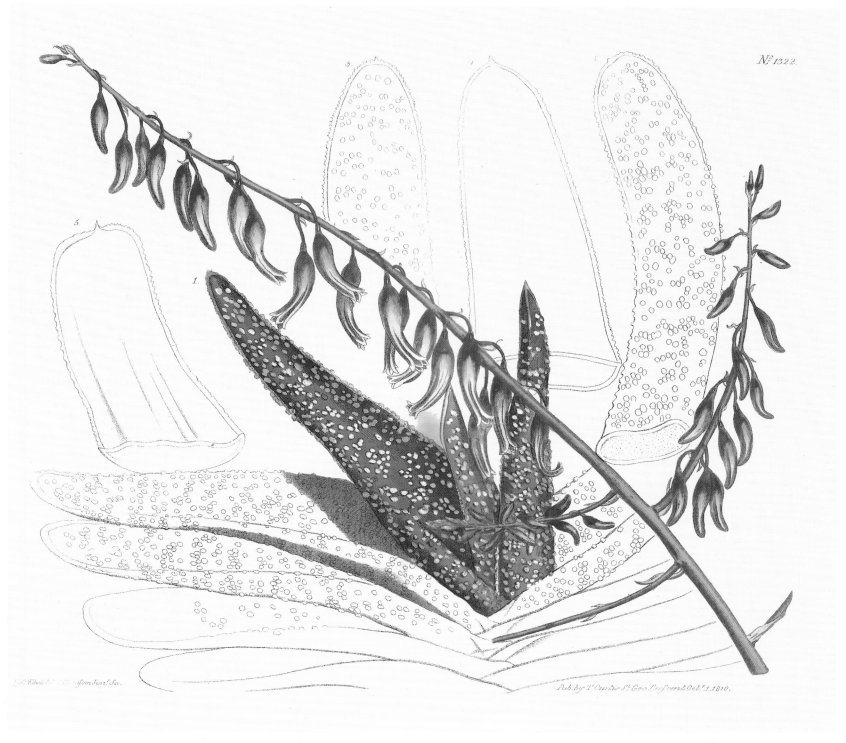

No. 1322.

315 *Aloe lingua* (1322 1810 SE)

ton, who preceded Miller, had it engraved, with several other succulents, on a plate which is prefixed to Dr. Blair's *Botanic Essays*, and which he inscribed to the Doctor, betwixt whom and Mr. Fairchild there appears to have subsisted a great degree of intimacy: the Essays were printed in 1720.

This species is a native of the Cape, and flowers in June, but not regularly so, increases very fast by offsets: Mr. Aiton makes it as he does all the aloes indiscriminately, dry stove plants, but it may be kept in a good greenhouse, taking care to place

it in the driest and most airy part, and to guard it at all times from much wet, but more especially in the winter season.

PHYLLOMA ALOIFLORUM.

THE BOURBON ALOE.

Lomatophyllum purpureum.

PLATE 317

Stem in our oldest specimens about eight feet high, and nearly the thickness of a

man's thigh; *leaves* smooth, about three feet long, two to three inches broad at their base, of a clear green colour; *corolla* about three-parts of an inch long, with the circumference of a common quill, yellow suffused with brownish red on the outside. Native of the Island of Bourbon. Introduced into this country in 1766, by Mons. Richard. A stove plant.

Our drawing was made from a specimen that flowered at the Apothecaries Garden, Chelsea, in June last, where it often ripens its fruit, which is about the size and shape of a bullace-plum.

S.Edwards del. *Pub. by W.Curtis St Geo Crescent Mar.1 1800.* *F.Sansom sculp*

316 *Aloe perfoliata var. succotrina* (t. 472 1800 SE)

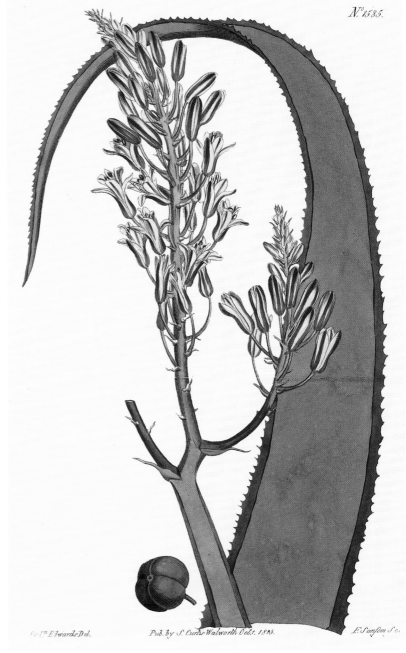

F.1. Edwards Del. *Pub. by S. Curtis Walworth Octr. 1813.* *F.Sansom Sc.*

317 *Phylloma aloiflorum* (t. 1585 1813 SE)

LILIACEÆ-ASPARAGACEÆ

EUSTREPHUS LATIFOLIUS.
BROADEST-LEAVED EUSTREPHUS.

Eustrephus latifolius.

PLATE 318

A genus instituted by the very able Botanist Brown, from whose, as yet unpublished, work the above characters have been, by his kind permission, extracted. It is a twining greenhouse shrub, lately introduced from Botany Bay; varies with leaves two or three times broader than those shown in the present figure.

Our drawing was made from a plant that flowered this summer at Messrs. Whitley and Brame's nursery, Old Brompton. Has been mistaken by the gardeners for *Medeola angustifolia.*

LILIACEÆ-ASPHODELACEÆ

ANTHERICUM ALOOIDES.
ALOE-LEAVED ANTHERICUM.

Bulbine alooides.

PLATE 319

A very old and very frequent inhabitant of our greenhouses. Native of the Cape of Good Hope, and cultivated by Dillenius in Sherard's Garden, at Eltham. We have to thank Mr. Haworth for the specimen.

ANTHERICUM LILIASTRUM.
SAVOY ANTHERICUM OR
ST. BRUNO'S LILY.

Paradisea liliastrum.

PLATE 320

Botanists are divided in their opinions respecting the genus of this plant; Linnæus considers it as an *Anthericum,* Haller and Miller make it an *Hemerocallis.*

It is a native of Switzerland, where, Haller informs us, it grows abundantly in the Alpine meadows, and even on the summits of the mountains; with us it flowers in May and June.

It is a plant of great elegance, producing on an unbranched stem about a foot and

318 *Eustrephus latifolius* (t. 1245 1809 SE)

319 *Anthericum alooides* (t. 1317 1810 SE)

half high, numerous flowers of a delicate white colour, much smaller but resembling in form those of the common white lily, possessing a considerable degree of fragrance, their beauty is heightened by the rich orange colour of their antheræ; unfortunately they are but of short duration. Miller describes two varieties of it differing merely in size.

A loamy soil, a situation moderately moist, with an eastern or western exposure, suits this plant best; so situated, it will increase by its roots, though not very fast, and by parting of these in the autumn, it is usually propagated.

Parkinson describes and figures it in his *Parad. Terrest.* observing, that "divers allured by the beauty of its flowers, had brought it into these parts."

320 *Anthericum liliastrum* (t. 318 1795 SE)

ANTHERICUM REVOLUTUM.
CURLED-FLOWERED ANTHERICUM.

Trachyandra revoluta.

PLATE 321

Descr. A fleshy *rootstock* from which descend several thick fleshy subsusiform fibres or roots. *Stem* upright, strict, round, compressed, paniculately and divaricately branched; *inflorescence* racemose; *racemes* several, straight, many-flowered, rather close;

pedicels rather shorter than the diameter of the corolla, filiform, upright, diverging but little; *bracts* shorter than these, membranous, ovate, convolute, awned-acuminate; *corolla* six-parted, revolutely radiate, at their base turbinately convergent for a very short space; *segments* linear-oblong, somewhat concave, obtuse, white, traversed by a green keeled line without, slightly unguiculate and marked with a kind of double yellow stain at the base within, inner ones nearly twice the broadest; *filaments* entirely hypogynous, not adnate to the segments, than which they are somewhat shorter, attenuately filiform, erect, fasciculately convergent, flattened downwards, and adpressed to the germen, where they are tomentosely pubescent, particularly the alternate ones, which are somewhat higher; *anthers* short-oblong; *style* erect, longer than stamens, filiformly slender, slightly curved; *stigma* an inconspicuous point; *germen* green, small, hexagonally obovate, perforated by three small pore-like apertures, from each of which issues a small drop of crystalline liquid, as in *Hyacinthus orientalis.*

A native of the Cape of Good Hope; cultivated in 1731, by Miller. Our drawing was made at the Nursery of Messrs. Whitley and Brame's, Old Brompton.

321 *Anthericum revolutum* (t. 1044 1807 SE)

322 *Asphodelus ramosus* (t. 799 1804 SE)

ASPHODELUS RAMOSUS.
BRANCHED ASPHODEL OR KINGSPEAR.
Asphodelus ramosus.
PLATE 322

The White or Branched Asphodel has roots composed of many thick fleshy fibres, to each of which is fastened an oblong tuber, as large as a small potato; the leaves are long and flexible, having acute edges, they grow in irregular clusters from the crown of the root, among these come out the stalks, which rise more than three feet high, sending out several side branches which are naked; the upper parts of these are adorned with many star-shaped flowers, which are white with a purplish line running longitudinally along the outside of each segment. They grow in long spikes, flowering successively from the bottom upwards. They appear the beginning of June and the seeds ripen in autumn.

Native of the south of Europe. Immense tracts of land in Apulia are covered with it, and it affords good nourishment to the sheep. Cultivated in 1596, by Gerard. Hardy. It does not increase very fast by roots, nor should it be often transplanted, for that will weaken it, so that the flower stems will not rise so tall, nor produce so

many flowers, as when left undisturbed for some years; therefore the best way is to propagate it by seeds. Mart. *Millers Dictionary* Clusius says, that on his way from Lisbon to Seville, he saw roots turned up by the plough of fifty pounds weight and upwards.

LILIACEÆ-ASPIDISTRACEÆ
ASPIDISTRA LURIDA.
DINGY-FLOWERED ASPIDISTRA.
Aspidistra lurida.
PLATE 323

Mr. Robert Brown has suggested, that there exists some affinity between this plant with *Tupistra* (*Bot. Mag* t. 1655), as established by Mr. Ker, whose generic character of our present subject in the *Botanical Register* we have adopted, with some little alteration. The flowers we examined had an eight-cleft, not six-cleft limb. The most remarkable character in the parts of fructification is the large stigma, filling the faux of the corolla, which is, in the *Register*, not unaptly compared to a mushroom in miniature.

Our drawing was taken in Mr. Colville's stove in the King's Road, in March last; but we could obtain no certain information of the country from whence it came.

323 *Aspidistra lurida* (t. 2499 1824 JC)

324 *Colchicum byzantinum* (t. 1122 1808 SE)

LILIACEÆ – COLCHICACEÆ
COLCHICUM BYZANTINUM.
BROAD-LEAVED COLCHICUM.
Colchicum byzantinum.
PLATE 324

Bulbs of this species were received by Clusius, while at Vienna, in 1598, from Constantinople. It has never yet been taken up as a species in any systematic enumeration of plants known to us. The bulb is the largest, the leaves the broadest, and the flowers the most numerous of any of the genus; the size of the first being equal to a man's fist, the breadth of the outermost leaf measuring sometimes near six inches, and we have seen from sixteen to twenty flowers thrown up in succession. The filaments are alternately shorter, and marked on the outside at the base with a tawny spot. The foliage is in perfection about the middle of May; the bloom early in the autumn.

Although cultivated here from the days of Parkinson, is now a rare plant in our gardens. Seems to be perfectly hardy.

S. Edwards del. Pub. by W. Curtis. St Geo. Crescent Mar.1.1809. F. Sansom sculp.

325 *Convallaria bifolia* (t. 510 1801 SE)

The specimen, from which our drawing was made, was the produce of a bulb imported from Holland last year.

LILIACEÆ-CONVALLARIACEÆ

CONVALLARIA BIFOLIA.
LEAST SOLOMON'S SEAL.

Maianthemum bifolium.

PLATE 325

There are few genera in which the parts of fructification vary so much, both in form and number, as in *Convallaria*; Linnæus makes three divisions of the species, first, such as have bell-shaped flowers, as Lily of the Valley; second, such as have funnel-shaped, as Common Solomon's Seal; and third, such as have wheel-shaped, as the present plant; the unripe spotted berry is said to afford a mark of distinction common to the whole; but how few are there who have an opportunity of seeing this in all the different species?

Most of these plants are ornamental, and many of them have been long cultivated in our gardens for their fragrance, and the beauty of their foliage or flowers; the pre-

sent small and delicate species was cultivated and figured by Mr. Miller in 1739.

It seldom rises above the height of four or five inches; the flowering stem is usually furnished with two, sometimes only one leaf, and is terminated by a loose spike of white flowers which appear in May, and with us are rarely succeeded by fruit.

"It is a native of the North of Europe, Holland, Germany, Switzerland, and Carniola. Mr. Miller gathered it near Haerlem and the Hague, where Mr. Ray had gathered it before on the 28th of May in flower." *Mart. Millers Dictionary*

Is a hardy perennial, increasing greatly by its creeping roots, on which and on other accounts, it is best kept in pots with the smaller alpines; plants which are regarded by me as so many beautiful cabinet pictures, to others they will not appear in the same light.

S. d. Edwards Del. Pub. by S. Curtis Walworth Aug.1.1811. F. Sansom Sc.

326 *Smilacina borealis* (t. 1403 1811 SE)

SMILACINA BOREALIS.
NORTHERN SMILACINA.

Clintonia borealis.

PLATE 326

Smilacina borealis was introduced into this country in 1778, by Dr. Solander, from Newfoundland and the neighbourhood of Halifax in Nova Scotia. We find also a

one-flowered smaller specimen, brought from the north-west coast of America, by Mr. A. Menzies, in the same Herbarium, which very probably belongs to a species distinct from both. We joined it with *umbellata* of Desfontaines, which was found by Michaux. Both species are hardy, and bloom together in June.

UVULARIA CHINENSIS.
BROWN-FLOWERED UVULARIA.

Disporum cantoniense.

PLATE 327

This singular as well as new species is (as we learn from the Banksian Herbarium) a native of China, and flowered two years ago in the Kew Gardens. Our drawing was made in September last from a plant that bloomed in Mr. Hibbert's conservatory at Clapham.

The following description is taken from a recently dried specimen, in which however the flowers were so far destroyed by pressure that we could not make out

327 *Uvularia chinensis* (t. 916 1806 SE)

S. d. Edwards del. Pub. by T. Curtis, St Geo. Crescent Sep.3.1806. F. Sansom sculp.

either the form or even site of the nectary, nor discover whether all or only the alternate segments terminated in the same kind of blunt spur-like knob.

Stem herbaceous, about a foot and half high, angular, subgeniculately flexuose, distantly leafy, branched upwards, branches simple, corymbosely arranged, patent: *leaves* ovate-lanceolate, acuminate, shortly petioled, nerved; those of the stem broader, elliptic, distant; those of the branches narrower, farther acuminate, and more closely set together; *racemes* one to four-flowered, rameous, axillary to the leaves, *pedicels* sasciculate; peduncle shorter than the sascicle, which last has a leafy bract at their base of the same form as the upper leaves, so that where there is a raceme it appears as if there were two opposite leaves; *corollas* cernuous, longer than pedicels, cupped-campanulate, brown without, knottedly angular at the base as if shortly and bluntly spurred; *stamens* equal to corolla and pistil; *filaments* subulate-linear, two to three times longer than the anthers; *germen* turbinately triquetral, several times shorter than the style, *stigmas* patent, revolutely recurved. This species differs from all its congeners yet known in the length of the filaments.

ly veined, generally somewhat twisted upwards, outer broader sublanceolate, inner more linear, all intersected on the inside by a longitudinal slender two-ridged furrow, terminated at the base by a small oblong melliferous green cavity, where they are also somewhat thickened, obsolutely turberculate and striate; on the outside gibbous; *stamens* twice as short as the corolla, upright, loosely surrounding the pistil; *filaments* inserted at the base of the corolla between the segments and the germen, membranous, linear, somewhat dilated at their base, inner rather shorter; *anthers* three times longer than these, linear-oblong, subsagitate, upright, fixed by their base, generally terminated by a small membranous inconspicuous mucro; *germen* green, obovate, obsoletely trigonal, six-furrowed, the corner furrows deepest; *style* longer than germen, straight, sulcately trigonal, as if of three filiform ones grown together; *stigmas* linear, but little shorter than style, recurvedly divergent, inwards glandularly pubescent. The whole plant is devoid of scent. Blooms the beginning of May. Perfectly hardy.

Our drawing was made from a plant imported last year by Mr. Williams, of Turnham-Green, from North America.

329   Uvularia perfoliata α (t. 955 1806 SE)

UVULARIA GRANDIFLORA.
LARGE YELLOW UVULARIA.
Uvularia grandiflora.
PLATE 328

According to Michaux, native of the highest mountains of Canada and Carolina. *Root* creeping; *stem* a foot or more high, round, enveloped downwards by several convolute streakedly membranous alternate unequal root-sheaths, upwards leafy and dichotomously branched; *branches* leafy, lax, flexuose, nutant; *leaves* many, alternate, perfoliate, lanceolate-ovate, undulate at the base, on the upper surface nerved-lineate, beneath hoary and covered with a close short velvety pubescence; *peduncles* filiform, rameous, axillary, one-flowered, recurved furnished about their middle with a leaflike *bract*, from one to four, bending into one rank; *corolla* yellow, pendulous, cernuous, turbinately campanulate, about an inch and half long; *segments* very slightly cohering at their base, oblong, striatulate and subreticulate-

328   Uvularia grandiflora (t. 1112 1808 SE)

UVULARIA PERFOLIATA (α).
PERFOLIATE UVULARIA.
Uvularia perfoliata.
PLATE 329

Since we have not seen the living specimen of this species, we do not pretend to add to or alter what has been said of the plant in the *Exotic Botany.* According to the figures, our plant seems to us to partake equally of Dr. Smith's *flava* and *perfoliata.* Michaux has two varieties, possibly his *perfoliata* (α) is the *flava* of Dr. Smith. We strongly suspect all these plants will be found to be mere varieties of each other: *perfoliata* (α) was found by Michaux in Canada and on the very high mountains of Carolina; *perfoliata* (β) in the mountains of middling height in Carolina and Virginia. Miller says the species is perfectly hardy, and should be planted in a hazel loam not too stiff nor wet; may be propagated by parting the roots about Michaelmas, but not oftener than every third year. Blooms in April and May.

LILIACEÆ-HEMEROCALLIDACEÆ

HEMEROCALLIS GRAMINEA.
NARROW-LEAVED DAY-LILY.

Hemerocallis minor.

PLATE 330

We have figured this species under two rather different appearances; the more entire one from a specimen actually raised from Siberian seeds, as its possessor Mr. Loddiges informed us; the single flower belonged to one that had long been cultivated in this country, probably a scion of the individuals imported in the days of Parkinson.

We have no doubt of this being a distinct species from *Hemerocallis flava*, from which it differs in having a mere scariose and shorter spathe: a corolla more truly campanulately ringent and ventricose; besides a pistil that exceeds but little the anthers, and is shorter than the corolla; the style is also thicker, tapers less, and the stigma more evidently trifid than in *flava*. Varies in the number of flowers. Blooms nearly at the same time as *flava*. The flowers are but slightly fragrant. Quite hardy and of easy culture.

331 *Hemerocallis caerulea* (t. 894 1805 SE)

330 *Hemerocallis graminea* (t. 873 1805 SE)

LILIACEÆ-HOSTACEÆ

HEMEROCALLIS CÆRULEA.
CHINESE DAY-LILY.

Hosta ventricosa.

PLATE 331

After the very detailed descriptions in the works of Redouté and Ventenat of this now not uncommon plant, it would be superfluous to add any further description to that contained in the specific character, which seems to distinguish it from *Hemerocallis japonica*, of which it has been deemed a variety by Willdenow.

A native of China; thought to bloom best in the stove; but thrives very well in a greenhouse; and some cultivators assure us, that it succeeds in the open ground better than with any other treatment.

Introduced by George Hibbert, Esq. Seeds freely, and is easily propagated by offsets. Our drawing was taken from a small few-flowered specimen.

LILIACEÆ-HYACINTHACEÆ

ALBUCA MAJOR.
LARGER ALBUCA.

Albuca major.

PLATE 332

Scarcely to be distinguished from *minor* but by its more robust stature and upright growth, as also perhaps by a bulb more apt to produce numerous offsets and somewhat smaller in proportion to the plant than that of *minor*. Our plant was formerly thought to be of Canadian origin, but is now well known to be a native of the Cape of Good Hope; was introduced here by Mr. William Malcolm, in 1767.

332 *Albuca major* (t. 804 1805 SE)

ALBUCA SETOSA.
BRISTLY-ROOTED ALBUCA.

Albuca setosa.

PLATE 333

Descr. *Leaves* about a foot and a half long, and about half an inch over towards their base; *stem* somewhat higher than these; *pedicels* two to three inches long, straight, about the thickness of a crow-quill; *bracts*

Pub. by S. Curtis Walworth Aug.t 1. 1812.

Syd.m Edwards Del. F. Sansom Sc.

N.o 1481.

333 *Albuca setosa* (t. 1481 1812 SE)

brownish; *corolla* rather more than an inch long, yellowish with a broad green stripe down the middle of each segment; *germen* green; *style* yellow, green at the angles; *capsule* brown, about the size of a filbert. Flowered in May; scent resembling that of bitter almonds, which however could only be perceived by smelling close to the bloom. Introduced by Mr. Masson in 1795, from the Cape of Good Hope.

ALBUCA VIRIDIFLORA.
GRASS-GREEN ALBUCA.

Albuca viridiflora.

PLATE 334

The thick laminæ which form the *bulb* are so compact as to give it the appearance of being solid, with somewhat of the look of a turnip-radish; *leaves* a foot or more long, about two lines broad near the base; *stem* round, about the thickness of a common pen, rather higher than the leaves; *peduncles* about two inches long; *bracts* sphace-late, brown, tapered; *flowers* scentless, about an inch in length, of a deep green colour, having a mixture of yellow in the inner segments; *anthers* pale.

Native of the Cape of Good Hope. Introduced into the Kew Gardens, by Mr. Masson, in 1794.

334   *Albuca viridiflora* (t. 1656 1814 SE)

335   *Albuca vittata* (t. 1329 1810 SE)

ALBUCA VITTATA.
RIBAND ALBUCA.

Ornithogalum vittatum.

PLATE 335

Bulb about the size of a pigeon's egg: *stem* (in our specimen) rather shorter than the *leaves*, which were about five or six inches long; *flowers* yellow; each petal-like segment intersected by a bright green vertical stripe or fillet.

Not recorded by any author known to us. Differs from *Anthericum albucoides* (the *Ornithogalum albucoides* of Thunberg's *Prodromus*? and, as far as we can judge from the specimen in the Banksian Herbarium, the *Ornithogalum secundum* of Jacquin and Willdenow) in having narrower leaves without a cartilaginous edging and striate on the outside; in having cernuously pendulous and not upright corollas; as well as in having alternate stamens with a bidentately alate membrane that reaches only half their length. But *Anthericum albucoides* (according to our conception of the genera) is, as well as this, an *Albuca*, not an *Ornithogalum*, much less an *Anthericum*. Blooms in the latter end of the summer. Native of the Cape of Good Hope, from whence it was introduced into this country by Mr. G. Hibbert, of Clapham.

EUCOMIS PUNCTATA.
SPOTTED-LEAVED EUCOMIS.

Eucomis comosa.

PLATES 337 AND 338

The trivial name is taken from the curious dotting on the stem and leaves. – Introduced by Mr. John Græfer, in 1783, from the Cape of Good Hope. Flowers in July. Its scent seems to us not unpleasant. The *leaves* do not lie flat on the ground as those of many of the species do; but are upright and divaricately patent; *pedicels* little longer than the corolla, about equal to the bractes, which are somewhat coloured and concave; *corolla* stellately patent and parted almost to the base; *filaments* shorter than corolla, connate, but only for a very little distance, divergent, somewhat incurved; both filaments and corolla are at first white, but turn green in time. *Germen* ovate-sastigate; style curved. A common greenhouse plant, of most easy culture.

HYACINTHUS RACEMOSUS.
STARCH HYACINTH.

Muscari neglectum.

PLATE 336

The *Hyacinthus racemosus* and *botryoides* are both cultivated in gardens, but the former here figured is by far the most common; *racemosus* and *botryoides*, though different words, are expressive of the same meaning, the former being derived from the Latin term *racemus*, the latter from the Greek one βοτρυς, both of which signify a bunch of grapes, the form of which the inflorescence of these plants somewhat resembles, and hence they have both been called Grape Hyacinths, but as confusion thereby arises, we have thought it better to call this species the Starch Hyacinth, the smell of the flower in the general opinion resembling that substance, and leave the name of Grape Hyacinth for the *botryoides*.

The *Hyacinthus racemosus* grows wild in the corn fields of Germany, in which it increases so fast by offsets from the root as to prove a very troublesome weed, and on this account it must be cautiously introduced into gardens. It flowers in April and May.

We have found the nurserymen very apt to mistake it for the *botryoides*, a figure of which it is our intention to give in some future number.

336   *Hyacinthus racemosus* (t. 122 1790 SE)

Publish'd as the Act directs June 1. 1790 by W.Curtis St George's Crescent.

155

337 *Eucomis punctata* (t. 1539 1813 SE)

338 *Eucomis punctata* (t. 913 1806 SE)

LACHENALIA LANCEÆFOLIA.
SPOTTED COPPERAS-LEAVED LACHENALIA.
Ledebouria revoluta.

PLATE 339

Leaves many, lying in a crowded circle round the stem, copperas-coloured, spotted, somewhat convolute upwards, and cowled at the base. *Stem* round, attenuated downwards, weak, generally recumbently assurgent, rachis interruptedly many-angled, owing to the decurrent bracts, of which many are barren and fit close to the side or under the sterile ones, all small and subulate. *Flowers* with deflex filiform pedicels, three times longer than the corolla, sparsely, but often crowdedly, disposed in an oblong raceme. *Corolla* regular, deep-

ly six-parted, virescent upwards, within thickset with liver-coloured confluent dots, segments with their apices glandularly thickened and inflectedly-retuse, linear-oblong, equal, inner ones recurved to the base, outer ones revolute and thence shorter; when impregnation has taken place these all unroll, and converging protect the germ while it ripens into a capsule. *Stamens* upright, adnate to the claws of the segments, shorter than style and corolla. *Style* inclined, slightly curved, rather shorter than corolla. *Germ* elevated within the corolla on stipitate receptacle.

A native of the Cape. Bulb and seed we have not an opportunity of observing, but their description will be found in Jacquin. We have seen a specimen having only three flowers and very narrow leaves. Flowers in October.

LACHENALIA ORCHIOIDES (α).
SPOTTED-LEAVED ORCHIS-LIKE LACHENALIA.
Lachenalia orchioides.

PLATE 340

This is a far more ornamental variety than that which has been already given in this present work; it is likewise very fragrant.

Our drawing was made at Mr. Loddiges's Nursery at Hackney. Native of the Cape of Good Hope.

339 *Lachenalia lanceaefolia* (t. 643 1803 SE)

340 *Lachenalia orchioides* α (t. 1269 1810 SE)

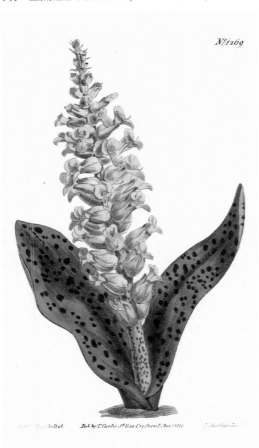

LACHENALIA QUADRICOLOR.
FOUR-COLOURED LACHENALIA.
Lachenalia aloides.

PLATE 341

We have no hesitation in pronouncing this to be a very distinct species from *Lachenalia pendula*, of which Willdenow considers it only a variety. It appears indeed to us to have greater affinity with *Lachenalia tricolor*, though sufficiently different from that also. The flowers chiefly differ from those of *pendula*, in having longer peduncles, the outer petals much shorter, and the inner more spreading at the mouth; they are also more distant, growing alternately on the scape, which is weaker. The leaves are much longer and more channelled, one of them longer than the other, and, as Jacquin remarks, erect at first, but reclined from above the middle; they come out from the bulb fistular and split open as they advance, and those of the young offsets not opening at all, have the appearance of a different plant growing in the same pot.

Our drawing was taken at Mr. Woodford's, Vauxhall, where it flowered the first time in February 1801, from bulbs imported from the Cape the preceding year.

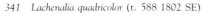

341 *Lachenalia quadricolor* (t. 588 1802 SE)

342 *Lachenalia tricolor* β *luteola* (t. 1020 1807 SE)

LACHENALIA TRICOLOR (β.) *LUTEOLA*.
YELLOW-FLOWERED LACHENALIA.
Lachenalia tricolor.

PLATE 342

From the specimen, preserved in the Banksian Herbarium, we find that the variety *tricolor* (α) of *Hortus Kewensis*, is the *Lachenalia quadricolor*, varying with spotted leaves; to which also the *tricolor* of the first volume of Jacquin's *Icones Plantes Rarairoes* belongs. These species are but too nearly allied; *quadricolor* however is altogether a slenderer plant, having narrower leaves, more channelled and acuminate, and not recumbent from the base, from whence they are on the contrary upright for some distance; the inner segments of its corolla are besides about twice the length of the outer, while the same in *tricolor* are only about one-third longer. Both propagate abundantly by offsets; and flower early in the spring. Quite scentless.

Our drawing was made at Mr. Williams's Nursery, Turnham-Green. A native of the Cape of Good Hope.

MASSONIA LATIFOLIA.
BROAD-LEAVED MASSONIA.
Massonia depressa.
PLATE 343

A native of the Cape of Good Hope, where it was found by Thunberg and Masson in Rogge-Veld country. Introduced into Kew Gardens by Mr. Francis Masson, in 1775.

Our drawing was taken at Mr. Woodford's from rather a small specimen. Is of easy culture, requiring to be kept in the greenhouse, where it flowers very early in the spring.

343 *Massonia latifolia* (t. 848 1805 SE)

ORNITHOGALUM SQUILLA (α).
COMMON RED-ROOTED SEA-ONION OR OFFICINAL SQUILL.
Urginea maritima.
PLATE 345

This well known vegetable is a native of all the countries bordering on the Mediterranean, as also of Brittany and Normandy; it has been found growing in the very sand of the seashore, and again, at the distance of a hundred miles inland, for instance, at the foot of the Estrella mountains; so that, as Link observes, *maritimum* is rather a fallacious appellation. By the Spaniards it is

called *Cebolla albarrana*. The bulbs are annually imported by our druggists, for whose purposes both varieties are used indifferently: they are esteemed powerfully diuretic, and administered chiefly in dropsical and asthmatical cases.

It blooms in July and August, the leaves appearing in October and November. Miller says the plant soon decays in our gardens, and attributes the decline to want of sea-water, which cannot, however, well be the cause, as its natural situation is often at a great distance from the sea, as we stated above; with us it has been preserved for these three years in vigour, planted in a large garden pot and sheltered during winter in a common garden frame; nor do we yet discover the least symptom of decay. The root is frequently as big as a child's head, and often, when fresh imported, throws out the flowering stem while lying in the shop windows; the spike is sometimes a foot or more in length; pedicels rather short, filaments nearly equal; seed-vessel alately three-lobed, a shape that Gærtner terms *molendinaccus*; seeds black, flat, chaff-like.

SCILLA AUTUMNALIS (α).
PURPLE-FLOWERED AUTUMNAL SQUIL.
Scilla autumnalis.
PLATE 344

We suspect our present variety to be of continental extraction, although the species is a native of our island; growing in several of the western districts, and has even been found in the neighbourhood of London. The bracts (which are generally obsolete or so inconspicuous that they have been overlooked and stated not to exist by most authors) were very evident, though minute, in the present specimen, which flowered in Mr. Hibbert's garden; Guettard, in his account of the plants growing about Estampes, is the only author we remember who mentions their presence; he terms them *tuberculi mamillares*. Desfontaines found this species on the coast of Africa with blue flowers; as did Link and Hoffmansegg in Portugal, where, as they state, its inflorescence precedes foliation; a circumstance also observed by Dr. Sims in this country, who supposes that when the leaves accompany the flowers, it is the less

natural mode, occasioned by a particular wet season; blooms from August to September.

The Portuguese Professor of Botany, Brotero, observes that the variety which he found in the province of Estremadura was twice the size of that which grew in the province of Beira; he does not notice the peculiarity in the flowering mentioned by Link and his fellow traveller.

The leaves grow on through the winter, dying away in the spring, after the manner of those of *Ornithogalum squilla.*

344 *Scilla autumnalis* α (t. 919 1806 SE)

SCILLA BREVIFOLIA.
ROOTSHEATHED CAPE SQUILL.
Dipcadi brevifolium.
PLATE 346

When the rootsheath does not unfold, but remains rolled together, enclosing the lower part of the foliage, (which is the case in many specimens where the root has grown somewhat deeper in the ground than that of ours) then the leaves have the appearance of being very short; and Thunberg's name characterizes the species much better than in the individual represented in our figure, where this is unrolled and the leaves

N.° 918

Pub. by T.Curtis, S.t Geo. Crescent Apr. 1. 1806. *Syd. Edwards del. F. Sansom sculp.*

345 *Ornithogalum squilla* α (t. 918 1806 SE)

lie open their whole length. *Scape* some-times nearly twice the length of the leaves, which are from two to near three inches long, and about a line and half broad. Comes very near to the *Hyacinthus corymbosus* of Thunberg, already given by us under the name of *Massonia corymbosa*; but which, we now think, should have been referred to *Scilla*. It differs, however, from that, in having a scape that is not shorter than the leaves, a raceme that is not erect and corymbose, by its large rootsheath and nearly obsolete bracts.

Imported from the Cape of Good Hope, by Messrs. Lee and Kennedy, in whose collection it flowered last January; and, as far as we can find, for the first time in any European garden.

SCILLA ESCULENTA.
MISSOURI SQUILL OR QUAMASH.

Camassia esculenta.

PLATE 347

Descr. *bulb* less than a common walnut; integuments brown; *scape* about a foot high; *leaves* rather shorter, broadest of them little more than half an inch over; *flowers* scentless, of a blueish grey or ash colour, about an inch in diameter when expanded; *anthers* yellow.

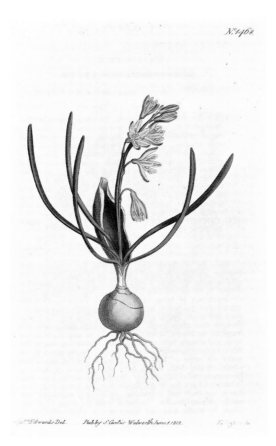

346 *Scilla brevifolia* (t. 1468 1812 SE)

We have added the synonym from the work of Mr. Pursh, in consequence of a communication that gentleman was so obliging as to make to us, in which he assured us, that Mr. Fraser's plant, from which our drawing has been made, was of the same species as that he had in view; otherwise we should have doubted its being so, not perceiving the slightest irregularity in the corolla of several specimens we examined. We have not had an opportunity of seeing the figure in Mr. Pursh's work, which is not yet published.

The specific name of Quamash that gentleman makes use of, is the appellation given to the plant by certain Indians in the neighbourhood of the Missouri River, in whose country it is spontaneous, and where it serves them as a principal article of food during the winter. The specimens we saw, in our judgment, seemed to belong to *Scilla* and not to *Phalangium*.

A hardy plant. Blooms in May. Our drawing was made from a plant imported by Mr. Nuttall, which flowered at Mr. Fraser's Nursery, in Sloane Square.

348 *Erythronium americanum* (t. 1113 1808 SE)

347 *Scilla esculenta* (t. 1574 1813 SE)

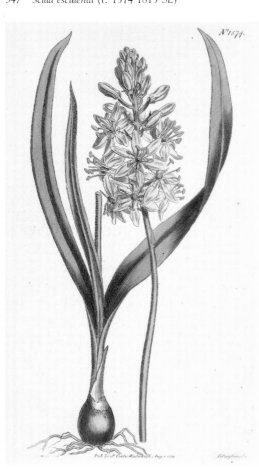

LILIACEÆ

ERYTHRONIUM AMERICANUM.

YELLOW-FLOWERED DOG'S-TOOTH-

VIOLET.

Erythronium americanum.

PLATE 348

Bulb solid, ovate pyramidal, about the size of a filbert, covered with membranous dark brown coats; *leaves* coriaceous, two, distich, lanceolately elliptic, intersected by a longitudinal furrow, carinately ribbed beneath, glaucous-green, variegated with liver-coloured blotches, (when looked at through a magnifying glass, are found to be shagreened or roughened by minute pointed tubercles) standing on narrow convolute petioles, the one of which envelopes the other, while both sheath the lower part of the one-flowered naked scape, with which they are concrete below; *corolla* deep yellow; outer segments broader and more reflex; *filaments* inserted between the base of the pistil and that of the corolla, upright, linear, flat, submembranous, adpres-

sed to the germen, longer than the *anthers*, which are yellow; *style* green, stigmatose opening, pubescent within, projecting beyond the stamens; *germen* green, obovate, obsoletely trigonal, three times shorter than style, corners furrowed.

Native of North America, and but recently introduced into our gardens. Differs from the European species, with which it has been generally confounded, in having a green triquetrally club-shaped style, not terminating in three recurvedly patent foldingly channelled stigmas; nor did we perceive any traces of the nectaries found at the bases of the segments of the corolla in *Dens canis*, nor of the transverse appendages of the three inner ones of the same. But of this circumstance we cannot speak with certainty, as the bloom was considerably faded when we obtained it for examination. Sent to us in bloom last April, by Mr. Loddiges, of Hackney, and also by Mr. Salisbury, of the Botanic Garden, Brompton.

349   *Fritillaria imperialis* β (t. 347 1796 SE)

350   *Fritillaria latifolia* γ *lutea* (t. 1538 1813 SE)

FRITILLARIA IMPERIALIS (β).
YELLOW CROWN IMPERIAL.
Fritillaria imperialis f. *lutea.*

PLATE 349

In the already so often cited Pallasian Herbarium, at Mr. A. B. Lambert's, there are many specimens of *verticillata* (Willdenow *Species Plantarum* 2. 91) under the name of *altaica*, collected in Asiatic Russia and southern Siberia; in these we find so close a resemblance to *imperialis*, that we strongly suspect that they are but one and the same species; and that the differences, which chiefly consist in the number and size of the flowers and leaves, have been merely produced by culture; in *verticillata*, however, the foliage is whorled and very regularly so, which is only partially and very inconstantly the case in *imperialis.*

FRITILLARIA LATIFOLIA. (γ.) LUTEA.
YELLOW FRITILLARY.
Fritillaria collina.

PLATE 350

The present variety has been considered by Mr. Marschal and some others, as a distinct species from *latifolia*; but as no characters, beyond those of size and colour, have been adduced to separate the species, we being unable to detect any others, have continued them as varieties. All are found on Caucasus; the yellow in particular near Kasbek. The capsule is obtuse-angular. Mr. Marschal observes, that in garden specimens, the leaves are more conspicuously alternate, or placed at wider distances from each other than in spontaneous ones. All are perfectly hardy.

FRITILLARIA MINOR.
LESSER ALTAIC FRITILLARY.
Fritillaria meleagroides.

PLATE 351

Of the genus *Fritillaria*, so called from *fritillus* a *dicebox*, on account of the shape of the flower, though the chequered blossom rather recalls the idea of a *diceboard*, nineteen species are enumerated by Sprengel, all remarkable for their large and gracefully drooping flowers, which render them universal favourites with cultivators. Of these, the greater number, perhaps the only legitimate species, are natives of central or southern Europe or northern Asia. The present new species was discovered by Professor Ledebour, in pastures of the Altai Mountains, and having flowered at Carlowrie, near Edinburgh, early in May of the

351 *Fritillaria minor* (t. 3280 1833 JM)

present year, we are indebted to Dr. Graham for the following description and remarks.

This plant was obtained by David Falconar, Esq. from Mr. Goldie, who brought it from Russia. It varies a little from the wild state. I have native specimens both from Dr. Fischer of St. Petersburg and from Professor Ledebour. The former are smaller, but the inflorescence is larger, and the leaves, which are longer and narrower, are collected nearer to the flower. Even in a wild state, it appears from Ledebour, that occasionally, though rarely, there are more flowers than one on the stem, and the two lowest leaves are sometimes subopposite.

I cannot but think that this plant scarcely differs more from F. *meleagris* than some of the acknowledged varieties of this species. The great length of the pendulous part of the stem or peduncle, which Ledebour considers characteristic, and which is figured in his beautiful illustrations of the *Flora Altaica*, is not possessed by my native specimens, nor by Mr. Falconar's plant, and the flower in the figure is much less lurid, and longer in proportion to its breadth, than any of these.

Bulb roundish, white, about the size of a small hazel nut, with many slender roots from its base. *Stem* (in native specimens, from seven inches to a foot high, in the

cultivated specimen one foot ten inches) erect, simple, single-flowered in native plants, and almost always so in such, according to Ledebour, in the cultivated ones three-flowered, promoso-glaucous, brown and speckled towards its base, obscurely three-sided, naked for a considerable way above the base.

FRITILLARIA PERSICA. (α.)
LARGEST PERSIAN FRITILLARY.

Fritillaria persica.

PLATE 352

Fritillaria persica is probably of Persian origin. The root is observed to be free from the offensive smell of its congener the Crown-imperial; but to make up for this the taste of it is, according to John Bauhin, horribly bitter. It appears to be perfectly hardy, and easily propagated by its bulbs; yet is less common than it deserves, being a very desirable flower.

352 *Fritillaria persica* α (t. 1537 1813 SE)

LILIUM BULBIFERUM.
ORANGE LILY.

Lilium bulbiferum.

PLATE 353

"The common orange or red Lily is as well known in the English gardens as the White Lily, and has been as long cultivated here. This grows naturally in Austria and some parts of Italy. It multiplies very fast by offsets from the roots, and is now so common as almost to be rejected: however, in large gardens these should not be wanting, for they make a good appearance when in flower, if they are properly disposed; of this sort there are the following varieties: The orange Lily with double flowers, The orange Lily with variegated leaves, The smaller orange Lily.

These varieties have been obtained by culture, and are preserved in the gardens of florists. They all flower in June and July, and their stalks decay in September, when the roots may be transplanted and their offsets taken off, which should be done once in two or three years, otherwise their branches will be too large, and the flower-stalks weak. This doth not put out new roots till towards spring, so that the roots may be transplanted any time after the

353 *Lilium bulbiferum* (t. 36 1788 JS)

N.º 1591

354   *Lilium japonicum* (t. 1591 1813 SE)

stalks decay till November. It will thrive in any soil or situation, but will be strongest in a soft gentle loam, not too moist."
Millers Dictionary

Bears the smoke of London better than many plants. Varies with and without bulbs on the stalks.

LILIUM JAPONICUM.
WHITE ONE-FLOWERED JAPAN LILY.

Lilium brownii var. *viridulum*.

PLATE 354

We have to thank Mr. Aiton for the opportunity of publishing a figure of this rare and ornamental plant. It flowered in the Kew Gardens, in the open ground, in the month of July last. *Stem* about two feet high; *leaves* nearly a span and half long, but narrow in proportion to their length; *flower*

about a span long, white, usually suffused with purple along the middle of the back of the outer segments; *anthers* of a deep yellow colour; *style* and *stigma* green.

The *Lilia* from China and Japan appear to us so pre-eminently ornamental, that we regret to find so many of the recorded ones (especially *speciosum* and *longiflorum*) from those parts still strangers to our collections. The present species was imported from China, by the Directors of the East India Company, in 1804.

163

N.º 893

Syd. Edwards del. F.Sanfom sculp.   *Pub. by T.ºCurtis, Sᵗ Geoᵉ Crefcenᵗ Dec.1.1805*

355   Lilium martagon (t. 893 1805 SE)

LILIUM MARTAGON.
TURK'S-CAP LILY.
Lilium martagon.

PLATE 355

A native of the Austrian mountains and of some other parts of Germany. Becomes in our gardens a large plant, between three and four feet high, or more. *Corolla* glossy, glazed like porcelain, varies in its colour from purple, to whitish purple and white. *Leaves* coarse and harsh. *Bracts* often double. Distance between the whorls of leaves about the length of the leaves. *Pedicels* long, ascendently patent. *Stamens* far shorter than the corolla. *Style* clubbed, twice longer than germen. Perfectly hardy; and flowers about July or August.

There are two Austrian specimens in the Banksian Herbarium, the one with a naked, the other with a pubescent stem; the former is figured in Jacquin, and is a slenderer smaller plant, but we can hardly think them specifically different.

LILIUM MONADELPHUM.
MONADELPHOUS LILY.
Lilium monadelphum.

PLATE 356

Descr. *Stem* two to three feet high; *corolla* of a light shining yellow colour thinly speckled on the inside with small oblong brown speaks; pollen light yellow; *style* and *stigma* green; scent very strong and pungent, to us disagreeable.

Differs from *pomponium* by leaves that

are not narrowed downwards, and which are blunter, shorter, and broader than in that; by the pedicels, which are twice shorter than the flower; by the limb of the corolla, which is not bent back for more than about half its length; by the absence of all warty excrescences on the inner side of the segments; by its monadelphously cohering filaments; by a pale yellow pollen, a germen three times shorter than the style, and a stigma that is more elongated.

Native of Mount Caucasus and the adjoining region; whence the seed from which our specimen was raised had been received by Messrs. Loddiges, of Hackney. Hardy. Flowers in June.

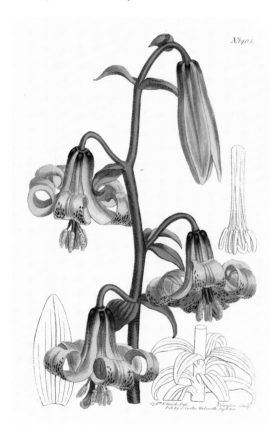

356 *Lilium monadelphum* (t. 1405 1811 SE)

LILIUM PENSYLVANICUM.
PENNSYLVANIAN LILY.
Lilium dauricum.
PLATE 357

The only mention of this species, that we have been able to find, is in a work of Catesby, where we are told that it is a native of Pennsylvania, was cultivated here in the garden of Mr. Peter Collinson, and flowered in 1745. A specimen from the above collection is deposited in the Banksian Herbarium.

The affinity with *Lilium bulbiferum* is so great that we can hardly bring ourselves to consider it as specifically distinct; the most availing differences we have been able to select are the following: in our plant the stem is generally one-flowered and ridged with only five decurrent subulate angles, in *bulbiferum* this is generally many-flowered and closely beset with numerous angle-like ridges; in *pensylvanicum* the four or five upper leaves are whorled and nearly equal to the corolla in length, but not so in *bulbiferum*; all the leaves of the former are also far more distant, and the peduncle and outside of the corolla more woolly; besides it is altogether a far smaller, tenderer, and more lax plant with a corolla more turbinately narrowed. The bulb about twice as big as a filbert, and sends out numerous creeping shoots, by which it propagates most rapidly; a single root in three or four years in a light rich soil and warm situation soon forms a very large tuft. Although we have seen above thirty otherwise fine specimens, we have never yet met with a growing one that had a pistil, which will account for the absence of that organ in our drawing; however that which flowered at Peckham was complete. Blooms in June,

357 *Lilium pensylvanicum* (t. 872 1805 SE)

but not freely except in the soil and situation above directed.

Catesby's figure of the plant is a very good one; he says the stem generally reaches sixteen inches; in our plant this was nearly two feet high.

LILIUM SUPERBUM.
SUPERB LILY.
Lilium superbum.
PLATE 358

This splendid native of North America was introduced by Mr. Peter Collinson, from Pennsylvania, about the year 1738. Michaux found it growing in moist grassy spots in Carolina. Spontaneous specimens have seldom more than three flowers in a kind of umbel; but cultivated carefully, and kept in a moist shady border of bog-earth, it will rise to the height of five feet and produce a thyrse of from twelve to fifteen flowers.

Differs from *Lilium martagon* in having a bulb as white as ivory, not of a reddish-yellow; in having narrower, linear-lanceolate, tender, not obovate-lanceolate subcorrugately veined harsh leaves; has also much shorter internodes. The plant adduced by Linnæus and all his successors from Miller's work, by way of a synonym to this, is quite a distinct species, most probably the large yellow-spotted many-flowered variety of the European *L. pomponium*; of this any one that attends to its description may easily convince himself. Blooms in July and August; scentless; seeds freely and is easily propagated by the numerous offsets it produces; tolerably hardy; at least we never lost any in the severest winters by cold merely; the bulbs sometimes rot in very wet seasons.

MELANTHIUM EUCOMOIDES.
DWARF MELANTHIUM.
Androcymbium eucomoides.
PLATE 359

Bulb tunicated, ovate, acuminate, integument dark brown. *Caudex* sometimes wholly under ground, and nearly obsolete, at

N.º 936

Pub. by T.Curtis, S.t Geo: Crescent June 1.1806.

Lilium superbum.

Syd.Edwards del.F.Sansom sculp.

358   *Lilium superbum* (t. 936 1806 SE)

other times three to four inches above it, covered by the imbricate cowled equitant bases of the *leaves*, which are four to six or even more, alternate, distich, oblong-lanceolate, recurved, smooth and somewhat shining with a middle longitudinal furrow, the upper ones ovate-lanceolate, sheathing the one to eight flowered umbel by the sinus formed of their cowled bases; *peduncles* hid by the leaves, one-flowered, about an inch long, equal, thick, triquetral, attenuated downwards. *Corolla* terminal, somewhat herbaceous, petals campanu-

lately radiating from the crown of the peduncles; *ungues* thick, fleshy, compressedly columnar; laminæ submembranous, streaked, incurved at their summits, and subgibbous outwards, rolling inwards they embrace the bases of the filaments which are brown, rumid, and stand on the upper extremity of the ungues, incurved, round, the length of laminæ and styles; *anthers* linear-oblong, purplish brown above the points of the petals; pollen yellow. *Styles* patent upwards. *Stigmas* small brown points. Seeds about the size of those of

mustard. An inhabitant of the Cape, to be treated as a greenhouse plant. Flowers in February.

Our drawing was taken at the garden of Mr. Woodford, Vauxhall, a never-failing source of rare and new plants.

359 *Melanthium eucomoides* (t. 641 1803 SE)

Melanthium monopetalum.

Many-flowered Melanthium.

Wurmbea monopetala.

PLATE 360

360 *Melanthium monopetalum* (t. 1291 1810 SE)

A greenhouse plant from the Cape of Good Hope. Introduced into Kew Gardens, by Mr. Masson, in 1788. We did not see the living specimen. In the enumeration of the species of this genus, which is given in *Bot. Mag.* t. 994, the synonymy belonging to *pumilum*, has been by mistake added to *monopetalum*. The *Melanthium pumilum* of Willdenow belongs most probably to another genus; our *M. pumilum* is his *Wurmbea pumila*.

Narthecium americanum

American Narthecium.

Narthecium americanum.

PLATE 361

In our fasciculus for the preceding month, we had given this plant for the *Narthecium glutinosum* of Michaux. In so doing, we had entirely relied on the authority of Mr. Pursh, a learned, acute, and zealous Botanist, with whose abilities the world is likely soon to become more satisfactorily acquainted, by a *Flora of North America*, which he has now in the press. He had shown the plant to Dr. Barton, a very eminent American naturalist, the friend, and sometimes the companion of Michaux in botanical excursions, and that gentleman had assured him of its being the plant we gave it for; add to this, that he had found it in abundance in the districts mentioned as the places of its abode by Michaux; who, if this is not the plant, has omitted to record it at all. Yet when we were lately shown a spontaneous American specimen in the Banksian Herbarium, of a *Tofielda* (the *Narthecium* of Jussieu) which had been noted by Mr. Dryander, as the probable *N. glutinosum*; we own the above authority lost all weight with us, and we regretted that we had been decided by collateral evidence, however strong, against that contained in an author's description of his plant. The specimen, besides a more immediate coincidence as to genus, has the rough clammy scape ascribed to his species by Michaux; a character which, as we observed in our former account, was wanting in our plant, and which we now find to be equally wanting in the spontaneous ones of Mr. Pursh. Considering it as distinct from *ossifragum*, we have ascribed to it the present name; the species being unnoticed in any work known to us. We ought to observe that Mr.

361 *Narthecium americanum* (t. 1505 1812 SE)

Pursh, as well as ourselves, have been always fully aware that the *Narthecium* intended by Michaux, was that of Jussieu, and not the present; and this we had from the first stated as our chief scruple, when we applied to Mr. Pursh; but he remained, and still does remain confident that he is right. He may be so; but the evidence of Michaux himself would not now convince us, that our plant was that which he had in view when he instituted his *Narthecium glutinosum*.

Liliaceæ – Trilliaceæ.

Medeola virginiana.

Indian Cucumber.

Medeola virginiana.

PLATE 362

Leaves whorled, six to eight in the lower, three in the upper whorl; *stem* scarcely a foot high, the thickness of a duck-quill. Common in most parts of the United

362 *Medeola virginiana* (t. 1316 1810 SE)

States of North America; where it grows in wettish woods; and is known, according to Mr. Barton (by whom a good coloured plate of it is given in the *Elements of Botany*,) by the appellation of Indian Cucumber, from the taste of the root, which is eaten by the Indians. Cultivated by Miller in 1768, who has however given an erroneous description of the root. Hardy. Blooms about June. Should be planted in bog-earth.

Our drawing was made from a plant sent us by Messrs. Loddiges, Nurserymen, at Hackney; by them it was kept in small garden pots. Flowered about June.

TRILLIUM CERNUUM.
NODDING-FLOWERED TRILLIUM.
Trillium cernuum.
PLATE 363

After the detailed description in Dr. Smith's *Spicilegium*, we need not make any addition in this place, except it be to remark, that a perfect trilocular fruit, such as represented in his figure, is in this genus

at least dubious. The receptacle of the seeds is in this species formed by a projection going off from the middle of three of the sides, but terminating with a thickened extremity before it reaches the centre of the fruit. In such a construction, of course, the shrinking of the receptacles of the seeds may occasion what appears to be a three-celled ovary to become one-celled in the ripe fruit. Moreover a difference in the length of the receptacle of the seeds in the different species of the same genus, extending in one nearly or quite to the centre of the fruit, in another less than half-way towards the centre, though evidently making no essential difference, will give in the former case the appearance of a three-celled, in the latter that of a one-celled fruit. This observation will probably explain the seeming contradiction in the formation of the fruit in this genus. Whether the three seminal receptacles in any case perfectly unite in the centre, as described by Mr. Salisbury in *Paradisus Londinensis*, No. 35, deserves to be further examined; in this species they are certainly free towards the centre and attached to the sides of the fruit only.

A hardy plant, requiring shade, and to be planted in bog-earth. Found by Michaux in mountainous places in Upper Carolina, by Kalm in Canada, and by Mr. Menzies in Nova Scotia.

363 *Trillium cernuum* (t. 954 1806 SE)

LILIACEÆ – YUCCACEÆ
YUCCA FILAMENTOSA.
THREADY ADAM'S NEEDLE.
Yucca filamentosa.
PLATE 365

According to Michaux a native of the western parts of Carolina and Virginia, growing on wilds near the sea-shore, with a stem rising sometimes to the height of five feet. An old inhabitant of our gardens, having been cultivated in them as far back as 1675. Hardy. Very ornamental; flowers about September or October. Is not uncommon in our nurseries; propagated by suckers.

LINACEÆ
LINUM ARBOREUM.
TREE FLAX.
Linum arboreum.
PLATE 364

Contrary to what we observe in most of the plants of this genus, the present very rare and no less beautiful species of flax forms

364 *Linum arboreum* (t. 234 1793)

N.º 900

Pub. by T. Curtis St. Geo: Crescent Jan. 1. 1806　　　　　*Syd. Edwards del. F. Sansom sculp.*

365　*Yucca filamentosa* (t. 900 1806 SE)

(if not a tree, as its name imports) a shrub of the height of several feet, which begins to flower in the greenhouse in March, and continues to be more or less covered with blossoms to the close of the summer.

It is a native of the Levant, from whence it was introduced to this country in the year 1788, with a profusion of other vegetables, by John Sibthorp, M. D. the present celebrated Professor of Botany in the University of Oxford; who, for the laudable purpose of promoting the science in which he is so eminent, and of enriching the Oxford collection, already rendered most respectable by his unwearied labours, meditates, as we are informed, a second journey into Greece.

Hitherto this plant has produced no seeds in this country and it is with difficulty increased by cuttings.

Our figure was drawn from a plant which flowered in the spring with Messrs. Grimwood and Co. Kensington.

LINUM AUSTRIACUM.
AUSTRIAN FLAX.

Linum austriacum.

PLATE 366

The Austrian Flax is nearly allied to the common and the perennial Flax; it has however much shorter peduncles, and con-

sequently a more compact panicle, which gives it a different habit; this difference is aided too by the peduncles being reflected whilst the flower is in bud.

The general habit is well expressed in *Tabernæmontanus*, but the calyx is incorrectly represented as acute. It is a hardy perennial, flowers in June and July, and may be propagated by parting its roots.

Our drawing was taken at the Botanic Garden, Brompton.

366 *Linum austriacum* (t. 1086 1808 SE)

367 *Linum quadrifolium* (t. 431 1799 SE)

LINUM QUADRIFOLIUM.
FOUR-LEAVED FLAX.

Linum quadrifolium.

PLATE 367

Our plant accords exactly with the *Linum quadrifolium* of Linnæus, and as such it is regarded at the Royal Garden, Kew, where we saw it in flower this spring, 1798; it agrees also with the description of Ray, so far as relates to its specific character, quoted by Linnæus, but the flowers of Ray's plant are described as blue, it is most probably therefore the *quadrifolium* of Linnæus, but not of Ray.

The stalks of this species rise to the height of about two feet, are much branched at their summits, on which are produced numerous yellow flowers, smaller than those of *L. arboreum* or *flavum*, to either of which, as an ornamental plant, it must be allowed to be inferior; yet it is not without its share of elegance and beauty.

It is a native of the Cape, newly introduced to our greenhouses, flowers in May and June, and is increased by cuttings.

LOASACEÆ

LOASA NITIDA.
SHINING-LEAVED LOASA.

Loasa nitida.

PLATE 368

The genus *Loasa* first occurs in Adanson's *Familles des Plantes*; but the characters were better ascertained by Jacquin in his *Observationes Botanicæ*; from whose authority only, it appears to have been inserted into the twelfth edition on Linnæus's *Systema Naturæ*, where the orthography is changed to *Loosa*, perhaps by an error of the press only; but continued in the future editions, and by Schreber in his *Genera Plantarum*; the original spelling is, however, restored by Jussieu, Lamarck, and Willdenow. The name is supposed to have been given by Adanson, in honour of some unknown Spanish Botanist.

The genus was at first added by Jussieu to his natural order of *Onagræ*; but has been since raised by him into a separate family, under the name of *Loaseæ*, containing, besides the present genus, only *Mentzelia*,

its near affinity with which was remarked by Jacquin.

Our plant, which was communicated by our kind friend Mr. Walker, appears to be a different species from the one published in the *Botanical Register*, t. 667, under the name of *Loasa tricolor*. By a comparison both with the figure and description of *nitida* in the *Annâles*, and with a specimen preserved in the Lambertian Herbarium, we have very little doubt of its belonging to that species. It is particularly remarkable for the dark shining green colour of the upper surface of the leaves.

The whole genus has probably more or less of the stinging quality of the common nettle. Of the virulence of the present species we have ourselves had personal experience, the effects of a puncture at the end of the thumb being felt, not continually indeed, but at intervals, especially on first rising in the morning, for six days. The sensation was chiefly a burning heat in the part, not accompanied with the intolerable itching that sometimes follows the sting of a nettle. A tender annual. Propagated by seeds which should be sown on a hot-bed in the spring. Native of Lima, in Peru, according to Dombey, where it grows among the rocks. Mr. Walker raised it from seeds received from Chili.

368 *Loasa nitida* (t. 2372 1823 JC)

369 *Lagerstroemia indica* (t. 405 1798 SE)

LYTHRACEÆ

LAGERSTRŒMIA INDICA.
INDIAN LAGERSTRŒMIA.

Lagerstromia indica.

PLATE 369

Of this genus, named in honour of *Magnus Lagerstroem*, Director of the Swedish East India Company, there is only one species as yet known, and that a native of China, Cochinchina, and Japan; it is described minutely by Thunberg, also by Rumphius, and very characteristically by Kaempfer.

According to these authors, in its native country it grows to the height of six feet, or more, acquires a stem the thickness of one's arm, and produces flowers the size of the garden Clove, which are very showy, no wonder therefore that the natives should be in the practice of planting it about their houses and their gardens.

The petals are curiously crisped or curled, each petal resembling, in miniature, a leaf of some of our varieties of cabbage: Kaempfer compares them to the mesentery. According to Mr. Aiton, it was introduced to the Royal Garden at Kew, by Hugh, Duke of Northumberland, in 1759.

It flowers from August to October; but in the greenhouse, where it is recommended

by Mr. Aiton to be kept, it is not a very ready blower, – in the stove it blossoms more freely. May be increased, without difficulty, from cuttings.

370 *Malpighia glabra* (t. 813 1805 SE)

MALPIGHIACEÆ

MALPIGHIA GLABRA.
SMOOTH-LEAVED BARBADOES-CHERRY.

Malpighia glabra.

PLATE 370

A shrub, seldom rising above six or seven feet in the West Indies, according to Brown, though Miller says there are some trees upwards of ten feet high in England.

It is cultivated in the West Indies for the sake of its acid pulpy fruit, in size and shape somewhat resembling our cherries. According to Jacquin, these are seldom eaten raw, but are generally made into a preserve with sugar. He remarks however that he and his two companions, when overcome with thirst in a long journey, ate them from the tree in very large quantities without suffering any inconvenience in consequence. It sometimes bears fruit in this country, but small and very thin of pulp.

Requires to be preserved in the stove

through the winter, but in the middle of summer is the better for being exposed to the open air. Flowers in the winter and also in June and July, at which time we received the plant from which our drawing was taken from Mr. Loddiges, and observed the flowers, during the day, to be sweet-scented not unlike those of jasmine.

Introduced by Miller in 1757, who received the seeds from the King of France's gardener at Trianon, Mons. Richard.

MALVACEÆ

ALTHÆA FLEXUOSA.
SERINGAPATAM HOLLYHOCK.

Alcea rosea.

PLATE 371

The Hollyhocks in Linnæus's system formed a genus of themselves under the name of *Alcea*; but the number of segments in the calyx not being very constant, this character has been thought too slight; and the genus has been suffered to immerge in *Althæa*; an alteration adopted both by Schreber in his *Genera Plantarum* and Willdenow in his new edition of the *Species Plantarum*. In plants so subject to vary it is not very easy to distinguish real species from mere varieties, and whether this will continue to preserve its characters, after a few years cultivation, is at present dubious. The Dwarf Chinese Hollyhock, a few years since held in high estimation, is now hardly to be found in its genuine state.

The flowers of all that have hitherto been raised, proved single; the stem is about two feet high, somewhat zig-zag from leaf to leaf, beset with rigid patent hairs, the petioles long and hairy, the leaves three, five, and seven-lobed, crenate, villous; peduncles solitary, erect, one-flowered; inner calyx frequently six-cleft as well as the outer; capsules hispid. For this plant we are indebted to Mr. Whitley, of Old Brompton, who raised it from seeds sent by Lady Gwillim from Madrass, under the name of the Seringapatam Hollyhock.

N.º 892

N.º 882

Syd Edwards del   Pub. by T. Curtis, St. Geo: Crefcent Dec.1.1805.   F.Sanfom sculp

371   *Althaea flexuosa* (t. 892 1805 SE)

Syd Edwards del   Pub. by T. Curtis, St. Geo: Crefcent Nov.1.1805.   F.Sanfom

372   *Hibiscus palustris* (t. 882 1805 SE)

FUGOSIA HETEROPHYLLA.

VARIOUS-LEAVED FUGOSIA.

Cienfuegosia heterophylla.

PLATE 373

A very pretty shrub, named by Cavanilles in honour of Bernard Cienfuegos, a Spanish botanist of the sixteenth century, and now, we believe, first cultivated in England, from seeds sent home from St. Martha, by our collector, Mr. Purdie, in 1845. At the Syon Gardens, where our figure was made, plants flowered in October of the same year. The general appearance of the blossoms is not much unlike those of *Turnera ulmifolia*; but when the centre of the flower is examined, each of the five petals will be found to have a rich scarlet or blood-coloured pectinated spot, the teeth or rays arranged with the most perfect regularity. Mr. Spach has, we think, correctly referred the *Redoutea* of Ventenat to *Fugosia*; for there seems to be no generic distinction. The present species was originally found in the Island of St. Thomas and on the banks of the Orinoco. Its specific name is derived from the varying form of the leaves, very evident in our dried specimens, but less remarkable in cultivated ones.

HIBISCUS PALUSTRIS.

MARSH HIBISCUS.

Hibiscus moscheutos.

PLATE 372

The Marsh Hibiscus is a native of North America, and seems to have been very early introduced into Europe, being mentioned by Dodonæus as a foreign plant cultivated in the gardens of Holland. It does not occur under this name in Michaux's *Flora of North America*, but we suspect that what he has described, as the *Hibiscus moscheutos* of Linnæus, is the same plant; indeed we very much doubt whether both species are not in reality the same. Be this as it may, we have no doubt but that our plant is the *palustris* of Linnæus, having

373 *Fugosia heterophylla* (t. 4218 1846 WF)

375 *Nuttallia digitata* (t. 2612 1826 CMC)

374 *Hibiscus surattensis* (t. 1356 1811 SE)

a perennial root, and speaks of it as forming a large wide-spreading shrub, with extremely tough branches, but green and not ligneous. The latter he says is herbaceous, with weak trailing stems, unable to support themselves without the assistance of some neighbouring bush. The flowers of both are similar to those of our plant, which exactly corresponds with his description of the latter. Some of the leaves are three-lobed, others five-lobed. The leaves of all these plants are gratefully acid, and, on that account, are used as culinary herbs.

Native of the East Indies, cultivated by Philip Miller, in 1768. It is a tender annual, and must be raised in a hot-bed or stove. Flowers in July; rarely ripens its seeds with us. Is very beautiful, though without scent, and its flowers are expanded but a few hours, and that in fine weather only.

had an opportunity of comparing it with a specimen from Kalm in the Banksian Herbarium, which however does not appear to differ from the *Hibiscus moscheutos* of the same collection. In both, the peduncle and petiole appear rather to be united at the base than to grow the one out of the other.

It is a perfectly hardy herbaceous plant, but will rarely flower in our gardens without the aid of artificial heat.

HIBISCUS SURATTENSIS.
PRICKLY-STALKED HIBISCUS.

Hibiscus surattensis.

PLATE 374

The variety *Hibiscus surattensis* β of Linnæus, Narinam-pouilli of the *Hortus Malabaricus*, is probably a distinct species from *Hibiscus surattensis*. Perhaps Loureiro's plant, which differs from ours in being a shrub of the growth of six feet or more, and in having flowers saffron-coloured within and very red without, also belongs to that, or is different from both.

Rumfe also describes two species or varieties of his *Herba crinalium*, the *domestica* and *sylvestris*. To the former he ascribes

NUTTALLIA DIGITATA.
DIGITATE-LEAVED NUTTALLIA.

Callirhœ digitata.

PLATE 375

This plant, which appears to be a new genus of the natural order of *Malvaceæ*, having the calyx of a *Sida* and the fruit of a *Malva*, was discovered by Professor Nuttall,

in the Arkansa territory, and has been published from his manuscript, in Barton's *Flora*, where the name of *Nuttallia* was given to it in honour of its discoverer, one of the most learned Botanists in America, to whose researches we are indebted for the knowledge of many of the rare vegetable productions of North America.

This fine hardy perennial was communicated by Robert Barclay, Esq. of Bury-Hill, in whose collection it was raised from seeds received from Mr. Nuttall. There is said to be another species of this genus in the Botanic Garden at Philadelphia.

NUTTALLIA PAPAVER.
PAPAVER-LIKE NUTTALLIA.

Callirhœ papaver.

PLATE 376

In the *Exotic Flora*, at t. 171 and 172, I had the pleasure of figuring two distinct species of the present genus, detected by Mr. Nuttall on the Arkansa River. Their discoverer has justly remarked, that this genus, of which the species are hardy, ornamental, and perennial, "appears to afford an additional link of connection

376 *Nuttallia papaver* (t. 3287 1833 RG)

between the Genera *Sida* and *Malva*." Had he been acquainted with the present individual, he would have found his idea still further strengthened, for here, with a habit altogether that of the other *Nuttalliæ*, there is the involucre of a *Malva*. The presence of this involucre does indeed appear to me to distinguish the species at once both from *N. pedata* and *N. digitata*: and this is constant in the wild specimens sent from Covington, Louisiana, by Mr. Drummond, in the spring of 1833, as well as in all the cultivated ones raised from seeds transmitted by the same indefatigable Naturalist, and from the same place. These seeds have been distributed among different gardens, and have probably produced flowering plants in several collections.

Scarcely was our drawing finished, from the Glasgow Botanic Garden specimens, when I had the satisfaction to receive a beautiful figure (made by Dr. Greville), and a description from Dr. Graham, done from plants of the Edinburgh Botanic Garden, both of which are here given in preference to my own. It appears to be quite hardy, and is highly ornamental.

377 RIGHT: *Sida cristata* (t. 330 1796)

SIDA CRISTATA.
CRESTED SIDA.
Anoda cristata.
PLATE 377

Dillenius has figured and described this plant in his *Hortus Elthamensis* as an *Abutilon*: Linnæus in his *Species Plantarum* has ranked it with the *Sida's*, in which he has been followed by Professor Murray, Messrs. Aiton and Cavanille; but Professor Gmelin, in the last edition of Linnæus' *Syst. Nat.* has made another new genus of it, by the name of *Anoda*; as his reasons for so doing are by no means cogent, we join the majority in continuing it a *Sida*.

It flowered in the garden of Mr. Sherard, at Eltham, in 1725, and was introduced from Mexico, where it is a native: Mr. Aiton considers it as a stove plant, as he does the *Tropæolum majus*, and other natives of South America; strictly speaking they may be such, but if raised early, and treated like other tender annuals, this plant will flower and ripen its seeds in the open ground, as we have experienced at Brompton.

It grows to the height of three feet, or more, producing during the months of July and August a number of blossoms in succession, which are large and showy; the stigmata in this flower are curious objects, resembling the heads of fungi in miniature.

Pub. by W. Curtis St. Geo. Crescent Nov. 1 1796

378 *Sida hastata* (t. 1541 1813 SE)

SIDA HASTATA.
HALBERT-LEAVED MEXICAN SIDA.
Anoda acerifolia.
PLATE 378

The specific name of halbert-shaped is so little applicable to the plant from which our figure was taken, that we were at first inclined to suspect that it was a distinct species; but we have seen such great variation in plants raised from the same seed, that we conclude no dependence can be placed upon the form of the leaves. The peduncles, in all the specimens that we have seen, when full grown, are twice the length of the leaves.

Our plant was communicated by Mr. Kent, from his collection at Clapton, where it flowers in the stove from March to the middle of summer, and ripens its seeds freely. Said to be introduced in 1799, by the Marchioness of Bute. Native of Mexico. Is usually treated as a stove plant, but being annual, or at most biennial, the seeds may be sown in a common hot-bed early in the spring, and the plants planted out in the open air by the latter-end of May, where they will, in favourable weather, ripen their seeds, by which alone they can be propagated.

N.2441.

379 *Melastoma granulosa* (t. 2441 1823)

MELASTOMACEÆ

MELASTOMA GRANULOSA.
COMMERSON'S MELASTOMA.

Tibouchina granulosa.

PLATE 379

Melastoma granulosa owes its specific name to the granulated appearance of the upper surface of the leaves, arising from a number of callous excrescences, terminated by a short adpressed bristle. These are more remarkable in the dried state from the shrinking of the parenchymatous substance of the leaf; but were sufficiently evident, in our plant, while growing.

Our drawing of this beautiful shrub, by far the most splendid of any species of *Melastoma* that has as yet flowered in this country, was taken at the fine collection at Bayswater, belonging to the Count De Vandes. It grows to the height of ten feet. A plant of this height, covered with its pendent flowering branches, must make a most splendid appearance.

Native of Brazil. Requires to be kept in the stove, where it flowers, in this country, in the month of August.

MELASTOMA MALABATHRICA.
CINNAMON-LEAVED MELASTOMA OR
BLACK STRAWBERRY TREE.

Melastoma sanguineum.

PLATE 380

It is singular, that of this very numerous genus, of which eighty-five species are enumerated by Willdenow, not one should be found in the *Kew Catalogue*. Several of them have been introduced of late years; but, of all that we have seen, this is the handsomest, and is otherwise interesting, as being the one from which the name of

380 *Melastoma malabathrica* (t. 529 1801 SE)

the genus was framed by Professor Burman. This signifies black mouth, a name given to it by the vulgar, from its effect on the mouths of the children who ate of the fruit, which is filled with a black pulp. Being a native of Ceylon and other parts of the East Indies, it must with us, always require to be kept in a stove, where it forms a handsome shrub.

MELIANTHACEÆ

MELIANTHUS MINOR.
SMALL MELIANTHUS OR
HONEY-FLOWER.

Melianthus comosus.

PLATE 381

There are few flowers that do not secrete from some kind of a glandular substance, honey, or nectar, to a greater or smaller amount; in those of the present genus, this liquid is particularly abundant, even dropping from the flowers of the M. *major*, in considerable quantity; in the present species it flows not so copiously, but is retained in the lower part of the blossom,

and is of a dark brown colour, an unusual phenomenon.

There are only two species of this genus described, the *major* and the *minor*, both of which are cultivated in our nurseries; the *major* is by far the most common, the most hardy, and the most ornamental plant; its foliage indeed is peculiarly elegant: this species will succeed in the open border, especially if placed at the foot of a wall with a south or south-west aspect, taking care to cover the root to a considerable depth with rotten tan in severe frosts: the *minor* is always kept in the greenhouse, in which, when it has acquired a certain age, it flowers regularly in the spring, and constantly so, as far as we have observed of the plants in Chelsea Garden; Mr. Aiton says in August, and Commelin the summer through.

The *Melianthus minor* grows to the height of three, four, or five feet; its stem, which is shrubby, during the flowering season is apt to exhibit a naked appearance, having fewer leaves on it at that period, and those not of their full size; but this, perhaps, may in some degree be owing to the plant's being placed at the back of others. The foliage when bruised has an unpleasant smell.

It is a native of the Cape, and, according to Mr. Aiton, was cultivated by the Duchess of Beaufort, in 1708; is propagated readily by cuttings.

381 *Melianthus minor* (t. 301 1795)

382 *Broussonetia papyrifera* (t. 2358 1822 JC)

MORACEÆ

BROUSSONETIA PAPYRIFERA.
PAPER-MULBERRY TREE.

Broussonetia papyrifera.

PLATE 382

The Paper-Mulberry tree is a shrub of but little beauty; but, both in Japan and in the South-sea islands, is of the utmost importance for economical purposes. In Otaheite, as we are informed by Captain Cook, in his relation of his first voyage, the finest and whitest cloth worn by the chiefs and principal persons of the island is entirely manufactured from the inner bark of this tree by a simple process of beating; and in Japan the same species is cultivated in great quantity, for the purpose of making paper of different kinds, by a process in which the bark is reduced to a pulp, to be afterwards spread into sheets of greater or less thickness, upon similar principles, though by different contrivances, to what are used in the manufacture of European paper, except that it appears that the Japanese employ vegetable mucilages only, and neither animal gluten nor alum, which is probably the reason that their paper is more bibulous than ours. A full description of the

Japanese process for making paper from the Paper-Mulberry may be seen in Kæmpfer's *Amænitates*, which has been translated into several of the Encyclopædias and Dictionaries of the day.

In young plants the leaves are more or less divided into lobes, but in adult shrubs they are generally entire, as seen in our plate, in which the upper figure represents a flowering branch of the female, and the lower one of a male plant. This tree has been long cultivated in our gardens; according to the *Hortus Kewensis* before 1751, by Peter Collinson, Esq. It appears by Mons. Poiret's account in Lamarck's *Encyclopédie* that it had been long cultivated also in the Paris gardens, but that the male plant only was known, till Mons. Broussonet, in his travels, met with the female in some garden in Scotland, and transmitted cuttings of it. The fruit being from that time known, it was found not to belong to the genus Morus, though nearly allied to it. Mons. L'Heritier gave it the name of *Broussonetia*; but his unfortunate death prevented its publication, till adopted by Ventenat, in his *Tableau du Règne Végétal*.

Native of Japan and the South-sea islands. Flowers from February to September. Propagated by layers, cuttings, or seed. Communicated by John Walker, Esq.

MYRTACEÆ

FABRICIA LÆVIGATA.
SMOOTH FABRICIA.

Leptospermum lævigatum.

PLATE 383

The genus *Fabricia* was first established by Gærtner, who has given an excellent figure of the fruit, and has been confirmed by Dr. Smith in the third volume of the *Transactions of the Linnean Society*.

This shrub has been twenty years in this country, but we have not heard of its having flowered any where; the specimen from which our drawing was taken, bloomed last May in the Botanic Garden belonging to the Dublin Society, whence it was kindly transmitted to us in a recent state.

383   *Fabricia laevigata* (t. 1304 1810)

GENETYLLIS MACROSTEGIA.
LARGE-INVOLUCRED GENETYLLIS.

Darwinia macrostegia.

PLATE 384

We have alluded to this *Genetyllis* as one of the two beautiful species of the genus the discovery of which in West Australia had given such pleasure to Mr. Drummond, and as having been received by us from the Bristol Nursery, Messrs. Garaway, Mayes, and Co. It is scarcely less beautiful, and certainly not less curious, than the G. *tulipifera*. It is a smaller plant; the leaves are much narrower, more sparse; the coloured involucres are perhaps more numerous, but smaller, not so spreading at the mouth, and the foliola are narrower, and all of a uniform brick-red colour. In writing on the G. *tulipifera*, Dr. Lindley says "that plant should be compared with the G. *macrostegia* of Turczaninoff." We think, however, our friend has done right in not adducing the latter as a synonym to that species. The present one accords so much better with the short description of G. *macrostegia*, that I think there can be little doubt that this is the species that was in view, and

that G. *tulipifera* was quite unknown to him. It proves to be as hardy as the others; and Messrs. Garaway and Mayes observe that it requires plenty of light and air, a compost of good peat and sand, with a little charcoal intermixed, and a moderate supply of water, especially in winter. It is the case with this and G. *tulipifera*, that the more hardy its treatment the brighter the colour of the bracts. Both have the merit of continuing in flower three or four months at a time. Their involucres are of a dry, membranaceous character, and would probably retain their colour and form for a long time in a dried state, like the xeranthemums and other so-called Everlastings.

384   *Genetyllis macrostegia* (t. 4860 1855)

MELALEUCA SQUARROSA.
MYRTLE-LEAVED MELALEUCA.

Melaleuca squarrosa.

PLATE 385

The leaves of this plant are described by Mr. Brown, as opposite; by Sir James Smith as both opposite and scattered, as they were in the one from which our drawing was made. In most specimens, however, that we have seen, they were entirely opposite and decussate; they are

385 *Melaleuca squarrosa* (t. 1935 1817)

usually obscurely five-nerved, and the broader ones seven-nerved. Some leaves, or bracts like leaves, grow among the flowers, which generally show more or less a disposition to become verticillate; but the whorls are seldom so distinct as they were in the plant from which our drawing was taken.

The filaments are collected into five bundles, connected at the base only, and so slightly, that Smith has observed that it is not very easy to decide whether it belongs to *Melaleuca*, or to the very nearly-related genus, *Metrosideros*; between which genera, the distinction, he remarks, is more artificial than natural.

Our drawing was taken from a specimen communicated by John Walker, Esq. in May 1815, from a plant that had stood two winters against a south wall, with no other protection than a mat during frost. A very fine spreading shrub, nearly three feet high, was sent us last summer, by Messrs. Barr and Brookes, of the Northampton Nursery, Newington-Green.

Native of New South Wales and of Van Diemen's-Island, and is generally treated as a hardy greenhouse shrub. Flowers most

part of the summer. Introduced about the year 1794. Propagated by cuttings.

The whole plant is aromatic and pungent, and the dried flowers, when rubbed, have a particularly grateful aromatic scent.

METROSIDEROS CITRINA.
HARSH-LEAV'D METROSIDEROS.
Callistemon citrinus.
PLATE 386

Though many species of this genus have been raised from seeds, brought within these few years from the South Seas, where they are said to be very numerous; this is, we believe, the only one that as yet has flowered in this country: our drawing was made from a plant which blossomed toward the close of last summer at Lord Cremornes, the root of which had been sent from Botany Bay; previous to this period we have been informed, that the same species flowered both at Kew and Syon House; as it is without difficulty raised both from seeds and cuttings, young plants of it are to be seen in most of the nurseries near town; it would seem that they do not flower till they are at least five or six years old.

386 *Metrosideros citrina* (t. 260 1794 SE)

Metrosideros is a name given originally by Rumphius in his *Herb. Amboin* to some plants of this genus, the term applies to the hardness of their wood, which by the Dutch is called Yzerhout (Ironwood): Forster in his *Gen. Pl.* figures this and another genus on the same plate, under the name of *Leptospermum*; Schreber in his edition of the *Gen. Pl.* of Linnæus, unites *Metrosideros, Melaleuca, Leptospermum*, and *Fabricia*, under the genus *Melaleuca*; Gœrtner in his elaborate work on the seeds of plants, makes separate genera of these, agreeably to the ideas of Sir Joseph Banks, and Mr. Dryander, who on this subject can certainly boast the best information.

We cannot, without transgressing the allotted limits of our letter-press, give a minute description of the plant figured; suffice it to say, that it is an evergreen shrub, growing to the height of from four to six or more feet, that its leaves on the old wood feel very harsh or rigid to the touch, and when bruised give forth an agreeable fragrance, the flowers grow in spikes on the tops of the branches, and owe their beauty to the brilliant colour of the filaments.

METROSiDEROS VIRIDIFLORA.
GREEN-FLOWERED METROSIDEROS.
Callistemon salignus.
PLATE 387

This species, which appears to us to be an undescribed one, approaches very near to *Metrosideros saligna*; but differs in having less flexile branches, leaves quite smooth, darker green, smaller, more rigid and pungent, not so much narrowed at the base, and more evidently petioled; calyx, corolla, and stamens all green; the latter much longer, and pointing downwards. The flowers grow in a crowded spike, at first quite at the extremity; the terminal shoot not appearing till some time after the flowers are fully expanded.

This handsome shrub was raised from seeds by Messrs. Whitley, Brame and Milne, and communicated in flower last June.

Native of New Holland. Appears to be a hardy greenhouse shrub, which can be propagated by cuttings; but whether it is equally hardy with *Metrosideros saligna* has not been as yet ascertained.

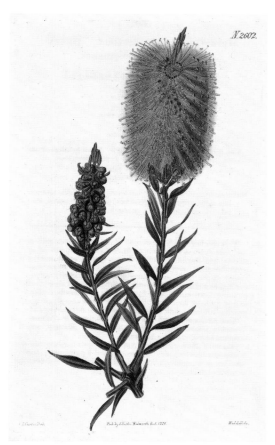

387   *Metrosideros viridiflora* (t. 2602 1825 JC)

PSIDIUM CATTLEIANUM.
PURPLE FRUITED GUAVA.

Psidium cattleianum.

PLATE 388

The specimen of this fine fruit, from which our drawing was taken, was sent us by our lamented friend, the late John Walker, Esq. It was originally introduced into this country from China, about the year 1817, by Mr. Brookes, of the Ball's Pond nursery. The fruit is said to exceed in flavour that of any of the known species of Guava, several of which are cultivated both in the East and West Indies, and from one or more of these the Guava jelly is prepared.

The first account we have of this handsome tree is from William Cattley, Esq. in the fourth volume of the *Transactions of the Horticultural Society*. In this gentleman's conservatory at Barnet two crops of fruit were produced from one tree in the same year; a fine figure of a fruit-bearing branch, from the pencil of Mr. Hooker, is added, and also some remarks by the Society's very zealous secretary, who applied the name of *cattleianum* to it. An illustration of the botanical character of the genus, as well as of this particular species, may be seen in

Lindley's *Collectanea Botanica*, together with a fine figure of a flowering branch and separate fruit.

The flower is very little larger than that of the common Broad-leaved Myrtle, which it is not unlike. The fruit contains a juicy pulp, sweet, with some acidity. In the one we tasted, perhaps from being too ripe, we could not discover the delicious flavour described by Mr. Lindley.

May be propagated by cuttings, and these, with good management, Mr. Cattley observes, may be brought into fruit the second year. It seems to be a fast grower, Mr. Cattley's plant, when purchased, being only twelve inches high, had, in two years, attained the height of three yards.

388   *Psidium cattleianum* (t. 2501 1824 JC)

MUSACEÆ

MUSA COCCINEA.
SCARLET BANANA.

Musa coccinea.

PLATE 389

Native of China and Cochinchina. Dr. Roxburgh says that it is cultivated as an exotic in the Botanic Garden at Calcutta, where it rarely produces perfect seed, any more than with us in Europe. We could

find no traces of a sixth fertile stamen in the female corolla, nor of a sixth sterile one in the male. Loureiro is the first who has described the species, but is mistaken in his synonyms, as is Dr. Martyn as to the plant that writer intended. The fertile stigma is erroneously represented both in the dissections given in Dr. Roxburgh's drawing and in the plate of the *Botanist's Repository*. Requires to be kept in the bark-bed of a stove, where it flowers from Christmas to March. Said to have been introduced into this country by Mr. Evans, of Stepney, in 1792. We are obliged to Lord Stanley for the specimen from which our drawing was made.

NEPENTHACEÆ

NEPENTHES DISTILLATORIA. MAS.
PITCHER PLANT: MALE.

Nepenthes mirabilis.

PLATE 390

Lid at first closed, afterwards raised to about a right angle with the oblique opening of the pitcher, and never again closed. Before the opening of the lid, rather more than a drachm of limpid fluid was formed within each of the largest pitchers of our specimen. This had a subacid taste, which increased after the rising of the lid, when the fluid slowly evaporated. My friend Dr. Turner perceived it to emit, while boiling, an odour like baked apples, from containing a trace of vegetable matter, and he found it to yield minute crystals of superoxalate of potash, on being slowly evaporated to dryness. The pitcher whose contents Dr. Turner analysed was a large one; it had not opened; and the whole fluid weighed only sixty-six grains. The upper part of the pitcher decays first; and the line at which this is observed, is often quite defined. Our largest pitchers measure six inches and a half from the highest part of the oblique mouth to the lowest part of the curvature at their base; the greatest circumference four and a half inches.

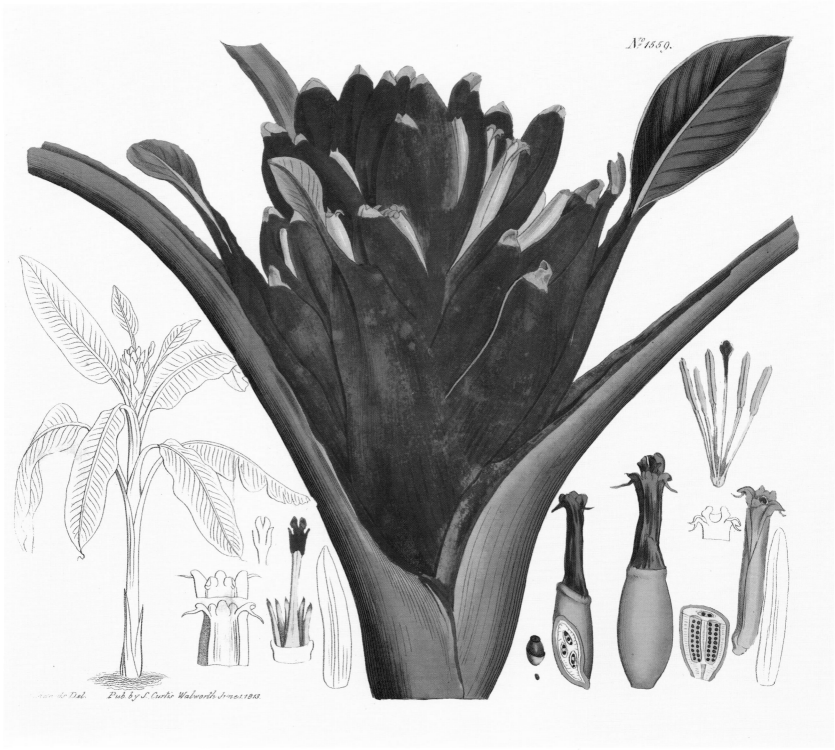

389 *Musa coccinea* (t. 1559 1813 SE)

Nepenthes phyllamphora.

Ventricose Pitcher Plant.

Nepenthes mirabilis.

PLATE 391

There are probably several undescribed species of this very curious genus, but our plant seems to agree so well with the description of Loureiro, that we have very little doubt of its belonging to the same species; nor does it differ much from that of Rumphius, which is quoted as a synonym by Willdenow.

The great curiosity of this plant consists in the pitcher-formed appendices to the leaves, which are said to contain sweet, clear water, even in dry weather. According to some authors the water rises from the roots, and is secreted into the vessels before the lid of the pitcher has ever been opened, and Rumphius observes that, in this state, these curiously constructed vessels contain the most water, the quantity of which diminishes after the lid opens, though even then it fills again in the course of the night, and evaporates in the day; but after the lid is quite shrivelled, the water entirely disappears. Loureiro, however, has a different opinion, and attributes the presence of the liquid to the reception and preservation of the night dews by the spontaneous opening and shutting of the lid; what is the real fact does not seem to have been as yet positively ascertained. In our plant, cultivated in the stove, the young pitchers, before the lid opened, were, Messrs. Loddiges observe, about one-third filled with a sourish tasted water; but after the lids opened, the water entirely evaporated.

Opposite:

390 *Nepenthes distillatoria Mas.* (t. 2798 1828 WJH)

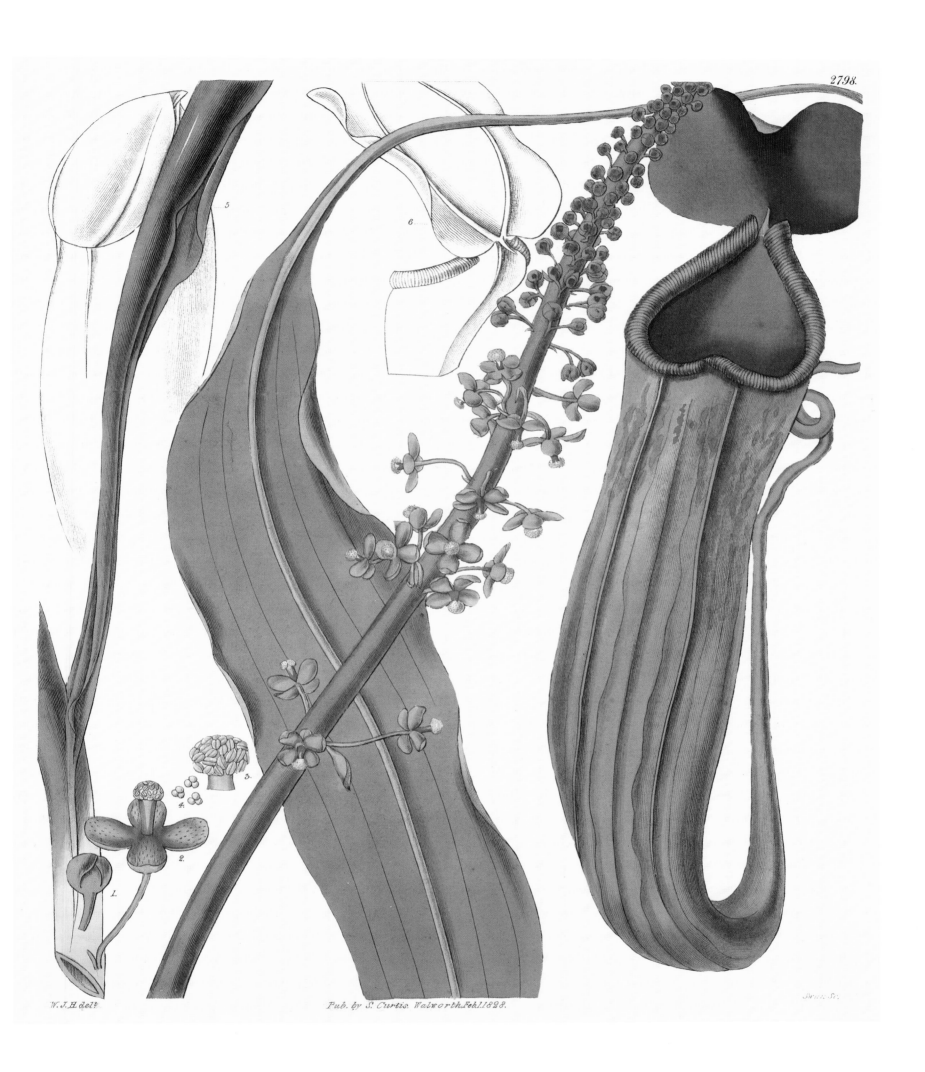

W.J.H. delt.

Pub. by S. Curtis, Walworth, Feb.1.1828.

Swan Sc.

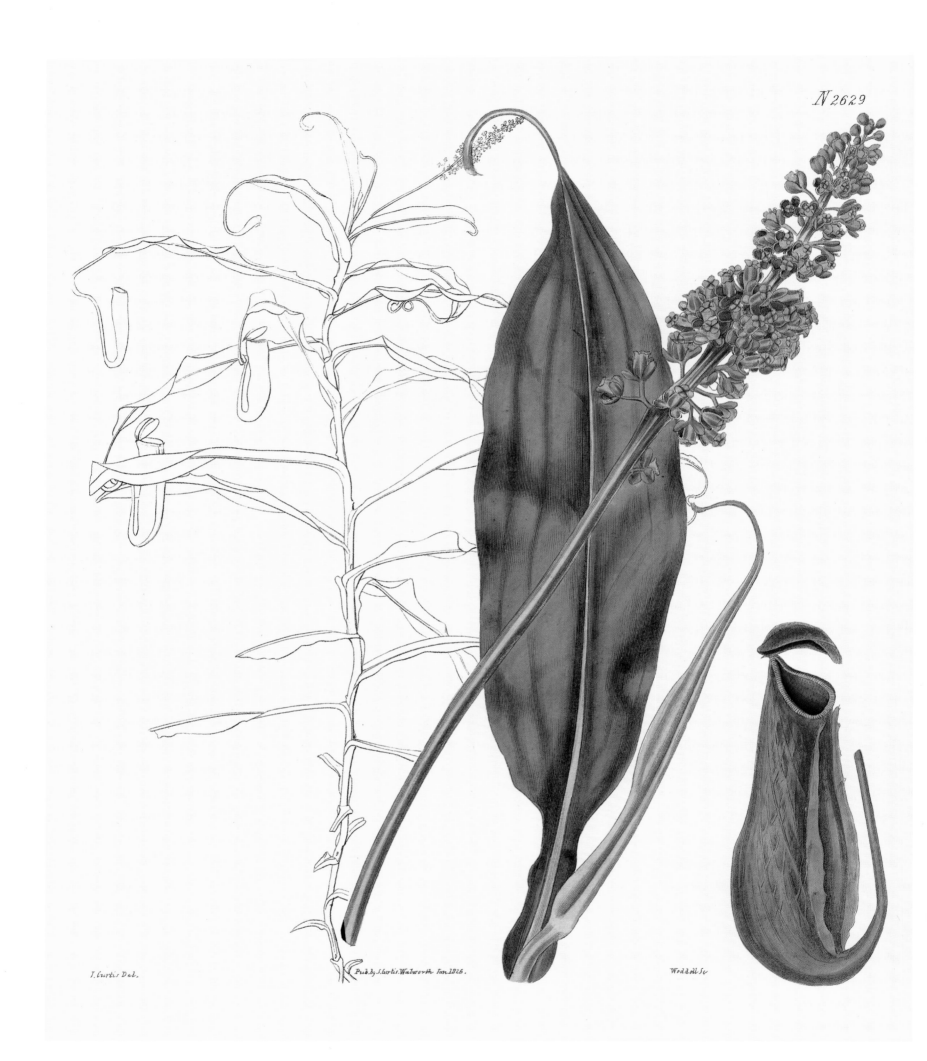

J. Curtis Del.

Pub. by S. Curtis. Walworth. Jan. 1826.

Weddell Sc

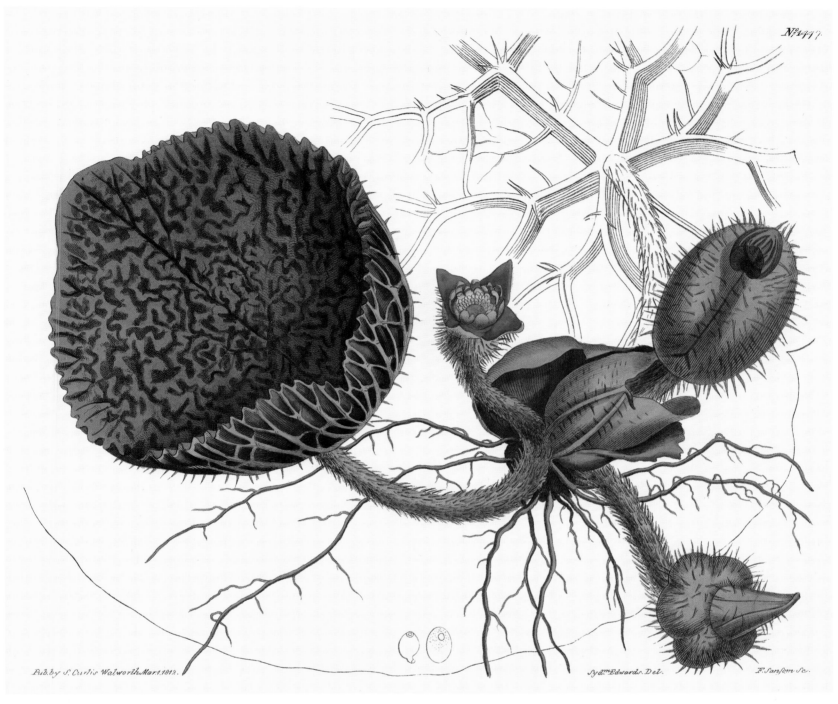

392 *Euryale ferox* (t. 1447 1812 SE)

Native of Cochinchina, Ceylon, and the Molucca Islands, growing in moist, mountainous districts, and both Loureiro and Rumphius remark, that it is very difficult to cultivate; the latter once succeeded, but the plant did not thrive well, and produced much smaller pitchers.

Our Drawing was taken at Messrs. Loddiges and Sons, in July, 1825, from the female plant; the male has probably not been as yet imported into this country.

OPPOSITE:
391 *Nepenthes phyllamphora* (t. 2629 1826 JC)

NYMPHÆACEÆ

EURYALE FEROX.

PRICKLY EURYALE.

Euryale ferox.

PLATE 392

This curious plant is a native of the East Indies, and has been cultivated in China, according to the pretensions of the Chinese writers, more than a thousand years before the commencement of the Christian era. The seeds which are involved in an insipid pulp, supposed to be of a cooling quality, are farinaceous, and considered as a wholesome food.

The leaves, which float upon the surface of the water, sometimes exceed three feet in diameter, and are covered on both sides with sharp curved spines. The under surface is of a deep bluish purple colour, curiously supported by spongy ribs, which rising from the centre of the leaf, where the petiole is inserted, are dichotomously branched over the whole. These ribs have considerably more perpendicular thickness than width, like the rafters of a house, and are covered with spines at first soft but becoming hard with age. The leaf, while in bud, is curiously folded up, and enclosed in an involucre, which bursts as the leaf expands.

Introduced by the Marquis of Blandford,

183

393 *Nelumbium speciosum* (t. 903A 1806 SE)

NELUMBIUM SPECIOSUM.
SACRED BEAN OF INDIA.

Nelumbo nucifera.

PLATE 393

The *Nelumbium* is no longer found in Egypt, but is common in most parts of the East Indies, and appears to be held in high estimation in China, where there are several varieties, if not distinct species. Is said to occur likewise in the West Indies, but it appears to us probable that this is a different species.

The seeds of this plant preserve their vegetative properties for very many years; which makes it the more surprising, that such a very ornamental and fragrant flower should not more frequently occur in our stoves; but its proper culture does not seem to be as yet well understood. It requires a deep cistern with a considerable depth of mud for its roots. The ancient Egyptians planted the seeds in balls of mud or clay, mixed with chaff, and thus sunk them in the water; perhaps this practice might be successfully imitated.

Although seldom reared to perfection in this country, it bears the severe cold of Peking with impunity. Probably, if attention were paid to obtain seeds from the coldest climes in which it is found, we

in 1809. Our drawing was taken at James Vere's, Esq. in August last, where it was cultivated with other tropical aquatics in a cistern, placed on a hot-bed, and covered with a melon-frame. Under this treatment the seeds were perfected, by which the plant is readily propagated. And as it is cultivated in the lakes and pools at Peking, though not to the same perfection as in the southern provinces, there is some reason to hope it may be found not to stand in need of artificial heat. The name of *Euryale* was first given to this plant by R. Salisbury, Esq. in the *Annals of Botany*; and five years afterwards, inadvertently, that of *Anneslea* in the *Botanist's Repository*.

might be more successful in cultivating it, with little or no artificial heat; at present, we believe, it has not with us been made to flower out of the stove.

Our drawing was first sketched from a very fine plant in blossom at Mr. Liptrap's, in the year 1797. Introduced in 1784, by the Right Hon. Sir Joseph Banks, Bart.

NYMPHÆA ADVENA.
THREE-COLOURED WATER LILY.
Nuphar advena.
PLATE 394

The full description given in *Hortus Kewensis*, and translated by Professor Martyn in his very valuable edition of *Miller's Dictionary*, renders it unnecessary to say more here than that we have remarked one of the three external calycine leaflets to be usually larger than the other two, and more or less yellow; sometimes it grows as large as the internal ones and resembles them in colour. The internal petals like calycine leaflets are likewise somewhat unequal in size and vary in colour, being more or less tinged with dull purple within. The petals, as these parts have been usually called in

394 *Nymphea advena* (t. 684 1803 SE)

this genus, in number sixteen, are so small as scarcely to appear in the figure, being very nearly concealed by the reflected anthers.

It is a native of North America, and hardy enough to bear the cold of our winters, but does not blow very freely.

Our drawing was taken at Messrs. Whitley and Brame's, in June 1802, where it flowered, in a cistern, in the stove. Introduced by Mr. William Young in 1772. Unassisted by artificial heat, it generally flowers in July.

NYMPHÆA NITIDA.
CUP-FLOWERED WATER LILY.
Nymphæa nitida.
PLATE 396

That this species, which is very nearly related to *Nymphea odorata* (*Bot. Mag. t. 819*) is really distinct, we are persuaded by the observations of Mr. Anderson, Gardener to James Vere, Esq. of Kensington-Gore. This intelligent cultivator finds that the roots afford the most discriminative characters in this genus, and at once point out a real difference between these two nearly allied species. In *Nymphea nitida* the root-stock is perpendicular and does not seem ever to acquire any considerable length, whereas in *N. odorata*, this part extends horizontally along the mud, in the same manner as in *alba*. *Nymphæa nitida* seems to require the constant heat of a stove or hot-bed to preserve it alive, whilst *odorata* is now found to be quite hardy.

We have not been able to learn of what country *N. nitida* is a native, but from the above circumstance it probably belongs to a tropical clime. The flowers are without scent. We are not yet satisfied whether the sinking of the veins below the surface of the leaf, which in this instance was the case on both sides, be a constant and permanent character, or variable according to the age of the leaf or from other accidental circumstances. Is propagated by offsets, Blossoms in august. Drawn at Mr. Vere's garden in August.

NYMPHÆA ODORATA.
SWEET-SCENTED WATER LILY.
Nymphæa odorata.
PLATE 397

We have no doubt but that this plant is a very distinct species from *Nymphæa alba*, to which it however approaches very nearly. In the form of its leaves it is apt to vary considerably, so that perhaps a distinguishing character cannot be well established from this alone; probably a better one might be found in the stigma, the rays of which we believe are always more erect and incurved. It is a native of North America, and is met with, according to Michaux, from Canada to Carolina, for we have little hesitation in referring his *alba* to this species. Its flowers are very sweet-scented, much like those of *Nymphæa cærulea*, in which it differs from *Nymphæa alba*, the flowers of which are entirely scentless.

Our drawing was made at Messrs. Whitley and Brame's, from a plant that flowered in the stove in the month of August 1801, out of the collection of the Marquis of Blandford. It is far less common than *Nymphæa cærulca*, requires the same treatment, supposed to be not hardy enough to bear our winters without protection from the frost.

395 *Nymphea pygmea* (t. 1525 1813 SE)

396 *Nymphea nitida* (t. 1359 1811 SE)

397 *Nymphea odorata* (t. 819 1805 SE)

Nymphæa pygmæa.
Pigmy Water Lily.
Nymphæa tetragona.
PLATE 395

Nymphæa pygmæa was certainly brought to this country from China, where, on the authority of Mr. William Ker, it is indigenous; yet, upon comparing it with Pallas's own specimens, now in the possession of A. B. Lambert, Esq. it appears to us to be decidedly the same as his *tetragonanthos*, the *tetragoma* of Mons. Georgi. Native of eastern Siberia; and, if we mistake not, the figure in Gmelin's *Flora Sibirica* rather be-

longs to this than to our *nitida*, to which it is referred in the new edition of *Hortus Kewensis*. The character of the sinking of the veins on the under, as well as upper, side of the leaf is common to both these species.

The name of *tetragona* was given to the Siberian plant, from the receptacle being exactly square, which gives in some degree the same form to the base of the flower. We did not advert to this circumstance when we had the living plant before us, but, from the drawing, it appears to have been the same in ours; and Mr. Salisbury, in describing this part, says it is slightly quadrangular.

Treated as a stove plant, blossoms freely, not always at the same season. Our specimen flowered in the elegant collection of Mr. Kent, in August last, and it was in bloom about the same time in the Royal Gardens at Kew.

186

398 *Nymphea rubra* (t. 1280 1810)

also. Introduced into the Kew Gardens by the Right Hon. Sir Joseph Banks, Bart. and K.B. Our drawing was taken from a plant which flowered in August 1808, at Mr. Woodford's, late of Rickmansworth in Hertfordshire. We have seen it repeatedly in flower at Mr. Vere's, Kensington-Gore, where, with several other species, it is cultivated in a cistern, placed on a common hot-bed.

OLEACEÆ

JASMINUM NUDIFLORUM.
NAKED-FLOWERING OR WINTER JASMINE.

Jasminum nudiflorum.

PLATE 399

One of the many interesting discoveries in China of Mr. Fortune on his first visit to that country, though not then a new discovery; for, according to Dr. Lindley, it had been distributed in a dried state from the Imperial Russian Chinese Herbarium under the erroneous name of *Jasminum angulare*, a species of the Cape of Good Hope, with white flowers growing on the peduncles in threes.

When first described by Dr. Lindley, in the valuable journal of the Horticultural Society of London, it was considered a valuable greenhouse plant, a winter bloomer, and continuing in flower for a length of time. But in the *Botanical Register* the further information was given that it was likely to prove hardy; for "this species," writes Mr. Fortune, "was first discovered in gardens and nurseries in the north of China, particularly about Shanghae, Loochou, and Nanking. It is a very ornamental dwarf shrub, and I have no doubt of its being perfectly hardy in this country (England). It is deciduous; the leaves falling off in its native country early in autumn, and leaving a number of large prominent flower-buds, which expand in early spring, often when the snow is on the ground, and look like little primroses."

Nothing can be more accurate than this statement. The shrub proves perfectly hardy; it flowers in the middle of winter (our drawing was made from a plant on the open wall in December, 1851), and the fallen

399 *Jasminum nudiflorum* (t. 4649 1852 WF)

blossoms on the frosty and snowy ground look like primroses. It is to be regretted that the foliage, scanty at best, does not appear at the same time with the leaves. Our specimen, not fully developed, was drawn in April. The plant is, like other jasmines, easily propagated by layers or cuttings.

DESCR. A twiggy *shrub*, from four to eight feet high, with long, opposite, dark-green *branches*, exactly quadrangular, the angles somewhat winged. *Leaves* opposite, petiolate, trifoliolate. *Petiole* rather shorter than the leaves. *Leaflets* ovate, the middle somewhat obovate, acute, glabrous, ciliated. *Flowers* lateral, opposite, solitary, arising from scaly buds, on short rather thick *petioles*. *Scales* ovate-acuminate, tinged with brown. *Calyx* with a short *tube*, the *limb* cut into six, spreading, linear, acute segments. *Corolla* full yellow, hypocrateriform; the *tube* slightly widened upwards; *limb* spreading horizontally, of five, obovate or obcordate, slightly-waved segments. *Stamens* two, inserted above the middle of the tube of the corolla, and quite included. *Filaments* very short. *Anthers* oblong-sagittate. *Ovary* globose. *Style* longer than the tube of corolla, a little thickened upwards. *Stigma* globose, emarginate.

NYMPHÆA RUBRA.
RED-FLOWERED WATER LILY.

Nymphæa rubra.

PLATE 398

We have made mention in the 29th volume, No. 1189, of the further division of this genus by Mr. Salisbury into Nymphæa and Castalia and bore our testimony to the propriety of this separation. Dr. Smith, in the *Prodromus Floræ Græcæ*, in adopting this division, has, we think very properly, retained the ancient name of *Nymphæa* for the genus which contins the most numerous and splendid species, and applied to the Yellow Flowered Water-lilies that of *Nuphar*, a name, which if not given to the same species by Dioscorides himself, has at least been added in some of the manuscripts of this author's works.

This magnificent species is a native of the East Indies. We learn from Dr. Roxburg's manuscript, that this species is not unfrequent in Indostan, growing in pools of fresh water, and in rivers, where there is little current. And that the seeds are eaten both raw and boiled, and esteemed wholesome; and in times of scarcity the roots

Cha.ˢ M.ᶜᵘʳᵗⁱˢ.Del.   Pub. by. S. Curtis. Walworth. Dec 1825.   Widdell Sc.

ONAGRACEÆ

FUCHSIA ARBORESCENS.
LAUREL-LEAVED FUCHSIA.

Fuchsia arborescens.

PLATE 400

For an opportunity of presenting our sub-scribers with a figure of this very fine shrub, we are indebted to our friend Robert Barc-lay, Esq. who kindly sent us the whole plant, in full flower, in October last, which the head gardener, Mr. David Cameron, informed us had been treated as a green-house plant; but being placed out of doors in the summer, had been suffered to root out of the pot into the ground where it stood. Whilst perhaps it flowered the best on this account, it was probably owing to the necessity of cutting off the protruded roots, that the flowers all dropped off before the drawing could be quite finished; depriving us of the opportunity of making a detailed description of the parts of fructi-fication.

Mr. Barclay had his plant from the Sloane Street Nursery, where it was raised from seeds brought from Mexico, by Mr. Bullock, ticketed *Fuchsia arborescens.* Several persons have received seeds of the same, under this name from that country; which makes it probable, that it has already, or will be so called in the Mexican publications; we have, therefore, adopted it, though with us we believe it has not yet reached a height exceeding three or four feet, and is only a shrub. Mr. Tate informs us, that he has since raised many plants of it, from seeds sent him by R. P. Staples, Esq. to whose kind favours he is indebted for above two hundred new, or rare species from Mexico.

Cultivated, at present, as a greenhouse shrub; but perhaps may hereafter be found hardy enough to bear our winters without protection.

OPPOSITE:
400 *Fuchsia arborescens* (t. 2620 1826 CMC)

401 *Fuchsia decussata* (t. 2507 1824)

FUCHSIA DECUSSATA.
CROSS-BRANCHED FUCHSIA.

Fuchsia magellanica var *gracilis.*

PLATE 401

Raised from seeds sent from Chili, in 1822, by Mr. Cruikshanks, through Francis Place, Esq.

Hitherto the plants have been kept in the greenhouse; but some are now planted in the open air and are expected to prove as hardy as the *Fuchsia coccinea.*

FUCHSIA SERRATIFOLIA.
SERRATED-LEAVED FUCHSIA.

Fuchsia austromontana.

PLATE 404

Ruiz and Pavon have justly remarked of this, *"planta dum florida perpulchra."* Its flowers are among the largest and most lovely of this lovely genus, and the leaves are handsome likewise, they and the stems being deeply tinted with red. The species was imported by Messrs. Veitch of Exeter, through their collector Mr. William Lobb, who detected it in Peru, probably at Muna,

where it was first discovered in moist and shady places by the original describers Ruiz and Pavon. It has been already exhibited at Chiswick, when the large silver-gilt medal was awarded to it, and other prizes in the Rooms of the Horticultural Society and the Regent's Park Garden; and the plant has excited great admiration. At present it is considered a hothouse plant; but in all probability it will be found to bear the open air during the summer months, when it will prove more ornamental than any species yet in cultivation among us. We possess fine native specimens gathered in Peru by Mathews, at Panahuanca and at Pangoa and at Huamantanga, gathered by our friend Mr. Maclean.

Note: *Fuchsia austromontana* is the correct name for the plant illustrated here; *Fuchsia denticulata* is the correct name for *Fuchsia serratifolie.*

LOPEZIA RACEMOSA.
MEXICAN LOPEZIA.

Lopezia racemosa.

PLATE 402

Some plants have a claim on our attention for their utility, some for their beauty, and some for the singularity of their structure, and the wonderful nature of their eco-nomy; in the last class we must place the present plant, the flowers of which we recommend to the examination of such of our readers as may have an opportunity of seeing them; to the philosophic mind, not captivated with mere show, they will afford a most delicious treat.

We first saw this novelty in flower, towards the close of the year 1792, at the Apothecaries Garden, Chelsea, where Mr. Fairbairn informed me, that he had that season raised several plants of it from seeds, communicated by Dr. J. E. Smith, who received them from Madrid, to which place they were sent from South America, and where the plant as Mons. Cavanille in-forms us, grows spontaneously near Mex-ico. In October 1793, we had the pleasure of seeing this plant again in blossom in the aforesaid garden, raised from seeds which ripened there the preceding year, but un-fortunately from the lateness of their flowering, and the very great injury the plants had sustained from the Cobweb Mite (*Acarus teliarius*) vulgarly called the Red Spider, there seemed little prospect that the seed-vessels would arrive at perfection.

The seeds were sown by Mr. Fairbairn, in March, and the plant kept in the greenhouse till very late in the summer, when to accelerate their blowing, they were removed into the dry stove: it is worthy of remark, that these plants, even late in the autumn, show no signs of blossoming, but the flowers at length come forth with almost unexampled rapidity, and the seed-vessels are formed as quickly, so that if the flowers were not very numerous, their blossoming period would be of very short duration; future experience may perhaps point out the means of making the plant blow earlier: in Spain, the blossoms appeared later than here, Mons. Cavanille observed them in the Royal Garden, in November and December, most probably in the open ground, as no mention is made of the plants having been preserved from the weather.

It was not till long after our description was taken, that we had an opportunity of seeing Mons. Cavanille's most accurate and elegant work, in which this plant is first figured and described; we have selected the most essential parts of his generic character, and adopted his specific description: there is one point, however, in which we differ from him; the part which he regards as the fifth petal, we are inclined to consider rather as that indescribable something, called by Linnæus the nectary, it is indeed of little moment whether we call it a Petal or a Nectary, but there are several reasons why, strictly speaking, we cannot regard it as a Petal: in general the number of Petals correspond with the number of the leaves of the Calyx, those of the latter are four; the base of this Nectary originates deeper than the claws of the Petals, springing in fact from the same part as the Filament, its structure, especially the lower part of it, is evidently different from that of the Petals, corresponding indeed as nearly as possible with that of the base of the filament. – *Vid. Descer.*

Mons. Cavanille was induced to call this plant *Lopezia*, in compliment to Th. Lopez, a Spaniard.

402 *Lopezia racemosa* (t. 254 1798 SE)

ŒNOTHERA MISSOURENSIS.
MISSOURI EVENING PRIMROSE.
Oenothera missouriensis.

PLATE 403

The flowers of the Missouri Evening Primrose are large and showy. In the denticulation of the leaves, and the length of the tube of the calyx, it resembles *longiflora*, but is a much smoother plant, and differs materially in the fruit, which is smooth, oval, four-winged, and stands on a footstalk instead of being cylindrical and hispid. The root is said to be perennial.

Found by Mr. Nuttall in the neighbourhood of the Missouri in North America, who brought many novel and curious plants from that country; some of which that flowered at Liverpool last year, he kindly transmitted us recent specimens of. But our draughtsman being unfortunately absent on a journey into Wales at the time, we had no opportunity of availing ourselves of them for this work.

We do not find that this species has been before noticed: it seems to differ from every one described by Michaux or by Pursh, whose valuable *Flora*, speedily to be published, we have been favoured with the opportunity of consulting. Flowers in June and July.

403 *Oenothera missourensis* (t. 1592 1813 SE)

ŒNOTHERA ROSEA.
ROSE-COLOURED ŒNOTHERA.
Oenothera rosea.

PLATE 405

Of the several different species of this genus growing in our garden at this present writing (eleven in number) two only are of a red or purple colour, the one here figured, and another with a larger flower, which we purpose soon to publish under the name of *purpurea*. The present species, Mr. Aiton informs us, was introduced in 1783 by Mons. Thouin, from Peru.

It has been considered as a greenhouse plant, and a perennial; we find it to be more hardy than greenhouse plants in general, and scarcely entitled to the distinction of a perennial.

It may be increased by cuttings and seeds, the latter of which are plentifully produced. It rarely exceeds a foot in height; its rose-coloured flowers expand during the whole of the day, and are produced during most of the summer months.

To guard against accidental severity of weather, sow its seeds in the spring with tender annuals; when the plants have acquired a proper age and the season is favourable, plant them out singly in the open border.

OPPOSITE:
404 *Fuchsia serratifolia* (t. 4174 1845 WF)

Tab. 4174.

Reeve, Bro. imp

Fitch, del. et lith

405 Oenothera rosea (t. 347 1796)

407 Oenothera viminea (t. 2873 1828 WJH)

Nuttall, who gave seeds of it, with his name attached, to Robert Barclay, Esq. of Burry Hill, to whom we are indebted for the communication of the plant from which our drawing was taken, in September, 1824.

406 Oenothera triloba (t. 2566 1825 JC)

ŒNOTHERA TRILOBA.
DANDELION-LEAVED EVENING PRIMROSE.

Oenothera triloba.

PLATE 406

In Dr. Barton's *Flora* the capsules are described as entirely radical, but in our plant, after the flowering was over they were raised upon a short stem. The flowers in his figure are smaller than with us, and more decidedly three lobed at the point. There is a near affinity between this species and the *acaulis* of Cavanilles, the *grandiflora* of the *Flora Peruviana*, which also, under cultivation, becomes caulescent, and to a greater degree, as appears by the figure given of it in the *Botanical Register*; but that species has white flowers, and differs in the form of its capsules, and in other respects. *Triloba* is not a good name, we think that *taraxacifolia* would have been better, but having been published under the former in America, we do not hold it right to change it.

A hardy annual or biennial. Native of the arid and almost denuded Prairies of the Red River, in North America, where it was first discovered, in 1819, by Professor

ŒNOTHERA VIMINEA.
LARGE PURPLE-FLOWERED TWIGGY EVENING PRIMROSE.

Godetia viminea.

PLATE 407

Descr. *Stem* annual, erect, glabrous, pale, almost white and polished, three to four feet high, branched, with many long, slender, twiggy branches. *Leaves* three to four inches long, alternate, shortly petioled, upper ones sessile, quite entire, glaucous. *Flowers* sessile in the axils of the superior leaves. *Segments* of the calyx acuminate, something more than half the length of the corolla. *Petals* large, of a fine and bright lilac colour, roundish-cuneate, waved, spreading, minutely crenulate at the extremity. *Stamens* four long and four short: *Anthers* linear-oblong, longer than the filaments. *Style* almost as long as the anthers.

Stigma four-cleft, deep purple, the segments patent. *Capsule* rounded, an inch or more long, with eight longitudinal furrows, tapering upwards, downy.

Allied to *Oenothera purpurea*, from which it is abundantly distinct. It is a handsome and hardy annual; and if the seeds be sown in the open border in the spring, the plants will continue to blossom throughout the summer. *Douglas.*

Introduced to the garden of the Horticultural Society, by Mr. David Douglas, in 1827. It was discovered by that most zealous Naturalist, in the interior of northern California: and it flowered for the first time in this country in the month of June, 1828.

ORCHIDACEÆ

ACANTHOPHIPPIUM JAVANICUM.
JAPANESE ACANTHOPHIPPIUM.

Acanthophippum javanicum.

PLATE 408

Cult. From the circumstance that the roots of this orchid adhere firmly to the inside of

408 *Acanthophippium javanicum* (t. 4492 1850 WF)

ADA AURANTIACA.
DEEP ORANGE-FLOWERED ADA.
Ada aurantiaca.
PLATE 409

The flowering specimen of this rare Orchidaceous plant was sent to us in January of the present year by our excellent friend Mr. Bateman, from his collection at Biddulph Grange, Congleton. It is a native of New Granada, and was discovered in the Pamplona, at the height of 8500 feet above the level of the sea, by Mr. Schlim, and has been hitherto only known by the description given by Dr. Lindley in his valuable *Folia Orchidacea*. It is there recognized as a new genus, "differing from *Brassia* in some important particulars: – 1, the lamellæ of the lip are confluent and membranaceous; 2, the lip is parallel with the column, and solidly united to the base of it; 3, the column is twice as long as in other *Brassias*, and thin-edged at the base; 4, the caudicle is short and obovate while the gland is circular." It flowered with Mr. Bateman in January, 1864.

410 *Aganisia ionoptera* (t. 7270 1892 MS)

the pot in which it grows, we may infer that its natural habitat is in rocky places, where there is but little soil, and which are subject to a considerable degree of dryness during a part of the year. With us it grows freely, if potted in loose, turfy, peat soil, and kept in the warm division of the Orchideous house. It should be planted a few inches above the level of the mouth of the pot, and supported by a substantial drainage; for plants of this habit, when potted in loose soil, are very liable, by their gravity, to sink below the margin of the pot – which not only gives the plant an unsightly appearance, but causes the pseudobulbs to become crowded and weak. This precaution is the more necessary, from the downward tendency of the pseudo-bulbs (a circumstance common to many bulbous-rooted genera), each successive formation being produced from the base of the previous ones, and being sessile in their attachment to them. They are thus liable to become, in time, a crowded mass in the pot. When this happens, it is advisable to divide the mass, and select the younger and healthier pseudo-bulbs, to be repotted in the manner described above.

409 *Ada aurantiaca* (t. 5435 1864 WF)

AGANISIA IONOPTERA.
Aganisia ionoptera.
PLATE 410

The genus *Aganisia* was established by Lindley in the *Botanical Register* (1839, Misc. No. 65, and 1840, t. 32) on a single Demeraran species (*Aganisia pulchella*). Lindley says of the genus, "if its column were produced into a foot, and the lower sepals unequal at the base, it would be a *Maxillaria*." To this are added by Bentham in the *Genera Plantarum*, and Reichenbach in various publications, about eight other species.

Aganisia ionoptera is a native of Peru, where it was found by the collector Wallis, who sent it to Linden, from whom the plant here figured was obtained at the International Horticultural Exhibition of Brussels in 1891. It flowered in the Royal Gardens in June, 1892.

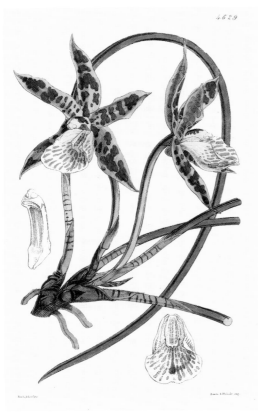

411 *Bifrenaria hadwenii* (t. 4629 1852 WF)

BIFRENARIA HADWENII.
MR. HADWEN'S BIFRENARIA.

Scuticaria hadwenii.

PLATE 410

Communicated by Isaac Hadwen, Esq., of Liverpool, from the stove of his garden, in June 1851. It has a good deal the habit of *Maxillaria* (*Scuticaria*) *steelii*, and it is no wonder that horticulturists placed it in the same genus; but Dr. Lindley observes that it departs from *Scuticaria* in the pollen-masses, and he refers it to *Bifrenaria*, though differing somewhat from that genus.

It is a native of Brazil, and appears to have been first imported by Mr. Hadwen from Rio Janeiro. We have received plants at Kew from the same country, through our valued friend Mr. Miers, of Temple Lodge, Hammersmith. It flowered with Mr. Hadwen in May, with us in September.

Cult. This orchid requires to be kept in the tropical Orchid house. It is strictly epiphytal, and the appearance of newly-imported plants leads us to suppose that it grows in rather exposed and dry situations. At the Royal Gardens it grows on a suspended block of wood, and has flowered. The wood should be slightly inclined, in order to favour the pendulous habit of the plant.

CALANTHE MASUCA.
PURPLE-FLOWERED CALANTHE.

Calanthe masuca.

PLATE 412

Native of India; – according to Dr. Lindley, of "Nepal, Bengal, Ceylon, and probably Java." It blossomed in 1842 with Messrs. Rollisons, at Tooting, but, though a handsome and really striking plant, it had never been figured. Our fine tuft of the plant at Kew, which blossomed in July and August, was derived from Mr. Clowes' collections.

Cult. This, being an East Indian terrestrial Orchid, requires to be grown in a moist tropical stove. It thrives in turfy peat containing a small portion of loam. On account of its soft fleshy roots adhering to the sides of the pot, it is desirable to use a shallow wide-mouthed pot, in order to avoid tearing the roots by frequent shiftings. In summer it may be freely watered, but the pot must be well drained, so as to allow the water to pass off freely. Shading is necessary during bright sunshine. In winter it should be placed in a drier atmosphere, and especial care must be taken that no water be allowed to lodge in the folds of the young leaves.

412 *Calanthe masuca* (t. 4541 1850 WF)

CATASETUM CALLOSUM VAR.
GRANDIFLORUM.
TUMOUR-LIPPED CATASETUM;
LARGE-FLOWERED VAR.

Catasetum callosum var *grandiflorum.*

PLATE 413

This singular plant, of which the flowers may, I think, be likened to the body and legs of a great spider, is from the rich collection in Syon Gardens, and was received by His Grace the Duke of Northumberland from Columbia. Notwithstanding the large size of the blossoms, and the slightly dissimilar form and different colour of the lip, I fear it can only be considered a variety of *Catasetum callosum* of Dr. Lindley, and I am the more confirmed in this opinion from afterwards receiving from Syon a smaller state of the same plant, exactly, as it were, intermediate between the two. Its long pendent spikes of dingy purple flowers, of which the floral coverings are singularly divaricated, the three upper pieces being applied to the back of the column, the two lower to the underside of the lip, are produced in December.

CATTLEYA FORBESII.
MR. FORBES' CATTLEYA.

Cattleya forbesii.

PLATE 414

Descr. Parasitic. *Stem* six to eight inches tall, slightly swollen, and hence somewhat bulbous, sheathed with long, membranous, cylindrical scales, and bearing at its extremity two oblong, firm and fleshy, patent *leaves*, from the centre of which, and from within a subcylindrical but carinated and slightly compressed sheath, arises the rounded peduncle, four to five inches long, single-flowered, but jointed and bearing one or two bracts, as if occasionally two or more-flowered. *Flower* large, handsome. *Sepals* and *petals* spreading, yet incurved, almost exactly similar to each other, of a yellowish-green colour, linear-lanceolate, faintly striated, often with a brownish tint. *Lip* externally whitish, cylindrical from the involuted sides, and much curved, three-lobed at the extremity, the central lobe white and crisped at the margin, yellow, and bearing three to four elevated lines in

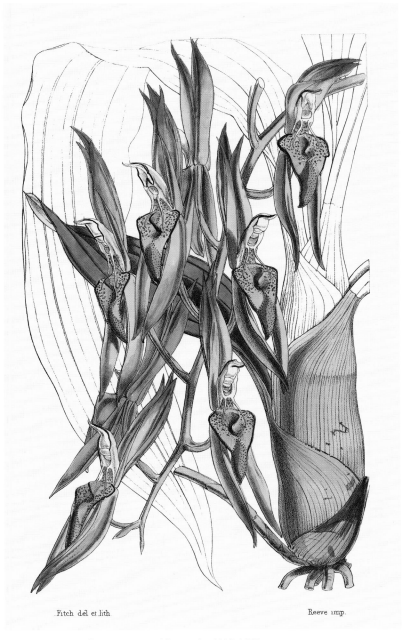

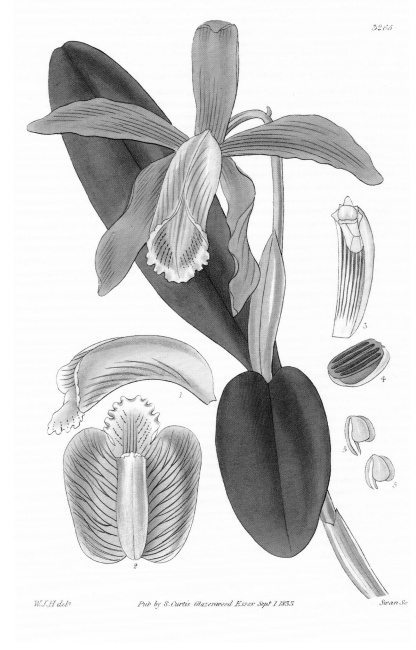

413 *Catasetum callosum var. grandiflorum* (t. 4219 1846 WF)

414 *Cattleya forbesii* (t. 3265 1833 WJH)

the centre, lateral lobes obtuse, slightly crenate and reflexed at the extremity. Within, the lip is very beautiful, having a broad, deep yellow, elevated line in the centre, the yellow gradually passing into rose-colour at the margin, and the whole is marked diagonally with forked, deep red, elevated lines, most branched near the margin. *Column* appressed to the labellum, semiterete, whitish, grooved within, and marked with red lines. *Stigma* large, convex, very glutinous. *Anther* sunk into a recess on the top of the column, four-celled, white, the cells dark brown.

A native of Brazil, and introduced to the Gardens of the Horticultural Society at Chiswick, by their Collector, Mr. Forbes. Our specimen, in the two seasons in which it has flowered, (in June 1832 and 1833,) produced only a one-flowered peduncle,

whereas Mr. Lindley represents two blossoms on the flower-stalk. But as if to make up for the deficiency, the size of our flower is much greater.

CATTLEYA LINDLEYANA.
DR. LINDLEY'S CATTLEYA.
X *Brassocattleya lindleyana.*
PLATE 415

This, which we cannot find to be anywhere described, was lately sent to us from Bahia, by our valued correspondent C. H. Williams, Esq. In aspect it much resembles *Lœlia*; but the pollen-masses are four and not eight. It flowered with us in September, 1863, not long after the plant was imported.

CATTLEYA PUMILA.
DWARF CATTLEYA.
Laelia pumila.
PLATE 416

The small size of this plant, the minute, rounded pseudo-bulbs and the narrow leaves, together with the obtuse, short, and almost simbriated lip, will, I think, clearly distinguish this very beautiful species of *Cattleya* from those hitherto described. It was received from the Essequibo by John Allcard, Esq., in whose collection it flowered last year, and who kindly sent the well executed drawing here engraved, from the pencil of Mrs. Withers.

Descr. There is evidently a horizontal stem, or *rhizoma*, throwing out stout radicles below, and minute *pseudo-bulbs* above,

195

415 *Cattleya lindleyana* (t. 5449 1864 WF)

which latter are at first clothed with sheathing scales, and afterwards seem to enlarge, till on the falling away of the leaves they are two inches long and naked, always rounded and striated. *Leaf* solitary, terminal, coriaceous, four to five inches long, scarcely an inch broad, linear-oblong, nerveless. *Flowers* solitary, arising from a

416 *Cattleya pumila* (t. 3656 1838 AW)

membranaceous sheath at the base of the leaf, drooping, of a beautiful blush-purple colour. *Sepals* spreading, oblong, the upper one reflexed. *Petals* larger and broader, waved at the margins. *Lip* large, three-lobed, the two lateral lobes involute, enclosing the *column* with the tube thus formed, the middle lobe short, reflexed, waved and crisped, almost laciniated.

417 *Cirrhopetalum ornatissimum* (t. 7229 1892 MS)

CIRRHOPETALUM ORNATISSIMUM.

Cirrhopetalum ornatissimum.

PLATE 417

Cirrhopetalum ornatissimum was first described from specimens stated to have been received from Assam, the reputed native country of the specimen here figured; but as, according to a figure in the collection of drawings belonging to the Botanical Gardens of Calcutta, it is a native of Sikkim, its more exact locality is probably the outer ranges of the Himalaya Mountains, from Sikkim eastwards. In the above-mentioned figure the sepals and petals are yellowish-green, and the red streaks are broken up into purple dots. In the plate given in Warner's Orchid Album the leaves are broadly elliptic with rounded retuse tips, dark green with no yellow margin, the

bracts are longer and the flowers much larger, of a dull purplish blue, the lateral sepals end in longer tails, and the petals have an almost black purple centre and greenish border; it doubtless represents a variety.

C. ornatissimum was received at Kew from the Royal Botanical Gardens of Calcutta in 1890 (under the erroneous name of *Bulbophyllum mannii*), and flowered in the tropical orchid house of Kew, in September, 1891.

CŒLOGYNE HUMILIS.

DWARF PLEIONE.

Pleione humilis.

PLATE 418

This pretty pleione, although long since introduced and figured, had been lost to the country for many years; no doubt through inattention to its habits and constitution. Fortunately a fresh supply of plants was recently obtained (through Dr. Anderson, of the Calcutta Botanic Gardens) from Sikkim by the Royal Gardens at

418 *Coelogyne humilis* (t. 5674 1867 WF)

OPPOSITE:

419 *Cycnoches loddigesii* (t. 4215 1846 WF)

Fitch del.

Reeve imp.

Kew, and it was here that the one represented in the plate flowered last winter. It is quite a mountain plant, having been found on the Indian Alps, in Nepal, Sikkim, and Bhutan, at an elevation of seven to eight thousand feet, growing among moss in shady places, and even on the trunks of trees. Dr. Hooker met with several varieties during his travels in the Himalaya, where this and other species take the place of our autumn crocuses, throwing up masses of gay flowers after the leaves have disappeared. Excepting *Cœlogyne maculata*, which is found two thousand feet lower, all the pleione section of *Cœlogyne* are easily cultivated in the shadiest part of the coolest house; and they form a most interesting group, to which other fine species, not yet introduced, will, I trust, ere long be added. They require to be grown in a pot.

CYCNOCHES LODDIGESII.
MR. LODDIGES' SWANWORT.

Cyncnoches loddigesii.

PLATE 419

This very striking Orchideous plant, the species upon which the genus was founded, is a native of Surinam, and was introduced from thence, by Messrs. Loddiges through J. H. Lance, Esq. As may be expected, it requires great heat and moisture, and, thus treated, it flowers readily in the autumnal months, at which season our specimen bloomed in the Royal Gardens of Kew. The column, long and slender and much convex, has not inaptly been compared to a swan's neck, whence, as is well known, the generic appellation is derived; but to us it appears to have a still greater similarity to a Cobra de Capella, the swollen and dilated apex below the anther very accurately representing the inflated throat of that dreaded reptile, while the colour and marking serve to increase the resemblance.

CYPRIPEDIUM ARIETINUM.
RAM'S-HEAD LADIES SLIPPER.

Cypripedium arietinum.

PLATE 420

In the *Cypripediums* which we have before figured, as in most of the genus, the two lower external petals are united together, and stand directly opposite the upper one; so that the four petals stand crosswise, which has been considered as part of the generic character: but in this species, from the lower petals being separate and distant, the arrangement is quite different.

The name of *arietinum* was given by Mr. Brown, from the resemblance which the flower, in some positions, bears to the head of a sheep.

Our drawing was taken in May 1811, from a plant that flowered with Messrs. Whitley, Brame and Milne; but as we had no opportunity of seeing the original, we could not publish it, till we were enabled this spring to examine living plants communicated by Messrs. Chandler and Buckingham, who imported the roots last year from Montreal in Canada. Requires the same treatment as the other American Cypripediums.

420 Cypripedium arietinum (t. 1569 1813 SE)

CYPRIPEDIUM MACRANTHON.
LARGE-FLOWERED LADIES SLIPPER.

Cypripedium macranthum.

PLATE 421

This beautiful species of *Cypripedium*, quite new to our collections, is said by Amman to be found at Tobolsk, and by Gmelin to be frequent in all Siberia, within the 58° of latitude, in open places, or in woods composed of scattered birches.

Seeds had often been sent by Dr. Fischer of St. Petersburg to the Glasgow Botanic Garden; but we never succeeded in cultivating the plant until last year, when roots were presented to us by the same liberal Botanist. One of these, from which the present figure and description were made, blossomed under the protection of a frame in May, 1829.

Cypripedium macranthon appears to be nearly allied to the C. *ventricosum*, which I only know by the figure of Sweet's *Brit. Fl. Garden, New Series*, t. 1. But there the two innermost segments of the perianth are much narrower, and longer than the lip, the mouth of the lip is larger, and with a small cleft at the lowest extremity, and is not so regularly notched as in our plant. The whole colour too is a deeper purple.

CYPRIPEDIUM PARVIFLORUM.
YELLOW LADIES SLIPPER.

Cypripedium parviflorum.

PLATE 422

This species of Ladies Slipper is an inhabitant of North America, from New England to North Carolina. It comes very near to the European species, and we suppose has been mistaken for the same by Michaux in whose specific description *confertis* seems to be an error of the press for *contortis*. It is a taller plant, more pubescent; lateral or interior petals longer, narrower, and more curled; and the nectarium or slipper is of a plain yellow colour without veins.

OPPOSITE:
421 Cypripedium macranthon (t. 2938 1829 WJH)

W.J.H.delt

Pub.by S. Curtis.Walworth   Oct.1.1829

Swan Sc.

422 *Cypripedium parviflorum* (t. 911 1806 SE)

CYPRIPEDIUM ROEZLI.

Phragmipedium longifolium.

PLATE 424

The nearest ally of this magnificient species is undoubtedly *Cypripedium longifolium* which differs in its much smaller stature, narrower leaves, spreading sheaths of the purple scape, shorter, more obtuse dorsal sepals, and colour of the flower. In all essential characters they agree very closely indeed, and the almost identical structure and form of the lip and sexual apparatus suggest the possibility of their being races between which intermediates will be found. For horticultural purposes *C. roezli* is incomparably the finest of the two, not only in colour, but on account of its size, it being by far the largest of the genus hitherto discovered. Probably these species would hybridise with facility, but I see nothing to be gained by such a proceeding, *C. longifolium* presenting no one superiority but the bright red colour of its scape.

Cypripedium roezli is a native of New Grenada, where it was found by Roezl on the banks of the Dagua river, which, according to Regel, occupies a valley between two ranges of the Andes. I find, however, no such river on the map, but a small town of Dagua on the western decliv-

ity of the Andes, near the Bay of Choco. The specimen here figured flowered at Messrs. Veitch's establishment in January, 1874. It is said to flower perennially and profusely, a statement inconsistent with the habits of any plants in continuous health, but which, if taken with the caution to be used in accepting the laudatory advertisements of choice plants, may be regarded as evidence of its being a very free flowerer.

DENDROBIUM ATROVIOLACEUM.

Dendrobium atroviolaceum.

PLATE 423

Of all dendrobes known to me I cannot recall amongst recent discoveries one so strikingly unlike its congeners in coloration, and at the same time so beautiful in this respect, as *Dendrobium atroviolaceum*. As Mr. Rolfe observes in his description of it, its nearest ally is *Dendrobium macrophyllum*, A. Rich. a noble species, with broad leaves, over a foot long, and hairy inflorescence. Technically, both belong to

423 *Dendrobium atroviolaceum* (t. 7371 1894 MS)

the section *Stachyobium*, of *Dendrobium*, and to the rather heterogeneous subsection of *Speciosæ*; but whether or no they may be included in the latter, they with a few other Far Eastern species form a small group distinguished by the long clavate stem or pseudobulb, with two, rarely three terminal coriaceous leaves, and a terminal raceme of flowers, with a deeply three-lobed lip. The group includes species with hairy and with glabrous inflorescence. Of the hairy flowered are the original *D. macrophyllum*, which ranges from Java to the Philippines and New Guinea; and *D. gordoni*, Horne (*Journ. Linn. Soc.* xx. 372), from the Fiji Islands; and of the glabrous-flowered are *D. atro-violaceum*, *D. chloropterum*, Reichb. F. & S. Moore (in *Trim. Journ. Bot.* 1878, 137, t. 196) from New Guinea, and *D. trigrinum*, Rolfe (*Annals of Botany*, vol. v. p. 507) from the Solomon Islands. In Veitch's *Manual* (*Dendrob.* p. 60) *D. macrophyllum* is referred to the sub-section *Calostachyæ* of sect. *Eudendrobium*, which is, I think, an error.

D. atroviolaceum was introduced from New Guinea in 1890; and the specimen here figured was received from F. Wigan, Esq., of Clare Lawn, East Sheen, in December of last year.

DENDROBIUM BRYMERIANUM.

Dendrobium brymerianum.

PLATE 425

This is certainly the most beautiful of the orange-coloured dendrobes, and the most singular; nothing can exceed the elegance of the long-branched fimbriation of the lip, and the flowers themselves are the largest of the section. Reichenbach first described it as a connecting link between the sections *Stachyobium* and *Dendrocoryne*. One of its nearest figured allies is the well-known *Dendrobium fimbriatum* from which it widely differs in the narrower longer sepals and petals, and in the form and enormously long fimbriation of the lip. Dr. Reichenbach further remarks that all the six flowers he examined had a strong tendency to become triandrous, which seems to be the case in our specimen also;

OPPOSITE:

424 *Cypripedium roezli* (t. 6217 1876 WF)

6217

W Fitch del et Lith

Vincent Brooks Day & Son Imp

425 *Dendrobium brymerianum* (t. 6383 1878)

he describes the bracts as half as long as the pedicel and ovary, which is not the case in the specimen here figured.

Dendrobium brymerianum was dedicated by its describer to W. E. Brymer, Esq., M.P., of Islington House, Dorchester, who first flowered it in 1875, the plant having, it is supposed, been one of Mr. Lowe's importations from Burma. It has since then been flowered in great perfection by Mr. Salt, of Fernichurch, Shiply, and of Messrs. Veitch, to whom I am indebted for the opportunity of having it figured.

DENDROBIUM DEVONIANUM.
THE DUKE OF DEVONSHIRE'S
DENDROBIUM.

Dendrobium devonianum.

PLATE 426

Assuredly one of the most delicate and most lovely of all Orchideous plants, and worthy to bear the name of that distinguished nobleman, the Duke of Devonshire, who has done so much to encourage Horticulture and Botany. It is a native of the Khoseea hills, East Indies, and bears this name in Mr. Paxton's *Magazine of Botany*,

vol. vii. I do not find it anywhere fully described. Our plant, from which the accompanying figure was made, is from the collection of the late Mr. Clowes. It flowered with us in September, 1847. The charm of this plant is confined wholly to its flowers: the stems and foliage possess no attractions. Except in the colour and markings and pubescence, the flowers have a considerable resemblance to those of *Dendrobium fimbriatum*. The leaves are widely different.

Cult. This belongs to the caulescent section of *Dendrobium* and, being of a weak and slender habit, its appearance does not offer much inducement to the cultivator; but what it wants in look as a plant, is amply compensated by its lovely flowers, which render it worthy of a place in every Orchideous collection. It requires to be kept in the warm Orchideous house; and as the stems are weak and naturally pendulous, it should be suspended from the roof of the house, either attached to a block of mossy wood, or in an open wire basket containing loose turfy peat mixed with chopped sphagnum moss; or the block of wood or wire basket may be dispensed with, by fixing the plant on a sod of solid sphagnum, which remains firm and sound a long time, and keeps entirely free from insects and fungi. During its season of growth it must receive the usual stimulus of

426 *Dendrobium devonianum* (t. 4429 1849 WF)

heat and moisture, and shading from the mid-day sun in summer. After the stems have attained their growth, they will begin to lose their leaves: water must then be gradually withheld, and the plant may be more freely exposed to the sun. The flowers are produced on the leafless stems during the dry season, a character common to many of the species in the section of *Dendrobium* to which the present one belongs. It increases by lateral shoots, which emit roots and continue to grow while attached to the old stems.

427 *Dendrobium fimbriatum var. oculatum* (t. 4160 1845 WF)

DENDROBIUM FIMBRIATUM; *VAR.*
OCULATUM.

FRINGE-LIPPED DENDROBIUM; *VAR.* WITH
SANGUINEOUS EYE.

Dendrobium fimbriatum var. *oculatum.*

PLATE 427

A native of Nepal, whence plants have from time to time been sent to our stoves by Dr. Wallich. It first blossomed in the Liverpool Botanic Garden, as stated in the *Exotic Flora*: and the flowers were of an uniform golden yellow. Our present plant, in the Royal Botanic Gardens of Kew, has a dark blood-coloured eye-like spot in the centre of the labellum, which adds greatly to the beauty of this otherwise very charming plant. This state of it, Dr. Lindley considers that of the native specimens. It flowered with us in September, 1843.

DENDROBIUM LAEVIFOLIUM.

Dendrobium laevifolium.

PLATE 428

Dendrobium laevifolium is a recent introduction by Sir Jeremiah Colman of Gatton Park, Reigate, to whose courtesy we owe the opportunity of figuring this most charming plant. It was collected by Mr. J. C. Frost on Rossell Island, one of the Louisiades, an archipelago of small islands situated in the direct continuation of the south-eastern-most point of New Guinea. It grows there, so Sir Jeramiah informs me, on moss-covered saplings, only six to seven centimetres in diameter, in the mist-belt of the mountains at an altitude of 360 to 450 m. and in a perpetually moist atmosphere.

Dendrobium laevifolium belongs to the section *Oxyglossum* which comprises over fifty species, all but a few endemic in New Guinea. They are noteworthy on account of their general habit of which our species is a characteristic example and of the fact that a number of them which moreover

428 *Dendrobium laevifolium* (t. 9011 1924 LS)

have showy flowers grow in assemblages large enough to become attractive objects in the scenery. According to Schlechter they are, like our species, generally confined to the mist-belt of the mountains, but in the south-eastern part of Dutch New Guinea, for instance on Mount Goliad, they occur at all levels up to the summit, often growing on rocks.

The cultivation of *D. laevifolium* does not appear to be difficult as long as it is in harmony with the conditions of its native habitat. Mr. J. Collier, Sir Jeremiah's gardener, writes that at Gatton Park *D. laevifolium* is planted in a shallow pan suspended high up near the glass-roof of a house with intermediate temperature and a rather moist atmosphere and it is never allowed to go very dry. Under such conditions it thrives very well and flowers freely and regularly.

429   *Dendrobium pierardi* (t. 2584 1825 WJH)

DENDROBIUM PIERARDI.

PIERARD'S DENDROBIUM.

Dendrobium aphyllum.

PLATE 429

This species of Dendrobium has a near affinity with *Dendrobium cucullatum* from which it is especially distinguished by the form of the labellum. As in that, the stems are naturally either pendulous, or prostrate, though drawn erect in our figure. It is

a beautiful parasite, native of Chittagong and of various parts of the Delta of the Ganges. Introduced into the Calcutta garden by Mons. Pierard, from whom Dr. Roxburgh gave it its specific name. Our drawing was made from a plant that flowered in the collection at Spofforth by the Hon. and Rev. Wm. Herbert, who informs us that he received it from Dr. Carey "that it is cultivated at Calcutta, by tying it on a smooth branch of a tree, water being constantly conducted to it by a string through a small aperture in a vessel above; that, so treated, it hangs down the length of six feet, covered with flowers after the leaves decay, at which time, it is stated by Dr. Carey to be one of the most beautiful objects in the vegetable kingdom." At Spofforth Mr. Herbert says, that "it thrives pretty well in several situations, but best in moss, running horizontally in a dampish situation. The more equal temperature of our stoves prevents its losing its leaves as regularly as it does at Calcutta, but they generally fall from the part which produces the flowers at least." Messrs. Loddiges state, that they have found it thrive pretty well, fastened to a damp wall in the stove, without earth, but sprinkled occasionally with water. It flowers in March, and the blossoms last in perfection a long time.

DENDROBIUM VICTORIAE-REGINAE.

Dendrobium victoriæ-reginæ.

PLATE 430

When not quite thirty years ago the discovery of this orchid was announced, the plant was acclaimed as the first "blue" *Dendrobium*. Although this was hardly correct, even if we make allowance for a considerable latitude in the application of the colour-term, the orchid marked then, and probably still does, the nearest approach to blue in a *Dendrobium*-flower. At any rate, the plant was undoubtedly a valuable acquisition from the gardener's standpoint; for if properly grown — and this does not seem difficult — it makes a really good display with its handsome and freely produced flowers. Botanically, too, it was interesting as it appeared to have no very close ally, and indeed its affinity was sought in more than one direction. This uncertainty was not surprising, confused as the condition of the taxonomy of *Dendrobium* was at the time. Today, with a somewhat better insight into the natural constitution of this unwieldy genus it is not so difficult to place.

Distribution. – Montane zone of the Philippine Islands, 1800 m. – 2400m.

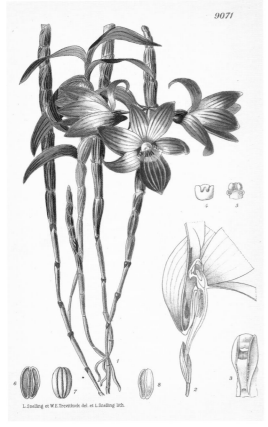

430   *Dendrobium victoriae-reginae* (t. 9071 1925 LS & WE)

EPIDENDRUM ALOIDES.
ALOE-LEAVED EPIDENDRUM.

Cymbidium simulans.

PLATE 431

The present epidendrum is figured and described in Rheede's *Hortus Malabaricus* from whence we learn that it is parasitical to several trees in India, but most frequently found on the *Strychnos nux vomica*.

A few years since, my friend Mr. Vere, of Kensington, received this plant from India, by the kindness of his neighbour J. Devaynes, Esq. Placed in a pot of earth and plunged in the tan pit of the stove, it grew, increased, and now flourishes, but has not blown: with Messrs. Grimwood and Wykes, the plant has flowered this summer; instead of plunging it in the tan, they

431   *Epidendrum aloides* (t. 387 1797)

set it on the flue of the stove; and to this variation in its treatment, its flowering is perhaps to be attributed.

It is of more ready growth than parasitical plants in general, and is increased by parting its roots.

432   *Epidendrum ciliare* (t. 463 1799 SE)

EPIDENDRUM CILIARE.
FRINGED EPIDENDRUM.

Epidendrum ciliare.

PLATE 432

The rare and singular species here represented, a native of the warmer parts of America, and the West Indies, flowered with Mr. Whitley, Nurseryman, in February 1799, and at irregular periods before that time; he informs me that it is not constant as to the time of its blowing, and that though the plant flowers with him, it never assumes a fine healthy green appearance, he propagates it by dividing its limbs or branches, which often put forth small roots; the plant grows in a pot, in a mixture of loam and peat or bog-earth, and is kept constantly plunged in the tan-pit of the stove.

EPIDENDRUM ELONGATUM.
LONG-STALKED EPIDENDRUM.

Epidendrum elongatum.

PLATE 433

As the *Epidendrum secundum* of Jacquin has not yet been seen by us, we cannot clear up the difficulties which have hitherto attended this species. We are however inclined to regard the *Epidendrum elongatum* and *secundum* of Jacquin, and the *suscatum* of Smith, as three distinct species. Our plant is undoubtedly the first of these; differing in no respect from Jacquin's figure, except in the colour of the flower, which with him is more resembling redlead. The flowers are not fecund, the leaves not emarginate nor of a dark purple red as in *secundum*; and the serrated nectarium seems sufficient to distinguish it from both the other species. If the *Epidendrum secundum* described by Solander be not different from either, we suspect that it belongs to this, as does undoubtedly the specimen so named in the Banksian Herbarium.

Our drawing was taken at E. J. A. Woodford's, Esq. in May last, from which time it continued in flower during nearly the whole of the summer. Native of the West Indies. Requires the same treatment as the rest of the genus.

433 *Epidendrum elongatum* (t. 611 1802 SE)

EPIDENDRUM LINEARIFOLIUM.
NARROW-LEAVED EPIDENDRUM.
Epidendrum bractescens.

PLATE 434

A native, probably, of Mexico. It was received at Kew as one of the collection of the late Mr. Clowes, but the name, if it had any, was effaced on the label. It does not appear to be anywhere described: but its affinity is doubtless with a group of *Epidendrum* which I have called *Encyclia*, and not far removed from *E. gracile*, Lindl. *Bot. Reg.* t. 1765, from the Bahamas; differing, however, abundantly from it in the much more slender and graceful character of the whole plant, in the smaller and even (not corrugated) pseudo-bulbs, much narrower and longer leaves, and in the small lateral lobes of the labellum. The colour and markings of the flower are different. The lip here, and especially the lobes, are most beautifully veined with purple. Flowers in June.

Cult. *Epidendrum* was the common name originally applied to the plants now called Epiphytal Orchids, of which twenty-five species are recorded to have been introduced into the gardens of this country previous to the beginning of the present century. A few were known in Miller's time, for under the word *Epidendrum*, in his

Dictionary, he states that these plants come from the West Indies, and that several kinds of soil had been tried for cultivating them, but without success; and he therefore considered it unnecessary to say more about them. There can be no doubt that the want of success in growing orchids at that time was not entirely owing to improper soil, but rather to their not being placed in a suitable atmosphere. Even in our time, we remember seeing a very extensive collection of Brazilian Orchids potted in common soil, which in a short time all perished; but when we also recollect that they were placed within a foot of a hot brick flue, that the stunted appearance of the other plants in the house indicated a dry atmosphere, and that no shading from the sun was used, we cannot be surprised at the death of the "*Epidendrums.*" The name is now restricted to a genus which contains above one hundred and fifty described species, the whole of which are natives of the West Indies and America, chiefly within or near the tropics. They vary much in size and aspect, some having showy flowers, while others are very inconspicuous and only of interest to the botanist. The species figured grows and flowers freely in the tropical Orchid house, attached to a

434 *Epidendrum linearifolium* (t. 4572 1851 WF)

block of wood suspended from the roof of the house; it may also be grown in a shallow pot or pan, planted in turfy peat, which should be kept open with potsherds; and, like other small orchids, it should be placed near the glass, shading it during bright sunshine.

435 *Epidendrum sinense* (t. 888 1805 SE)

EPIDENDRUM SINENSE.
CHINESE EPIDENDRUM.
Cymbidium ensifolium.

PLATE 435

This plant belongs to the genus *Cymbidium* of Swartz, and is very nearly allied to *Epidendrum ensifolium* of Linnæus, figured by Dr. Smith, in his *Spicilegium Botanicum*; so nearly indeed that, perhaps, some may be inclined to consider both as varieties. It is a large plant, the leaves wider and more evidently nerved, the flowers larger, darker coloured, and more nodding; the bract below each flower is above two-thirds the length of the germen, whereas in *ensifolia* it is scarcely one-third the length; and the germen is much curved, which in *ensifolia* is nearly straight. But even these distinctions, slight as they are, we can hardly insist upon, unless we had seen more specimens of both in flower: there is however a considerable difference in the general appearance, and cultivators think them distinct. We have a drawing of the other plant by us, and perhaps, when we publish this, we may be able to speak more decidedly upon the subject.

A native of China, from whence it was introduced by the late Mr. Slater; has been hitherto treated as a stove plant, but does not require so much heat as the West Indian species, thriving luxuriantly in the conservatory.

EULOPHIA GUINEENSIS.
SIERRA LEONE EULOPHIA.

Eulophia guineensis.

PLATE 436

The name of *Eulophia* was given by Mr. Brown from the notable crest towards the base of the labellum in the other species, but which is not remarkable in this.

This beautiful plant of the family of the *Orchideæ* is a native of the west coast of Africa, and was communicated to us by Messrs. Loddiges and Sons, who, as we are informed in their *Botanical Cabinet*, received a parcel of them in the autumn of 1822, procured by Mr. Walter Hawkins

436 *Eulophia guineensis* (t. 2467 1824 JC)

from the islands of Loss, on the west coast of Africa, between the ninth and tenth degree of north latitude. Requires to be kept in the stove. Flowered in September, and continued in flower till November.

EULOPHIA STREPTOPETALA.
TWISTED-PETALED EULOPHIA.

Eulophia streptopetala.

PLATE 437

In one of the flowers on our specimen, there is a remarkable monstrosity. One of the segments of the inner perianth is reflected, and assumes the appearance of the outer perianth, and on each side of the perfect anther there is an abortive but distinct appearance of two others, making the whole number five. Mr. Brown remarks, that the appearance of one abortive stamen on each side of the perfect one in many *Orchideæ*, brings them within the ternary arrangement so common in monocotyledonous plants; and Dr. Hooker shows, that in *Epidendrum fuscatum, Bot. Mag.* t. 2844, the three anthers are all perfected; but the singular monstrosity which I have noticed, would show that the tendency exists to carry our plant forward to the quinary arrangement of *Dicotyledones*.

We received our plant in 1828 from the garden at Kew, where so much has been done lately to extend the high reputation of that noble collection. It has been kept in the stove, and flowered in April, growing in a pot, among pieces of bark. *Graham.*

GRAMMATHOPHYLLUM ELLISII.
MR. ELLIS'S GRAMMATOPHYLLUM.

Grammangis ellisii.

PLATE 438

The Rev. William Ellis, in a letter addressed to Dr. Lindley, from Hoddesdon, dated August 23rd, 1859, writes: – "Among the plants which I brought from Madagascar was a large-bulbed plant, something like *Anguloa Clowesiana*, only the bulbs are square instead of being round. I found it growing on a branch of a tree about the size of a man's leg, and stretching over a river

at about twenty-five feet above the water. The roots were abundant, but short, white, fleshy, and matted together, a little larger than the roots of *Ansellia Africana*. The bulbs were seven or eight inches long, and one and a quarter inch square, but last year it made a bulb eleven inches long and nearly two inches wide on each of the four sides. The leaves are one and a half to two feet long, about the size, but not so curved as those of *Angræcum sesquipedale*, and less fleshy than the *A. eburneum*, but, like all the Angræcums, growing on opposite sides of the crown of the bulb: each bulb has five or six leaves. The flower-spike, as in the case of the *Anguloa*, comes up with the young growth, and this year two young bulbs were accompanied by a flower-spike; each one damped off, but the other reached about two feet in length, and at the end furthest from the bulb bore between thirty and forty flowers. The flowers began to open three weeks ago, and as they opened slowly, I thought it would last longer, but on my return on Saturday from the country I found the flowers fading rapidly. I have therefore cut the spike, and send it to you; some of the flowers are, I hope, yet in a state of sufficient preservation to enable you to determine its species. Mrs. Ellis has also made a coloured drawing of some of the flowers, and a sketch of the whole plant." Such is the first notice of this fine plant on its blossoming in Mr. Ellis's Orchideous house; and from the spike there mentioned, aided by the very beautiful drawing of Mrs. Ellis, the accompanying plate has been executed; the dissections are by Mrs. Crease; and I am indebted to Dr. Lindley for the specific name and character and the following remarks:-

The genus *Grammatophyllum* is so nearly allied to *Cymbidium* that the two may possibly be united hereafter. They differ, however, first, in the presence of a sac at the base of both the column and lip; and, secondly, usually in the pollen-masses of *Grammatophyllum* being attached towards each extremity of a lunate gland. The first of these characters is the more important; the second can only be regarded as subordinate. It is in the first that the plant before us corresponds with *Grammatophyllum*; in the second it approaches *Cymbidium*. As to habit, the first of these two genera includes very dissimilar plants; G.

OPPOSITE:
437 *Eulophia streptopetala* (t. 2931 1829 WJH)

W.J.H.delt

Pub.by S.Curtis. Walworth. Aug.t 1.1829.

Swan Sc

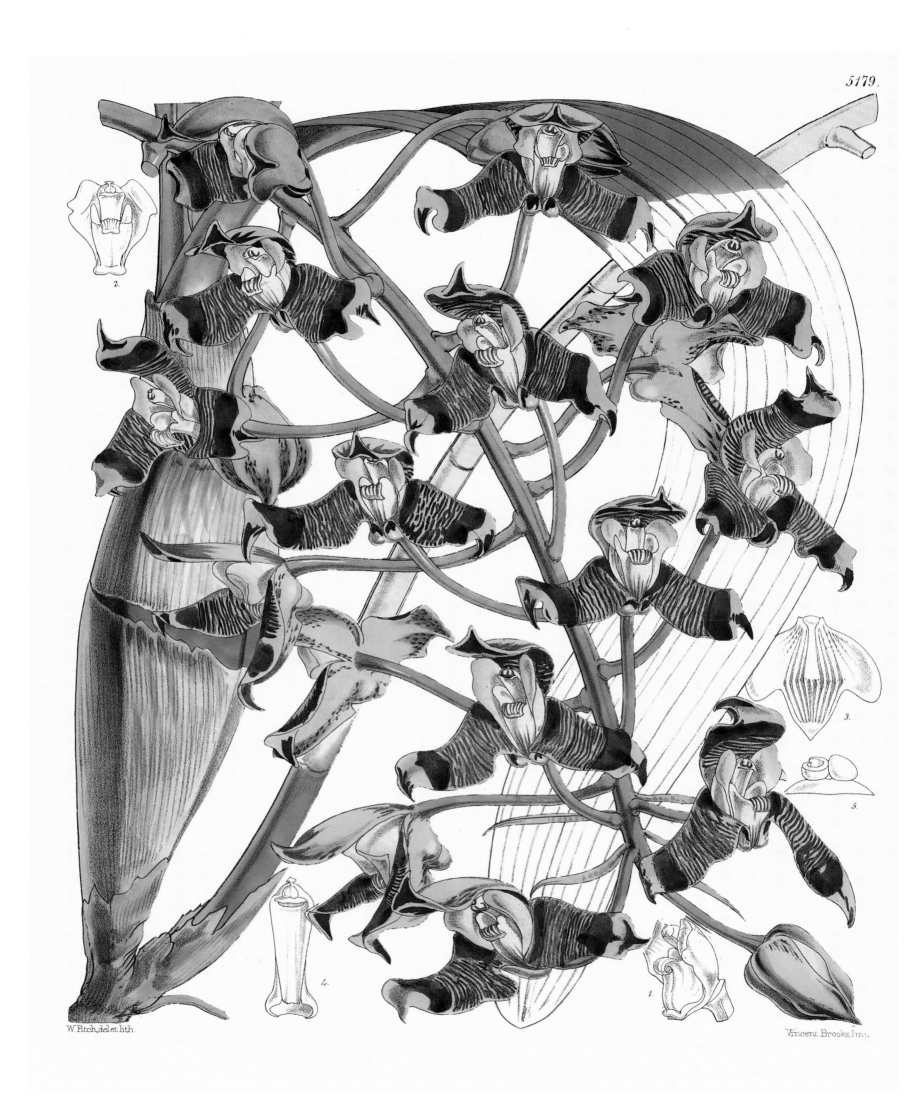

W.Fitch,del.et lith.

Vincent Brooks, Imp

speciosum (see *Bot. Mag.* t. 5157) being caulescent, this and G. *multiflorum* being pseudobulbous; a circumstance exactly analogous to what occurs in the great genera *Dendrobium, Epidendrum, Oncidium,* etc.

As a species, G. *ellisii* is very distinctly characterized by its broad leaves, short petals, gibbous lateral sepals, and smooth lip, which has one stout median rib, separating at the isthmus into three short slender ridges. The anther is moreover crested with a small pedicellate tubercle.

KEFERSTEINIA GRAMINEA.
GRASS-LEAVED KEFERSTEINIA.
Kefersteinia graminea.
PLATE 439

This curious orchid was not known in cultivation when Dr. Lindley named and described it as *Zygopetalum gramineum.* It is from Popayan, on the west side of the Andes, where it was discovered by Hartweg, and it has since been found in the

439   Kefersteinia graminea (t. 5046 1858)

OPPOSITE:
438   Grammatophyllum ellisii (t. 5179 1860 WF)

Caraccas by Linden, Funcke, and Schlim. We derived our plant from the Imperial Gardens of St. Petersburg, and we learn that it exists in gardens under the name of "*Huntleya fimbriata.*" Three species of the genus are described by Reichenbach fil.

440   Laelia praestans (t. 5498 1865 WF)

LÆLIA PRÆSTANS.
ADMIRABLE LÆLIA.
Lælia præstans.
PLATE 440

At first sight this rare and beautiful plant might be mistaken for a large variety of another Lælia, with which we have been long familiar under the various names of *Cattleya pumila,* C. *marginata,* or C. *pinelli,* but it is in reality perfectly distinct. Professor Reichenbach was the first to distinguish it, and he has given a most faithful representation in one of the Plates of his *Xenia Orchidacea,* his specimens have been obtained from the rich collection of Consul Schiller, of Hamburg. In this country the plant is still extremely rare, and I am not aware of its having bloomed except in the collections of Mr. Day and Mr. Marshall.

It was from a plant that flowered finely in the garden of the latter gentleman that the accompanying figure was prepared.

L. præstans comes from the island of St. Catherine, and should be treated like other Brazilian *Lælias* and *Cattleyas* from the same locality; but it prefers a block of hard wood to a pot, and it should always be placed near the glass. Its flowering season is November, and the blossoms are exceedingly durable.

LIMODORUM FALCATUM.
FRAGRANT LIMODORUM.
Neofinetia falcata.
PLATE 441

This pretty little plant is also very fragrant. It is a native of Japan, where, according to Thunberg, it grows on the mountains among shrubs; but as this traveller had no opportunity of gathering the plants from their place of growth, it must be uncertain whether it grew on the earth, on rocks, or parasitically on trees; by the manner in which it puts forth its roots, if they can be so called, we should judge that its natural situation was not on the soil. Our plant was cultivated in the garden of the Horticultu-

441   Limodorum falcatum (t. 2097 1819 JC)

ral Society as an air plant, being suspended from the roof of the stove in a basket with only a little moss in it; and was communicated by the society's gardener, Mr. Charles Strachan, in May last.

It was first cultivated in England by Sir Abraham Hume, at Wormleybury, who received the plant from the East Indies, through the late Dr. Roxburgh.

MASDEVALLIA LINDENI.

Masdevallia coccinea.

PLATE 442

This is another of that remarkable group of *Masdevallias* which have attracted so much attention amongst Botanists and Horticulturists of late, from the singular form and colouring of their sepals, and of which *Masdevallia veitchiana* Reichb. f. (*Bot. Mag.* t. 5739) and *M. ignea* (*Bot. Mag.* t. 5962) are examples. All these present a wonderful similarity in the form and structure of the petals, lip, and column, which are concealed in the tube of the perianth, and appear as if reduced in size and suppressed as to function in favour of the three outer

442 Masdevallia lindeni (t. 5990 1872 WF)

sepals, which, by their gorgeous colouring, if not by their form also, no doubt attract insects to fecundate the species by cross fertilization. Of this type many more species have yet to be imported, especially from New Grenada. Altogether upwards of fifty species of this singular genus exist in our Herbarium at Kew, the genus extending from Cuba and Mexico to Rio de Janeiro.

M. lindeni was flowered at the Glasnevin Gardens by Dr. Moore, F.L.S., who obligingly transmitted it for figuring, in June of the present year. It was supposed to have been received by him amongst a batch of Central American Orchids, collected by Roezel; but André states that it was introduced by G. Wallis from New Grenada in 1869.

MASDEVALLIA SHUTTLEWORTH.

Masdevallia caudata.

PLATE 443

The rapid increase in number of imported species of *Masdevallia* is certainly the most striking feature in the history of the orchid culture of the past ten years. No less than thirteen have been figured in the *Botanical Magazine* within that period, and only four before it; whilst at least double that number are in cultivation in individual collections of the first-class.

The geographical limits of the genus seem to be limited to the northern and western countries of South America, where they inhabit cool-temperate humid regions. *Masdevallia shuttleworthii* was discovered, by the traveller whose name it bears, in the United States of Colombia, when collecting for Mr. Bull.

I am indebted to W. H. Punchard, Esq., of Poulett Lodge, Twickenham, for the loan of the specimen here figured, which is believed to be unique; it flowered in March of the present year. Native of the United States of Colombia.

443 Masdevallia shuttleworth (t. 6372 1878 WF)

NEOTTIA ORCHIOIDES.
FROSTED-FLOWERED NEOTTIA.

Stenorrhynchus lanceolatus.

PLATE 444

444 Neottia orchioides (t. 1036 1807 SE)

For this very rare and beautiful plant, which we believe has never been before figured, we are indebted to E. J. A. Woodford, Esq. at whose seat, near Rickmansworth, it flowered in May last, in the stove.

When closely inspected it appears covered over with pellucid and white dots, much resembling hoar-frost. Is said by Swartz to grow in the most arid places among grass in Jamaica.

N.º 1374

445   *Neottia speciosa* (t. 1376 1811 SE)

NEOTTIA SPECIOSA.
RED-FLOWERED NEOTTIA.
Stenorrhynchus speciosus.
PLATE 445

The *Neottia speciosa* is a native of the West India islands, and, of course, requires to be kept constantly in the bark stove. Willdenow doubted whether the figure published by Mr. Andrews in the *Botanist's Repository* might not represent a different species from Jacquin's plant. Our drawing, however, being certainly done from the same species as the former, leaves no room to doubt of the identity of all three. The colour of the leaves, as given in the *Botanist's Repository*, is much too dark a green, and the veining is falsely depicted; but Willdenow has laid too much stress upon

the small undulation at the margin of the leaf, represented by Jacquin as giving an appearance of its being crenated; for not unfrequently this particular crispature is altogether wanting, as in one of the leaves in our figure.

Our drawing was made several years ago from a plant that flowered in December, at Mr. Woodford's, at Vauxhall, who imported it from the island of Barbados. Is easily propagated by its roots.

NEUWIEDIA LINDLEYI.
Neuwiedia lindleyi.
PLATE 446

The singular Malayan genus *Neuwiedia* is here for the first time figured from a living specimen. It was founded by Blume in 1834 on a Javan plant (*N. veratrifolia*) of which only two specimens were seen, a flowering and a fruiting, and of which the descriptions (his own, and a later by Reichenbach) are very incomplete, and are insufficient to distinguish it from some later described species. The genus comprises five more or less imperfectly distinguished spe-

446   *Neuwiedia lindleyi* (t. 7368 1894 MS)

7368

cies, namely *N. zollingeri* of Java and *N. griffithii* of Malacca, both of Reichenbach, *N. calanthoides*, Ridley, from New Guinea, *N. curtisii*, Rolfe, of Penang and Sumatra, and the subject of the accompanying plate. The tribe to which it belongs, *Apostasieæ*, has been the subject of an elaborate memoir by Mr. Rolfe, in the *Journal of the Linnæan Society*. In it Mr. Rolfe rightly separates the *Apostasieæ* from *Cypripedieæ*, with which they are united in the *Genera Plantarum*, and the above enumerated species are all described.

N. lindleyi was received at the Royal Gardens, Kew, in July, 1887, from Mr. Ridley, F.L.S., Superintendent of the Singapore Gardens, and (as Mr. Watson informs me) developed its flowers very slowly in mid-winter, 1893–4. *N. griffithii* is also in cultivation at Kew, and will, I hope, appear in this work in due course, when it flowers.

447   *Odontoglossum praenitens* (t. 6229 1876 WF)

ODONTOGLOSSUM PRÆNITENS.
Odontoglossum prænitens.
PLATE 447

Reichenbach describes this as an interesting addition to our knowledge of *Odontoglossa*, allied to *O. triumphans*, but with smaller flowers, and as suggesting the suspicion that it might prove to be a hybrid between that species and *O. tripudians*: it however differed in the shape of the lip so much that he was obliged to abandon this idea. On the other hand, this justly celebrated Orchidologist speaks doubtfully of the specific value of *O. prænitens* in saying that it "*may prove* as good a species as *O. nevadense.*"

O. prænitens is a native of New Grenada, whence it was collected by Mr. Gustave Wallis for Messrs. Veitch, who forwarded the specimen here figured in April, 1875.

this description in January, 1845. Dr. Lindley alludes to its close affinity with *Oncidium cavendishianum*, "so much so as to seem a mere variety of it; but it is in reality quite distinct." My own investigation would rather lead me to consider the two as forms of one and the same kind, and that the species is liable to considerable variation; the more especially as our *O. pachyphyllum*, is considered by Dr. Lindley a state of *O. cavendishianum*. To me, our present plant seems to correspond better with Mr. Bateman's original figure of *O. cavendishianum* than our *O. pachyphyluum* does.

lobed at the back, placed at the point of a thin, ovate, membranous, white *pedicel* whose margins are revolute, and which has a large brown gland at the base. *Germen* small, lineari-clavate, striated.

From the stove of the Glasgow Botanic Garden, to which the plants were liberally communicated by the late Baron De Schack, from Trinidad. The species blossomed in 1826, and again in June, 1827. It is among the most singular and most beautiful of the extensive parasitic family with which our hothouses are now so abundantly stored; and is well named *Oncidium papilio* by Mr. Lindley.

ONCIDIUM BICALLOSUM.
TWO-WARTED ONCIDIUM.
Oncidium bicallosum.
PLATE 448

An inhabitant of Guatemala, whence it was introduced to our stoves by Mr. Skinner, who sent it to Woburn Abbey, as well as to Mr. Bateman: and it is now, with the Woburn Orchideous collection, in the gardens of Kew, where we do not find it difficult to flower. Our drawing was made in October, 1843, and the plant is now again in blossom at the time of drawing up

448 Oncidium bicallosum (t. 4148 1845 WF)

ONCIDIUM PAPILIO.
BUTTERFLY ONCIDIUM.
Oncidium papilio.
PLATE 449

Descr. *Bulb* somewhat orbicular, compressed, dark purple; bearing a single, elliptical, one-nerved, coriaceous *leaf*, of a purple-brown colour, spotted and blotched with green, the spots smaller on the underside. *Scape* two to three feet long, springing from the base of the bulb, flexuose, jointed, with sheathing, membranous bracteæ at the joints, lower articulations terete, very slender, spotted with purple, upper ones very much compressed, sharp at the edges and quite ancipitate. *Flowers* solitary, or two, at the end of the scape, very large and beautiful. Three posterior *petals*, at least three inches long, linear, the margins revolute, the back lurid green, the inside deep purple: two *anterior* petals decurved, subfalcate, lanceolate, waved, bright yellow, with transverse red-brown blotches, longer than the lip. *Lip* two inches long, deep yellow, pendent, three-lobed, two lateral lobes forming a cordate base to the lip, and dotted with reddish-brown, having a three-lobed, whitish crest, spotted with red, the middle lobe two-toothed at the base; terminal lobe cordate, its sides involute, its margins waved; a broad irregular band of red-brown runs along just within the margin. *Column* short, yellow, fringed at the upper margins with glandular soft spines, of which the upper one on each side is the longest, lower down bearing two, yellow, fleshy wings, obscurely fringed with glands at the extremity. *Anther-case* helmet-shaped, two-celled. *Pollen Masses* two-

PAPHINIA CRISTATA.
CRESTED PAPHINIA.
Paphinia cristata.
PLATE 450

A very curious and really handsome Orchideous plant, native of Trinidad and New Granada, first published by Dr. Lindley as a *Maxillaria*, and then very justly raised by him to the rank of a new genus. In our plant the flowers are large, and the markings are of a deeper and more chocolate-brown colour; and there is a slight difference in the form of the lip, but not enough to justify its being considered a new species. Our plant was received from Mr. Purdie. It flowers in the Orchideous stove in August.

PHALAENOPSIS GRANDIFLORA.
LARGE-FLOWERED INDIAN
BUTTERFLY-PLANT.
Phalæonopsis amabilis.
PLATE 451

Dr. Lindley first distinguished this as a species from the well-known and universal favourite, *Phalænopsis amabilis*, in the *Gardeners' Chronicle*, and we cannot do better than transcribe his remarks thereupon: – "A small plant of this noble epiphyte was exhibited on the 7th of September, last year (1847), before the Horticultural Society, by J. H. Schroder, Esq., of Stratford Green, when it received the silver Bank-

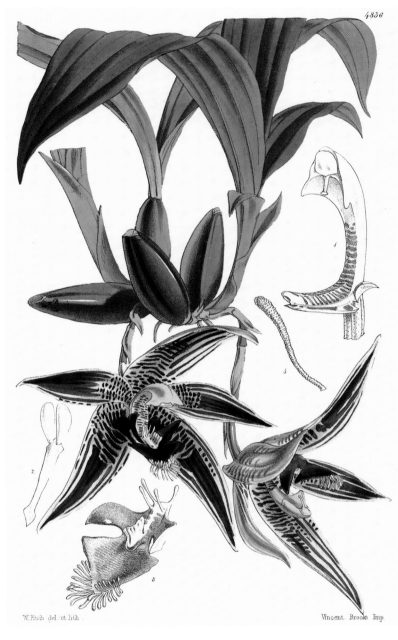

449 *Oncidium papilio* (t. 2795 1828 WJH)

450 *Paphinia cristata* (t. 4836 1855 WF)

sian medal. It was not supposed at that time to be a distinct species from the *Phalænopsis amabilis*, but was regarded merely as a fine variety. Upon a comparison of it with the Manilla species, it proves however to possess so many points of difference, that no doubt can be entertained of its being really distinct. Its flowers are four times as large, the petals do not overlap the back sepal, nor have they the small point which is invariably present in *Phalænopsis amabilis*; the lip is very narrow, much shorter than the lanceolate sepals, and its chief lateral lobes are somewhat wedge-shaped, with the angles rounded off. The distribution of colour, too, is different; there is a large stain of deep yellow on the front edge of the chief lateral lobes of the lip, and the cirrhi are yellow, not white."

Such are the distinguishing characters given by the botanist who has made the Orchideous plants almost the study of his life – to which he adds, in the specific definition, "the longer leaves mucronated at the point." Whether these marks are permanent or not, the *Phalænopsis grandiflora* is eminently deserving of a figure in the pages of the *Botanical Magazine*, the more so as no coloured figure of it has yet been published. It is a native of Java, and said to have been introduced to Europe by Messrs. Veitch and Sons, of the Nurseries, Exeter and Chelsea. Our figure is taken from a fine flowering specimen in the Royal Gardens of Kew.

SACCOLABIUM DENTICULATUM.

TOOTHED SACCOLABIUM.

Gastrochilus acutifolius.

PLATE 452

Said to be a native of Khasya in eastern Bengal, introduced to our stoves in 1837, and among the Orchideous collection bequeathed to Kew by the late Mr. Clowes. It is a plant of little show, but the flowers are exceedingly beautiful when minutely examined, and they are prettily variegated in regard to colour. It flowers with us in November.

451 *Phalanopsis grandiflora* (t. 5184 1860 WF)

452 *Saccolabium denticulatum* (t. 4772 1854 WF)

SOBRALIA MACRANTHA.
LARGE-FLOWERED SOBRALIA.

Sobralia macrantha.

PLATE 453

This belongs to a very fine genus of Orchideous plants, as Dr. Lindley observes, having reed-like stems and handsome flowers, natives of tropical America; and the finest of all the species is the one here figured for the first time, from plants growing in the Royal Gardens, collected by Mr. Skinner in Guatemala. Our figure is no exaggerated representation of the plant: in point of colour it falls far short of reality, for it is of that deep purplish-rose colour, which every botanical artist knows is so difficult to imitate upon paper.

Cult. The plant producing this splendid flower, belongs to a genus of terrestrial Orchids of a pecular habit, having slender reed-like, leafy stems, varying from two to ten or more feet in height, which spring from a fascicle of thick fleshy roots. The species now figured is a native of Mexico, and is found to thrive best when kept in the cool division of the Orchideous house, the average winter temperature ranging between 55° and 60°. A light free soil suits it, which should be composed of a mixture of sandy peat and light loam, with the addition of a little leaf-mould. On account of its thick fleshy roots it is necessary to give it more pot-room than its slender habit would seem to require; and as the roots are not inclined to go deep, wide shallow pots or pans are to be preferred, taking care to have the pot properly drained so as to allow free watering and syringing during summer, without the chance of the mould becoming saturated. Too much water should not be given in winter, during which season it is apt to be attacked by *thrips*. If these are not checked in time, the plant will soon assume a sickly appearance, owing to the cuticle of the under-side of the leaves having been destroyed by this minute but troublesome insect. Repeated fumigation with tobacco does much to keep them under, but it is advisable to remove the plant to a convenient place and apply the syringe to the under-side of the leaves, taking care that the water is at a proper temperature. It is increased by separating the roots, which requires to be done very carefully, so as not to break them.

STANHOPEA TIGRINA.
TIGER-SPOTTED STANHOPEA.

Stanhopea tigrina.

PLATE 454

Perhaps no Orchideous plant is more calculated to attract attention than the present, whether we consider the large size of its blossoms, their strange form and almost waxy consistence, their singular markings, or the powerful fragrance they exhale, scenting the whole stove, and almost too strong to be agreeable; but which is considered to resemble a mixture of Melon and Vanilla. The species is now not uncommon in our collections, and is said to have been introduced to them by Messrs. Low, of Clapton, from Xalapa in Mexico. Like the other *Stanhopeas* it is easily cultivated, only requiring to be suspended from a beam of the stove in a wire basket filled with Sphagnum and other mosses, through which the flower-stalks penetrate downwards and hang below the basket, the pseudo-bulbs and leaves being seen above. During the present and for several months in the summer, our plants in the Royal Botanic Gardens flowered in the highest degree of perfection, and from one of them this representation was made. It is the best marked and most distinct of all the genus.

TRICHOPILIA SUAVIS.
SWEET TRICHOPILIA.

Trichopilia suavis.

PLATE 455

Native of Central America, like the other two known species of the genus, from which this is extremely distinct, having very different pseudo-bulbs and leaves, and longer flowers, with the sepals and petals only slightly twisted. It is powerfully fragrant. The very fine specimen here figured was sent to us by Messrs. Lucombe, Pince, and Co., in April of the present year, 1852.

Descr. *Pseudo-bulbs* extremely compressed, almost foliaceous, orbicular, aggregated, bearing a solitary, broad, elliptical,

OPPOSITE:
453 *Sobralia macrantha* (t. 4446 1849 WF)

Fitch, del et lith.

Reeve, Benham & Reeve, imp

Fitch del.

Reeve imp.

coriaceous *leaf*, contracted at the base into a short, laterally compressed *petiole*. From the base of a pseudo-bulb the *peduncle* emerges, and is pendent, bearing three or more large and highly fragrant *flowers*, bracteated at the insertion of each flower; *bracts* ovate, thin, membranaceous, white, streaked with brown. *Ovary* long, clavate, angled, pale green. *Sepals* and *petals* spreading, white or cream-coloured, lanceolate, acuminate, nearly straight or only slightly twisted. *Lip* very large, projecting forward, white or cream-coloured in its groundcolour; the lower half or claw is convolute upon the column, but enlarged suddenly upwards so as to constitute a funnel-shaped petal, with a very large oblique limb; this *limb* is three-lobed, spotted with pale purple, yellow in the throat, the lateral lobes waved and crenated, the middle lobe very large, slightly deflexed, emarginate or retuse at the apex, the margin crisped and crenulate. *Column* very long, terete, expanding at the apex in front into a large convex fleshy *stigma*, and bearing at the back of the anther a four-lobed hood, each lobe beautifully fringed with long cilia. *Anther-case* helmet-shaped, acuminated. *Pollen-masses* on a narrow cuneated *caudicle*, with a small *gland* at the base.

456 *Vanda cristata* (t. 4304 1847 WF)

455 *Trichopilia suavis* (t. 4654 1852 WF)

OPPOSITE:
454 *Stanhopea tigrina* (t. 4497 1850 WF)

VANDA CRISTATA.
CRESTED VANDA.

Vanda cristata.

PLATE 456

This has not much beauty to recommend it; but the lip is large, and prettily striped and variegated with blood-colour and yellow upon a velvety ground: and as far as the labellum is concerned, Dr. Wallich was quite correct in saying "*flos exquisitæ pulchritudinis.*" To that liberal gentleman we owe the possession of the species at the Royal Gardens of Kew, where it blooms in the latter end of winter and early in spring, enlivening the stove at that season with its variegated flowers. It inhabits trees in Nepal, where also its flowering season is the spring.

VANDA SUAVIS.
FRAGRANT VANDA.

Vanda tricolor.

PLATE 457

An extremely lovely Orchideous plant, the flowers richly blotched and spotted with blood-purple on a pure white ground, so clear and distinct that they look as if they were made of porcelain. Dr. Lindley refers to it my *Vanda tricolor* (*Bot. Mag.* t. 4434) which I had taken to be the *V. tricolor* of Lindley, but which that author makes var. *flava* of his more beautiful *V. suavis*. Dr. Reichenbach, on the other hand, maintains that it is the true *tricolor*. The differences in fact are more in colour than in structure; so that the description at *Bot. Mag.* t. 4434 may answer for the present species. Here the ground colour of the flower is pure china-white, the exterior spotless: the inner face of the sepals and petals is streaked and spotted with purple. The lip is deep purple in the lower half, with three white lines or streaks on the disk; the rest of the lip is paler purple, the whole destitute of spots. The species inhabits Java, but is yet, we believe, rare, and much prized, as it deserves to be, in collections.

457 *Vanda suavis* (t. 5174 1860 WF)

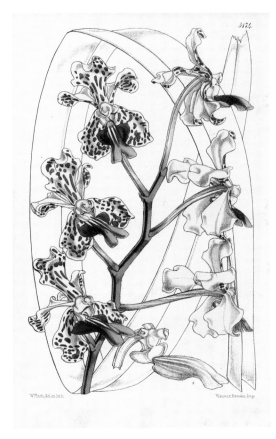

217

458 *Vanda watsoni* (t. 8109 1906 MS)

VANDA WATSONI.
ANNAM.

Vanda watsoni.

PLATE 458

Vanda watsoni Rolfe, is a distinct and attractive species, which was discovered in the interior of Annam by Mr. W. Micholitz, a collector for Messrs. Sander & Sons, by whom it was introduced to cultivation, and at whose request it was dedicated to Mr. W. Watson, Curator of the Royal Botanic Gardens, Kew. It flowered at the Royal Botanic Gardens, Glasnevin, early in 1905. It is the third member of a curious little group, characterized by having narrow or acute leaves and racemes of moderate-sized flowers, all of which have now been figured in this work. The two others are *V. kimballiana*, Reichb. f. (t. 7112) and *V. amesiana*, Reichb. f. (t. 7139), both natives of Upper Burma. A fourth species with terete leaves has also been figured, namely, *V. teres*, Lindl. (t. 4114), but that has far larger flowers, which are markedly different in structure.

The plate was prepared in February last from materials furnished by Messrs. Sander, with the help of a living plant in the Kew collection which had previously been received from them. It flowers freely in winter under tropical treatment.

PÆONIACEÆ

PÆONIA ANOMALA.
JAGGED-LEAVED SIBERIAN PÆONY.

Pæonia anomala.

PLATE 459

Pæonia anomala has for the most part five capsules, which are not upright, but spreading. The root, in its native soil, is said to grow very large, dividing into tuberous branches a foot long, yellow on the outside and white within, smelling like Florentine Iris. There are two varieties, the one having flowers of a pale, the other of a more intense purple colour.

Native of Siberia, consequently considered as a hardy perennial. Yet we have frequently observed, that it perishes in the winter. This is probably owing to the wetness, not to the cold of our climate; though many plants which, in their native soil, are covered with snow, are liable to injury from the latter cause; partly, perhaps, from the want of this natural defence, and partly from beginning to vegetate too early, and being then cut off by our spring frosts. We do not know that it has yet been put in practice; but we should recommend the roots to be taken up, as soon as the foliage is all decayed, and

459 *Pæonia anomala* (t. 1754 1815)

preserved in dry sand, protected from the frost, during the winter, planting them out early in the spring.

Introduced in 1788, by John Bell, Esq. Flowers in May and June.

PAEONIA CLUSII.

Pæonia clusii.

PLATE 460

The beautiful paeony here figured is met with in the valleys of the mountains of Crete and our illustration has been prepared from a plant grown by Mr. G. P. Baker in his garden at Sevenoaks. This was raised from the seed he collected in the deep gorge of Samaria in the south of the island and in an article in the *Gardeners' Chronicle* (1933) Mr. Baker describes how he found this paeony on the outskirts of a primeval forest of *Cupressus sempervirens* var. *horizontalis*. The late Mr. S. C. Atchley of the British Legation at Athens also found the paeony in the same place and distributed seed to several gardens in England.

P. clusii, as far as is known, is only found in the Island of Crete. It is allied to the *officinalis* group of paeonies with the lower leaves much dissected into twenty-one or more segments. It differs from *P. officinalis* L. by the segments being smaller and narrower, and in having white flowers sometimes flushed with pink, and also in being a dwarfer plant. Further it has proved to be a diploid while *P. officinalis* is a tetraploid. In the living plant the pink colour of the stem and petioles and the cup-shaped flower give this paeony a distinct appearance and a peculiar charm.

P. clusii is a beautiful plant for the garden, growing about one foot high. The white cup-shaped flowers with their golden stamens are very attractive, set off by the cut-leaved foliage and the pink stem. It is not a strong grower in cultivation and seems to do best in a sheltered place where the early sun does not reach it. It flowers in English gardens in mid-May. Distribution. – Crete.

460 *Paeonia clusii* (t. 9594 1940 LS)

PÆONIA MOUTAN.
THE MOUTAN OR
CHINESE TREE-PÆONY.
Pæonia suffruticosa.

PLATE 462

The *Moutan*, though cultivated in China about fourteen hundred years, is considered in that ancient empire, according to the missionaries, as rather of modern introduction. The Chinese writers seem to differ in their accounts with regard to its origin, some attributing it to a particular process of culture, by which the common Paeony has been converted into this magnificent shrub, sometimes attaining, as it is said, in the province of Lo-Yang, the soil and climate of which is particularly favourable, the height of eight or ten feet; whilst others, perhaps with more probability, say it was first discovered growing among the mountains in northern China, whence it was brought into the southern provinces, and cultivated with the same rage as Tulips have been in Europe, and with a similar effect of producing numerous varieties, some of which, from their beauty and rarity, have been known to sell in China for a hundred ounces of gold. Notwith-

standing the Chinese Florists differ from the European, in rejecting all variegated flowers, considering such as contrary to nature, they enumerate two hundred and forty species, as they are called, many of them of exquisite beauty and delightful fragrance.

For the introduction of this valuable acquisition to our gardens, we are indebted to Sir Joseph Banks, who instructed several persons trading to Canton, to inquire for the moutan, the name by which it is known in China; in consequence of which numerous specimens were sent to this country, most of them however perished in the voyage. Since that time several varieties have been imported in a growing state, but we have not seen any that were remarkable for the fragrance of their flowers.

Propagated in China by seeds, the only way to obtain new varieties, also by parting the roots, by layers and cuttings, and they generally inoculate the buds of different varieties upon the several branches of the same root. When the time of flowering approaches, they carefully remove all superfluous buds, and protect those that are left from the scorching heat of the sun. It is sufficiently hardy to bear the cold of our climate, but to have it bloom well it is necessary to protect it by a glass frame.

Flowers in May and June, and sometimes with us perfects its seeds in September and October. Introduced about the year 1794.

PAPAVERACEÆ

ARGEMONE MEXICANA.
MEXICAN ARGEMONE OR
PRICKLY POPPY.
Argemone mexicana.

PLATE 461

This species of argemone is a native of Mexico, and the West Indies, where we should suppose it to be a very common and noxious weed, from the name there given it of *Fico del inferno*, or the *Devil's Fig*: it has long been introduced to this country; Gerard, who cultivated it with success, ludicrously attributes its nickname to a different source: "The Golden Thistle of Peru, called in the West Indies, Fique del inferno, a friend of mine brought it unto me from an iland there, called Saint Johns

Iland, among other seedes, what reason the inhabitants there have to call it so it is unto me unknown, unless it be bicause of this fruite, which doth much resemble a figge in shape and bignesse, but so full of sharpe and venemous prickles, that whoever had one of them in his throte, doubtless it would sent him packing either to heaven or to hell."

Miller mentions it as a plant of no great use or beauty, in the latter point of view Clusius, who was one of the first to figure and describe it, and Gerard, thought differently; its foliage is certainly beautiful, somewhat like that of the Milk Thistle, its blossoms are large and showy, though not of long duration; like the Celandine, the whole plant abounds with a yellow juice, which flows out when it is wounded; it differs from the poppy, to which it is nearly related, in having a calyx of three leaves.

Though a native of a very warm climate, it is cultivated with as much facility as any annual whatever; in the gardens about London, where it has once grown, and scattered its seeds, it comes up spontaneously every spring, flowers in July and August, and ripens its seeds in September; these are large, somewhat round, of a black colour, with a beautiful surface; a light rich soil and warm situation suits it best.

461 *Argemone mexicana* (t. 243 1793 SE)

No 1154

Pub by T. Curtis S^o Geo. Crescent Nov 1. 1808.   *Syd. Edwards et. F. Sansom Sculp*

462   *Paeonia moutan* (t. 1154 1808 SE)

BOCCONIA CORDATA.
HEART-LEAVED BOCCONIA.

Macleaya cordata.

PLATE 463

The *Bocconia cordata* is a hardy herbaceous perennial, which, for the singularity of its foliage and fine large feathery panicles of flowers, is well deserving a place in every large garden. It is, when viewed at a distance, that its peculiar appearance is more especially striking.

The stamens are very numerous, about thirty, and the capsule according to Jacquin, contains four seeds inserted in the margin; in the germen we have observed sometimes four and sometimes six ovula. The filaments are long and hair-like; stigma sessile, two-lobed.

Native of China, from whence it was introduced into this country by Sir George Staunton, Bart. in 1795. It is propagated by dividing its roots; thrives best in a light loamy soil. It flowers in August and September.

PASSIFLORACEÆ

PASSIFLORA QUADRANGULARIS.
SQUARE-STALKED PASSION-FLOWER.
OR GRANADILLA

Passiflora quadrangularis.

PLATE 464

Cultivated in gardens in the West Indies, but whether indigenous there seems doubtful. The fruit is as large as a swan's egg; its pulp is eaten with wine, either with or without the seeds, and much esteemed for its supposed cooling quality. From its quick growth and thick foliage, it is well suited

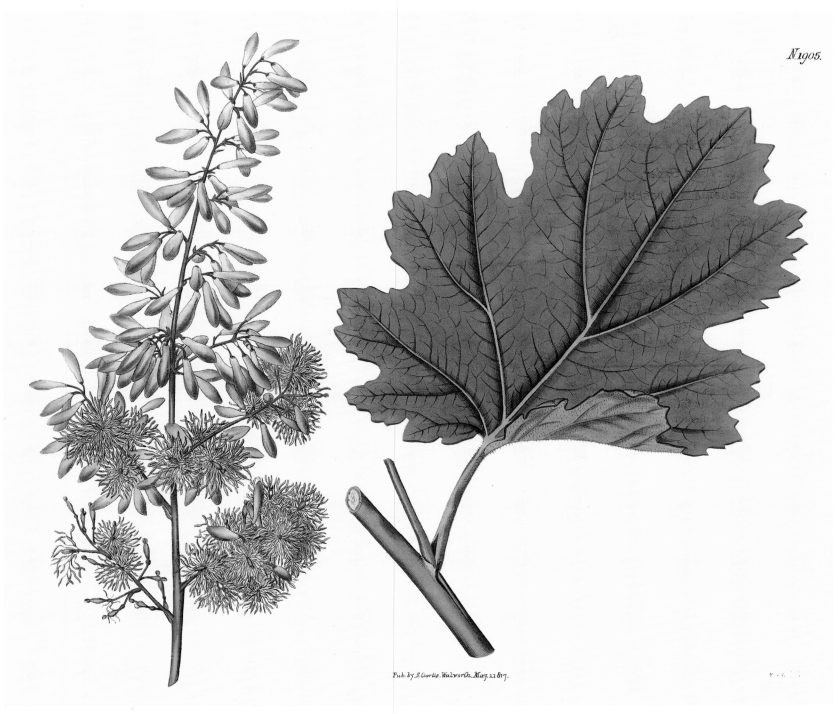

N.1905.

Pub. by S.Curtis. Walworth. May 22 1817.

463 *Bocconia cordata* (t. 1905 1817)

for forming arbours and covered walks, but Jacquin observes that they are apt to be infested by venomous serpents, who choose the Passion-flowers, more especially this species and the laurel-leaved, for their abode, well knowing that their favourite prey, the squirrels, no where more abound, these animals being fond of these fruits.

Requires the constant protection of the stove, of which it is one of the greatest ornaments. Propagated by cuttings or by seeds, which last are seldom produced here. Flowers in August and September.

PASSIFLORA TUCUMANENSIS.
LARGE-STIPULED PASSION-FLOWER.

Passiflora tucumanensis.

PLATE 465

This new species of Passion-flower was discovered by Mr. Tweedie, at St. Jago and Tucuman, at the eastern foot of the Cordillera of Chili, inhabiting, though rarely, the woods. It is a free grower, and flowered copiously the second year in the stove of the Glasgow Botanic Garden, in the month of July. It is no. 1173 of Mr. Tweedie's collections sent in 1836.

PHILYDRACEÆ

PHILYDRUM LANUGINOSUM.
WOOLLY PHILYDRUM.

Philydrum lanuginosum.

PLATE 466

This is certainly not a plant of much beauty, but will recommend itself to the Botanist by the very singular construction of its flowers. It is truly, as the name imports, a lover of water, and will not thrive at all unless the pot containing it is plunged deep in water; but so treated and kept in an airy part of the stove, it grew to a very great size and produced plenty of ripe

Pub. by S. Curtis. Walworth. Jan. 1. 1819.

465 *Passiflora tucumanensis* (t. 3636 1838 WF)

seeds, at Mr. Woodford's at Vauxhall, where our drawing was taken in June last.

It is a native of New Holland, of China, and Cochinchina, and from the latter place specimens were sent into Europe.

466 *Philydrum lanuginosum* (t. 783 1804 SE)

OPPOSITE:
464 *Passiflora quadrangularis* (t. 2041 1819)

POLEMONIACEÆ

PHLOX AMŒNA.

FRASER'S HAIRY PHLOX.

Phlox amœna.

PLATE 467

Mr. Fraser first discovered *P. amœna* in 1786, near the Santée Canal, in South Carolina, and never met with it in any other place. He has several times before attempted to introduce it into England, but without success until the present year.

From the size and brilliancy of its flowers, it must be deemed a valuable acquisition to our gardens. Flowers in May, June, and July. Being a native of the southern state it will probably be a little tender.

467 *Phlox amoena* (t. 1308 1810)

POLYGONACEÆ

POLYGONUM ORIENTALE.

TALL PERSICARIA.

Polygonum orientale.

PLATE 468

Of the genus *Polygonum*, the present well-known native of the East, as well as of India, is the principal one cultivated in our gardens for ornament, and is distinguished

468 *Polygonum orientale* (t. 213 1792)

not less for its superior stature than the brilliancy of its flowers; it will frequently grow to the height of eight or ten feet, and become a formidable rival to the gigantic sunflower.

There is a dwarf variety of it, and another with white flowers; it has been observed to vary also in point of hairiness.

It flowers from July to October, and produces abundance of seed, which, falling on the borders, generally comes up spontaneously in the spring; but it is most commonly sown in the spring with other annuals: when the seedlings appear, they should be thinned so as to stand a foot apart. This plant requires very little care, and will bear the smoke of London better than many others. Was cultivated by the Duchess of Beaufort, in 1707. *Ait. Kew.*

The stipulæ on the stalk are deserving of notice, being unusual in their form, and making it look as if beruffled.

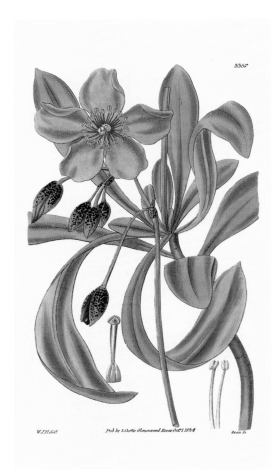

469 *Calandrinia discolor* (t. 3357 1834 WJH)

CLAYTONIA ALSINOIDES.
CHICKWEED CLAYTONIA.

Montia sibirica.

PLATE 470

This species is usually taken for *Claytonia sibirica*, to which it is very similar, but differs in the size and form of its cauline leaves, which in the latter are more than twice as large and of a rhomboid shape, more remarkably veined, and more narrowed at the base, but connate; it has also larger flowers, and one of the racemes generally bears a pair of leaves similar to the first; the other bracts are all narrow and not like the first. In habit it bears some resemblance to *Stellaria media* or common Chickweed.

It appears by the specimens preserved in the Banksian Herbarium that our plant is a native of Nootka Sound, where it was discovered by Mr. Menzies. Communicated by Mr. George Graves. Flowers in May, June and July, and in moist ground will maintain itself by its scattered seeds, without other trouble than keeping clear from weeds.

471 *Claytonia virginia* (t. 491 1800 SE)

PORTULACACEÆ

CALANDRINIA DISCOLOR.
TWO-COLOURED-LEAVED CALANDRINIA.

Calandrinia discolor.

PLATE 469

Among many other novel plants which adorned the Glasgow Botanic Garden in the year 1824, three species of *Calandrinia* were not amongst the least beautiful, *C. grandiflora* of Dr. Lindley, which we received from the Horticultural Society of London; *C. speciosa*, for which we are indebted to Messrs. Young of Epsom; and *C. discolor*, from Mr. Fischer's collection at Gottingen, the subject of the present plate. I regret that of the two last I am ignorant of their native country: but if we may judge from their general affinity with the *C. grandiflora*, they are from Chili. Similar, however, as they are in aspect, they are totally different as species. They succeed well, treated as greenhouse plants, or better still if planted during the summer months in the open border, where both the flowers and foliage attain a larger size and a brighter hue. Flowering season July and August.

470 *Claytonia alsinoides* (t. 1309 1810 SE)

CLAYTONIA VIRGINICA.
VIRGINIAN CLAYTONIA.

Claytonia virginica.

PLATE 471

The variety with broader lanceolate leaves mentioned in *Hortus Kewensis*, is probably the *Claytonia caroliniana* of Michaux. It occurs also with flowers of a deeper rose colour: in our plant the petals are white streaked with red veins. Jussieu has placed *Claytonia* in his natural order of *Portulaceæ* together with *Montia*, to which it has certainly a very near affinity. If Clayton's observation be correct, that the seed is monocotyledonous, perhaps it should be brought nearer to the *asphodeli*, to which family it approaches in general habit, in having a tuberous root, a scape in part embraced by the leaves, which are not always exactly opposite, a two-valved persistent calyx in some respects resembling a spathe, a corolla decaying before it falls off, a trifid stigma, and a three-valved capsule. This is however one-celled, and contains three kidney-shaped seeds, or rather lentiform, with a notch at the part from whence the umbilical cord issues, by means of which it is connected with the bottom of the capsule. The embryo of the seed is rolled round a farinaceous perisperm.

A native of moist woods in Virginia and New England. A hardy perennial. Flowers in May. Propagated by seeds or by the tuberous roots. Requires a moist soil in a shady situation. Introduced by Mr. J. Clayton before 1759.

PRIMULACEÆ

ANDROSACE PUBESCENS.
DOWNY ANDROSACE.

Androsace pubescens.

PLATE 472

A lovely little alpine, belonging to a genus notoriously difficult to keep in cultivation. It is a native of the lofty mountains of Dauphiny, the Pyrenees, and Swiss Alps, at elevations of seven to nine thousand feet, and often occurs near the glaciers, on whose detritus it likes to grow. For the

472   *Androsace pubescens* (t. 5808 1869 WF)

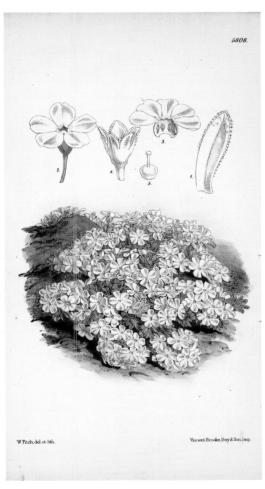

plant here figured I am indebted to Mr. Backhouse, of York, in whose splendid collection of Alpines it appears to flourish. Beautiful as this species is, it cannot compare with the *A. glacialis* of the Tyrolese and Enghedien Alps, which carpets the rocks with sheets of the most lovely rose-purple, and is the choicest of all Alpines known to me.

Descr. A small, densely-tufted alpine, forming low mossy patches six inches broad and upwards, much branched; branches one inch long. *Leaves* crowded, rosulate, one-eighth to one-fourth of an inch long, linear-oblong, or oblong-obovate, obtuse, ciliate with forked hairs, and more or less pubescent. *Flowers* excessively numerous, solitary at the ends of the branchlets; peduncles short, slightly swollen at the base of the calyx, nearly glabrous. *Calyx* campanulate, five-lobed to the middle; lobes ovate, obtuse, ciliate, and slightly pubescent. *Corolla* white with a faint yellow eye, one-third of an inch in diameter; tube short, subglobose; lobes obovate, emarginate. *Stamens* included. *Ovary* subglobose, stigma capitate.

ANDROSACE SPINULIFERA.

Androsace spinulifera.

PLATE 473

Androsace spinulifera, so named on account of the spinescent or at any rate pungently mucronate tips of the leaves, particularly of those of the resting rosette, has a wide distribution, vertical and horizontal, in south-western and western China. It ranges from the mountains of the Yangtse-Tali divide to north-west Szechuan and from 2400 to 3600 m., and it is locally very common. On the edges of dry shady pine-forests, which, according to Forrest, seem to be the most favourable position it sometimes covers acres of ground to the exclusion of all other herbage, and here it attains also its greatest beauty. On dry barren limestone-conglomerate at the lower limit of its range the same explorer found it much stunted and more "spinous" than elsewhere. At high altitudes it becomes similarly dwarfed with the leaves often hardly exceeding three centimetres in length and very grey. The other extreme is represented by specimens from intermedi-

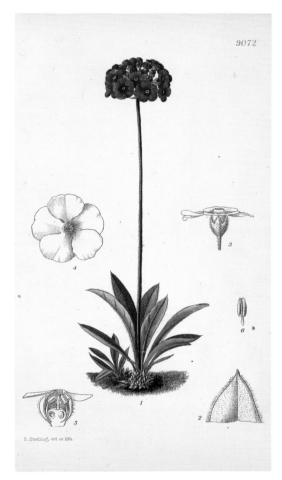

473   *Androsace spinulifera* (t. 9072 1925 LS)

ate stations where the summer-leaves may attain a length of more than fifteen centimetres and a correspondingly greater width. The flower-stalks are mostly very short at first, so that dense flower-heads are formed, but they grow out to one or two centimetres as the fruit ripens; individuals, however, are found in which this lengthening of the flower-stalks occurs already on the opening of the flowers, or it may be that only some lengthen out whilst the others remain comparatively short. Extreme cases with long flower-stalks (1.5–2.5 cm.) and long narrow leaves (15 cm. by 1.2 cm.) represent Knuth's *A. praitiana* from Tachienlu. A suite of specimens obtained by Wilson in the same district (uplands around Tachienlu) connects this *Prattiana*-state so intimately with the dwarf condition that one is forced to consider these dimensional characters as dependent on the vigour of the plant or as subject to fluctuation of a wide range. The differentiation of the leaves into scale-leaves, forming a resting rosette, and normal foliage-leaves is repeated in *A. strigillosa*, a native of Upper Sikkim and Chumbi (3000–4200 m.), although the scale-leaves of the latter are not quite of the same nature, being linear, softer and clothed with a brownish wool; the foliage-leaves are also broader and distinctly differentiated into blade and stalk. Otherwise there is not much difference. Franchet in fact described our plant originally as a variety of *A. strigillosa*. Other species more distantly related to our plant are *A. aizoon* from the western Himalaya and *A. coccinea* (*Bot. Mag.* t. 8653) with practically the same distribution as *A. spinulifera*; but in both we have only one set of leaves in simple sempervivum-like rosettes.

A. spinulifera, like *A. strigillosa*, forms tufts of rosettes from a common collar, which often passes into a short strong and woody root-stock. It is quite hardy, but seems – at least at Kew – to suffer in the winter from the damp. Where it can be given protection from excessive moisture during its resting season, it should do well if planted at the same time in a light, well-aired soil with some lime in it. The colour of the flowers which varies from the deepest rose-purple and crimson to rose makes our plant one of the most attractive of the genus. The specimen which served for the preparation of the plate was raised at Kew from seed received from Edinburgh under Forrest's No.21242. This seed was collected in dry stony "lime-pastures" on the mountains east of Youngning (27° 48′ N. by 101° E.), south-west Szechuan, at an altitude of 3000–3300 m. The colour of the flowers of this number is described on Forrest's label as "rose, drying purple, tube yellow."

Distribution. – Common in the high mountains north of the Tali basin, also in southern and central Szechuan to the Tibetan frontier, 2500–3000 m.

ANDROSACE VILLOSA.
HAIRY ANDROSACE.
Androsace villosa.
PLATE 474

Notwithstanding all the pains that Von Wulfen, in Jacquin's *Collectanea*, has taken to establish a distinction between his *Androsace villosa* and *chamœjasme*, we con-

fess ourselves still to have been at a loss to decide to which of these species our plant belongs, nor can we persuade ourselves that the reverend author has satisfactorily established a specific distinction between them. If really different, we should be inclined to consider our plant as the one intended by Linnæus, Scopoli and Jacquin in his *Flora Austriaca*, under this title, and that figured in Jacquin's *Collectanea*, as a new species not noticed by any preceding author.

The hairiness of the leaves in the cultivated plant, at least, is not at all to be depended upon; in one we saw last year at Mr. Loddiges, the leaves so thickly covered with long white hairs, as to give the whole a hoary appearance; in the same this year the leaves are of a deep green colour, with comparatively few hairs; nor are they in all specimens equally obtuse at the point; those in the one from which our drawing was taken being much more acute than in Mr. Loddiges's plants, though undoubtedly the same species. Haller says it has both obtuse and lanceolate leaves; indeed the whole of his excellent description leaves no room to doubt of the identity of his plant with ours.

Propagated by parting the roots. Though perfectly hardy with respect to cold, these alpine plants are sure to be soon lost, unless planted in a pot; and as they flower very early, they succeed best if sheltered by a hand-glass or common glass frame. During the summer it is necessary to keep them entirely in the shade.

474 *Androsace villosa* (t. 743 1804 SE)

475 *Cyclamen coum* (t. 4 1787)

CYCLAMEN COUM.
ROUND-LEAVED CYCLAMEN.
Cyclamen coum.
PLATE 475

Grows wild in many parts of Italy and Germany, and is sometimes found with white flowers; if the season be mild, or the plants sheltered from the inclemency of the weather, this species will flower as early as February, or much earlier by artifical heat.

As it grows naturally in woods and shady places, it will thrive best in a mixture of bog-earth and loam placed in a north border; if planted in the open border, it will require to be covered with a hand-glass during winter, and in the spring, when in bloom; the more usual method with Gardeners is to preserve them in pots in a common hot-bed frame, the advantage of this method is that they may, at any time, be removed to decorate the parlour or the study.

The plants of this genus admit of but little increase by their roots; the best method of propagating them is by seed, which should be sown soon after they are ripe in boxes or pots, and covered about half an inch deep, placing them where they may have only the morning-fun, till the beginning of September, when they may be removed to a warmer exposure.

PRIMULA AMOENA.

Primula elatior subsp. *meyeri*.

PLATE 476

This Caucasian Primula was first described in 1808 but in the diagnosis was included a plant which was known later as *P. sibthorpii* Hoffmannsegg (otherwise *P. vulgaris rubra*). This early association of two different plants has tended to obscure the story of this species and particularly its record in cultivation. Grown no doubt first in Europe at St. Petersburg (now Leningrad), plants brought from there to Mr. Neill of Canonmills (a few hundred yards from Edinburgh Botanic Garden), flowered freely in a cold frame, one umbel producing eighteen flowers. Recent introductions have not yet overtopped this record. One of Mr. Neill's plants was figured in this magazine in 1833, but unfortunately the plate is inaccurate and does not do justice to the plant, and, moreover, does not agree with the description. The colour of the corolla is shown as a very pale dull lilac or as a slaty-blue, although in the text it is given as "purplish-lilac," whilst the hairs on leaves, scape, and calyx are omitted from the drawing, though fully noted in the text. We were therefore glad to take the opportunity of figuring this species again, when plants flowered in 1938 with Major F. C. Stern.

P. amoena is found throughout the Caucasus and is recorded also from Armenia and Lazistan in north-east Turkey. It is stated to occur at various elevations from one thousand metres to as high as four thousand metres. Like its ally *P. elatior* Schreber, it is a variable plant and some half-dozen forms have been described showing divergences in height, in shape of leaf and degree of hairiness, in the number and size of the flowers, in colour of corolla and in length of capsule. The present figure can be regarded as a good example of the typical plant. *P. amoena* is closely akin to *P. elatior* and is sometimes regarded as a variety or subspecies of that widespread plant. It bears somewhat the same relationship to *P. elatior* as *P. sibthorpii* does to *P. vulgaris*; these two last have no evident scape. The chief distinction between *P. amoena* and *P. elatior*, it must be admitted, is the colour of the corolla, for the flowers of *P. elatior* are consistently yellow. (There is the same contrast between the other two plants quoted in comparison.)

Distribution. – Throughout the Caucasus and into Lazistan in north-east Turkey.

476   *Primula amoena* (t. 9593 1940 LS)

A. PRIMULA EROSA.

B. PRIMULA CAPITATA, VAR.

Primula glomerata.

Primula capitata.

PLATE 477

Primula erosa belongs to a common type of Himalayan Primulas, that of which *P. denticulata* is the prevalent form, and *P. capitata* the rarer. In their usual states they are distinguished as follows: *P. denticulata* by having sparingly mealy or glabrous finely toothed leaves, that are not fully developed till after flowering, and which are surrounded at their bases by fleshy scales, formed by the arrested outer leaves on the crown of the rootstock; it bears a large or small depressed globose head, the flowers of which are lilac or purple, and all open together.

P. erosa differs from *denticulata* in its much slenderer habit, in always (except on young parts) wanting the meal on the

477   *Primula capitata and erosa* (t. 6916 1887 MS)

leaves, which are developed at flowering time, are translucent with strongly erose and denticulate margins, and have a strongly reticulated surface, and the petioles are often red; the umbels are loose or dense-flowered, and the flowers in our garden specimens are of a far deeper purple than is usual in *denticulata*.

P. capitata differs greatly in habit from both the above; it is confined to the eastern Himalaya, has finely denticulate leaves, often snow-white with meal beneath, but sometimes not so, a tall also mealy scape and globose densely crowded head of sessile flowers which open slowly, and the uppermost unexpanded ones are depressed and imbricate over one another like the tiles of a house. The corolla is of a very deep purple blue, the tube and calyx both short.

P. erosa is found throughout most parts of the Himalaya, but I did not observe it in Sikkim. It is known in gardens as *P. capitata*, var. *crispa*. Both it and the *P. capitata* here figured were raised from seeds sent by Dr. King, of the Calcutta Botanical Gardens.

227

PRIMULA LACINIATA.

Primula laciniata.

PLATE 478

Primula laciniata was described from material collected in 1914 by Dr. Limpricht who made two gatherings under nos. 1799 and 1958. These were obtained in an area not far from Tatsien-lu in the district of Dawo, growing in wet places or near springs in the vicinity of Lama temples at an elevation of 3900 metres. The originals show flowers collected at end of June and beginning of July and it is unlikely that any seed was secured. E. H. Wilson, however, found the same plant in July, 1908, and specimens under Wilson 3147 are in the herbaria of Kew and Edinburgh. He describes it as a herb of six to nine inches, with purple flowers, found in wet stony places north-east of Tatsien-lu. Again there is no record of seed and Wilson's sheets either remained unidentified or were allocated near *P. incisa* Franch. The introduction of the plant into cultivation is due to Dr. Harry Smith of Upsala who obtained fruiting specimens in the beginning of September, 1934, under no. 11741 (Herb. Upsal. and Herb. Edin.). The locality is given as "*Sikang*: Taofu (Dawo) distr.:

478   *Primula laciniata* (t. 9584 1939 LS)

Taining (Ngata): South pass; loco argilloso secus rivalum; circ. 3700 m." Wilson records the locality as in west Szechwan, Limpricht in east Tibet and Harry Smith in Sikang, but all refer to the same area – it is only the provincial terms and boundaries that have fluctuated.

Through the courtesy of Dr. Harry Smith seed was obtained by Edinburgh Botanic Garden and plants were flowered in June, 1937. Plants sent to Kew flowered also at the same time. The figure is based on stronger plants presented to Kew by Lord Aberconway which flowered on May 28, 1938. It may be noted that the first plants raised from seed seemed to represent anything but a *Primula* and could easily be mistaken in their early stages for some member of the *Umbelliferae*.

Distribution. – China: western Szechwan.

479   *Primula villosa* (t. 1161 1808 SE)

PRIMULA VILLOSA.

MOUNTAIN PRIMULA.

Primula hirsuta.

PLATES 479 AND 480

Mr. Miller, in the Sixth Edition of the Abridgment of his *Gardener's Dictionary*, mentions only four primulas, exclusive of the *Auricula*, the two first of which are named erroneously, and of the two last not

480   *Primula villosa* (t. 14 1787)

a syllable is said either as to their place of growth or culture.

The plant here figured, has been introduced pretty generally into the Nursery-Gardens in the neighbourhood of London within these few years: Mr. Salisbury informs me, that a variety of this plant with white flowers, brought originally from the Alps of Switzerland, has for many years been cultivated in a garden in Yorkshire.

It is not noticed by Linnæus: Professor Jacquin, in his *Flora Austriaca*, has figured and described a primula, which, though not agreeing so minutely as could be wished with the one we have figured, is nevertheless considered by some of the first Botanists in this country as the same species; he gives it the name of *villosa*, which we adopt, though with us it is so slightly villous as scarcely to deserve that epithet.

It varies in the brilliancy of its colours, flowers in April, and will succeed with the method of culture recommended for the Round-leaved Cyclamen.

OPPOSITE:
481   *Banksia aemula* (t. 2671 1826 CMC)

C. Curtis Del.   Pub by J. Curtis, Walworth Aug. 1816.   Weddell Sc.

PROTEACEÆ

BANKSIA ÆMULA.
RIVAL BANKSIA.
Banksia æmula.
PLATE 481

Our drawing of this rare species of *Banksia*, was taken at the Count de Vandes garden, at Bayswater, in January, 1825. The gardener informed us he had the name from Mr. Brown, and it appears to correspond with the Character given in his *Prodromus. Banksia æmula* has a near relation to *serrata*, but differs in the leaves being more deeply serrate, and especially in the size and form of the stigma. Its flowering in the winter season may perhaps have occasioned the colour to be greater, than it might have been, had the plant had the enjoyment of more sun.

BANKSIA ERICÆFOLIA.
HEATH-LEAVED BANKSIA.
Banksia ericfolia.
PLATE 482

The *Banksia*, a genus so named in honour of its first discoverer, the President of the

482   *Banksia ericaefolia* (t. 738 1804 SE)

Royal Society, in a voyage round the world with Captain Cook, is very nearly allied to *Protea*, and like that appears to contain a great number of species of very various forms and size. Our present plant forms a handsome shrub, thrives freely, and has flowered in several collections.

The beauty of the flower consists very much in the length of the style; which, from the stigma being long retained within the anthers, is fancifully bent into a loop: when the efflorescence is complete, the petals expand and set the stigma at liberty. The flower is considered by some as monopetalous, but the petals in *Banksia ericæfolia* at least, adhere so slightly at the base only, that they can hardly be kept from separating when removed from the receptacle. The germen in this species is surrounded with brown hairs very like that of many of the *Proteaceæ*. We could not discover any other calyx than the squama of the *Amentum*, in no respect like that described by Gærtner. A native of New Holland. By no means tender, and may be kept in a greenhouse with *Proteas* and other Cape shrubs. Propagated by seeds and by cuttings.

EMBOTHRIUM SPECIOSISSIMUM.
THE WARATAH.
Telopea speciosissima.
PLATE 483

The Waratah is allowed, both by the natives and the settlers in New South Wales, to be the most splendid of all their vegetable productions; and the former are said also to find an agreeable repast in sucking the tubular flowers, which abound with honey.

Mr. Loddiges's and some other collections contain this valuable and rare shrub, but we have not heard that it has as yet flowered in any but in that of Emp. J. A. Woodford, Esq. in Hertfordshire, where our drawing was taken in May last. Propagated by layers, or by seeds imported from New Holland.

PROTEA ACAULIS.
STEMLESS PROTEA.
Protea acaulis.
PLATE 484

Descr. *Stem* short, bent down. *Leaves* obovate-oblong, veined, rigid, margins cartilaginous and recurved. *Bracts* of the *Involucrum* imbricated, the inner ones longest, smooth except some villosity at the margins, yellowish, tipped with red. *Pappus* at the base of the germen reddish brown, chaffy and bristly. *Claw* of the distinct *petal* filiform, twisted: *limb* ovate acute, unarmed: *anther* a little shorter than the limb. *Style* subulate, incurved: *stigma* acute, retained a long time together with the anther in the embrace of the petals.

The colour of most of the *Proteas*, both in the leaves and flowers, is more or less tinged with red according as they are more or less exposed to sun and air.

This fine specimen of *Protea acaulis* was communicated near the end of May in 1818.

PROTEA GRANDIFLORA, α. *LATIFOLIA*.
BROAD-LEAVED GREAT-FLOWERED
PROTEA.
Protea nitida.
PLATE 485

There are several species of *Protea* with much larger flowers than this, which has probably acquired the name of *grandiflora* from comparing it with *Protea scolymus*, a much smaller, but somewhat related species.

Mr. Brown remarks that it sometimes varies with linear-oblong leaves, and is then hardly to be distinguished from *Protea abyssinica*, a species known to us only by the figure, and account of it in the appendix to Bruce's travels.

The *Protea grandiflora* is said to form a tree eight or ten feet high. Native of the Cape of Good Hope, where it was detected by Professor Thunberg. Introduced to the Kew garden, by Mr. Francis Masson, in 1787. Our drawing was taken several years ago, by the late Mr. Sydenham Edwards not long after its first establishment, from a plant out of the collection of George Hibbert, Esq. Flowers in May and June. Requires to be kept in an airy greenhouse.

N.º 1128

Pub. by T. Curtis S.ᵗ Geo. Crescent Aug 1.1808.   Syd. Edwards Del. F. Sansom Sculp.

483   *Embothrium speciosissimum* (t. 1128 1808 SE)

PROTEA NANA.

Protea nana.

PLATE 486

On the authority of Aiton's *Hortus Kewensis*, *Protea nana* was introduced into England in 1787 by Francis Masson, a collector sent to South Africa from Kew; and it seems surprising that so attractive and striking a plant should have been lost to cultivation. In this respect it has shared the fate of a vast number of equally handsome or even handsomer species of *Protea* and its allies, not to mention other South African plants that ornamented the greenhouses of our grandfathers. Of *Protea* itself, a genus containing upwards of sixty known species, about one-half have, previous to the first quarter of this century, been both cultivated and figured in Europe, chiefly in England.

Protea nana is a native of rocky places in the Cape Town district. The plant figured was raised from seed sent to the Royal Gardens by Professor MacOwan, Director of the Cape Town Botanical Gardens. It flowered in a cool greenhouse.

RANUNCULACEÆ

ACONITUM UNCINATUM.
HOOK-FLOWERED WOLF'S-BANE.

Aconitum uncinatum.

PLATE 490

The leaves of this species, a native of North America, are less deeply divided than in any other with which we are acquainted; a character that distinguishes it at first sight. The flowers resemble those of *A. cammarum*, but the point of the

231

Pub. by. S. Curtis. Walworth. May.1.1819.

Weddell. Sc.

485 *Protea grandiflora* α *latifolia* (t. 2447 1823)

486 *Protea nana* (t. 7095 1890 MS)

OPPOSITE:
484 *Protea acaulis* (t. 2065 1819)

helmet-shaped petal turns inwards, instead of being reflected, as it usually is in the last mentioned species; the side-petals are kidney-shaped and appear ciliated, when viewed through a lens; the lower petals are unequal. This plant has been supposed to be the *Aconitum japonicum* of Thunberg, which that Botanist describes as having flowers very similar to *A. lycoctonum*, and must be therefore altogether different. The Japan species, we suspect, has never been seen in this country, though its name occurs in some of our catalogues.

It is more from the comparison of our plant with the specimen in the Banksian Herbarium, than from its exact agreement with the descriptions of Linnæus and Michaux, that we consider it to be the *uncinatum*.

The very curious nectaries in this genus, and which really are receptacles of honey, are called by Jussieu petals, together with the minute coloured excrescences, surrounding the germens; and what Linnæus calls corolla is considered by him as the calyx.

A hardy perennial. Flowers in September. Requires no particular treatment.

ANEMONE HORTENSIS.
STAR ANEMONE OR BROAD-LEAV'D GARDEN ANEMONE.

Anemone pavonina.

PLATE 487

We are more and more convinced, that in our eagerness for novelties, we daily lose plants by far more ornamental than the new ones we introduce; the present, a most charming spring plant, with which the Gardens abounded in the time of Parkinson, is now a great rarity; its blossoms, which are uncommonly brilliant, come forth in April, and, like those of many other plants, appear to advantage only when the sun shines.

It may be propagated either by seeds, or by parting its roots in autumn, in the former way we may obtain many beautiful varieties. It prefers a light loamy soil and moderately exposed situation.

Thomas Penny, of London, is another variety; but if so, the calyx, which appears below the flower in the figure, must be an error. Our plant has frequently petals

487 *Anemone hortensis* (t. 123 1790)

stained with purple on the outside, especially when past its prime. It is one of the most showy of the alpine plants, prefers a moist situation and bog-earth. Introduced to this country in 1773, by the late Earl of Bute. Flowers in April and May.

Roots of a variety of this plant with scarlet double flowers are imported from Holland, under the name of *anemonoides*, and sold at a high price.

ANEMONE NARCISSIFLORA.
NARCISSUS-FLOWERED ANEMONE OR WIND FLOWER.

Anemone narcissiflora.

PLATE 488

The *Anemone narcissiflora*, although rarely met with in our collections, is a very common plant on the high mountains, in the south of Europe; and in Siberia, according to Gmelin, from the River Yenisi nearly to the 54th degree of Northern latitude. We have seen dried specimens also from Mount Caucasus. Is said by Clusius to be sweet-scented, which we could not perceive. This plant varies very much in stature and in the size of its flowers; and the *Anemone fasciculata* of the *Species Plantarum* is one of these varieties. Most probably too, Clusius's *Ranunculus montanus* with a purple flower, which he had not seen himself, but received the description and drawing of it from his friend Dr.

488   *Anemone narcissiflora* (t. 1120 1808 SE)

AQUILEGIA HYBRIDA.
TWO-COLOURED COLUMBINE.

Aquilegia × hybrida.

PLATE 489

This beautiful *Columbine* came up in considerable numbers, among the seedlings of *Aquilegia canadensis*, and may perhaps be a hybrid production between that species and *vulgaris*. It appears to us however to be the same as the Siberian variety of *Aquilegia vulgaris* in *Hortus Kewensis*, which is said to be permanent. If so, it might be considered as a valuable acquisition; but as some of the flowers came entirely blue, and others altogether white, it is to be feared that it may not be easy to preserve its peculiarities, and that further experience may not justify our having made a distinct species of it.

It is propagated by seeds only, at least the experienced cultivator who introduced it, has not yet been able to succeed by any other mode. Is perfectly hardy, bearing the severest frosts of our climate without injury.

489   *Aquilegia hybridia* (t. 1221 1809)

The leaves have none of the purplish hue of *A. canadensis*, and are more pubescent, feeling very soft on both sides; on which account the seedling plants were readily distinguished as they grew together; they do not however appear to be materially different in form. The stem is somewhat taller, and the whole plant larger. The nectaries of the flowers are incurved, but not so much so as in *vulgaris*.

It is a hardy perennial. Flowers in May and June. Propagated by seeds or parting its roots.

ATRAGENE ALPINA, VAR. AUSTRIACA.

Clematis alpina.

PLATE 491

The *Atragene alpina* from Siberia and that from Austria, if not distinct species, are certainly permanent varieties. Our plant is undoubtedly the Austrian kind, and was first introduced to this country by Mr. Loddiges, who raised it from seeds sent from Crane above fourteen years ago, and in his garden it has flowered freely for several years past, as also in some others to which it has been extended.

ATRAGENE AMERICANA.
AMERICAN ATRAGENE.

Clematis verticillaris.

PLATE 492

Previously the *Atragene austriaca* (see above), of which the *alpina* from Siberia has been generally considered as a variety, we observed that these plants were probably distinct species. We are now able to ascertain that they really are so, and here we add a third, a native of North America, *Atragene americana*.

Atragene capensis and all the other species mentioned by Willdenow, except perhaps *Atragene zeylanica*, probably do not belong to this genus; which is chiefly distinguished from *Clematis* by the presence of the nectaries or internal petals, and by its very singular manner of growth; every gemma (to which there appears to be nothing similar in *Clematis*) producing as it were a distinct plant, consisting of two or four leaves, with a peduncle bearing a solitary flower in the centre. These plants are connected together by sarmentous stalks, but on very elevated mountains the *Atragene austriaca* is entirely destitute of these stalks, and the whole plant consists merely of two radical leaves with a solitary flower, supported on a scape. It was in this form only that the plant had occurred to Haller, at the time he wrote his *Historia Stirpium Helvetiæ*; probably also Linnæus had not seen it in any other, when he described the leaves as radical, and called the peduncle a scape: and even in cultivation the seedling plants will sometimes flower before any running shoot appears.

The plant now figured flowers nearly at the same time with *Atragene austriaca*, a month later than *sibirica*, is hardly less ornamental, and has the exclusive advantage of being agreeably scented. Was raised from seeds from North America, by Mr. Loddiges; appears to be perfectly hardy, and to produce seeds freely, by which it may be propagated without difficulty, and makes a very desirable addition to our climbing shrubs.

S.Edwards del.   Pub. by W.Curtis St Geo: Crescent Sep. 1.1801.   F.Sansom sculp.

Syd.Edwards del.   Pub. by T. Curtis, St Geo: Crescent Nov.1 1805.   F.Sansom sculp.

S.E. del. F.S. sculp.   Pub. by T. Curtis St Geo Crescent. Dec.1.1808.

CLEMATIS CYLINDRICA.
LONG-FLOWERED VIRGIN'S-BOWER.
Clematis crispa.
PLATE 493

We were informed by Mr. Loddiges, who communicated the plant to us, that it has been many years in Messrs. Gordon and Thompson's garden at Mile End, who probably obtained it from North America.

It has more affinity with *Clematis crispa* than with *viorna*, but we apprehend is distinct from both. From the latter it is distinguished by the flowers being more cylindrical, with petals far thinner, and curled at the edges; from the former, by the petals being never rolled back, as in that, and by the arista of the seeds not being naked; and from both, by the leaflets being much narrower, never cordate, nor growing by threes, as the lower ones generally do in both the other species.

This plant may be the *Clematis reticulata* of Michaux, but he describes the leaflets as being obtuse at both ends, whereas ours are acute; and says the veins, which form the network, are prominent on both sides the leaf; whereas ours are, as in most other plants, prominent on the under surface and depressed on the upper.

It is perfectly hardy, but as it seldom perfects its seeds with us, must be propagated by laying down the branches, or parting the roots in the spring. Flowers in July or August, and continues flowering till checked by the frosty nights.

CLEMATIS NANNOPHYLLA.
DWARF CLEMATIS.
Clematis nannophylla.
PLATE 494

The Dwarf Clematis which is the subject of our plate was discovered by the explorer Przewalski in Kansu in 1872. From his material and from additions secured in 1875 in the same province by Piasezki, Maximowicz published a brief diagnosis, referring the new species to the section *Flammula* and placing it in proximity to *C. fruticosa* Turcz.

The introduction of the species to cultivation was somewhat fortuitous. We owe the plant to Farrer who with Purdom was collecting in Kansu in 1914–15. Farrer sent

494 *Clematis nannophylla* (t. 9641 1942 LS)

home his gatherings of seeds for distribution, but, in these years of war, plant records were not kept with precision. No mention of it appears in *The Plant Introductions of Reginald Farrer* by E. H. M. Cox (1930), where the number 321 is correctly attributed to *Allium purdomii*. Farrer labelled the dried specimens of his *Clematis* 321A and also his seeds but misquoted the same in his book (p. 282). Whatever be the reason, this dwarf species has been long overlooked and there is no evidence that it has survived in cultivation except in Edinburgh. Although in Farrer's eyes it was deemed to be tender, its habit and attractive small flowers merit a trial in the open where a sunny exposure in rock-garden conditions with a light soil and sharp drainage may induce it to mound itself into the bushy form described by Farrer. Distribution. – China; Kansu.

HELLEBORUS HYEMALIS.
WINTER HELLEBORE OR ACONITE.
Eranthis hyemalis.
PLATE 495

Grows wild in Lombardy, Italy, and Austria, affects mountainous situations, flow-

ers with us in February, and hence is liable to be cut off by severe frosts. "Is propagated by offsets, which the roots send out in plenty. These roots may be taken up and transplanted any time after their leaves decay, which is generally by the beginning of June till October, when they will begin to put out new fibres; but as the roots are small and nearly the colour of the ground, so if care is not taken to search for them, many of the roots will be left in the ground. These roots should be planted in small clusters, otherwise they will not make a good appearance, for single flowers scattered about the borders of these small kinds are scarce seen at a distance; but when these and the Snowdrops are alternately planted in bunches, they will have a good effect, as they flower at the same time, and are much of a size." *Miller's Gard. Dict.*.

495 *Helleborus hyemalis* (t. 3 1787)

HELLEBORUS NIGER.
BLACK HELLEBORE
OR CHRISTMAS ROSE.
Helleborus niger.
PLATE 496

As our Publication seems likely to fall into the hands of such as are totally unacquainted with Botany, or botanical writings, it must plead as an apology for our

496 *Helleborus niger* (t. 8 1787)

often explaining many circumstances relative to plants, which may be well known to adepts in the science.

This plant derives its first name from the black colour of its roots, its second from its early flowering and the colour of its petals, which, though generally milk-white on their first appearance, have frequently a tint of red in them, which increases with the age of the blossom, and finally changes to green; in some species of hellebore, particularly the *viridis*, the flower is green from first to last.

Black Hellebore grows wild on the Appenine and other mountains, preferring such as are rocky. If the weather be unusually mild, it will flower in our gardens in the open borders as early as December and January; it may indeed be considered as the herald of approaching spring.

Like most other Alpine plants, it loves a pure air, a situation moderately moist, and a soil unmanured; as the beauty of its flowers is apt to be destroyed by severe frosts, it should be covered during the winter with a hand-glass, or if it be treated in the manner recommended for the Round-Leaved Cyclamen, it may be had to flower in still greater perfection.

It is propagated by parting its roots in autumn: neither this species nor the *hyemalis* thrive very near London.

NIGELLA HISPANICA.
SPANISH FENNEL-FLOWER.
Nigella hispanica.
PLATE 497

Nigella hispanica is at once distinguished from *N. damascena* by the want of the leafy involucre, with which the flower of the latter is curiously surrounded; and from all the other species, by the styles becoming so patent as to form a radiated crown to the top-shaped fruit. The back of the separate capsules stand out in angles, and are covered with glandular excrescences.

That this is Miller's *latifolia*, appears from his specimen preserved in the Banksian Herbarium.

Although cultivated in our gardens as long ago as the days of Parkinson, and bearing more showy flowers than any of the other species, and equally hardy, yet it is far less common than Love in a Mist, whose singular involucre appears to have much attracted the attention of florists.

Native of Spain and the coast of Barbary. Is an annual, and requires the same treatment as *Nigella damascena*; flowers in June and July, and ripens its seeds in August.

497 *Nigella hispanica* (t. 1265 1810 SE)

498 *Nigella orientalis* (t. 1264 1810 SE)

NIGELLA ORIENTALIS.
ORIENTAL FENNEL-FLOWER.
Nigella orientalis.
PLATE 498

According to Morison, the *Nigella orientalis* was introduced into this country, from Aleppo, by the Rev. Mr. Harrington, chaplain to the factory there. It is a hardy annual. Drawn at Mr. Salisbury's Botanic Garden. Flowers in July and August.

RANUNCULUS PARNASSIFOLIUS.
PARNASSIA-LEAVED CROWFOOT.
Ranunculus parnassifolius.
PLATE 499

In the autumn of 1796, I received roots of this and several other rare and curious Alpine plants from Mr. Neckar de Saussure, at Geneva, and have been so fortunate as to bring the present plant to flower with me early in the summer of 1797, and to show signs of ripening some of its seeds: it grew with me in a small pot of loam and bog-earth, sheltered during the winter in a frame.

499 *Ranunculus parnassifolius* (t. 386 1797)

parting its roots in autumn; it may also be raised from seeds, which ripen frequently on strong healthy plants: to succeed in its cultivation, we should plant it in a composition of loam and bog-earth, and place it in a north border, taking care that it does not suffer from want of watering in dry summers. Was cultivated by Mr. Miller, in 1759. *Ait. Kew.*

*The Turkish species is now distinguished as *Trolius ranunculiaus.*

500 *Trollius asiaticus* (t. 235 1793 SE)

Mr. Aiton informs us, that this species was introduced by Messrs. Kennedy and Lee, in 1769, but there is no mention made of its flowering; small indeed is, we believe, the number of Botanists who have seen this plant in flower, as neither Linnæus, Murray, or Gmelin, refer to any figure of it; this has proved an additional inducement for us not to let the present opportunity slip of presenting to the botanical world a figure of this rare and precious jewel of the Alps.

TROLLIUS ASIATICUS.
ASIATIC GLOBE-FLOWER.
Trollius asiaticus.
PLATE 500

Of this genus, two species only have as yet been discovered, the one a native of Great Britain, the other here figured the produce of Siberia and Cappadocia*, both hardy, perennial, herbaceous plants; the latter, more particularly, from the bright orange colour of its flowers, held in high estimation as an ornamental plant, and flowering in May and June. This species, as yet rare in this country, is usually propagated by

RHAMNACEÆ
PALIURUS VIRGATUS.
NEPAL CHRIST'S-THORN.
Paliurus spina-christi.
PLATE 501

Paliurus virgatus is a native of Upper Nepal, from whence it was introduced to our gardens a few years ago, by seeds received from Dr. Wallich. We do not, however, find it recorded among the Nepalese species of *Zizyphus* described in the second volume of the *Flora Indica.* The plant, from which our drawing was taken, is growing in the Botanic Garden, Chelsea. It is now six feet high, and produced flowers for the first time in this country, in August and

501 *Paliurus virgatus* (t. 2535 1824 JC)

September last. It is perfectly hardy. Its drooping branches, and shining green leaves render it a pleasing object in the shrubbery. The *Paliurus vulgaris*, very inaptly named *australis* by Gærtner, is essentially distinguished from our plant, by its decumbent stem, pubescent branches, the leaves never cordate at the base, its more numerous flowers, and lastly by the wing of the fruit having an uneven crenated margin. The proper place for *Paliurus* in the Linnean System is evidently Pentandria Trigynia, and not Pentandria Monogynia.

For the above article we are entirely indebted to Mr. David Don, who has now in the press an account of the plants of Nepal.

ROSACEÆ
CORCHORUS JAPONICUS,
VAR. β. FLORE PLENO.
DOUBLE-FLOWERED JAPAN CORCHORUS.
Kerria japonica.
PLATE 502

The *Corchorus japonicus*, though of very late introduction, is likely to be soon common, as it increases very fast by suckers which the roots throw up in numbers, and strikes most readily from cuttings. At present it is treated as a greenhouse, sometimes as a stove shrub, but will probably be found sufficiently hardy to bear the cold of our winters in the open air as well as the *Ophiopogon japonicus* which likewise grows spontaneously about Nagasaki.

The single-flowered variety has not, to our knowledge, been ever seen in Europe: that with double flowers was introduced into Kew Gardens in 1805, by Mr. William Kerr; from whence it has already spread into most of the principal collections about London. It is cultivated both in Japan and China as an ornamental shrub.

Our drawing was taken from a small plant in August last; but its more natural season of flowering appears to be in the spring: in Japan it blooms in February and the following months.

502   *Cochorus japonicus var.* β *flore pleno* (t. 1296 1810 SE)

503   RIGHT: *Dalibarda fragarioides* (t. 1567 1813 SE)

DALIBARDA FRAGARIOIDES.
STRAWBERRY-LEAVED DALIBARDA OR
BARREN STRAWBERRY.

Waldsteinia fragarioides.

PLATE 503

Descr. *Stems* creeping, bright red, hairy. *Leaves* ternate, on long channelled *footstalks* dilated and ciliated at the base: *leaflets* obovate, irregularly sawed and cut into lobes with ciliated edges, smooth, deep green, fading to a lurid colour. *Peduncles* axillary, longer than the petioles, bearing the flowers in a lax panicle, thinly haired. *Bracts* leaf-like, simple, or eared at the base. *Calyx* five-cleft: *segments* spreading, acute, hairy, *tube* top-shaped. There is here and there a little segment between the others, showing a disposition to become ten-cleft. *Corolla* yellow: *petals* oblong-ovate, scarcely equalling the calyx. *Stamens* many: *filaments* somewhat shorter than the petals, inserted into the back of a fleshy ring within the tube of the calyx, persistent after the petals are fallen off. *Germens* globose.

A hardy perennial. Native of North America. Introduced into the Kew Garden, by Mr. George Don. The plant, from which our drawing and description were taken, was brought from America, by Mr. Lyons.

MALUS HUPEHENSIS.
WILD APPLE FROM HUPEH.

Malus hupehensis.

PLATE 507

" . . . among the many plants it has been my privilege to add to gardens I count this most beautiful of the deciduous small trees. . . . and grateful am I of the honour of being the fortunate introducer of this Crabapple." So wrote E. H. Wilson of this very lovely and very free-flowering species, which was first brought into cultivation in this country by means of the seeds which he obtained on his expedition to western China.

In cultivation the species has proved to be outstanding in all respects, and has come to be regarded, both in Britain and at the Arnold Arboretum, as one of the finest of the crab-apples. It forms a small shapely tree with rather stiff, somewhat ascending, branches; it is extremely floriferous, usually fruits heavily, and is perfectly hardy. The flowers, produced in April, vary in colour; they may be pink in bud and pure white when open, or deep rose in bud and flushed with rose when open whilst a form with flowers wholly rose has been described. In 1930 the species received the Award of Garden Merit.

The species is unusual among crab-apples in breeding true from seeds when grown in close proximity to other species. Moreover, at the Arnold Arboretum Professor Karl Sax found that seeds were produced even by flowers whose anthers and stigmas had been cut off while the flower was still in the bud-stage.

The species proved to be a triploid, and since triploids can only be reproduced asexually, they are naturally stable species. This is the case with *M. hupehensis*, but it does not follow that the individual plants are completely uniform; in fact, judging from the herbarium material, there is quite considerable variation. The species is widely distributed in China, where it is found at the margins of woods, in thickets, and in scrub in mountainous and rocky areas up to 2500–3000 metres, and is commonly cultivated. Its wide distribution is no doubt due, in part at least, to the regular production of an abundance of seeds.

Distribution. – China, from the western provinces of Szechwan, Yunnan and Kweichow right across the country to the eastern provinces of Shantung, Kiangsu, Chekiang and Fukien.

504 *Prunus nigra* (t. 1117 1808 SE)

505 *Rosa bracteata* (t. 1377 1811 SE)

506 *Rosa semperflorens* γ *minima* (t. 1762 1815)

embassy to that country. It bears the cold of our climate very well, and is easily propagated by layers or cuttings.

At Mr. Malcolm's Nursery at Kensington, where our drawing was taken, there is a very fine specimen, planted against a wall, some of the branches of which did spread five or six feet; but it is now much reduced by the pruning knife. The leaves are evergreen, and the flowers fragrant: circumstances that add to its value.

PRUNUS NIGRA.
BLACK PLUM-TREE OR CANADA PLUM.
Prunus nigra.

PLATE 504

Upon a comparison of our plant with the specimen of *Prunus nigra* in the Banksian Herbarium, it appears to be undoubtedly the same; but in the *Hortus Kewensis*, it is called the black Cherry-tree. We have not seen the fruit, but suppose it to be a Plum, especially as there is a specimen in the same Herbarium, from the elder Bartram, of what he calls "the common native Plum of America," which appears to us to be the same species. Flowers in May. Said in the *Hortus Kewensis* to have been introduced by Messrs. Lee and Kennedy in 1773. Is perfectly hardy.

ROSA BRACTEATA.
MACARTNY'S ROSE.
Rosa bracteata.

PLATE 505

Native of China, whence it was introduced by Lord Macartny, on his return from his

ROSA SEMPERFLORENS (v.) MINIMA.
MISS LAWRENCE'S ROSE
OR FAIRY ROSE.
Rosa chinensis var. *minima* or
'Lawrenceana'.

PLATE 506

Several varieties of the *Rosa semperflorens*, differing in size, colour, and scent, have, within these few years, found their way into the different collections about town, and have generally been represented as fresh importations from China; we believe, however, that most of them have been raised from seed here. Every experienced cultivator knows, that the varieties to be obtained in this way are endless.

Our present subject is the most dwarfish Rose that has ever fallen under our notice, rarely producing any branches, so large as represented in our plate. We are inclined to consider it as a mere seminal variety, perhaps of hybrid origin; yet we cannot assert that it is not a distinct species. It is generally known among collectors by the name of Miss Lawrence's Rose.

The plant from which our drawing was taken, was communicated by Mr. Hudson, of the war-office. Flowers most part of the spring, and has an agreeable, though not powerful scent.

RUBUS BIFLORUS.
TWIN-FLOWERING RASPBERRY.
Rubus biflorus.

PLATE 508

Messrs. Veitch of Exeter received this really handsome Bramble from Nepal, and cultivated it for some time under the name of *R. leucodermis*, a name it well deserves, from the pure white of the stems of the plant, looking exactly as if they had been white-washed. Closely examined, the cuticle is found covered by an extremely mi-

507 *Malus hupehensis* (t. 9667 1946 LS)

nute, perfectly white, pulverulent substance. The name however of *leucodermis* is given by Mr. Douglas to a north-west American species, and adopted by Messrs. Torrey and Gray in their *Flora of North America*, which species we have been ourselves led to consider a variety of *Rubus occidentalis* of Linnæus. Our plant is identical with a Nepalese and Himalayan species in our Herbarium, which we believe to be the *R. biflorus* of Dr. Buchanan (Hamilton), and probably the *R. pedunculosus* of Don. It is quite hardy and ornamental, and very striking from its tall very white stems, and its copious white flowers produced in May and June, which are succeeded by the

good-sized and well-flavoured orange or rather deep amber-coloured fruit in the early autumn. We feel sure that this handsome and agreeable fruit would be worth cultivating for the table.

SPIRÆA TRIFOLIATA.

THREE-LEAVED SPIRÆA.

Gillenia trifoliata.

PLATE 509

To this genus both the flower-garden and shrubbery are indebted for some of their

chief ornaments. Of the hardy herbaceous species the *trifoliata* is considered as one of the most elegant; when it grows in perfection it certainly is a most delectable plant.

It is a native of North America, flowers in June and July, and was cultivated by Mr. Miller, in 1758. Being a plant much coveted, increasing but little, propagated with difficulty, and liable to be lost unless planted in a soil and situation highly favourable to it, it is scarce in the gardens about London.

It is usually increased by parting its roots; these might grow when made cuttings of. Miller says it is propagated by seeds, which should be sown on a shady border, soon

508 *Rubus biflorus* (t. 4678 1852 WF)

after they are ripe; if they are sown in the spring, the plants will not come up till the year after, and many times fail; they require to be very carefully weeded and attended to. The best situation for this plant is a north border; it loves moisture, and should be planted in light bog or peat-earth, or a mixture of it and a pure hazel loam.

509 *Spiraea trifoliata* (t. 489 1800 SE)

RUBIACEÆ

COFFEA ARABICA.
COFFEE-TREE.
Coffea arabica.

PLATE 510

As cultivated in our stoves, the Coffee-tree, if allowed sufficient space, makes a very handsome evergreen shrub, and will both flower and ripen its fruit. The flowers, which are very sweet-scented, especially after sunset, are so like those of Jasmin that it is not surprising that Botanists should at first have considered this tree as belonging to the same genus.

Coffee had been imported into every part of Europe, and used as a favourite beverage, long before it was known of what plant it was the product. Prosper Alpinus had seen the Coffee-tree, without fructification, in some gardens in Egypt; but the first intelligent botanical account was published by Ant. de Jussieu, in the memoirs of the Academy of Sciences in Paris in 1713. It was introduced to Europe by means of Witsen, a Burgomaster of Amsterdam and Chairman of the Dutch East India Company, who gave directions to the governor of Batavia to procure seeds from Mocha in Arabia Felix. These being sown in the island of Java, several plants were

510 *Coffea arabica* (t. 1303 1810 SE)

produced, and one was transmitted to Witsen about the year 1690, who presented it to the Botanic Garden at Amsterdam, of which he had been the founder. From the progeny of this plant not only the principal botanic gardens in Europe, but also the West India Islands, were supplied with this interesting tree. Within six years after its introduction into Holland, it appears to have been cultivated by Bishop Compton at Fulham.

Much has been written upon the effects of Coffee on the constitution, which by some are considered as highly salutary, and by others as very injurious. There is no possibility of reconciling accounts so contrary; but doubtless the effects are various upon different persons. One source of difference has not been sufficiently attended to, which is the mode of preparing and taking it; excessive roasting for instance must change its qualities altogether, and reduce it to the nature of charcoal; and what, as a grateful aromatic bitter, may, when taken pure, promote digestion, shall become altogether inimical thereto by being mixed with sugar and cream. If we expect to experience effects similar to what it produces upon the Arabs and Turks, we ought to follow their example, to use it as soon as roasted, and without admixture.

Flowers with us in August and September. Propagated by the berries, which must be sown soon after they are gathered, or they will not vegetate. Being native of Arabia Felix, within the tropics, requires to be kept in the stove, but should be allowed a free circulation of air, or the leaves become damp and covered with insects, which render the plant unsightly, and if not remedied will infallibly destroy it.

GARDENIA FLORIDA, FL. SIMPLICI.
SINGLE-FLOWERED CAPE JASMINE.
Gardenia jasminoides.

PLATE 511

This delightfully fragrant shrub flowered in June of the present year, in the noble gardens of Wentworth, where it was received from the East Indies, and is treated as a stove plant; and was obligingly communicated by Mr. Cooper, with the remark that it is probably different from the single-flowered state of *Gardenia florida*. In this doubt I partake myself, for it differs from

511   *Gardenia florida fl. simplici* (t. 3349 1834 WJH)

the only figure I am acquainted with, taken from the recent plant, namely, that of Mr. Ker, in the *Botanical Register*, – chiefly, however, in the greater length of the tube of the corolla, and in the leaves being much more crowded towards the extremities of the branches. Still I dare not venture to make it a new species, without an examination of the fruit, but prefer considering it a long-flowered *var.* of the *Gardenia florida*.

HAMELIA VENTRICOSA.
LARGE-FLOWERED HAMELIA.
Hamelia ventricosa.

PLATE 512

The name of *Hamelia*, of which there are several species, was given in honour of Mons. Henry Louis Du Hamel Du Monceau, Inspector-General of the French Marine, and author of several esteemed works on trees, by Professor Jacquin.

Brown, in his *History of Jamaica*, assigns an altitude of eight or ten feet to this tree; but if the synonym of Sloane, generally quoted, but which, we very much suspect, belongs to some other species, be correct, it becomes a very large and stately tree,

affording broad planks, of which there were formerly exported great quantities for the use of cabinet-makers, under the names of Spanish Elm and Princes Wood. With us, it must be cultivated in the bark stove, where it forms a flowering shrub, producing its yellow blossoms from September to November. Propagated by cuttings. Introduced in 1778, by Dr. Thomas Clark.

512   *Hamelia ventricosa* (t. 1894 1817)

RUTACEÆ

CORRÆA SPECIOSA.
RED-FLOWERED CORRÆA.
Correa speciosa.

PLATE 513

The whole plant, not excepting the corolla, is covered with a stellated pubescence, thicker and frequently ferrugineous on the underside of the leaf. The tube of the corolla has four lines, which may be supposed to mark out the adhesion of the four petals, but which we have not found to be separable without tearing. The leaves in different specimens vary from eliptical, to oblong-cordate; the apparent sinuosities of the margin arise from this part being unequally rolled back, rather than from any real incisure or denticulation.

As Sir James E. Smith had given the distinguishing characters of this species,

when describing *Corræa virens* in the *Exotic Botany*, and had called it *rubra*, this appropriate name ought to have been retained; when the three known species would have all derived their appellations from the colour of their flowers, *alba, virens,* and *rubra*; but as the nurserymen's favourite name of *speciosa* seems now to be generally adopted, we have rather fallen in with it, than run the risk of making any confusion, though, by so doing, we give up both the right of priority and the preferable name.

The genus was first established by Sir James E. Smith, in honour of that excellent Portuguese Botanist, Mr. Joseph Correa de Serra.

Native of New South Wales. First discovered by Sir Joseph Banks and Dr. Solander. Introduced in 1804. Propagated by cuttings. Requires to be protected from frost; but ought to have a free circulation of air. Thrives best in a mixture of light loam and peat-mould. Flowers in March, April, and May.

513   *Corraea speciosa* (t. 1746 1815)

DIOSMA FRAGRANS.
AROMATIC DIOSMA.
Adenandra fragrans.

PLATE 514

The whole plant is very aromatic, without any admixture of the foxy smell so offensive in several species; and is otherwise one of the most desirable of the whole genus.

Native of the Cape of Good Hope. Flowers in May, June, and July. Propagated by cuttings. First raised from seeds sent by Mr. Nevin, Collector to George Hibbert, Esq. by Mr. Knight, now of the Exotic Nursery, King's Road, Little Chelsea, by whom it was communicated to us.

514   *Diosma fragrans* (t. 1519 1813 SE)

DIOSMA PULCHELLA.
BLUNT-LEAVED DIOSMA.

Agathosma pulchella.

PLATE 515

Linnæus, in the twelfth edition of the vegetable kingdom in his *Systema Naturæ*, had adopted the division of the genus *Diosma*, proposed by Bergius; separating such as had the male and female flowers distinct and only three capsules, under the name of *Hartogia*: and this species, though it agreed in the latter respect only, was united with the new genus. But Linnæus soon found that in this polymorphous genus, there were no characters then discovered, sufficiently stable to ground a distinction upon; and in the thirteenth edition of the *Systema Vegetabilium* he again reduced the whole under *Diosma*.

515   *Diosma pulchella* (t. 1357 1811 SE)

Diosma pulchella is a very beautiful little shrub, producing its lively flowers in great profusion throughout most of the summer. Native of the Cape of Good Hope, requiring only to be protected from frost. Introduced into the Kew Garden by Mr. Francis Masson, in 1787.

DIOSMA SPECIOSA.
UMBEL-FLOWERED DIOSMA.

Adenandra umbellata.

PLATE 516

Although very nearly related to *D. uniflora*, we do not hesitate to consider this species as distinct from *Diosma uniflora*, although very nearly related to it, especially from the presence of a pair of remarkable glands at the base of the footstalks of every leaf, which in *uniflora*, is not entirely wanting, are barely visible in the old leaves only: a character first pointed out to us by Mr. George Loddiges. The habits of the plants are also considerably different, the leaves in *uniflora* are not only much smaller and narrower, but more revolute and more glaucous on the under surface; the calyx too is less punctate and more ciliate than in *speciosa*; the young branches are more decidedly quadrangular and pubescent. In variety (β), the *rugosa* of Donn, the glands at the base of the petiole are the same as in

516   *Diosma speciosa* (t. 1271 1810 SE)

speciosa, but perfectly smooth, not villous, as Thunberg describes his plant. Native of the Cape. Flowers in May and June. Requires the shelter of a greenhouse. Propagated by cuttings.

ZANTHOXYLUM NITIDUM.
SHINING-LEAVED ZANTHOXYLUM.

Zanthoxylum bungei.

PLATE 517

As we had not the opportunity of seeing this plant growing, we are not certain whether our plant is really the species to which we have referred it on the authority of Mr. Lindley, Botanist of the Horticultural Society; but from Dr. Roxburgh's account of his *Fagara nitida*, which is referred by his editor, Dr. Wallich, to *Zanthoxylum*, we have very little doubt about it.

According to Mr. John Reeves, who has been long a resident in China, and is well acquainted with the plants of the country, it is the *Fagara piperita* of Loureiro, with whose description, it in most respects agrees tolerably well; but it cannot be the *Fagara piperita* of Linnæus.

Our drawing of this rare shrub was taken at the Horticultural Society's greenhouse, in February 1824. We are informed by Mr. Sabine, that it has been received from China by the Society at various times, particularly in 1822, from Mr. John Potts. In China it forms an impenetrable fence. It is nearly hardy enough to be cultivated in the open ground.

517 *Zanthoxylum nitidum* (t. 2558 1825)

SAPINDACEÆ

XANTHOCERAS SORBIFOLIA.

Xanthoceras sorbifolia.

PLATE 522

This is one of the most attractive and interesting hardy garden shrubs that has been introduced for many years, and though introduced nearly twenty years ago, is rarely seen except in the botanical establishments or the gardens of those in search of novelties. It was discovered by the now venerable Dr. Bunge, formerly Professor of Botany at Dorpat, near Peking, some sixty years ago, on the occasion of his accompanying an overland mission to that capital from St. Petersburg; but was not introduced till Father David, the most laborious and successful of all explorers of the Chinese Flora, sent seeds to the Jardin de

Plantes at Paris about twenty years ago. According to a statement in the *Gardener's Chronicle*, Father David sent the plant in 1868, and as it flowered and was figured in the *Flore des Serres* in 1872, it must have been transmitted to Paris in a living state.

Xanthoceras sorbifolia is a beautiful free-flowering bush, with the habit of the Bladder-nut (*Staphylea pinnata*), to which it is allied. I am indebted to Mr. Lynch, of the Cambridge Botanical Gardens, for the fine specimens here figured, with flowers of both sexes, and where it blossomed in May, 1886, the females appearing a few days after the males. The leaves were fully developed in July. For the fine fruits I am indebted to the kindness of continental correspondents; the apple-shaped ones were received in August of last year from M. Max Cornu, of Paris, and were ripened in the Jardin de Plantes. The pyriform ones were received in October from M. J. Van Volxem, of Brussels. The seeds are described as being eaten by the Chinese.

SARRACENIACEÆ

SARRACENIA FLAVA.
YELLOW SIDE-SADDLE FLOWER OR PITCHER PLANT.

Sarracenia flava.

PLATE 518

The singular structure both of the flower and the leaves of this plant has long made it an object of curiosity, but the difficulty of cultivation continues to render it still a rarity in this country, though a common inhabitant of the swamps in North America from Carolina to Florida. The singularity of the flower consists principally in the stigma, which is spread over the parts of fructification like an umbrella. Between the angles of this umbrella the flaccid petals hang down somewhat in the manner as a woman's leg hangs over the pummel of the sidesaddle, which we suppose was the origin of the name given it by the first English settlers.

The leaves being hollow tubes capable of holding water, Linnæus ingeniously considered this curious conformation as a metamorphosis of the leaves of a *Nymphæa* into a form fit for receiving and retaining rain water. And we are told that "the hollow parts of the leaves have always water stand-

518 *Sarracenia flava* (t. 780 1804 SE)

ing in them, and the top or ear is supposed, in hot dry weather, to shrink, and fall over the mouth of the tube, and serve as a lid to prevent the exhalation of the water. In great droughts birds and other animals repair to these plants." There would be more probability in this hypothesis if these plants were found growing in dry places, but they will not live except in wet situations, where the roots can readily find water without the aid of these supposed reservoirs. In the cultivated plant we rarely find any water in the leaves; nor does it appear that the appendix at the end in this species ever closes upon the opening, so that the real purpose of this curious construction is probably not yet discovered. In some of the species a great number of insects find a prison, from which it seems they cannot easily extricate themselves, but what purpose the death of these can serve in the economy of this plant, or in any other of the fly-traps, is as yet totally unknown.

Miller recommends the pots to be kept constantly in water, and only protected from frost by a glass-frame in the winter; but we more usually see them kept in an airy part of the stove. In a manuscript journal of the late Mr. Thomas Collinson, he remarks having seen the *Sarracenia* (but whether the yellow or purple is not noted) flowering in the open air in the greatest perfection he ever saw, in the wet rock-work at the Duke of Athol's at Dunkeld.

519   *Sarracenia purpurea* (t. 849 1805 SE)

SARRACENIA PURPUREA.
BROAD-LIPPED PURPLE SIDE-SADDLE FLOWER OR PITCHER PLANT.

Sarracenia purpurea.

PLATE 519

The *Sarracenia purpurea*, being a native of Canada, should be sufficiently hardy to bear our winters in the open air, but, perhaps from some error in the treatment, it has seldom been made to flower without artificial heat; we should recommend its being planted in bog-earth, in a moist shady situation, where the ground is generally covered with moss.

There is however another species with purple flowers, the *Sarracenia psittacina* of Michaux, which we have seen at Mr. Woodford's, and this being a native of the more southern states of North America, is probably more tender.

Our drawing was made at Messrs. Lee and Kennedy's, Nurserymen, at Hammersmith, in the middle of last March, and we received a specimen in fine flower but imperfect in its foliage, in April of the preceding year, from Mr. Loddiges. Said in the *Hortus Kewensis* to be introduced by Mr. John Tradescant, jun. before the year 1640.

SAXIFRAGACEÆ

RIBES RESINOSUM*.
CLAMMY CURRANT.

Ribes orientale.

PLATE 520

It has been cultivated eight or nine years at Messrs. Fraser's, of Sloane Square, whose father first discovered it in the mountains of North America; it has been also some years in the garden of George Anderson, Esq. by whom we have been repeatedly favoured with specimens; but no where has it produced fruit: indeed from the smallness of the germen and the sphacelated appearance of the stigmas we suspect this species to be dioecious, and that we have only the male plant. Flowers in April and May. Propagated by cuttings.

*This species is, in fact, native from Greece eastwards to Siberia.

520   *Ribes resinosum* (t. 1583 1813)

521   *Ribes speciosum* (t. 3530 1836 WC)

RIBES SPECIOSUM.
SHOWY GOOSEBERRY.

Ribes speciosum.

PLATE 521

This fine *Ribes*, so remarkable, for its leaves resembling those of the White-thorn, and its flowers those of a *Fuchsia*, was first discovered by the venerable Menzies in California, during the voyage of Capt. Vancouver, and his beautiful drawing and description made on the spot, are now before me. It was introduced to our gardens by Mr. Collie, the surgeon of H. M. S. Blossom, in 1829. In native specimens, the leaves are smaller, and the racemes only two-flowered. In England the plants seem to be perfectly hardy: in Scotland it requires the protection of a wall, or the flowers will effectually, in most years, be destroyed, by our fickle springs. Its flowering season is April and May; its growth is rapid and vigorous during summer, and the plant is now becoming common.

OPPOSITE:
522   *Xanthoceras sorbifolia* (t. 6923 1887 MS)

247

523 *Saxifraga ceratophylla* (t. 1651 1814 SE)

SAXIFRAGA CERATOPHYLLA.

SHINING-CALYXED SAXIFRAGE.

Saxifragi ceratophylla.

PLATE 523

This is a very desirable little alpine plant, its foliage being a particularly bright green growing in hemispherical even tufts. It seems particularly suited to ornament rock-work, and in such a situation would probably bear our ordinary winters very well, though it will be safer to preserve some pots of it under a frame. Native of Spain. Flowers in June. Introduced in 1804.

SAXIFRAGA CRASSIFOLIA.

OVAL-LEAVED SAXIFRAGE.

Bergenia crassifolia.

PLATE 524

The term *grandifolia* would have been more applicable to this species of saxifrage than *crassifolia*, for it is not so much distinguished for the thickness as the largeness of its leaves; these are almost equal in size to those of our Broad-leaved Dock, red on the under and of a fine shining green on their

upper surface; they may be ranked indeed among the more handsome kinds of foliage; the flowering stems, according to the richness and moisture of the soil in which they are planted, rise from one to two or even three feet high; at top supporting a large bunch of purple pendulous flowers, which blossom in April and May, and, if the season prove favourable, make a fine appearance. Should cold winds prevail at the time of their flowering, which they are very apt to do, the plants should be covered with a hand-glass; or, if in a pot, it may be removed into the greenhouse, which they will not disgrace.

Is found spontaneously on the Alps of Siberia, and, according to Mr. Aiton, was introduced in 1765 by Dr. Solander. No plant is more readily increased by parting its roots, which may be done either in spring or autumn.

There is another saxifrage in our gardens exceedingly like this in appearance, but differing, in producing larger bunches of flowers, and in having larger, rounder, and more heartshaped leaves; Mr. Aiton regards this as a variety of the *crassifolia*, we are inclined to consider it as a species under the name of *cordifolia*.

524 *Saxifraga crassifolia* (t. 96 1789)

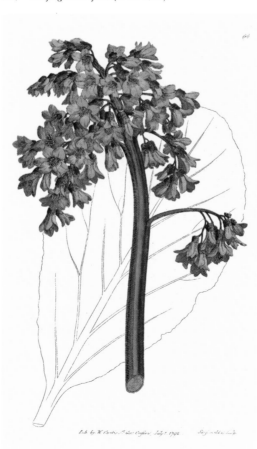

525 *Tiarella cordifolia* (t. 1589 1813 SE)

TIARELLA CORDIFOLIA.

HEART-LEAVED TIARELLA.

Tiarella cordifolia.

PLATE 525

Tiarella cordifolia usually, if not always, puts up a flowering stem immediately from the root, without leaves. Retzius has described, as a distinct species, one with a single sessile leaf on the scape. In the Banksian Herbarium are specimens gathered by Mr. Archibald Menzies, at Port Trinidad, on the north-west coast of America, which have very long simple assurgent stems, terminated with a spike of flowers, and having five or six leaves, placed alternately, and a pair of membranaceous stipulæ beneath each. This may well be considered as a distinct species, especially as the flowers are on pedicels much shorter than the flower. But the same Herbarium contains a specimen marked as belonging to *cordifolia*, and like it with respect to the length of the pedicels, communicated by Professor Peck: this has two leaves on the scape, and the lower leaf has the same stipulæ as Mr. Menzies's plant. Our character is intended to separate these plants; at the same time, it may perhaps be doubted whether they ought not to be considered as mere varieties of the same species.

The first notice we find of this plant is by Jo. Bodæus a Stapel, in his *Commentaries on Theophrastus*, who has given a characteristic representation of it, cut in wood. The figure in Herman's *Paradisus*, usually referred to this, can hardly belong to it. It is apetalous, has purple stamens, and what is still more material, the pedicels of the flowers are branched.

A hardy perennial, native of North America. Propagated by partings its roots.

SCHISANDRACEÆ

SCHISANDRA COCCINEA.
SCARLET-FLOWERED SCHISANDRA.
Schisandra coccinea.

PLATE 526

For the specimen of this very rare climbing shrub, from which our drawing was made, we are indebted to our friend John Walker, Esq. of Arno's Grove, Southgate. As it unfortunately produced only male flowers, our character of the female was necessarily borrowed from Michaux: that of the male we have made to correspond with our ideas of its structure from actual though too limited observation.

526 *Schisandra coccinea* (t. 1413 1811 SE)

Native of South Carolina and Georgia, therefore liable to be killed by the severity of our winters, unless protected by the shelter of glass. Flowers in June. Propagated by cuttings.

527 *Antirrhinum triste* (t. 74 1789)

SCROPHULARIACEÆ

ANTIRRHINUM TRISTE.
MELANCHOLY OR BLACK-FLOWER'D TOAD-FLAX.
Linaria tristis.

PLATE 527

Receives its name of *triste* from the sombre appearance of its flowers; but this must be understood when placed at some little distance, for, on a near view, the principal colour of the blossoms is a fine rich brown, inclined to purple.

It is a native of Spain, and of course a greenhouse plant with us, but it must not be too tenderly treated, as it loses much of its beauty when drawn up, it should therefore be kept out of doors when the season will admit, as it only requires shelter from severe frost, and that a common hot-bed frame will in general afford it.

It flowers during most of the summer months; as it rarely or never ripens its seeds with us, the usual mode of propagating it, is by cuttings which strike readily enough in the common way.

Miller relates that it was first introduced into this country by Sir Charles Wager, from Gibraltar seeds.

CALCEOLARIA ARACHNOIDEA.
COBWEB SLIPPERWORT.
Calceolaria arachnoidea.

PLATE 528

We received the seeds of this plant from our invaluable correspondent, Dr. Gillies, of Mendoza, in January last, having been collected by him in Chili. It has been treated like all the other species of the genus, and hitherto kept in the greenhouse. There is great probability that it may not produce seed; but it strikes very readily by cuttings, the branches even pushing down roots as they lie along the ground.

We fear it will be found more difficult to preserve the only other purple-flowered *Calceolaria* in cultivation (C. *purpurea,*

528 *Calceolaria arachnoidea* (t. 2874 1828 WJH)

Edin. Phil. Journ. 1827; which was also introduced through the Botanic Garden, Edinburgh, by seeds sent from our other excellent correspondent Mr. Cruickshanks, as it has hitherto produced very few seeds. An entirely new aspect has been given to our greenhouses within these few years, by the kindness of Dr. Gillies and Mr. Cruickshanks, particularly in most interesting additions from the genera *Fuchsia*, *Calceolaria*, *Salpiglossis*, *Schizanthus*, and *Loasa. Graham.*

CAPRARIA UNDULATA.
WAVED-LEAVED CAPRARIA.
Freylinia undulata.
PLATE 529

Capraria undulata forms a small straggling shrub, of little beauty except while in blossom, when its lively purplish flowers, growing near the extremities of the branches, make a pleasing variety.

Native of the Cape of Good Hope, whence it was introduced to the Kew Garden, by Mr. Francis Masson, in 1774. Requires the shelter of a greenhouse. Flowers in June. Communicated by Messrs. Loddiges and Sons, Hackney.

529   *Capraria undulata* (t. 1556 1813 SE)

CHELONE MAJOR
LYON'S CHELONE.
Chelone lyonii.
PLATE 531

This undescribed species of *Chelone* was introduced by the late Mr. Lyons, from Carolina. It differs from *Chelone obliqua* in its greater size, longer horizontal petioles, broader and more cordate leaves, tomentose underneath, and peach-blossom coloured flowers; but more especially in the number of spikes, which grow from the axils of the leaves as well as at the extremities of the branches, and are frequently crowded several together. The rudiment of the fifth filament is not half the length of the others, and perfectly smooth; in *obliqua* we have sometimes found them hairy at the base.

It is considered as a hardy perennial, and may be propagated by dividing its roots. Flowers in August and September.

DIGITALIS FERRUGINEA.
IRON-COLOURED FOX-GLOVE.
Digitalis ferruginea.
PLATE 532

Descr. *Root* perennial. *Stem* upright, rigid, from three to six feet high, clothed with lanceolate *leaves* quite entire or slightly toothed. *Spike*, or rather spike-like *raceme*, terminal, two or even three feet long, gradually tapering to the top; simple, or having a few short branches towards the base. *Flowers* crowded together, but solitary, on short peduncles, supported each by a single, lanceolate, marginated, reflexed bracte, of which the lower ones are much longer than the calyx, the upper ones shorter. *Calyx* five-cleft; the three upper segments erect, the two lower applied close to the corolla, all of them oval, very obtuse, and edged with a white membranaceous margin. *Corolla* drooping, dull yellow on the outside, within streaked with rusty purple lines: *tube* short, contracted: *faux* suddenly swelling, bellied: *limb* five-cleft: two upper *laciniæ* very short, nearly obsolete, rolled back; two lateral somewhat longer, acute; lowermost long, blunt, hollowed, thinly bearded. *Stamens* shorter than corolla; filaments inserted into the

tube of the corolla, equal, thickened at the base, sigmoid: *anthers* parallel: *lobes* divaricate. *Germen* superior, conical, bilocular; *style* the length of the stamens; *stigma* simple.

A hardy perennial, generally perishing after flowering; very shewy, from its stature and long tapering spike of flowers. Native of Italy. An old inhabitant of our gardens, being cultivated by Gerard above two hundred years ago. Our drawing was taken from a specimen, communicated by John Walker, Esq. of Arno's Grove; our description from one communicated many years ago, by Thomas Furley Forster, Esq.

530   *Digitalis lanata* (t. 1159 1808)

DIGITALIS LANATA.
WOOLLY-SPIKED FOX-GLOVE.
Digitalis lanata.
PLATE 530

Native of Hungary. Hardy. Flowers in June, July, and August. Propagated by seeds. Introduced, according to Donn, in 1790. Communicated by Messrs. Napier and Chandler, Nurserymen at Vauxhall, in 1807.

OPPOSITE:
531   *Chelone major* (t. 1864 1816)

Pub. by. S. Curtis. Walworth. Nov.r 1.1816.

Pub. by. S. Curtis. Walworth. June 1. 1816.

MIMULUS LUTEUS, *VAR.* YOUNGANA.
YELLOW CHILIAN MONKEY-FLOWER;
MR. YOUNG'S VARIETY.

Mimulus luteus.

PLATE 533

We have before stated our opinion that the *M. luteus* is subject to much variation, especially in the markings of its flowers. The present is certainly among the most beautiful, having the corolla of a rich full yellow, and every segment marked with a large blotch of a rich red-brown inclining to blood colour. It is perfectly hardy, and flowers in July and August in the Glasgow Botanic Garden, where it was received from Mr. Loddiges, under the name here adopted. We possess wild specimens of the same variety, from its native country Chili.

533   Mimulus luteus var. youngana (t. 3363 1834 WJH)

OPPOSITE:
532   Digitalis ferruginea (t. 1828 1816)

PENTSTEMON DIGITALIS.
FOX-GLOVE-LIKE PENTSTEMON.

Penstetmon digitalis.

PLATE 537

Descr. *Stem* erect, three feet high, roundish, purple at the lower part, green above. *Leaves* opposite, lanceolate, undulate, toothed, stem-embracing; top-ones ovate-acuminate; bottom-ones very much narrowed at the base. *Flowers* in a very long, terminal, trichotomous panicle, white, with purple streaks on the inside. *Bracts* cordate-acuminate. *Peduncles* erect. *Pedicels* mostly three together. *Calyx* small, five-cleft: segments revolute, shorter than the contracted tube of the corolla. *Corolla* covered on the outside with short, glandular, viscid hairs: *Tube* contracted, channelled on the upper side. *Faux* bell-shaped, open at the mouth, and somewhat hairy. *Limb* two lipped: upper-lip bifid, with smaller revolute laciniæ: under-lip trifid, with larger laciniæ. *Fertile stamens* four, unequal: *Filaments* curved: *Anthers*, before the expansion of the flower, kidney-shaped, purple at the back, and yellow from the escaping pollen in front: *sterile filament* somewhat longer than the fertile; straight; thinly covered towards the point with deflexed hairs. *Germen* superior, bilocular: *style* curved at the point; scarcely so long as the stamens.

Pentstemon digitalis is by far the finest species of this genus that we have seen, growing upright to more than three feet in height, and bearing a very large panicle of delicate white flowers, of which the size of our work would not admit half to be inserted.

Communicated by our friend Robert Barclay, Esq. to whom the seeds were sent by Professor Nuttall, in March, 1824, under the name which we have adopted, thinking it probable, that it may have been published by it in America; otherwise a substantive specific name should be confined to such species as have before constituted a different genus. A hardy perennial. Native of the Arkansa territory. Flowers in June and July.

PENTSTEMON MURRAYANUS.
MR. MURRAY'S SCARLET PENTSTEMON.

Pentstemon murrayanus.

PLATE 538

A native of San Felipe, in Texas: discovered by Mr. Drummond in 1834, and by him sent to our gardens, where it promises to be a very great acquisition, being remarkable for its stately growth, its singularly glaucous and large foliage, and for the number and size and rich colouring of the flowers. The seeds arrived rather late in the spring of 1835, so that, in the Glasgow Botanic Garden, the autumn advanced rapidly upon us before the blossoms were generally expanded. Under more favorable circumstances we may judge of the beauty of the plant, from the fact that, on one specimen, we counted eleven pairs of floral leaves, from the axils of which sprang two to four flower buds: and in one of the dried native specimens a single raceme had fifty-six blossoms. It will probably prove quite a hardy, herbaceous perennial. I am anxious it should bear the name of the skilful Curator of our Glasgow Botanic Garden, who has been the means of rearing so many of Mr. Drummond's plants, and to whose undeviating kindness and friendship that zealous Naturalist was greatly indebted for much of the success that attended his exertions.

RHODOCHITON VOLUBILE.
TWINING RHODOCHITON.

Rhodochiton atrosangiuneum.

PLATE 544

This plant, a native of Mexico, was received at the Botanic Garden, Edinburgh, from Mr. Low of Clapton, who had it from Berlin, and it has flowered very freely with us in the open border during September, and will no doubt continue to do so during October. It seems perfectly hardy, and is highly ornamental. I regret that I have not seen the original observations on the genus by Zuccarini; but I cannot agree with Mr. Don in uniting it with *Lophospermum*; though undoubtedly these Genera are very nearly allied.

SCUTELLARIA GRANDIFLORA.

LARGE-FLOWERED SCUTELLARIA.

Scutellaria grandiflora.

PLATE 534

This species approaches very near to the *Scutellaria orientalis*, especially to the variety found in Georgia, by Tournefort, and described in his travels: but besides that his plant has yellow flowers, ours differs in having much shorter spikes, corolla larger in proportion to the size of the bracts, leaves rounder, less tomentose underneath, but soft like velvet on both sides; the flowers are scentless, and, as well as the whole plant, intensely bitter. A hardy perennial. Flowers in July.

The specimen from which our drawing was made, was sent us by Mr. Loddiges, Nurseryman, who raised it from seeds sent him from Siberia.

534 *Scutellaria grandiflora* (t. 635 1803 SE)

VERBASCUM PHŒNICEUM.

PURPLE-FLOWERED MULLEIN.

Verbascum phoeniceum.

PLATE 535

The mulleins are all showy plants; this species, a native of the southern parts of Europe, having bright purple flowers is very

535 *Verbascum phoeniceum* (t. 885 1805 SE)

ornamental, and has been long thought worthy of cultivation, being seen in our gardens before the time of Gerard. Is a perfectly hardy perennial, "the roote (as Parkinson observes) abiding sundry yeares," though some have supposed it to be only biennial, an error still handed down in Martyn's *Miller's Dictionary*. May be easily propagated by parting its roots or by seeds, which however with us it rarely produces, though in some years abundantly. Succeeds best in a sandy loam with an eastern exposure; its stems, if not tied up, are liable to suffer from high winds. Blooms through the months of May and June.

VERONICA FORMOSA.

HANDSOME SPEEDWELL.

Hebe formosa.

PLATE 536

This pretty shrub has been long in cultivation at the Royal Gardens of Kew, raised from seeds sent from Van Diemen's Land, where it inhabits Mount Wellington. Lately it has been planted against a wall having an eastern aspect, and has been found to brave the winters, and to flower copiously in the summer-months. The flowers are a

deep and bright blue, produced at the end of almost every branchlet.

Cult. A neat-growing plant, which, with a few other species, belongs to a section of *Veronica* characterized as evergreen shrubs, having small, closely-set, decussate leaves, and forming Myrtle-like bushes. The old and well known *Veronica decussata* may be viewed as the type of the group. They are natives of high southern latitudes, being found in Van Diemen's Land, New Zealand, Falkland Islands, and Lord Auckland's and Campbell's Islands, in lat. 53°. As might be expected, from the nature of the climate of these southern lands, the two species known to us in a living state prove sufficiently hardy to bear the winter of this climate, when planted in sheltered situations, and protected during severe frosts. The species figured is a native of Mount Wellington, in Van Diemen's Land, and has been known to us for a number of years. Its neat habit makes it worthy of being kept in the greenhouse, where it produces its pretty racemes of light blue flowers in the spring. It grows readily in light loam and leaf-mould, and is easily propagated by cuttings, treated in the usual way; it also freely produces seeds.

536 *Veronica formosa* (t. 4512 1850 WF)

OPPOSITE:
537 *Pentstemon digitalis* (t. 2587 1825 JC)

J. Curtis Del.   Pub. by J. Curtis Walworth Aug. 1825.   Waddell Sc.

Pub by S.Curtis Glazenwood Essex March 1 1838

1

Swan Sc

WULFENIA CARINTHIACA.
CARINTHIAN WULFENIA.
Wulfenia carinthiaca.

The learned President of the Linnean Society, in the sixth volume of the *Society's Transactions*, has united *Pæderota* to this genus, with the exception of the Cape species, and the characters of the two seem to us to be but little different; but neither Willdenow, Schrader, nor Roemer and Schultes have adopted this change. *Wulfenia*, therefore, continues still to exist of a solitary species. It belongs to the natural order of *Scrophularinæ* the *Personatæ* of Linnæus.

Native of the loftiest Carinthian Alps, growing in a very rich soil. Appears to be rare even when indigenous, and does not occur in the last edition of the *Hortus Kewensis*.

A hardy perennial, not annual, though it has been frequently noted as such.

540   *Hebecladus biflorus* (t. 4192 1845 WF)

539   *Wulfenia carinthiaca* (t. 2500 1824 JC)

OPPOSITE:
538   *Penstetmon murrayanus* (t. 3472 1836)

SOLANACEÆ

HEBECLADUS BIFLORUS.
TWIN-FLOWERED HEBECLADUS.
Hebecladus biflorus.

PLATE 540

A very pretty Solanaceous plant, with graceful drooping two-coloured blossoms; a native of the Andes of Peru, about Tarma, Canta, Culluay, &c., according to Ruiz and Pavon, and collected in the same countries by Mr. Mathews, but only recently introduced in a living state by Mr. Veitch of Exeter, through Mr. William Lobb. It flowered in Mr. Veitch's Nursery in August 1845, and from a fine specimen kindly communicated by him, the accompanying figure is taken. It only requires a good greenhouse and may easily be increased by cuttings and probably by seed. The generic name is derived by Mr. Miers from ηβη *down*, and κλαδος *a slender stem*, in allusion to the character of some of the species. The genus includes a very natural group of *Solaneæ*, mostly natives of Peru and New Granada, and all from South America.

HYOSCYAMUS SCOPOLIA.
PENDULOUS-FLOWERED HENBANE.
Scopolia carnilica.

PLATE 541

Matthiolus, the first Botanist who noticed this plant, considered it as a species of Deadly Nightshade, and even described the fruit as being a black berry; by which he misled all the older Botanists. Scopoli, a Physician and celebrated Naturalist at Ydria in the Frioul, first gave a true description of the fruit, and having an opportunity of searching in the Salvantine mountain, near Goritia, where Matthiolus discovered it, was able to ascertain that his plant was the same. Although Scopoli pointed out the difference in the fruit, he continued to consider it nevertheless as a species of *Atropa*. Jacquin attempted to raise it to the dignity of a new genus, and named it, in honour of the above Botanist, Scopola; but Linnæus added it to the genus *Hyoscyamus*, with which, according to Gærtner, its fruit perfectly corresponds.

Notwithstanding these authorities, we are inclined to think, that the first ideas of the near affinity of this plant with the *Belladonna* were perfectly just. The habit and form of the corolla are the same in both; nor is there that difference in the

541   *Hyoscyamus scopolia* (t. 1126 1808 SE)

542 *Solanum campanulatum* (t. 3672 1838 WF)

543 *Solanum marginatum* (t. 1928 1817)

fruit which at first sight may appear so striking: if examined in an unripe state it is similar in both species, being bilocular with a large fleshy central receptacle. The difference consists in this, that as the fruit approaches maturity, the fleshy parts in *Belladonna* become more succulent and ripen into a dark-coloured juicy berry; whilst in our plant these parts evaporate, and the fruit becomes a dry capsule instead of a berry. Similar differences in the fruit of very nearly allied species, in other genera, are not wanting. The calyx can hardly be properly said to be inflated, being applied close to the tube of the corolla, and only becoming larger than the capsule from the shrinking of the latter in ripening.

The duration of this plant above ground is but short, for springing up in April, it goes speedily into flower, ripens its seeds in June or early in July; after which the stems

soon dry up, and the roots remain dormant in the earth till the following spring. It is a hardy perennial, and having creeping roots, will readily establish itself in any situation not too much exposed to the sun.

SOLANUM CAMPANULATUM.
BELL-FLOWER SOLANUM.

Solanum campanulatum.

PLATE 542

A very beautiful species of *Solanum*, for the first knowledge of which we are indebted to Mr. Brown, who found it about Port Jackson. The specimen here figured was communicated from the greenhouse of the Edinburgh Botanic Garden, in July, 1837.

Descr. *Stem* herbaceous, branched, and,

as well as almost the entire plant, hirsutely pubescent, and equally clothed in the same parts with numerous long, straight, slender, subulate *spines*, green at the base, the rest purple. *Leaves* petiolate, broadly-ovate, sometimes triangulari-ovate, deeply and irregularly lobed and angled, aculeated on both sides, the aculei confined to the midrib (which is often purple) and the veins. *Racemes* lateral and terminal, few-flowered. *Pedicels* almost as long as the flower. *Calyx* campanulate, five-cleft, persistent; the segments acute, at first spreading, afterwards connivent over the fruit, very prickly. *Corolla* large, handsome, purplish-blue, broadly campanulate, very indistinctly-lobed, lobes with an acute point, almost aristate. *Stamens* five. *Filaments* short. *Anthers* oblong-lanceolate, connivent, yellow.

OPPOSITE:
544 *Rhodochiton volubile* (t. 3367 1834)

Pub. by S. Curtis Glazenwood Essex Dec.r 1. 1834.

Swan Sc.

SOLANUM MARGINATUM.
WHITE-MARGINED NIGHTSHADE.
Solanum marginatum.

PLATE 543

The name of *marginatum* was given to this species, from a broadish white irregular stripe along the margin on the upper surface, which, however, is not always evident, either in the younger leaves, which are at first covered all over with a woolly powdery pubescence, or when they are grown old, but is most remarkable in the intermediate stage; for the white tomentum disappearing gradually from the upper surface, remains longer near the edge than on the rest of the leaf, and thus produces the white margin.

This shrub grows three or four feet high, and bears racemes of large flowers, not unlike those of the potato. The calyx is never reflexed, and has on the fruit the same kind of yellowish straight prickles as grow on the stem and on both sides of the leaves. The flower is white with a pale purple star, the rays of which proceed from the centre along the course of the laciniæ of the pubescent corolla.

Native of Palestine. Requires the protection of a good greenhouse. Introduced in 1775. Propagated by seeds, which are ripened with us in favourable seasons.

545 *Solanum pyracanthum* β (t. 2547 1825 JC)

A small shrub. Native of Madagascar, where it was discovered by M. Joseph Martin, and communicated by him to the Chevalier Lamarck. Introduced to the Kew Gardens from Paris, by M. Thouin, in 1789. Cultivated with us in the stove, where it sometimes produces ripe seeds. Flowers from August to October.

SOLANUM PYRACANTHUM. β.
ORANGE-THORNED NIGHTSHADE.
Solanum pyracanthum.

PLATE 545

Dunal, in his monograph of the genus *Solanum*, remarks, that the peduncles and calyxes of *Solanum pyracanthum* are sometimes very thorny, and at other times quite without thorns. In our plant, these parts were unarmed, the common peduncles cernuous, the flowers smaller, with reflexed petals, without any green star, and altogether not much resembling the figure in the *Exotic Botany* of Sir James E. Smith, but more like that of Jacquin, in his *Hortus Schœnbrunensis*. We have, however, very little doubt that it is one of the various appearances of the Orange-thorned Nightshade.

VESTIA LYCIOIDES.
BOX-THORN-LIKE VESTIA.
Vestia lycioides.

PLATE 546

The genus *Cantua*, to which our plant has been referred by Jussieu and other Botanists, belongs to the natural order of *Polemonicaceæ*; but Mr. Robert Brown, in the *Botanical Register* has referred Vestia to the *Solaneæ*; the justness of which arrangement has been since confirmed by Mr. David Don, from an examination of the fruit. This able young Botanist has likewise pointed out its near affinity to *Cestrum*, a genus also belonging to the family of *Solaneæ*.

There is only one species of *Vestia* at present known, for a full description of which we refer to Mr Don's observations on the natural family of plants called *Polemoniaceæ*, published in the Edinburgh Philosophical Journal, for October 1822.

It is entirely on the authority of Pavon's specimen now in the Lambertian Herbarium, that the synonym from the *Flora Peruviana* is added, for the figure cited from that work is so incorrect, especially from the addition of the capsule of a true *Cantua*, that we should not have thought it intended for our plant. It was most probably owing to this error as Mr. Don remarks, that Jussieu was led to unite it with his *Cantua*.

This handsome, but ill-scented, shrub is a native of Chili in South America. Is generally treated as a greenhouse plant; but, if the winter prove mild, will do very well without protection. Mr. Jos. Knight in the King's Road, Chelsea, had a very fine plant, which stood in the open air through the winter of 1721–2, flowered and produced fruit the following summer, but the severe frost of 1722–3 destroyed it. It is readily propagated by cuttings. Flowers in April, May, and June.

546 *Vestia lycioides* (t. 2412 1823 JC)

547   Hermannia alnifolia (t. 299 1795)

STERCULIACEÆ

HERMANNIA ALNIFOLIA.
ALDER-LEAVED HERMANNIA.

Hermannia alnifolia.

PLATE 547

Hermannia is a genus of plants named in honour of Dr. Paul Herman, a Dutch Botanist of great celebrity, author of the *Paradisus Batavus*, and other valuable works: twenty-six species are enumerated in the thirteenth edition of the *Syst. Nature* of Linnæus by Professor Gmelin, and eight in the *Hortus Kewensis* of Mr. Aiton; most of those in the latter work are cultivated in the nurseries near town: they form a set of the more hardy greenhouse plants, grow readily, and flower freely; their blossoms are for the most part yellow, and have a considerable affinity with those of the *Mahernia*.

The present species flowers very early in the spring, from February to May, producing a great profusion of bloom during that period; is a native of the Cape, and was cultivated by Mr. Miller, in 1728. It rarely ripens its seeds with us, but is readily increased by cuttings.

The Nurserymen near town regard this plant as the *grossularifolia* of Linnæus, calling another, equally common species, with longer and narrower leaves, *alnifolia*, and which does not appear to be described by Linnæus or mentioned by Mr. Aiton; our plant accords with the Linnæan description of *alnifolia*, and there is we think no doubt of its being the *alnifolia* of the *Hortus Kewensis*, and *Miller's Dictionary*.

548   Hermannia flammea (t. 1349 1811)

HERMANNIA FLAMMEA.
NIGHT-SMELLING HERMANNIA.

Hermannia flammea.

PLATE 548

Descr. A low shrub: *branches* weak, rough, reddish brown. *Leaves* wedge-shaped, truncated and usually three-toothed; sometimes, the outer teeth being truncated, the leaf becomes obsoletely five-toothed, naked. *Stipules* two, linear-lanceolate, nearly half the length of the leaf. *Flowers* grow in terminal racemes looking one way.

Peduncles nodding, two together, one of which is two-flowered, the other single-flowered. *Bracts* three, at the base of the peduncles, like the stipules, and from two to four smaller ones near the flower. *Calyx* campanulate, very patent, scariose. *Corolla* of five petals very much twisted, externally of a deep orange or flame-colour, internally a very pale yellow: *petals* remain long firmly twisted together, and are seldom completely expanded. *Stamens* five; *filaments* united. *Anthers* oblong, incumbent. *Germen* five-angled. *Styles* five, united, longer than the stamens.

The flowers are very odoriferous after sunset, but appeared to us to be scentless during the day. Jacquin says they smell like new hay, but does not mention whether by night or in the daytime.

This shrub flowers in the greenhouse, during most of the summer; was introduced from the Cape by George Hibbert, Esq. Native of the Cape of Good Hope and easily propagated by cuttings.

549   *Mahernia pinnata* (t. 277 1794)

MAHERNIA PINNATA.
WINGED MAHERNIA.
Hermannia pinnata.
PLATE 549

Linnæus, in his *Spec. Pl.* regarded this plant as a species of *Hermannia*; finding afterwards that it differed materially in its fructification from that genus, he made a new one of it in his *Mantissa*, by the name of *Mahernia*; still, however, the two genera are very nearly related: one principal difference consists in the nectaria of the *Mahernia*, which are very remarkable.

This species was introduced from the Cape, where it is a native, by Mr. Masson, in 1774, and is now very generally met with in our greenhouses. It produces its little bells, of a lively red when they first open, from June to August, or September; is a small delicate plant, and easily raised from cuttings.

STYRACEÆ

HALESIA TETRAPTERA.
FOUR-WINGED SNOW-DROP-TREE.
Halesia carolina.
PLATE 550

550 *Halesia tetraptera* (t. 910 1806 SE)

This fine shrub was named in honour of the learned and venerable Stephen Hales, D.D. F.R.S. by John Ellis Esq. who first raised it in this country from seeds sent over by Dr. Alexander Garden, in 1756. It is a native of South Carolina, where it grows by the sides of rivulets shaded by wood. Is perfectly hardy. Flowers in April and May; but not with us, as in America, entirely before the appearance of the leaves.

Propagated by seeds, and as these, in favourable seasons, are not unfrequently perfected here, we are surprised that a shrub of so much beauty should not be more generally met with in our pleasure-grounds. According to Dr. Garden, the fruit is also very pleasant to the taste.

551 *Styrax laevigatum* (t. 921 1806 SE)

STYRAX LÆVIGATUM.
SMOOTH STORAX.
Styrax americana.
PLATE 551

Neither the form of the leaves nor the number of stamens will, in this genus, afford permanent distinguishing characters; but the flowers of this species growing either solitary or in pairs from the axils of

the leaves and at the extremity of the branches, seems to be constant. It is a native of the bogs of Carolina and Georgia in North America, and sufficiently hardy to bear the cold of our ordinary winters. Propagated by layers, and by seeds procured from America. Introduced in 1765.

The stamens are connected in a ring at the base; in which account, some Botanists have referred this genus to the class Monadelphia.

TACCACEÆ

TACCA INTEGRIFOLIA.
ENTIRE-LEAVED TACCA.
Tacca integrifolia.
PLATE 552

As we had no opportunity of seeing the plant from which our drawing was made, we shall not attempt to add any further description to that contained in the generic and specific characters. In the former of these, at the suggestion of Mr. Brown, we have omitted that part which related to the anthers, as inapplicable to the present species. In the Banksian library we have seen a drawing of it done in India, in which the stem is upright, so that we should infer that its recumbent position in our specimen was accidental; perhaps the effect of artificial culture? An unrecorded species; lately sent from the East Indies by Dr. Roxburgh to Sir Abraham Hume, in whose hothouse at Wormleybury it blossomed in June last, probably for the first time in Europe. Mr. Brown observes, that the genus is intermediate between the *Aroideæ* and *Aristolochiæ*.

TECOPHILÆCEÆ

CYANELLA LUTEA.
YELLOW CYANELLA.
Cyanella lutea.
PLATE 553

Cyanella lutea seems to differ from *Cyanella capensis* in having a *stem* with only one or two upright branches, instead of one with

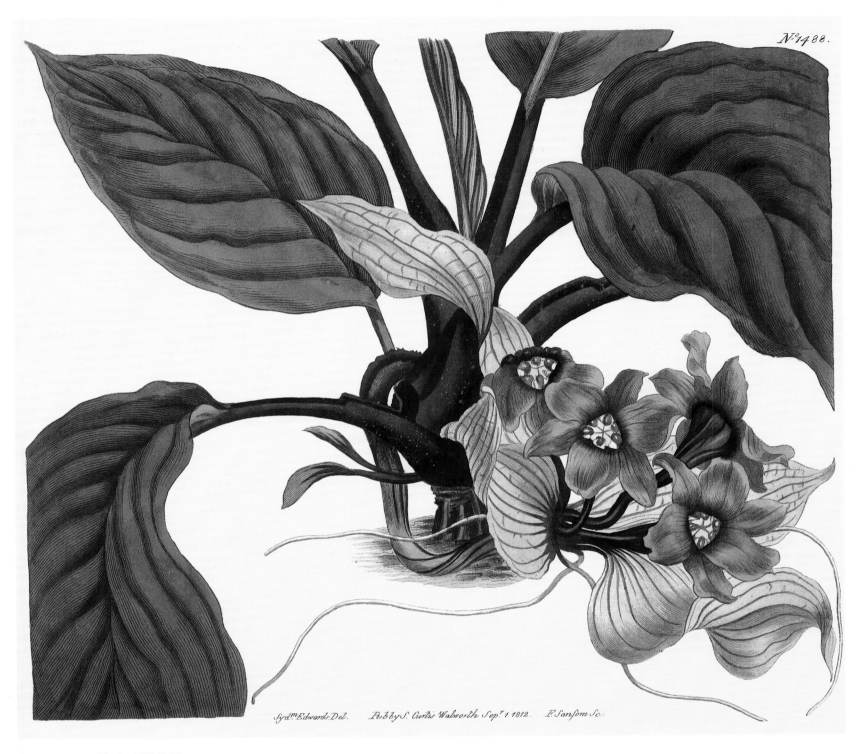

N° 1488.

Syd.^m Edwards Del.   *Pub. by S. Curtis Walworth Sepr 1 1812.*   *F. Sansom Sc.*

552   *Tacca integrifolia* (t. 1488 1812)

many branches and those horizontally patent or divaricate, in the *leaves* not being undulate, and in having a larger different coloured *corolla*; but we had no opportunity of comparing the living species together. Native of the Cape of Good Hope; from whence it was introduced into Kew Gardens by Mr. Masson, in 1788.

TEREBINTHACEÆ

MANGIFERA INDICA.

MANGO TREE.

Mangifera indica.

PLATE 554

Long and well as this has been known as the most valuable of tropical fruits, I can quote no good and faithful representation, save in the costly work of Jacquin. It is the more gratifying, therefore, that our plants in the stoves of the Royal Gardens are

bearing annually flowers most abundantly, and fruits, though comparatively sparingly. Fortunately, our plants are of the choicest kind of the East Indies, the *Muldah*, sent by Dr. Wallich to Kew, and the fruit has a remarkably fine flavour. Dr. Roxburgh, who had occasion to observe that "of this tree, though one of the most common in India, he had not met with any description which deserved the name," has given the best and fullest account of it, in the *Flora Indica* above quoted. Although cultivated generally throughout the warm parts of Asia, it does not appear to be certainly

553 *Cyanella lutea* (t. 1252 1810 SE)

known in a truly wild state. Dr. Wallich met with a tree (not in flower) which he considered to be this, "seemingly wild, near Hetouma, on the banks of the Karra or Karrara rivulet."

The ripe fruits, says Roxburgh, "are universally eaten, and esteemed the best fruit in India: jellies, preserves, tarts, pickles, &c., are made of them before they are ripe. The kernels are large, and seem to contain much nourishment, but they are made no use of except during times of scarcity and famine; when they are boiled in the steam of water, and used as an article of diet. The wood is of a dull grey colour, porous, yet pretty durable if kept dry, but it soon decays if exposed to wet. In very large old trees it acquires a light chocolate-colour towards the centre of the trunk and larger branches, and becomes hard, close-grained, and much more durable. From wounds made in the bark there issues a soft, reddish-brown gum-resin, which age hardens, and renders exceedingly like *Bdellium*. Laid on the point of a knife and held in the flame of a candle, it readily melts, catches flame, and burns with a crackling noise, emitting a smell resembling that of

Cashewnuts when roasting. Its taste is slightly bitter, with some degree of pungency. It dissolves almost entirely in spirits, and in a great measure in water: both solutions are milky, with a small tinge of brown."

THEACEÆ

CAMELLIA AXILLARIS.
AXILLARY-FLOWERING CAMELLIA.
Gordonia axillaris.
PLATE 558

Descr. *Flowers* solitary, axillary, in our specimen nearly terminal. *Calyx* of five leaves, obcordate, sphacelated at the tip, imbricate. *Corolla* five-petaled: *petals* obcordate, yellowish white, partly crumpled. *Stamens* very many, yellow: *filaments* unequal, connected at the base, falling off with, and holding the petals together: *anthers* ovate, versatile. *Germen* subglobular, four-celled: *style* erect, shorter than the longer stamens; *stigmas* four, divaricate. Properly indeed there are four styles closely approximate but separable without tearing! The *lower leaves* are serrate, the *upper* quite entire. Whether the germen is constantly four-celled, we have not yet had an opportunity of ascertaining.

An evergreen shrub. Appears to be rather more impatient of cold than the other camellias, but Mr. Milne thinks it will succeed very well in a good conservatory.

Has been several years in the Fulham Nursery, and is supposed to have been brought from China by Mr. Robarts, and presented by him to Messrs. Whitley, Brames, and Milne, with other camellias. It flowered for the first time December last.

THYMELÆACEÆ

DAPHNE ODORA.
SWEET-SCENTED DAPHNE.
Daphne odora.
PLATE 559

Daphne odora generally passed in our Nurseries for some years as the *indica*,

described by Osbeck as having opposite leaves and a stem only a span in height; which species has probably never been seen in this country. That, however, described as the *indica*, by Loureiro, seems to be very similar to *odora*, and may, perhaps, only be a variety of it with opposite leaves.

This plant is hardy enough to survive our winters in the open air; but flowering in the coldest season, from December to March, it requires protection on that account. Indeed, unless the season prove favourable, it frequently fails of flowering altogether, otherwise, it would be a most desirable acquisition; producing its highly fragrant flowers at a season when it has few rivals.

The figure by L'Heritier, quoted in the former edition of *Hortus Kewensis*, we believe was never published.

Introduced in 1771, by Benjamin Torin, Esq. Communicated by Messrs. Loddiges and Sons, by whom we are informed that it is propagated by cuttings; that the soil which suits it best is a mixture of loam and bog earth; and that its flowering is promoted by placing it on the flue of the stove.

DAPHNE PONTICA.
TWIN-FLOWERED DAPHNE.
Daphne pontica.
PLATE 555

Although the flowers of *Daphne pontica* are not showy, nor in fragrance nearly equal to that of several other species of this genus; yet the beauty of its foliage renders it well worthy of cultivation. It was first discovered by Tournefort near the coast of the Black Sea on hills and in woods. Pallas says it is found also in Siberia in the thick shady beech woods, between the ridges of the lofty mountains. It is sufficiently hardy to bear the ordinary cold of our winters; but being disposed to put forth young shoots, from which the flowers grow, early in the spring if the weather is mild, these are apt to be destroyed and the plant disfigured by the recurrence of later frosts; an inconvenience which probably might be avoided by planting it in thickets and under the shelter of trees.

Communicated by Messrs. Loddiges and Sons. Flowers in April and May. Propagated by seeds or cuttings.

OPPOSITE:
554 *Mangifera indica* (t. 4510 1850 WF)

4510.

Fitch del et lith.

R. B. & R. imp.

265

555 *Daphne pontica* (t. 1282 1810 SE)

556 *Gnidia simplex* (t. 812 1805 SE)

GNIDIA SIMPLEX.
FLAX-LEAVED GNIDIA.

Gnidia simplex.

PLATE 556

From a careful consideration of the description in the *Mantissa*, we were persuaded that this plant is the real *Gnidia simplex* of Linnæus, however different from the one usually known by that name in our nurseries and figured as such in the *Botanist's Repository*; and a comparison with the specimens in the Banksian Herbarium has confirmed our opinion. In no other known species are the flowers in every part yellow.

In transcribing the description from the *Mantissa*, where it is said the items are roughened with tubercles from the vestiges of the leaves, Reichard has by some accident added the figure four after *tuberculis*, and notwithstanding the sentence is thus made unintelligible, the leaves having before been said to be scattered, this blunder has been copied both by Willdenow and Martyn.

This pretty little shrub, a native of the Cape of Good Hope, has much the habit of *Struthiola erecta*, and requires a similar treatment, being hardy greenhouse plant.

Its flowers, which appear in August, are without scent. We received it from Mr. Loddiges of Hackney under the name of *Gnidia aurea*.

557 *Lachnaea buxifolia* α *virens* (t. 1657 1814 SE)

LACHNÆA BUXIFOLIA (α.) VIRENS.
GREEN BOX-LEAVED LACHNÆA.

Lachnæa buxifolia.

PLATE 557

This plant has been mistakenly called in the nurseries *Gnidia capitata*. Native of the Cape of Good Hope. Flowers in the spring. Requires to be kept in an airy light greenhouse. Propagated by seeds, difficulty by cuttings or layers. Introduced about 1800, by George Hibbert, Esq.

TILIACEÆ

ENTELÉA ARBORESCENS.
NEW ZEALAND ENTELÉA.

Entelea arborescens.

PLATE 560

Discovered in 1769, near Tigada, Tolaga, Opuragi, and Motuaro, in New Zealand, by Sir Joseph Banks and Dr. Solander. It grows in its native country into a small tree, the wood of which is remarkably light, and, for this property, is used by the natives to float their fishing nets with.

Enteléa belongs to the natural order of *Tiliaceæ*, and approximates the genus *Sparrmannia*, from which Mr. Brown distinguishes it by its want of the sterile filaments (*nectaria* of Linnæus), all of them in *Enteléa* bearing anthers; by its capsules being undivided to the base, and not as in *Sparrmannia* longitudinally dehiscent into six distinct valves; by the segments of the calyx being awned, and by the cells of the capsule containing many seeds, instead of only two, as described by Thunberg; but the value of this character is much weakened by Mr. Brown's observation, that the ovarium in *Sparrmannia* has certainly many ovula.

For this very rare plant, which perhaps never flowered in Europe before, we are indebted to Messrs. Whitley, Brame, and Milne, in whose stove, at Fulham, it blossomed in May 1823.

558 *Camellia axillaris* (t. 2047 1819)

559 *Daphne odora* (t. 1587 1813)

TURNERACEÆ

TURNERA ANGUSTIFOLIA.
NARROW-LEAV'D TURNERA.

Turnera ulmifolia var *angustifolia.*

PLATE 561

This plant here represented is generally known to the Nurserymen about London as the *Turnera ulmifolia,* or Elm-leav'd Turnera, its foliage however does not answer to the name, nor to the figures of the plant as given by Martyn in his *Cent. Pl.* and Linnæus in his *Hortus Cliffortianus,* which figures indeed are so similar that they look like copies of each other, these represent the true elm leaf; on the same plate of *Martyn's Cent.* there is given a very excellent figure of what he considers as another species of *Turnera,* vide Synon. and which Miller, who cultivated it about the year 1773, also describes as a distinct species, under the name of *angustifolia,* asserting,

from the experience of thirty years, that plants raised from its seeds have constantly differed from those of the *ulmifolia*; this is our plant, which on his authority we have given as a species, though Linnæus regards it as a variety.

Plumier gave to this genus the name of *Turnera,* in honour of Dr. William Turner, a celebrated English Botanist and Physician, who published an *Herbal,* black letter, folio, in 1568.

The present species is a native of the West Indies, and is commonly cultivated in our stoves, where it rises with a semishrubby stalk, to the height of several feet, seldom continuing more than two or three years; young plants generally come up in plenty from seeds spontaneously scattered, so that a succession is easily obtained.

It flowers from June to August. Its foliage has a disagreeable smell when bruised; its flowers are showy, but of short duration, and are remarkable for growing out of the footstalk of the leaf.

UMBELLIFERÆ

ERYNGIUM ALPINUM.
ALPINE ERYNGO.

Eryngium alpinum.

PLATE 562

John Bauhin, in his history, informs us, that he sent this plant to Gesner, whose figure of it published by Camerarius, though never quoted, is the only one before those of Jacquin and F. Miller, except Dalechamp's, which is at all characteristic of the species. Lobel's figure, so often copied, was originally but a very indifferent one, and, as mutilated by our Morrison, in his too usual manner, is no longer applicable to this plant or any other.

This hardy perennial, a native of the Alps in most of the southern parts of Europe, is worthy of a place in every curious garden, where its uncommon form and beautiful colour cannot fail to attract

J. Curtis Del.   Pub. by J. Curtis Walworth April 1. 1824.   Weddell Sc.

561   Turnera angustifolia (t. 281 1794)

562   Eryngium alpinum (t. 922 1806 SE)

OPPOSITE:
560   Enteléa arborescens (t. 2480 1824 JC)

the notice of every beholder. It does not owe its charms to the splendour of its blossoms, but to the floral leaves, or involucre surrounding the head of flowers, admired for their feather-like appearance and delicate blue colour; all the upper-parts of the plant partake of the same tint, which becomes in descending more and more dilute.

Propagated by seeds, or by cuttings of its root. Requires a dry soil, or is apt to perish from the humidity of our winters. Cultivated by Philip Miller in 1752.

FERULA PERSICA.
PERSIAN FENNEL-GIANT.
Ferula persica.
PLATE 564

Seeds of the *Ferula persica* were sent to Pallas from the mountains of Ghilan in Persia, supposed to be those of the plant producing the *Assa fœtida*. From these several plants were raised by the Professor at Petersburgh, and two of these were sent by Dr. Guthrie to the late Dr. Hope, Professor of botany in Edinburgh, one of which lived and produced seeds, and from this source probably sprung the plant in the Apothecaries garden at Chelsea, from which our drawing was made.

That this is the real plant producing the *Assa fœtida*, seems confirmed by the strong smell of that drug which pervades the whole herb, and indeed we have picked off small globules of true *Assa fœtida* that had exuded from the stem. At the same time it is evident that it is not the same species as described by the accurate Kæmpfer. This author, whilst he allows that the inhabitants of Chorasan and Laristan, the two provinces famous for this production, believe that their plants are of a different kind, convinced himself, by an examination of both, that there was no real difference between them: so that it must remain doubtful whether we have yet seen the true species producing the *Assa fœtida*; but from our present greater intercourse with Persia, it is probable that we shall not be long without more satisfactory information.

It appears from Kæmpfer's account that the plants which produce the drug in abundance, are confined to very limited districts, and that beyond these, their smell becomes much less powerful, and is at length so mild, that goats are very fond of

it, and fatten wonderfully upon it. An observation which does not tend to encourage the expectations entertained by the late Professor Hope, that this drug might hereafter be produced in our own country.

It is a hardy perennial. Flowers from May to July. Communicated by Mr. William Anderson, from the Botanic Garden at Chelsea.

VALERIANACEÆ
VALERIANA MONTANA (β.)
ROTUNDIFOLIA.
ROUND-LEAVED MOUNTAIN VALERIAN.
Valeriana rotundifolia.
PLATE 563

Valeriana tripleris, montana, and *rotundifolia* of Villars are very nearly allied. The cauline leaves of the first being, according to the just-named author, sometimes quite entire, it is not easily distinguished from *montana,* except by the more glaucous colour of the leaves.

Our present plant, which we take to be

563   *Valeriana montana β rotundifolia* (t. 1825 1816)

Weddell.

270

Pub. by S. Curtis Walworth July 1. 1816.

the *rotundifolia* of Villars, is the smallest of the three, scarcely exceeding the height of eight or ten inches. It seems to vary with leaves, sometimes quite entire and sometimes slightly toothed.

Haller, in his *Opuscula*, has sought out the synonymy with great labour, and reduces what had been considered by Caspar Bauhin and the Botanists of his time, as several species, to one and the same; Villars, from his own observations, thinks it right to seperate our plant from the *scrophulariæfolia* of Bauhin's *Prodromus*, in which he does not seem to have been followed by any more modern author. On this account we have considered the two as varieties only; which Villars himself acknowledges they may be, though he at the same time asserts that he had frequently found it difficult to distinguish the varieties of *tripleris* and *montana* from one another, but that he was never in danger of confounding the *rotundifolia* with any of the varieties of the other two.

A hardy perennial. Native of the mountainous regions of the south of Europe. Flowers in May and June.

VERBENACEÆ

CLERODENDRUM FRAGRANS.
FRAGRANT CLERODENDRUM.

Clerodendrum fragrans.

PLATE 565

Clerodendrum fragrans, is chiefly valuable for the sake of its very fragrant blossoms. It is a native of Japan and China, and, though generally treated as a stove plant, is not very tender. It has creeping roots, and we remember once to have seen an instance where it had been planted in the border of the conservatory, that the roots found their way through or under the brickwork, and the shoots came up in the open ground, in which situation the plants flourished and flowered very well during the summer; but perished in following winter.

PREVIOUS PAGE:
564 *Ferula persica* (t. 2096 1819 SE)
565 *Clerodendrum fragrans* (t. 1834 1816)

Willdenow, in his Enumeration of the Plants in the Berlin Garden, has quoted t. 57, of Kæmpfer's drawings published by Sir Joseph Banks, as a representation of our plant, but, as we think, without foundation. Communicated by John Walker, Esq. of Arno's Grove.

CLERODENDRUM MACROPHYLLUM.
BROAD LEAVED CLERODENDRUM.

Clerodendrum serratum.

PLATE 566

It appears, from the observations of Mr. Robert Brown, to be very doubtful if there are any real distinctive characters between *Volkameria* and *Clerodendrum*, and most, if not all, of the species which were once referred to the former genus, have been more lately united to the latter. Some species however, of which our present subject is one, differ remarkably from others, in the greater irregularity of the corolla: these may perhaps hereafter be formed into a separate genus.

Our plant has a near affinity with *Volkameria serrata* of Linnæus, but differs in having opposite leaves, tomentose underneath. One of the specimens united with that species in the Banksian Herbarium appears to agree nearly with our plant, but another with much narrower leaves in the same collection agrees better in the form of its leaves with the Linnean character, and we think that both can hardly be united under the same species. In the Lambertian Herbarium is a specimen of *Volkameria serrata*, on the authority of Dr. Francis Hamilton, which has its leaves growing by threes, and branches less decidedly quadrangular than in our plant: this is evidently the same as the *Tsjerom-Theka* of the *Hortus Malabaricus* vol. 4. t. 29. But in our present subject, besides the difference in the leaves, and more decidedly quadrangular branches, the fifth lacinia of the corolla is more different from the other four, forming a labellum distinct in colour and form.

Clerodendrum belongs to the natural order of *Verbenaceæ* of Jussieu and Brown, formerly called *Vitices* in the *Genera Plantarum* of the former author.

Our drawing was taken from a specimen communicated last August, by Robert Barclay, Esq. of Bury Hill, who raised it from seeds received from the Mauritius. Requires to be kept in the stove.

ZINGIBERACEÆ

ALPINIA CERNUA.
DROOPING ALPINIA.

Alpinia calcarata.

PLATE 567

We have, on the authority of Mr. Salisbury, that this plant was introduced by the late G. Slater, Esq. before the year 1790. Propagated by suckers. Flowers in June. Native of the East Indies. Communicated by John Walker, Esq. of Arno's Grove.

CURCUMA ZEDOARIA.
AROMATIC TURMERIC.

Curcuma aromatica.

PLATE 568

The rootstocks of this plant are aromatic and yellow within, but do not appear to be the same as the Zedoary of the shops, which is most probably the product of *Curcuma zerumbet*.

We are not certain that our plant is the same species as that described by Mr. Salisbury in the *Paradisus Londinensis*; as the leaves, independently of the white variegation, which is probably accidental, are not without some purplish tinge, and the fertile bractes were green, not white as in his figure and description.

It flowered in ther stove of the late Right Hon. Charles Greville, in May, before the appearance of the leaves.

The cultivation of these plants in this climate is attended with particular difficulty; and unless they are strong and healthy they seldom or never produce flowers; hence these can hardly be expected, except from newly imported roots. They require to be kept constantly in a high temperature, should have plenty of water while flowering, and very little after the leaves die. The great difficulty seems to be to keep up a sufficient heat and a due supply of fresh air at the same time.

L.Curtis.Del.   Pub.by J.Curtis Walworth, Dec.1.1814.   Weddell Sc.

Pub. by S. Curtis. Walworth. April.1.1817.

N.º 1546.

Syd.ᵗʰ Edwards Del.   Pub. by S. Curtis. Walworth. Ap. 1. 1813.   F. Sansom Sc.

568   *Curcuma zedoaria* (t. 1546 1813 SE)

OPPOSITE:
567   *Alpinia cernua* (t. 1900 1817 SE)

KÆMPFERIA ROTUNDA.
ROUND-ROOTED GALANGALE.

Kæmpferia rotunda.

PLATE 569

We have no doubt but that this plant is the *Kæmpferia rotunda* of Linnæus, and as little that it is the same as is figured by Jacquin in his magnificent work the *Hortus Schoen-brunnensis*, and since by Redouté in his

Liliacées under the name of *Kæmpferia longa*. Upon what grounds Jacquin considered it as a different species we can form no conjecture.

The flowers appear early in the spring, some time before the leaves, and have a very pleasing scent, especially as they dry. They grow immediately from the root, several in succession, but seldom more than one or two are open at the same time. The organs of fructification are very similar

275

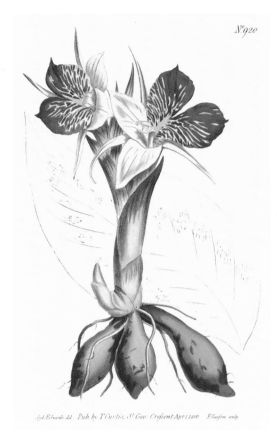

569 *Kaempferia rotunda* (t. 920 1806 SE)

570 *Fagonia cretica* (t. 241 1793 SE)

his *Curcuma zedoaria* yields the Zedoary; and we have observed, that the usual sophistication of this drug is by mixing Turmeric (*Curcuma longa*) with it.

Being a native of the East Indies, it requires the warmth of a stove. Propagated by cuttings.

From the Banksian Herbarium we learn that it flowered at Spring Grove in 1793, a year or two before which time, as we are informed by Mr. Dryander, it was introduced to this country by Sir George Yonge, Bart.

ZYGOPHYLLACEÆ

FAGONIA CRETICA.

CRETIAN FAGONIA.

Fagonia cretica.

PLATE 570

Clusius is the first author who has described and figured this plant, he is very minute in his description of it, noticing the exact number of its stamina; it is the more surprising, therefore, that he should have so little idea of generic character, as to rank it with the trefoils merely from the form of its leaves: Tournefort, born to illustrate the genera of plants, named it *Fagonia*, in honour of his friend and patron, Mons. Fagon, privy counsellor and consulting physician to Lewis XIV.

This species is a native of the isle of Candia, and was cultivated here by Mr. Miller, in 1739; it is an annual, and as it

to those of *Amomum exscapum*, as figured in the *Annals of Botany*, vol. 1. pl. 13.

The college of physicians, both of London and Edinburgh, upon the authority of Linnæus, have referred the Zedoary of the shops to this plant; but the form of the roots as they occur at our druggists corresponds much better with those of *Amomum zerumbet*. But the roots of the larger Galangale, which Loureiro supposes to be sold indiscriminately for Zedoary or Galangale, are, at least as they occur in our shops, totally different. Dr. Roxburgh thinks that

does not perfect its seeds with us in the open air, unless in very favourable seasons, it is usually treated as a greenhouse plant, its seeds should be sown in the autumn, as it thereby flowers earlier, and ripe seeds are with more certainty obtained.

It blossoms from June to August. Its branches are usually procumbent, about a foot in length, and require, if the plant be kept in a pot, to be tied up to a stick.

APPENDIX
Of Botanists and Gardeners

ADAMS, J.F. (1780–1833) botanist and collector in the Caucasus.

ADANSON, MICHEL (1726–1806) collected mainly in Senegal, and is commemorated in the Baobab, *Adansonia digitata*.

AITON, WILLIAM (1731–1793) born in Hamilton, Scotland; assistant to Philip Miller at the Chelsea Physic Garden, and later the first curator of the Royal Botanic Garden at Kew; author of *Hortus Kewensis* 1789, assisted by Dryander, Solander and Robert Brown (qqvv).

AITON, WILLIAM TOWNSEND (1766–1849), son of William, edited ed. 2 of *Hortus Kewensis* 1810–1813.

ALLCARD, JOHN FLS (c.1777–1855) had a collection of ferns, orchids and other exotics at Stratford Green.

ALSTROEMER, BARON CLAS, (1736–1794) a friend of Linnæus.

ANDERSON, DR ALEXANDER, MD FLS Curator of St Vincent Botanic Garden from 1783; collected plants in Guiana in 1791; died in St Vincent in 1811.

ANDERSON, THOMAS (1832–1870) born in Edinburgh; superintendent of Calcutta Botanic Garden 1861–1868.

ANDERSON, WILLIAM (1766–1846) born in Edinburgh; gardener to James Vere 1793–1814; Curator of the Chelsea Physic Garden 1815.

ATCHLEY, SHIRLEY CLIFFORD (c.1871–1936) 1st secretary of the British Legation in Athens, 1930–36, and author of *Wild Flowers of Attica* (1938).

BAKER, GEORGE PERCIVAL (1856–1951) of Sevenoaks; traveller, specialist in oriental fabrics, grower of rare plants especially irises and alpines.

BAKER, J.G. (1834–1920) born in Guisborough, Yorkshire; botanist at Kew, specializing in bulbous plants, and bromeliads.

BALE, THE REVD. SACKVILLE, of Withyam, Kent, (fl.1800).

BALLS, E.K. (1892–1984), collector in Turkey, Greece and South America; spent much of his later life in California.

BANKS, SIR JOSEPH (1743–1820) born in London; travelled with Captain Cook on his circumnavigation of the world in H.M.S. Endeavour (1768–71); established Kew as a Botanical Garden; President of the Royal Society 1778–1820.

BARCLAY, ROBERT (1751–1830) born in Philadelphia; had large gardens, first at Clapham, later at Bury Hill; one of the original supporters of and subscribers to the *Botanical Magazine*.

BARTON, WILLIAM P.C. (1756–1856) born in Philadelphia; author and illustrator of *A Flora of North America* (1821–1823), and a medical botany of North America.

BATEMAN, JAMES (1811–1897) of Biddulph Grange, Congleton; born in Bury, Lancashire; grower of exotic plants and especially of orchids; author of *A Monograph of Odontoglossum*, and *The Orchidaceae of Mexico and Guatemala*, an Elephant folio, one of the largest botanical books ever published. The garden at Biddulph Grange is at present being restored.

BAUER, FERDINAND LUKAS (1760–1826) born in Feldsberg, lower Austria, flower painter and botanist, who worked mainly in England, travelling with John Sibthorp (qv) to Greece, and with Flinders to Australia.

BAUER, FRANZ (1758–1840) brother of Ferdinand, worked for most of his life at Kew as a botanical illustrator, notably of orchids.

BAUHIN, KASPAR (1541–1626) born in Basle, and Johann (1560–1624), born in Lyon, early French botanists.

BEAUFORT, MARY, DUCHESS OF, née Capel (c.1630–1714) had a botanical garden at Badminton, Gloucestershire.

BELL, JOHN fl.1782; a nurseryman, perhaps at Isleworth, Middlesex.

BELLEVAL, PIERRE RICHTER DE (1558–1623) born at Chalons-sur Marne; early botanist, commemorated in the Scilla-like genus Bellevalia.

BIEBERSTEIN, BARON, F.A. MARSCHALL VON (1768–1826), collector in the Caucasus and author of *Flora Taurico-caucasica* (1808–1819).

BLAIR, DR PATRICK (c.1666–1728) of Dundee; author of *Botanic Essays*, describing sex in plants; imprisoned at Newgate for his part in the Jacobite rising of 1715, but pardoned through the influence of Sir Hans Sloane.

BLANDFORD, GEORGE SPENCER CHURCHILL, MARQUIS OF, later 5th Duke of Marlborough (1766–1840) made a large and extravagant garden at Whiteknights, Reading, now part of Reading University. One of the best customers of Lee & Kennedy, with the Empress Joséphine and Thomas Jefferson.

BRADLEY, JOHN (There were two seedsmen of this name, active in the 1790's, one at Leek, Staffordshire, the other at Dorking, Surrey).

BROOKES, SAMUEL of Balls Pond Nursery, Islington, c.1820, in partnership with Thomas Barr.

BROTERO, F. AVELLAR (1744–1828) of Lisbon, author of *Flora Lusitanica* (1804).

BROWNE, DR PATRICK MD (1720–1790) born at Woodstock, Co Mayo; author of *The Civil and Natural History of Jamaica* (1756), illustrated by G.D. Ehret (qv).

BROWN, NICHOLAS EDWARD (1849–1934) born Redhill, Surrey; Assistant Keeper at Kew 1909–1914, an authority on Cape plants.

BROWN, ROBERT (1773–1858) born in Montrose; visited Australia with Flinders 1801–1805; librarian and botanist to Sir Joseph Banks 1810–1825, after the death of Dryander, and author of books on the floras of Australia and Tasmania; first Keeper of Botany at the British Museum and President of the Royal Society 1849–1853.

BULLOCK, WILLIAM (c.1790–1840) was proprietor of a Museum of Natural History in Liverpool (1799–1811); collected plants in Mexico, 1822–1823 and 1827, and founded a museum in Cincinnati, Ohio.

BURMAN, J. (1706–1779), author of *Rariorum Africanarum Plantarum* (1738–1739).

BURTT, B.L. (b. 1913), botanist, now at the Royal Botanic Garden, Edinburgh, author of numerous books on the South African flora, and on *Gesneriaceæ*.

BUNGE, A.A. VON (1803–1890) of Kiev; botanist, collector and traveller in Asia.

BUTE, JOHN STUART, 3RD EARL OF (1713–1792) born in Edinburgh; botanist, patron of William Curtis, and 'principal manager' of the Royal Gardens at Kew. He had his own botanic garden at Luton Hoo, Bedfordshire, and at Highcliffe, Hampshire; Prime Minister 1762–1763.

CAREY, THE REVD. WILLIAM (1761–1834) born at Paulerspury, Northamptonshire; Baptist missionary in India; Professor of Sanskrit; founded botanic garden at Serampore, where he died.

CATTLEY, WILLIAM FLS (1788–1835), a merchant in Barnet; John Lindley's first patron and collector of plant drawings, commemorated by the orchid genus *Cattleya*.

CATESBY, MARK (1680–1749) born in Sudbury, Suffolk; traveller in North America, plant collector and painter, and author of *The Natural History of Carolina, Florida and the Bahama Islands*, and *Hortus Brittanico-americanus*, a treatise on growing North American trees in England.

CELS, JACQUES MARTIN (1743–1806), born at Versailles; nurseryman, and grower of rare plants. Flowers from his garden were the subject of Ventenat's *Descriptions des Plantes Nouvelles . . .* (1800) and *Choix des Plantes . . .* (1803), illustrated by Redouté among others.

CLARK, DR THOMAS MD (d.1792), island botanist and Curator of Bath Garden, Jamaica 1777–1787.

CLOWES, THE REVD. JOHN, (1777–1846) had an outstanding collection of orchids at Broughton Hall, near Manchester, and employed Jean Linden, among others, to collect for him.

CLUSIUS, CAROLUS (1526–1609) born in Atrecht, Artois; botanist, traveller, gardener and writer, responsible, while in Vienna, for the introduction of many plants from the Near East.

COLLIE, ALEXANDER (1793–1835) born Wantonwells, Aberdeen; surgeon with Captain Beechey 1825–1828, on H.M.S. Blossom 1829 and explored the country round Perth, Australia; also collected plants in California, Mexico and Chile.

COLLINSON, PETER FRS (1694–1768) born in London; a merchant trader with the American colonies; acted as agent for John Bartram's collections and helped finance Catesby's *Natural History of Carolina*; he also had fine gardens himself at Peckham, and then at Mill Hill.

COLLIER, J. gardener to Sir Jeremiah Colman.

COLMAN, SIR JEREMIAH VMH (1859–1942) of Gatton Park, Reigate, a noted grower of orchids, whose fortune was based on mustard.

COLVILL, JAMES, father and son; nurserymen on the Kings Road, specializing in South African plants.

COMPTON, HENRY (1632–1713), born at Compton Wynyates; Bishop of Oxford, then London; had large gardens and greenhouses at Fulham Palace, full of rare and new plants, which he made freely available to botanists.

COMMELIN, JAN (1629–1692), and Caspar (1668–1731); born in Amsterdam; authors of an account of the rare plants grown in the Botanic Gardens in Amsterdam (1697 and 1715).

CRUICKSHANKS, ALEXANDER; visited Chile 1825–1828.

CUNNINGHAM, ALLAN (1791–1839) born Wimbledon, Surrey; collected plants for Kew and visited Brazil with J. Bowie 1814–1816; and Australia 1816–1831; Superintendent of Sydney Botanic Garden 1836–1838.

DAVID, PÈRE ARMAND (1826–1900) born in France. Naturalist and traveller in Mongolia and western China, 1868–1870 and 1872–1874; introduced some new plants and animals from the Peking area.

DEVONSHIRE, 6TH DUKE OF, WILLIAM GEORGE SPENCER CAVENDISH (1790–1858) born in Paris. Employed Joseph Paxton at Chatsworth; President of the Horticultural Society 1838–1858.

DILLENIUS, JOHAN JACOB (1684–1747) born in Darmstadt; botanist who worked in Oxford, and wrote and illustrated *Hortus Elthamensis* (1732).

DOMBEY, JOSEPH (1742–1796) born in France; collector in Peru and Chile.

DON, GEORGE (1764–1814) botanist and author of *A monograph of the genus Allium* (1827).

DONN, JAMES (1758–1813) born in Monivaird, Perthshire; Curator of the University Botanic Garden, Cambridge 1794–1813, author of *Hortus Cantabrigiensis* (1796).

DOUGLAS, DAVID (1798–1834) born Scone, Perthshire; at Glasgow Botanic Garden 1820; collected plants for the Horticultural Society, mainly in western North America 1823–1833; killed in Hawaii after falling into a bull pit.

DRUMMOND, THOMAS (c.1790–1835); first Curator of Belfast Botanic Garden 1828–1831, and from 1831 collected plants for Glasgow in North America, notably in Texas and Louisiana.

DRYANDER, JAMES CARL (1748–1810) born in Gothenberg, Sweden; worked for Sir Joseph Banks after the death of Solander (qv); later librarian of the Royal Society.

DUHAMEL DE MONCEAU, HENRI LOUIS (1700–1782) born in Paris; Inspecteur General of the French Marine; author of books on trees and shrubs.

EHRET, GEORG DIONYSUS (1708–1770) born in Heidelberg; spent most of his life in London, especially associated with the Chelsea Physic Garden and married the daughter of Phillip Miller; one of the greatest botanical painters of the eighteenth century.

ELLIS, JOHN (c.1705–1776) born in Ireland; botanist and author of tracts on the treatment of tree seeds on long voyages and on useful plants, including in 1774, an account of coffee.

ELLIS, THE REVD. WILLIAM (1794–1872) of Hoddesdon; missionary in Polynesia and in Madagascar 1853–1865.

FALCONER, HUGH MD (1808–1865) born in Forres, Morayshire; Superintendent of Calcutta Botanic Garden (1848–1855), and Professor of Botany at Calcutta Medical College.

FAIRBAIRN, JOHN Curator of Chelsea Physic Garden 1784–1814.

FARGES, PÈRE PAUL GUILLAUME (1844–1912) born in France; missionary and collector in western China.

FEUILLÉE, LOUIS (1660–1732) born in Provence; botanist and collector in Peru and Chile; author of *Journal . . . de l'Amerique Meridionale et dans les Indes Occidentales* (1701–1712).

FISCHER, FRIEDRICH E.L. VON, (1782–1854), Director of the Botanic Garden at St Petersberg, collector in Russia.

FORBES, JOHN (1800–1823); collector for the Horticultural Society in Brazil, Madagascar and South Africa; died at Senna, Mozambique.

FOSTER, PROFESSOR SIR MICHAEL FRS FLS (1836–1907) born in Huntingdon; Professor of Physiology at Cambridge 1883–1903) and grower and breeder of irises.

FOTHERGILL, DR JOHN (1712–1780) born in Wensleydale, Yorkshire; a successful London physician, botanist, zoologist and gardener; had a private botanic garden at Upton, Essex.

FRASER, JOHN FLS (1750–1811) Nurseryman at Sloane Square, London in the 1780's; collected in Newfoundland 1783–1784, in North America 1785–1807; Nursery continued by his son John 1790's–1860's.

FUNKE, DR ALEXANDER; had a garden in North America c.1756.

GERARD, JOHN (1545–1612) born Nantwich, Cheshire; author of *The Herball* 1597.

GILMOUR, JOHN (1906–1986) botanist and writer; director of the Royal Horticultural Society's Garden as Wisley, and of the University Botanic Garden, Cambridge.

GMELIN, J.G. (1709–1755) and S.G. (1744–1774) his nephew, born in Tubingen; botanists and travellers in Siberia and the Caucasus.

GOLDIE, J. (1793–1886) collector in Russia and in Canada.

GOOD, PETER (died in Sydney 1803) in Calcutta 1796, and was assistant to Robert Brown on Flinders voyage to Australia 1801.

GORDON, JAMES (1708?–1780) gardener to Lord Petre and Dr Sherard, and later a nurseryman at Mile End, celebrated as a skilful raiser of American trees and shrubs from seed and cuttings.

GRAEFER, JOHN (d. 1802); partner with James Gordon the younger in the nursery at Mile End. Then in 1786 gardener to the Queen of Naples and later steward of Lord Nelson's estate in Sicily and gardener to James Vere at Kensington Gore.

GRAHAM, DR ROBERT, born in Stirling; Professor of Botany at Glasgow 1818 and at Edinburgh 1820–1845.

GRAVES, GEORGE FLS (1784–1839) married Mary Curtis and became part owner of the remainder of *Flora Londinensis*.

GRIFFIN, WILLIAM (d. 1827); nurseryman in South Lambeth and a good grower of bulbs.

GRIMWOOD, DANIEL (d. 1796) and Wykes of Kensington; nurserymen, seedsmen and introducers of many new plants; nursery closed in 1804.

GWILLIM, LADY wife of SIR HENRY, a judge in Madras; sent seeds of Indian plants back to England.

HALES, THE REVD. STEPHEN (1677–1761) born at Bekesbourne, Kent; scientist and author of *Vegetable Staticks*, one of the earliest treatises on Plant Physiology; commemorated in the genus *Halesia*.

HALLER, ALBRECHT VON (1708–1777); Swiss botanist and Professor of Botany at Gottingen; author of several Swiss floras.

HARTWEG, KARL THEODORE (1812–1871) born at Karlsruhr, Germany; collector for the Horticultural Society in Mexico and Guatemala 1836–1846, and in Madeira 1854.

HAWORTH, ADRIAN HARDY (1768–1833) born in Hull, but spent most of his life in Chelsea; grower of succulent plants and author of an early monograph of the *Mesembryanthemaceae*.

HEADFORT, 4TH MARQUIS OF, GEOFFREY THOMAS TAYLOUR (1878–1943); made a garden at Headfort, Co. Meath, where he grew many of the plants collected by George Forrest and others in the Himalaya.

HERBERT, HON. WILLIAM (1778–1847), son of the Earl of Carnarvon, vicar of Spofforth and Dean of Manchester, illustrator, botanist, skilful gardener and specialist on the *Amaryllidaceae*.

HIBBERT, GEORGE FRS (1757–1837) born in Manchester; West Indies merchant; had his own botanic garden at Clapham.

HODSON, NATHANIAL SHIRLEY; established a botanic garden at Bury St Edmunds, Suffolk in 1820.

HOPKINS, GEORGE; collected plants near Rio de Janiero in the 1830's.

HORSFALL, CHARLES of Liverpool; had a collection of plants at Everton; his wife drew five plates for the Botanical Magazine around 1835, and his son, J.B. Horsfall, of Bellamour, Staffordshire, contributed plants to the *Botanical Magazine* in 1865.

HUME, SIR ABRAHAM (1748/9–1838) born in London; with his wife, Lady Amelia nee Egerton, imported the first chrysanthemums from China to their garden at Wormleybury.

JACQUIN, NICOLAUS JOSEPH VON (1727–1817) born in Leiden; Supervisor of the Royal Gardens at Schonbrunn; botanist, follower of Linnaeus, and prolific author, mainly on Austrian and South African plants cultivated in Vienna, where he was from 1768 Professor of Botany and Chemistry and Director of the Botanical Gardens.

JENKINS, THOMAS (1800–1832) nurseryman of Gloucester Place and of Regent's Park.

JONES, SIR WILLIAM (1736–1794) Judge of the Supreme Court, Calcutta 1783–1794; botanist and Sanskrit scholar.

JUSSIEU, ANTOINE LAURENT DE (1748–1836) and his son A.H.L. de Jussieu (1797–1853); French botanists who established a more natural system of plant classification in contrast to the artificial Linnean system.

KENT, WILLIAM, (d. 1840) had a garden in Upper Clapton and later in Bath, Somerset.

KER-GAWLER, JOHN BELLENDEN (1764–1842) born at Andover, Hampshire; né Gawler, but changed his name to Bellenden Ker in 1804; botanist and specialist in South African *Iridaceae*.

KERR, WILLIAM (d. in Ceylon 1814); collector for Kew in China, Java and the Phillipines; superintendent of the gardens at the King's House, Colombo.

KNIGHT, JOSEPH (c.1777–1855) born in Bridle, Lancashire; gardener to George Hibbert (qv), and later had a famous nursery in the King's Road which was sold to Veitch in 1853.

KNUTH, REINHARD (1874–1957) German botanist, Professor in Berlin and specialist in the *Geraniaceae*.

LAMBERT, AYLMER BOURKE FRS (1761–1842) of Boyton; patron of botany and built an important library and herbarium; his most important works were A *Description of the genus Cinchona* 1797 (the source of quinine) and A *Description of the genus Pinus* 1824.

LANCE, JOHN HENRY FLS (1793–1878) born in Dorking, Surrey; barrister and judge in Surinam.

LEE, JAMES AND KENNEDY, LEWIS; nurserymen at the Vineyard nursery, Hammersmith, c.1745–1890 (see introduction).

L'HERITIER DE BRUTELLE, CHARLES LOUIS (1746–1800) born in Paris; magistrate, patron of botany, botanist and author of several books; visited London in 1786–1787, bringing with him the South American collections of Joseph Dombey.

LINDEN, JEAN J. (1817–1898) born in Luxembourg; studied in Belgium; collected in Brazil, Cuba, Mexico and elsewhere in South America; after returning to Belgium he started a famous nursery in Ghent.

LINDLEY, DR JOHN (1799–1865) born in Calton, Norfolk; botanist, assistant secretary of the Horticultural Society, a founder of the *Gardeners' Chronicle* and author of several books, notably on orchids. The library of the Royal Horticultural Society in London is based on his collection of books.

LINNAEUS, CAROLUS (1707–1778) born near Stenbroholt in Smaland, Sweden; biologist and professor at Uppsala; his *Species Plantarum* 1753, is the beginning of modern plant naming.

LOBB, THOMAS (1820–1894); collector for Veitch in India, Burma and the East Indies.

LOBB, WILLIAM (1809–1864), brother of Thomas; collector for Veitch in western South America 1840–1848, and in California and Oregon 1849–1857.

LODDIGES, GEORGE (1784–1846) son of Conrad (see introduction), nurseryman at Hackney, specialist growers of epiphytic orchids.

LOW, SIR HUGH (1824–1905) born at Clapton, London; son of Hugh Low who founded the famous nursery at Clapton. Entered the diplomatic service and served in Borneo, Perak and Malaya, sending back orchids and other exotics to Kew.

LUCOMBE, PINCE & CO., nurserymen in Exeter from 1720, after whom the hybrid oak, raised in 1765, is named.

LYNCH, RICHARD IRWIN (1850–1924) born in St Germans, Cornwall; Curator of the University Botanic Garden, Cambridge 1879–1919, and hybridizer of several good garden plants, e.g. *Bomarea xcantabrigiensis*.

MACARTNEY, LORD GEORGE; led an embassy to the court of the Chinese Emperor at Peking in 1792; the mission was a political failure, but brought back a few plants including the Macartney Rose (*Rosa bracteata*).

MALCOLM, WILLIAM (d. 1798); nurseryman at Kennington from 1758 and from 1782 at Stockwell.

MARTYN, JOHN (1699–1768) born in London; Professor of Botany at Cambridge 1732–1762; author and translator of numerous books on botany.

MARTYN, THOMAS (1735–1825), son of John; Professor of Botany and Curator of the University Botanic Garden from 1762. Author of revised edition of Miller's *Gardener's Dictionary* 1795.

MASSON, FRANCIS (1741–1805) born in Aberdeen; collector for Kew in South Africa.

MENZIES, ARCHIBALD (1754–1842) born in Aberfeldy, Perthshire; gardener at the Royal Botanic Garden, Edinburgh; surgeon and naturalist on Captain Vancouver's voyages 1791–1795.

MICHAUX, ANDRÉ (1746–1892) born at Versailles; collector in North America and author of *Flora Boreali-Americana*.

MICHAUX, FRANÇOIS ANDRÉ (1770–1855) born at Versailles; son of André, collector with his father and author of *The North American Sylva*.

MICHOLITZ, WILHELM (1854–1932) born in Saxony; collector, mainly of orchids, for Messrs Sanders of St Albans in the Phillipines, New Guinea and elsewhere in the East and in South America.

MIERS, JOHN FRS (1789–1879) of Temple Lodge, Hammersmith; collector in South America (1819–1838).

MILLER, PHILIP (1691–1771) born at Deptford or Greenwich; florist and nurseryman; then gardener at the Chelsea Physic Garden 1722–1770 and author of the *Gardener's Dictionary*.

MILN, fl.1810 nurseryman in the Brompton Road, with Whitley etc. (see introduction).

MOORE, ARMYTAGE-, HUGH (c.1873–1954) created the garden at Rowallane, Co Down.

MURRAY, STEWART (c.1759–1858) Superintendent of Glasgow Botanic Garden till 1852.

MUSSIN-PUSCHKIN, A.A. (1760–1805); Russian botanist and collector in the Caucasus.

NIVEN, JAMES (c.1774–1827) born at Pennicuick, Edinburgh; collctor at the Cape for George Hibbert, 1798–1803 and for Lee and Kennedy 1803–1812.

NORTHUMBERLAND, 1ST DUKE OF, Hugh Percy né Smithson of Alnwick and Syon House, patron of botany and horticulture.

NUTTALL, THOMAS (1786–1859) born at Settle; author of the *North American Sylva*, a supplement to Michaux's work.

PALLAS, PETER SIMON (1741–1811) born in Berlin; traveller in Russia and Siberia and author of *Flora Rossica* 1784–88.

PARKINSON, JOHN (1567–1650); botanist and herbalist; author of the *Paradisus* 1629.

PETRE, ROBERT JAMES, 8TH EARL OF, FRS (1713–1742); botanist and gardener of Thornton Hall, Essex; died of smallpox.

PITCAIRN, DR WILLIAM (1711–1791) physician to St Bartholemew's Hospital 1750–1780, keen gardener with a private botanic garden at Islington.

PLACE, FRANCIS. ESQ. of Charing Cross, London; introduced plants from Chile.

PLUMIER, PÈRE CHARLES (1646–1704) born in Marseilles; traveller, botanist, author and illustrator of early floras of Central America and books on ferns.

PORTLAND, 1ST EARL OF, HANS WILLEM BENTINCK (1649–1709) born in Holland; superintendent of the gardens of King William III and introducer of the first pineapple grown in England.

PORTLAND, 3RD DUKE OF, WILLIAM HENRY CAVENDISH-BENTINCK (1738–1809) of Welbeck Park, Nottinghamshire; patron of botany, gardener and collector.

PULTENEY, WILLIAM, OF BLANDFORD; possibly the son of Richard (1730–1801), a surgeon who died at Blandford, and was a historian of botany and author of *A General View of the Writings of Linnaeus*, 1781.

PURDIE, WILLIAM (c.1817–1857); collector in the West Indies and in South America for Kew.

REDOUTÉ, PIERRE JOSEPH (1759–1840) born in St Hubert, Belgium; botanical painter, worked mainly in Paris; visited London in 1787.

REEVES, JOHN FRS (1774–1856) born in West Ham, Essex; inspector of tea for the East India Company and went to China in 1812, where he collected plants and flower paintings, now in the Lindley Library.

RHEEDE TOT DRAAKSTEIN, HENDRICK ADRIAN VAN (1636–1691); author of *Hortus Malabaricus*, 1698–1703, a sumptuous flora of southern India.

RICHARD, M. visited the Île de Bourbon in 1766; gardener to the Kind of France at the Trianon 1757.

ROBIN, JEAN (1550–1629) born in Paris; gardener to the Kind of France, and grower of many new plants from North America; commemorated in the genus *Robinia*.

ROEZL, BENEDICT (1823–1885) born in Prague; from 1854 had a nursery in Mexico, and collected for Sander's nursery throughout America from Washington south to Bolivia.

ROLFE, ROBERT ALLEN (1855–1921) born at Ruddington, Nottinghamshire; botanist at Kew; founder and editor of the *Orchid Review*.

ROLLINSONS, MESSRS; nurserymen of Tooting, c.1830–1875.

ROXBURGHE, WILLIAM (1751–1815) born at Craigie, Ayrshire; collector in India and superintendent of the East India Company's garden in Calcutta 1793–1814. Author of *Plants of the Coast of Coromandel*.

RUDBECK, OLOF (1630–1702) and Olof (1660–1740), his son, early Swedish botanists.

RUMPHIUS, GEORG EBERHARD (1627–1702); Dutch traveller, botanist and author of an early flora of the Dutch East Indies.

RUPRECHT, FRANZ JOSEPH (1814–1870) born in Freiburg; botanist, algologist and traveller in northern and eastern Siberia.

RUSSELL, PATRICK (1727–1805); physician and botanist to the East India Company 1785–89, before Roxburgh.

SABINE, J. FRS (1770–1837) born Tewin, Hertfordshire; barrister and later secretary of the Horticultural Society 1816–1830.

SALISBURY, RICHARD ANTHONY, né Markham (1761–1829) born in Chapel Allerton, and had a botanic garden there and a garden at Mill Hill which had belonged to Collinson; was secretary of the Horticultural Society 1805–1816.

SCHILLER, CONSUL (fl 1858) had a collection of orchids in Hamburg, with over 1400 species.

SCOPOLI, GIOVANNI ANTONIO (1723–1788) born in Cavallese, Tirol; botanist and author of floras of the southern Alps.

SEALY, J. ROBERT (b. 1907); botanist at Kew.

SELLOW, FRIEDERICK (1789–1831) of Potsdam; a collector who accompanied Prince Neuwied on an expedition in Brazil.

SHERARD, WILLIAM (1659–1728) born in Bushby, Leicestershire; antiquary and botanist, consul at Smyrna (today Izmir) 1703–1716; founded a chair of botany at Oxford.

SHERARD, JAMES (1666–1738) brother of William; had a famous garden at Eltham in Kent, the subject of Dillenius' *Hortus Elthamensis* 1732.

SIBTHORP, JOHN (1758–1796) born in Oxford; succeeded his father as Sherardian Professor of Botany in 1784; travelled in Greece and Turkey in 1786 and 1794; author of *Flora Graeca*.

SKINNER, GEORGE URE (1804–1867) born in Newcastle-upon-Tyne; a merchant in Leeds and in Guatemala, where he collected orchids for James Bateman and for William Hooker; died in Panama.

SLATER, GILBERT (c.1753–1793) manager of East India Company ships, and imported plants to his garden at Leyton, including *Cymbidium ensifolium*.

SLOANE, SIR HANS (1660–1753) born in Killyleagh, Co Down; studied medicine and botany in France and at the Chelsea Physic Garden; visited Jamaica 1687–1688; his collection formed the basis of the British Museum.

SMITH, SIR JAMES EDWARD (1759–1828) born in Norwich; botanist and author of numerous floras, notably the early Australian flora *A Specimen of the Botany of New Holland* 1793.

SOLANDER, DANIEL CARL (1793–1782) born in Pitea, Sweden; arrived in England in 1760, and was botanist and librarian to Sir Joseph Banks from 1771. Accompanied Banks on the Endeavour 1768–71.

SPACH, EDOUARD (1801–1874) born in Strasbourg; botanist, and with H.F. Jaubert (1798–1784) author of a book of illustrations of new plants from western Asia.

STANLEY, JAMES, 10th Earl of Derby had an important garden in the early 18th C., and was a subscriber to Houston's expedition for the improvement of botany and agriculture in Georgia.

STAPLES, ROBERT PONSONBY; English consul in Latin America c.1820–1835, sent seed from Mexico to A.B. Lambert.

STAUNTON, SIR GEORGE LEONARD, BART. (1737–1801) born Cargin, Co Galway; visited Brazil; secretary to Lord Macartney in Madras 1781–1784, and in China 1792–1794, when he introduced several new plants.

STERN, SIR FRED (c.1884–1967) banker and gardener; subscriber to many expeditions for his chalk garden at Highdown, Sussex.

STEARN, PROF. WILLIAM T. FLS (b. 1911) born in Cambridge; librarian to the Royal Horticultural Society; botanist at the British Museum and author of numerous books of unparalled scholarship.

TELFAIR, CHARLES (1778–1833) born in Belfast; surgeon and supervisor of the botanic garden on Mauritius 1826–1839.

THOUIN, ANDRÉ (1747–1824); Professor of Agriculture in Paris.

TEMPLETON, JOHN (1766–1825) born in Belfast; a botanist in Northern Ireland.

THUNBERG, CARL PEHR (1743–1828) born in Jönkoping, Sweden; a pupil of Linnaeus; botanist and plant collector in South Africa, and in Japan; author of *Flora Capensis* 1811–1818, and *Flora Japonica* 1784.

TRADESCANT, JOHN (d. 1638) and his son John (1608–1662); both gardeners, the father to the Earl of Salisbury at Hatfield; the son an early collector in North America; they had a botanic garden and museum in Lambeth which formed part of the collection which became the Ashmolean in Oxford.

TURNER, DR WILLIAM, DEAN OF WELLS (1508–1568) born at Morpeth, Northumberland; protestant, author of many books on religion and natural history, including the celebrated *A New Herball* 1551, one of the earliest to be written in English.

TWEEDIE, JOHN (1775–1862) born in Lanarkshire; a gardener at Edinburgh Botanic Garden before he went to South America in 1825. Died in Buenos Aires in 1862.

VAHL, MARTIN HENDRIKSEN (1749–1804) born in Bergen; botanist and author of books on North American plants.

VAN VOLXEM, M.; nurseryman of Brussels.

VANDES, COMTE DE; had a garden in Bayswater.

VEITCH (see introduction); pre-eminent family of nurserymen between 1800 and 1920.

VILLARS, DOMINIQUE (1745–1814) of Grenoble; botanist and author of an early flora of the Dauphiné.

WALKER, THE REVD. JOHN (1731–1803) born in Edinburgh; Professor of Natural History at Edinburgh 1779–1803, and teacher of Robert Brown.

WALLICH, NATHANIEL, né Wolff (1786–1854) born in Copenhagen; studied under Vahl; surgeon to the Danish settlement at Serampore 1807; worked for the East India Company in 1813; superintendent of Calcutta Botanic Garden 1815–1841, and collected in Nepal; visited South Africa 1842–1843.

WALLIS, GUSTAV (1830–1878) born at Luneberg, near Hanover; after starting a nursery in south Brazil, which went bankrupt, he was commissioned by Jean Linden, a famous Ghent nurseryman, to collect up the Amazon, which he ascended to its source. Later he collected orchids for Messrs Veitch in the Phillipines, before returning to Columbia in 1872, and dying in Ecuador.

WARSCEWICZ, JOSEPH RITTER VON RAWICZ (1812–1866) born in Wilno, Lithuania; studied in Berlin and then collected in Guatemala for L.B. van Houtte of Ghent. Later he collected widely in Central America, and was one of the most important continental orchid collectors, before becoming, in 1853, Supervisor in Cracow Botanic Gardens.

WEBB, PHILIP BARKER (1793–1854) born at Milford, Surrey; traveller, botanist and author, with Sabin and Berthelot, of a large flora of the Canary Islands.

WHITLEY, BRAME AND MILNE; Nurserymen, in the Old Brompton Road (see introduction).

WIGAN, SIR F. (c. 1828–1907) had an important orchid collection at Clare Lawn, East Sheen.

WILLIAMS, C.H. had a nursery at Turnham Green in the 1860's.

WILSON, ERNEST HENRY (1876–1930) born in Chipping Camden, Gloucestershire; gardener at Kew 1897–1899; collected for Messrs. Veitch in China 1899–1902, and for the Arnold Arboretum 1906–1911; keeper of the Arnold Arboretum 1927–1930.

WITHERS, MRS AUGUSTA INNES (c.1793–1860s) of Lisson Grove, London; botanical painter to Queen Adelaide 1830, and to Queen Victoria 1864.

WOODFORD, EDWARD JOHN ALEXANDER (fl. 1790's) had a good garden with large greenhouses at Vauxhall.

YOUNG, WILLIAM, born in Philadelphia; and introduced many plants, notably the Venus Fly Trap to Kew in 1768.

APPENDIX

Of Artists

BOJER, WENCESLAS (1795–1856) born in Bohemia. Director of Royal Botanic Garden, Pamplemousses and plant collector in Mauritius, Madagascar and Zanzibar. Drew seven plates for the magazine.
PLATES 269 and 270.

CURTIS, CHARLES M. (c. 1795–1839) brother of John Curtis. Contributed plates to entomological, as well as botanical publications. Drew nine plates for the magazine.
PLATES 267, 375, 400 and 481.

CURTIS, JOHN (1791–1889) apparently no relation to the founder of the magazine. Contributed plates to volumes forty-six to fifty-three of the magazine.
PLATES 7, 15, 17, 35, 38, 48, 56, 67, 82, 85, 87, 91, 101, 106, 109, 117, 123, 129, 133, 144, 151, 169, 188, 196, 263, 265, 275, 296, 301, 307, 323, 368, 382, 387, 388, 391, 406, 436, 441, 501, 537, 539, 545, 546, 560 and 566.

CURTIS, WILLIAM (b. 1804) son of Samuel Curtis who was apparently no relation of the founder. Drew four plates for the magzzine.
PLATE 521.

DUNCOMBE, E. (fl. 1810–1820's) drew six plates for the magazine.
PLATE 147.

EDWARDS, SYDENHAM TEAST (1768–1819) son of a schoolmaster from Abergavenny. Trained in botany and botanical illustration by William Curtis. His first illustration appeared in the second volume in 1788. From 1788–1815 he was almost the sole artist. Many of the anonymous plates in this selection were drawn by Edwards.
PLATES 10, 12, 20, 22–24, 26–30, 32–34, 36, 39, 40, 41, 44–47, 49–51, 53–55, 57, 59, 61, 62, 64, 66, 68, 70, 74, 76, 77, 79–81, 86, 89, 90, 92, 94, 99, 102, 104, 105, 107, 111, 113, 114, 116, 119, 120, 126–128, 132, 134, 135, 138, 139, 143, 145, 146, 148–150, 152–154, 156, 157, 160, 161, 163, 167, 170, 171, 173, 175, 177–181, 183–187, 191, 195, 197, 199, 200, 202–210, 212–219, 221–223, 226–240, 242–245, 247–249, 251–254, 258, 259, 264, 266, 267, 272–274, 276, 277, 279, 280, 283, 284, 286, 288, 290–292, 295, 297–299, 302–304, 306, 308, 309, 311–322, 324–350, 352, 354–363, 365–374, 378–380, 386, 389, 392–397, 402, 403, 420, 422, 432, 433, 435, 444, 445, 461, 462, 466, 470, 471, 479, 482, 483, 488, 490–493, 497, 498, 500, 502, 504, 505, 509, 510, 514–516, 518, 519, 523, 525, 526, 529, 534, 535, 541, 550, 551, 553, 555–557, 562, 564, 567 and 570.

FITCH, WALTER HOOD (1817–1892). Trained by William Jackson Hooker. The most prolific botanical artist of the nineteenth century. He published over ten thousand drawings in all. Fitch was principal botanical artist on the magazine between 1834 and 1877, drawing some 2,700 plates. Resigned in 1878.
PLATES 60, 65, 95, 137, 172, 201, 220, 281, 373, 399, 404, 408, 409, 411–413, 415, 418, 419, 424, 426, 427, 434, 438, 440, 442, 443, 447, 448, 450–457, 465, 472, 508, 536, 540 and 542.

GLOVER, THOMAS (fl. 1830's) drew one plate for the magazine.
PLATE 125.

GREVILLE, ROBERT KAYE (1794–1866) was a friend of Sir Joseph Hooker and a wide-ranging naturalist. Drew the three hundred colour plates of algae and fungi in Scottish Cryptogamic Flora 1823–1828. Contributed sixteen plates to the magazine between 1824–1834.
PLATE 376.

HERBERT, HON. WILLIAM (1778–1847) son of the Earl of Carnarvon, vicar of Spofforth and Dean of Manchester, illustrator and botanist. Drew approximately sixty plates for the magazine between 1840–1847. He was an expert on the Amaryllis family and wrote the text for many of these entries.
PLATES 18, 19, 63, 69, 108, 124, 131, 136, 162, 246, 261, 390, 407, 414, 421, 429, 437, 449, 469, 511, 528 and 533.

MCNAB, JAMES (1810–1878) Curator, Royal Botanic Garden, Edinburgh. Drew approximately twenty-eight plates for the magazine.
PLATE 351.

NORTON, HON. MISS C.E.C. (fl. 1830's) drew two plates for the magazine.
PLATES 71 and 72.

ROSS-CRAIG, STELLA (b. 1906) was on the staff of The Royal Botanic Gardens, Kew from 1929–1960. Drew over four hundred plates for the magazine. Her finest work is Drawings of British Plants 1948–1974.
PLATES 21, 42, 194 and 211.

SHORT, CHARLES WILKINS (1794–1863) drew three plates for the magazine.
PLATE 100.

SMITH, MATILDA (1854–1926) was trained by Sir Joseph Hooker and was principal artist for Curtis's Botanical Magazine from 1878–1922. Drew over 2,300 plates for the magazine.
PLATES 115, 130, 410, 417, 423, 446, 458, 477, 486 and 522.

SNELLING, LILIAN (1879–1972) was trained by H J Elwes. Principal artist on the magazine from 1922 to 1952. Contributed to Royal Horticultural Society publications and F.C. Stern's A Study of the Genus Paeonia 1946.
PLATES 21, 42, 73, 164, 166, 182, 194, 211, 262, 428, 430, 460, 473, 476, 478, 494 and 507.

SOWERBY, JAMES (1757–1822). The Sowerby family are famous for their writings on natural history and the many hand coloured plates they produced. James Sowerby was trained by marine painter, Richard Wright. He is responsible for the majority of the plates in English Botany, which began in 1790. Drew over fifty plates for the magazine.
PLATES 25 and 353.

WITHERS, AUGUSTA INNES (c. 1793–1860) was a teacher of flower painting. Drew many of the plates for J. Bateman's Orchidaceae of Mexico and Guatemala 1837–1843. Contributed six plates to Curtis's Botanical Magazine.
PLATE 416.

YOUNG, MISS M. (fl. 1830's) drew nine plates for the magazine.
PLATES 71 and 88.

GLOSSARY

Of Botanical Terms

Anther the part of the stamen that contains the pollen.

Bract a modified leaf below a flower.

Calyx the outer, usually green parts of the flower, made up of sepals.

Carina keel (latin); usually of the boat-like part of a pea flower.

Corolla the inner, usually coloured parts of the flower, made up of petals.

Filament that part of the stamen which supports the anther.

Germen ovary (latin and archaic botanical); the part of the flower which contains the young seeds.

Inflorescence the part of the plant on which the flowers are born.

Integuments the parts of the flower which enclose the ovule, later forming the seed coat.

Keel usually refers to the boat-like part of a pea flower.

Leaflet part of a compound leaf, itself like a small leaf.

Legumen the fruit of a pea flower, the pod and the seeds.

Limb the main part of a petal or leaf, excluding the stalk.

Pappus the silky or woolly part of a fruit, usually of the daisy family, which helps with dispersal of the seed.

Pedicel the stalk of a flower.

Peduncle the stalk of the inflorescence.

Perianth the parts of the flower around the stamens and style, usually consisting of petals and sepals.

Raceme a simple inflorescence in which the flowers are arranged on short, nearly equal stalks on an elongated axis.

Radical leaves leaves emerging from the root, or from the base of the plant.

Receptacle the part of the stem onto which the petals and other parts of the flower are attached.

Spathe a large leafy bract, either wrapped round the inflorescence, or enfolding the young buds.

Stamen the part of the flower which holds the pollen, consisting, usually, of filament and anther.

Stigma the part of the flower which catches the pollen, usually on the apex of the style.

Stipule leaf- or scale-like tissue, inserted at the base of the leaf-stalk or petiole.

Style the part of the flower, usually in the centre, which joins the stigma to the ovary.

Vexillum the standard; the usually upright, outer petal of a pea flower.

Wings the two side petals of a pea flower, which lie along the keel (qv).

INDEX